AUGMENTED REALITY

How to Use This Book

Augmented Reality: Innovative Perspectives across Art, Industry, and Academia uses the augmented reality app Aurasma to augment the essays, interviews, and artist statements found throughout the book. To view these augments, follow these steps:

1. On your mobile device, download the Aurasma app from the iTunes Store (for iOS devices) or Google Play (for Android devices).
2. In the Aurasma app, search for **Parlor Press**.
3. Select "**Parlor Press's Channel**" in the Aurasma app and then "Follow."
4. Images throughout the book have been augmented, so simply point the Aurasma app to scan them and reveal the augmented overlays. Each trigger image capable of activating augmented content will include the Aurasma icon somewhere on the page.

http://apple.co/2aMHntF

Available on the App Store

http://bit.ly/2axta3g

GET IT ON Google play

AURASMA

Scan this page to watch
David Bowie - Heroes - Live Aid 1985

AUGMENTED REALITY

INNOVATIVE PERSPECTIVES ACROSS ART, INDUSTRY, AND ACADEMIA

Edited by Sean Morey and John Tinnell

Parlor Press
Anderson, South Carolina
www.parlorpress.com

Parlor Press LLC, Anderson, South Carolina, USA

Printed in the United States of America on acid-free paper.

SAN: 254-8879

Library of Congress Cataloging-in-Publication Data on File

978-1-60235-556-9 (paperback)
978-1-60235-557-6 (hardcover)
978-1-60235-558-3 (pdf)
978-1-60235-559-0 (ePub)
978-1-60235-560-6 (iBook)
978-1-60235-561-3 (mobi)

First Edition
1 2 3 4 5

Credits: Chapter opener images are from Unsplash.com. Used by permission. Frontispiece and book half title: NASA; Ch. 3: Matthew Bedford; Ch. 4: Ksenia Kudelkina; Ch. 5: Sebastian Pichler; Ch. 6: Jethro Stebbings; Ch. 7: Kevin Young; Ch. 8: Topich; Ch. 9: Samuel Scrimshaw; Ch. 10: Pierrick Le Cunff. Ch 1: Screenshot, *Vanilla Sky* (2001). © Paramount Pictures. Ch. 2: Glenn Scofield Williams from USA - Mount Hood over Fort Vancouver (2008) CC 2.0 license.

Cover image: Cesar Quintero, from Unsplash.com. Used by permission.
Interior design: David Blakesley; Cover design: Sean Morey

Parlor Press, LLC is an independent publisher of scholarly and trade titles in print and multimedia formats. This book is available in paper, cloth and eBook formats from Parlor Press on the World Wide Web at http://www.parlorpress.com or through online and brick-and-mortar bookstores. For submission information or to find out about Parlor Press publications, write to Parlor Press, 3015 Brackenberry Drive, Anderson, South Carolina, 29621, or email editor@parlorpress.com.

Contents

Acknowledgments *ix*

1 Introduction: A Medium in the Making 3
Sean Morey and John Tinnell

Part 1: Scholarly Articles

2 Designing, Arranging, and Assessing Augmented Places through Mobile Media Alignment 27
Brett Oppegaard

3 Potential Panels: Toward a Theory of Augmented Comics 47
Jason Helms

4 "Sergey Brin Is Batman": Google Glass and the Rhetoric of Adoption in Popular Networked Culture 65
Isabel Pedersen and Douglas Trueman

5 Life through the Screen: Location-Based Information and the Personalization of Space 83
Jordan Frith

6 "Augpunk": Imagining Alternative Futures for Augmented Reality through Science Fiction 99
Joseph P. Weakland

7 Gathering Memories with Augmented Reality 119
Jason Kalin

8 The Dream Deferred: Augmented Reality as Rhetorical Realism 137
Scot Barnett

9 SAZoo-AR, *Ethea*, and Computer Vision 155
Steve Holmes

10 When Geolocation Meets Visualization 177
Jason Farman

Part 2: Interviews

Interview 1: Sidney I. Dobrin 202

Interview 2: Blair MacIntyre 214

Interview 3: Christine Perey 228

Interview 4: Jay Wright 240

Interview 5: Maarten Lens-Fitzgerald 248

Interview 6: BC Biermann 256

Part 3: Artwork

BC Biermann

Augmented Architecture [NYC + LA, 2012] 266

Bowery Wall [NYC, 2012] 268

Wynwood Walls @ Art Basel [Miami, 2012] 270

Tamiko Thiel

Shades of Absence [Venice, Istanbul, Brooklyn, Los Angeles, 2011] 271

Clouding Green [Singapore, 2012-2013] 272

Reign of Gold [NYC, Berlin, Los Angeles, Sydney, Tampa, 2012] 273

Jasmine Rain (Birdcage) [Cairo, Tunis, Beijing, Boston, NYC, 2011] 274

Carnation Rain [Lisbon, 2011] 275

Conor McGarrigle

NAMAland [Dublin, 2010-2012] 276

Walking Stories [Dundrum, 2011] 278

Vineland [2013] 280

Where's Franco? [VENICE, 2011] 282

John Craig Freeman

Orators, Rostrums, and Propaganda Stands [2012-2013] 284

Flotsam & Jetsam [Singapore, Massachusetts, 2013] 286

EEG AR: Things We Have Lost [Liverpool, 2013] 287

Border Memorial: Frontera De Los Muertos [Arizona, 2012] 288

Water wARs [Venice Biennial and Brooklyn, 2011] 289

Tiananmen SquARed (Attributed to) 4 Gentlemen [Beijing, 2010] 290

Peace Doors [Belfast, 2010] 291

Bryan Leister

Goldman Sachs (Giant Blood Sucking Vampire Squid) [Denver, 2012] 292

Mood Analyticator [Denver, 2012] 294

Mark Skwarek

#arOCCUPYWALLSTREET [NYC, 2011] 296

The Bottomless Pit [Zero1 Biennial, 2012] 298

erasAR [USA, 2010] 299

Notes 301

Bibliography 325

Contributors 341

Index 347

Acknowledgments

We would like to thank David Blakesley for supporting our project from its inception and for providing deft guidance throughout. This collection casts a wide range of work and perspectives on a still-emerging medium; as editors, we also wanted to experiment with augmented reality as a publishing technology in the process. We needed a bold publisher. David encouraged us to pursue our broadest vision, and he always supplied good ideas when we needed to adjust our course. We would also like to thank Sid Dobrin, Laurie Gries, Jack Stenner, and Greg Ulmer for constantly pushing us to think deeply about the rhetorical, aesthetic, and historical facets of digital culture. John Craig Freeman's involvement in the collection was both essential and catalytic; in addition to suggesting layouts for the artwork, he put us in touch with several of the other artists who contributed to this book. We are grateful to him, BC Biermann, Bryan Leister, Conor McGarrigle, Mark Skwarek, and Tamiko Thiel for each providing images of their pioneering artworks. Thanks to Sid Dobrin for his thoughtful responses to our questions about augmented reality and the future of higher education. Many thanks also to BC Biermann, Maarten Lens-Fitzgerald, Blair MacIntyre, and Christine Perey for graciously taking time to talk with us at the 2013 South by Southwest Interactive Festival, and to Jay Wright for giving an extensive phone interview. Transcribing these interviews for print would have been inconceivable without Kim Tinnell's help and her admirable attention to detail. We would also like to thank the scholars who contributed their essays to this volume: Brett Oppegaard, Jason Helms, Isabel Pedersen, Douglas Trueman, Jordan Frith, Joseph Weakland, Jason Kalin, Scot Barnett, Steve Holmes, and Jason Farman; we hope readers gain as much from your insights as we did. Finally, this one's for Aubrey, Sofia, and Fisher: augmenting reality every day.

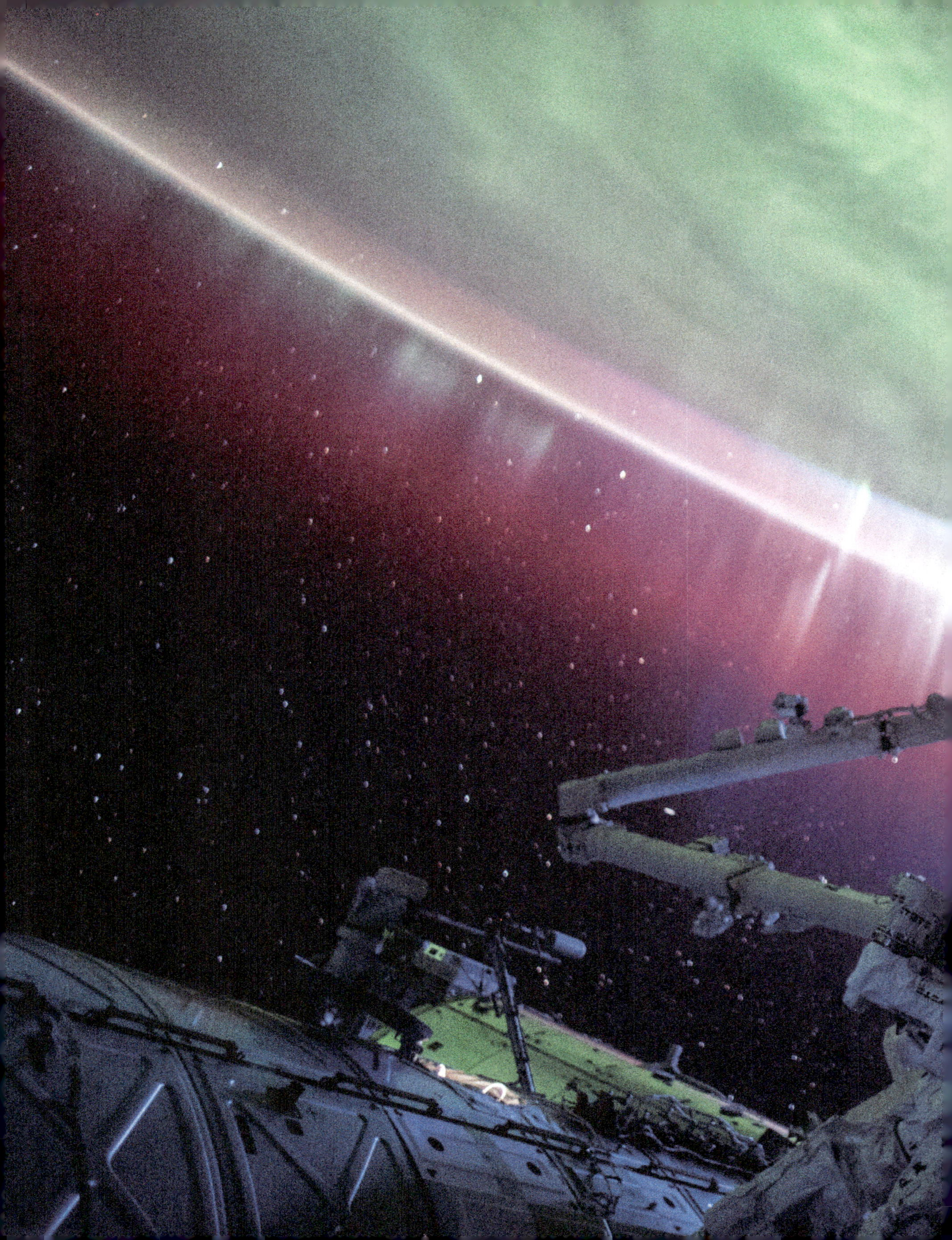

AUGMENTED REALITY

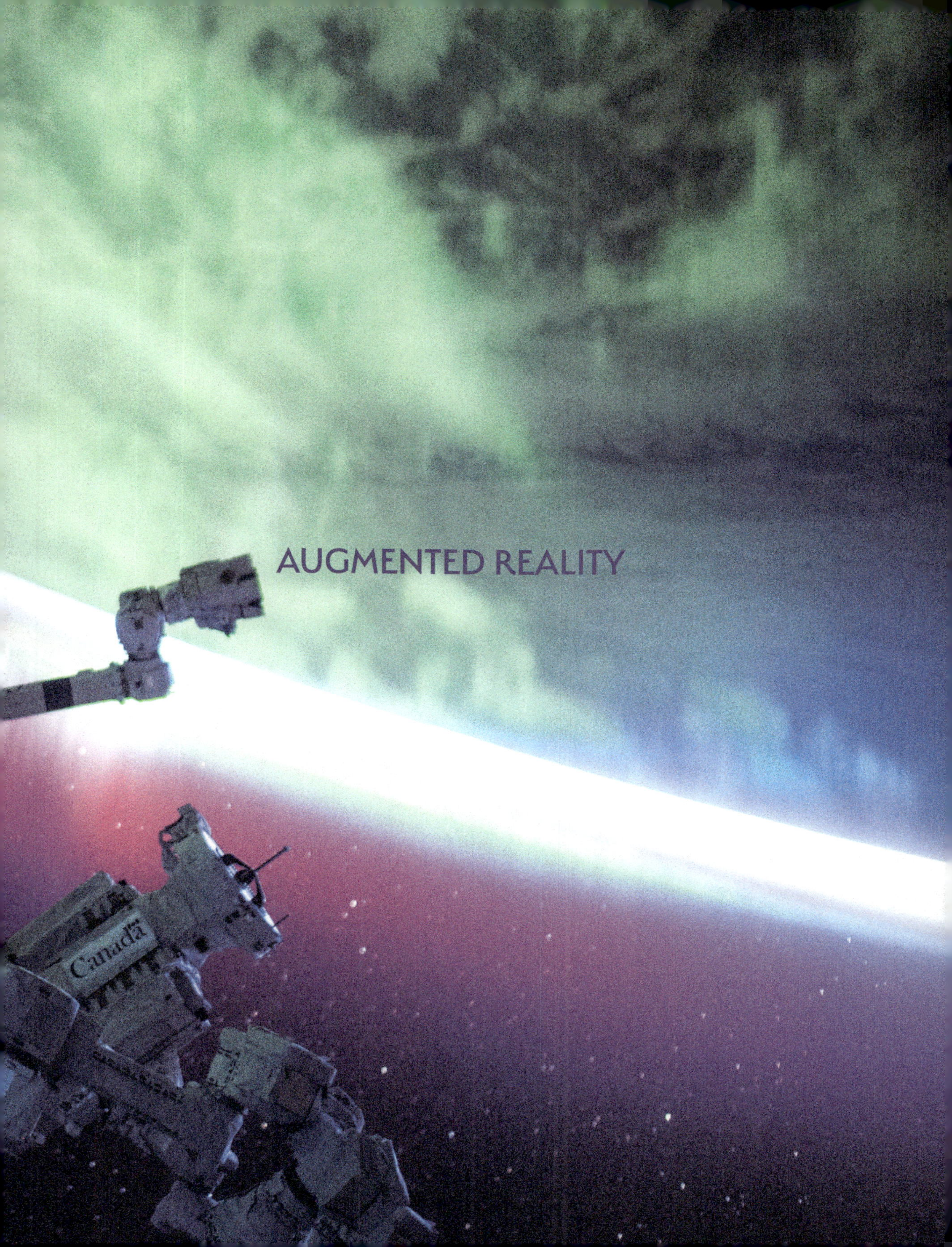

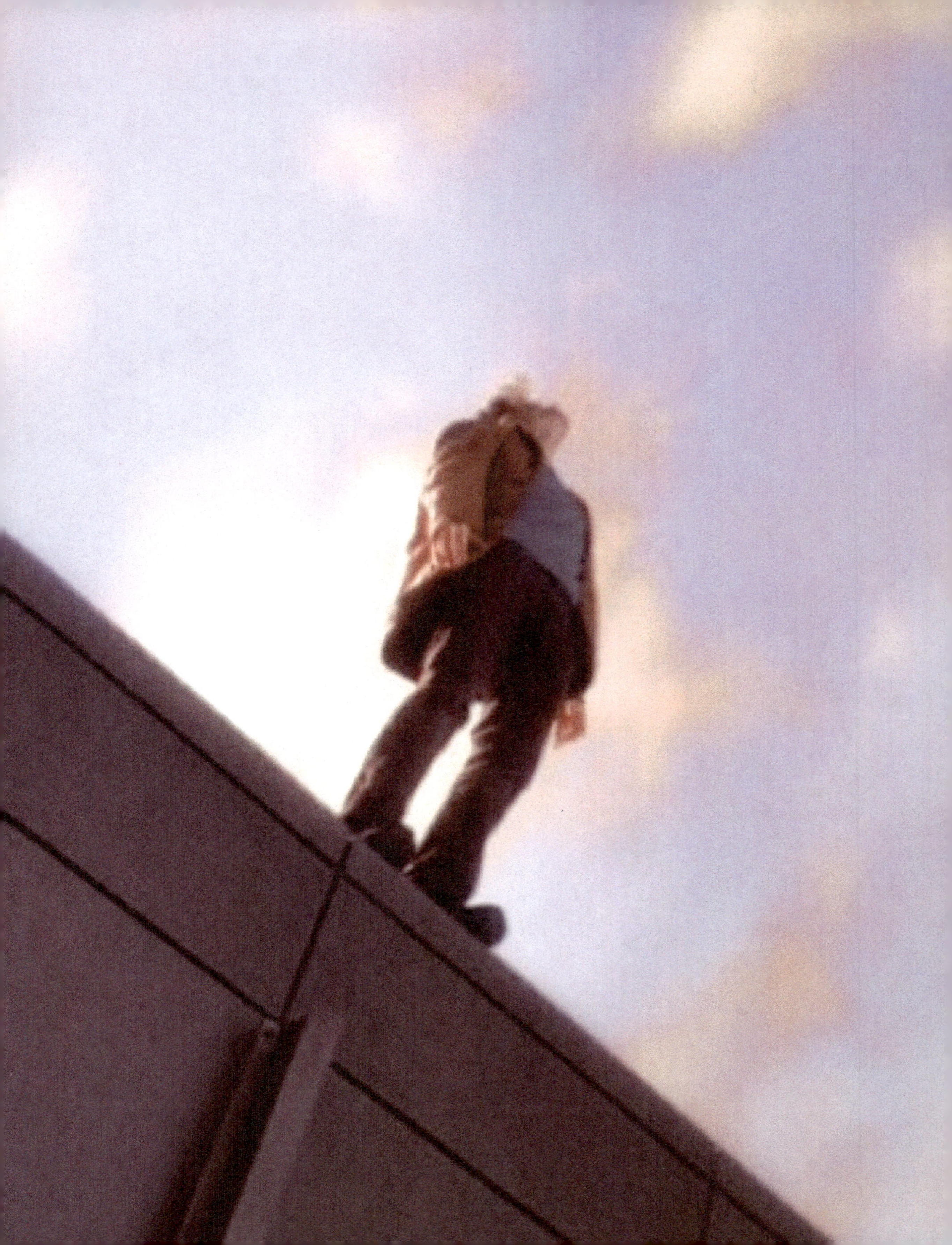

1 Introduction: A Medium in the Making

Sean Morey and John Tinnell

The final scene of *Vanilla Sky* dramatizes a central conflict of digital culture. The protagonist, David Aames, stands atop a Manhattan skyscraper located in the depths of his subconscious. He's facing what the film calls his "true moment of choice." He must decide whether to live forever in his personalized, computer-generated fantasy or to live out the rest of his mortal, earthly existence. Let's back up a bit.

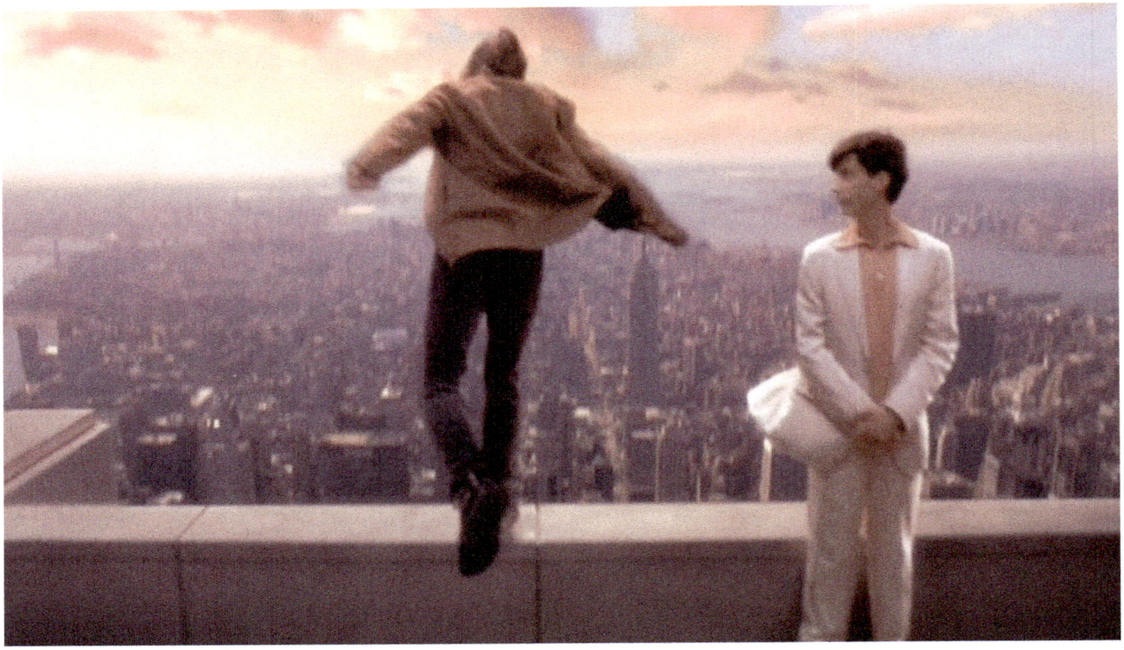

Figure 1. *Vanilla Sky*. © 2001 by Paramount Pictures.

AURASMA
Scan the image to view.

Vanilla Sky is a complicated film, precisely because viewers, like the protagonist, find it difficult if not impossible to decipher between digital dreams and material realities. Conceptually, the film performs something like a Derridean deconstruction of this conventional dichotomy, *almost* writing it under erasure—until the final scene. Immediately prior to that scene, we learn that David essentially signed his life over to a tech startup, paying a high price to do so. Months after a car accident left him isolated and disabled, David traded away his pain-ridden, conscious life for an account on the "lucid dream" biotech platform, wherein one's lived experience unfolds in a virtual world set to the music, images, and narratives he or she identifies with most. In this suspended state, the modes in which users interact with electronic media serve as basic commands David executes over anything; for instance, he can put his lifeworld on "pause" or summon tech support whenever a "glitch" occurs. A quintessentially sci-fi notion, the lucid dream is a hyperbolic extension of our increasing engagement with customizable online software of all sorts that variously filter and organize information on the basis of specific preferences each user selects. Pandora meets Second Life, inside of our brains.

In the penultimate scene, David's lucid dream has become a nightmare on account of a technical error, which effectively causes the program to render events that manifest his worst fears instead of his preferences and desires. That is, the lucid dream technology crashed, temporarily, but the system's administrator appears and assures David that the bug has been fixed and the software updated. On account of this mix up, though, the administrator offers David a money back guarantee of sorts: he can continue to bask in his lucid dream, or he can terminate the contract (i.e., wake up). The former enables David to be the author of his own (digital) life, so to speak, while the latter leaves him vulnerable to the unknown, otherness, spontaneity—to more *accidents*. The terms of the decision are irreconcilably *either/or*. Either David re-commits to total immersion in his user-generated virtual world (never to experience anything else), or he can elect for tech support to end the lucid dream and bring him back to "the world out there."

We might view David's moment of choice as a parable for an array of decisions that citizens in media-saturated societies make on a daily basis: Should I play another hour of *World of Warcraft* or should I go play football outside? Should I limit my kids' "screen time" or let them do as they wish? Should I respond to this text message while driving? Should I check my email now? Aside from GPS navigation, few routine digital activities function in concert with the situation at hand; rather, users assume a liaison role, ceaselessly orchestrating their attention from screens to something else and back again. Few among us are virtuosos. In the end, David decides to unplug from the lucid dream platform: "I want to live a real life. I don't want to dream any longer." In the context of the film's technological undertones, this statement is tantamount to saying "I want to live among accidents. I'm done with virtual reality." The film seems to insist that reality happens in unscripted and non-programmable moments, and that total immersion in virtual reality is the antithesis of living.

Since the release of *Vanilla Sky*—and we are certainly not implying causality here—scholarship in media theory has been quick to dispel any alleged separation of digital and physical worlds. Digital dualism, a now-popular phrase coined by Nathan Jurgenson in 2011, characterizes this critical tendency (which was practically an enthymeme during the 1990s) as an intellectual fallacy. Every digital bit owes its existence to physical atoms; every pixel that appears on screen does so on the shoulders of the inorganic matter that technologists have organized into the hardware, satellites, and other infrastructure supportive of networked computing. The digital is not immaterial, even though the form of the hardware often reveals little about the function of the software. Electronics bear serious material consequences, which, while this may be painfully obvious with phenomenon like e-waste, often elided the early adopters of cyberspace who quickly acclaimed the Web as new frontier cut off from earthly realities. Jurgenson also attacks the idea that what happens in so-called cyberspace stays in cyberspace, or that digital activity occurs in a vacuum. Even the most apparently benign videogames can influence the way we apprehend and act in "real world" situations. Email brought on a dramatic decline in postal mail, and cell phones have done the same for home telephones. Jurgenson ultimately argues that social networks, search engines, blogs, and other venues are no less real for being online. He cites numerous crowdsourcing protests and other digitally planned "offline" events as clear examples of how Internet activity regularly informs and organizes our social existence, to such a degree that it is becoming more and more absurd to speak of cyberspace or of the real world as if those spaces were neatly sealed off from one another.

And yet, many of the social media and mobile applications that Jurgenson and like-minded critics describe borrow their design and functionality from the virtual reality of the desktop metaphor. The overwhelming majority of software development in the age of smartphones has pushed the Web ever closer to the ubiquity famously envisioned by Mark Weiser, but the fine print of Weiser's manifestos have evidently been shrugged off. With his colleague John Seely Brown, Weiser proclaimed, "when computers are all around, so that we want to compute while doing something else . . . we must radically rethink the goals, context and technology of the computer and all the other technology crowding into our lives." While smartphones clearly extend the domain of digital media to a plethora of on-the-go use cases, many of the interaction modalities they mobilize still belong to what Weiser called the personal computing era. Mobile interfaces still require people to disengage from their surroundings in order to engage with digital content. In this sense, the mobile Web, at least in most of its current iterations, amounts to Weiser's worst nightmare. The ways in which one must interact with a desktop have now become regular ways of behaving anytime, anywhere. It has become all too normal to experience what critic Sherry Turkle calls "being alone together"—when people habitually devote their attention more to their tiny screens than to the person sitting across from them. It has become all too normal to have one foot in cyberspace while the other foot's on the gas pedal. While the digital and the physical are thoroughly entangled, we tend to encounter more knots than bonds.

The paradigm shift that AR beckons is as much about everyday ethics as it is technological utopias. Along with research in location-based and context-aware computing, ongoing developments in AR create and sustain transductive relationships between multimedia, humans, and the environments we inhabit—such that all three of these spheres affect and become affected by one another. To engage with digital content, in this paradigm, does not require disengagement from one's surroundings; indeed, enhancing one's perceptual and cognitive experience of the spatiotemporal *here and now* is precisely the ideal that orients AR. Unlike today's mobile Web, where—pragmatically speaking—we do have to choose between the digital and the physical, the scenarios enacted and imagined by emerging AR technologies reconfigure portions of the Web so that we might experience multimedia as an integral part of the landscapes and events unfolding around us. If screened for citizens of an AR-saturated society, the climactic scene that ends *Vanilla Sky* would seem more comedic than dramatic.

From Lab Prototype to Cultural Interface

Within the past five years, AR has emerged from research labs into a multitude of everyday settings. Mobile devices have replaced clunky head-mounted displays, dramatically increasing access to AR around the world. Distinct from traditional Web browsers, AR browsers (e.g., Layar, Junaio, Aurasma, etc.) utilize the camera view of smartphones to create a unique visual-tactile interface, which blends a person's gaze of the physical environment with texts, graphics, and other media files that have been "geotagged" to specific coordinates on the earth's surface. In addition, many AR browsers now incorporate computer vision and image tracking software, creating a more precise mode of aligning digital overlays on top of print media, building façades, signage, and other fixtures of the built environment. In the wake of these advancements, innovators in various fields today are optimistic about the potential for AR applications to enhance education, tourism, publishing, retail, architecture, manufacturing, and cultural heritage.

In fact, of the multitude of technologies being invented worldwide, the 2011 Horizon Report identified AR as one of two technologies most likely to change the face of higher education, beginning as early as 2014. Magazine publishers from *Esquire* to *Playboy* have sought to revitalize their print editions by incorporating AR icons that effectively link their pages to exclusive digital content. In such cases, the page and the screen operate in conjunction with one another, inciting new rhetorical possibilities. Writers, designers, and publishers have the opportunity to reconsider and reconfigure the borders that have delineated physical and digital worlds, as well as print media and the Web. Retailers oscillate between excitement and fear over the emergence of AR "pop-up stores," which bring e-commerce to a target audience at a particular place and time, without any brick and mortar expenses. Archivists and museum professionals around the world now display their digital collections out in the streets; in London and Philadelphia, the historical photographs of a city block are readily visible to smartphone users as they move through that same space.

Following cellphones, a multitude of everyday objects (watches, glasses, car windshields, books, etc.) are becoming networked "smart" objects. The 2012 announcement of Google Glass (i.e., "Project Glass"), for instance, envisions a bold future for AR beyond smartphones and tablets. While Google Glass may not support robust AR experiences in its first iterations, the intense promotion of the product has generated an unprecedented degree of buzz around AR in popular culture and tech journalism. Alexis Madrigal, a senior editor for *The Atlantic*, tested Google's Field Trip app and imagined how this geo-publishing platform might be experienced through the lens of Google Glass. Noting critical differences between locative AR apps and standard Web browsers, Madrigal concludes that the

> *"Augmented reality technologies support new writing and design spaces, which demand new principles to help orient production and interpretation amid this emerging dimension of digital culture."*

projected futures of AR demand "a new kind of media" that will challenge traditional assumptions about genre, audience, and context:

> No one publishes a city, they publish a magazine or a book or a website. If we've thought about our readers reading, we've imagined them at a breakfast table or curled up on the couch or sitting in their office. No one knows how to create words and pictures that are meant to be consumed out there in the world.

In short, the technological conditions of mobile and wearable AR support new writing and design spaces, which, in turn, demand new aesthetic and rhetorical principles to help orient acts of production and interpretation amid this emerging dimension of digital culture. *Augmented Reality* assembles a multidisciplinary cast of contributors with the aim to reflect on current practices, propose new concepts, and initiate critical conversations pertinent to AR's cultural development. As a preface to these efforts, we offer readers—especially those unfamiliar with AR—an overview of key scholarly contributions to AR discourse, beginning with landmark technical advances and then shifting toward recent inquiries across the arts and humanities.

Two important works on AR appear in the mid-1990s from Paul Milgram and Fumio Kishino, both engineering scholars, and Ronald T. Azuma, a computer scientist. Milgram and Kishino provide a seminal attempt to classify and taxonomize the early virtual reality technologies, which includes AR. In their article "A Taxonomy of Mixed Reality Visual Displays," the authors argue that rather than lump AR in with virtual reality, mixed reality and AR deserve their own space, so to speak, since they do not provide total immersion within a self-contained virtual environment as we see in *Vanilla Sky*. To illustrate these differences, Milgram and Kishino offer a "virtuality continuum" diagram, positioning the "real environment" on one end and "virtual environment" on the other, and placing "augmented reality" and "augmented virtuality" in-between these opposite poles.

Through this taxonomy, the authors problematize their own continuum to suggest that these poles aren't always opposite and that these categories sometimes blend together. As the authors argue, the very term "virtual reality" can be seen as a bit of an oxymoron or paradox, for the virtual should ideally seem to be the real (this paradox is somewhat explored in films like *The Matrix*). Using this logic, we might place "augmented reality" in the same camp. Even if an augmented or mixed reality isn't immersive via a room or headset, viewers can feel as if they are in a virtual environment as they become focused on the AR experience, and so the continuum can loop back on itself.

Milgram and Kishino point out a few other important variables for AR technologies, ones that continue to be problematic. The first is the extent to which an AR or MR system knows its world. An early example of this pertains to a head-tracking device on a head-mounted display, allowing the software to keep track of the user's head movements and "know" the world which it shares and creates with the viewer. Today, as GPS accuracy improves and networks of tagged locations and image patterns continue to become catalogued, AR becomes better at the "what and where" of images, migrating and extending World Knowledge to the Cloud for any device to use.

Secondly, the authors describe "Reproduction Fidelity," looking at both the hardware systems as well as the modeling and rendering techniques for how well technology can produce realistic images. For the authors, ultimate fidelity occurs on a 3D HDTV hardware system combined with 3D animation, making it nearly impossible for the viewer to distinguish reality from its augmentation. Nearly two decades later, as these devices are more widely available, we are seeing some realistic productions in AR artwork and more realistic blending of live action and digital animation. However, we are also seeing some examples, such as London Street Museum, that attempt to create a kind of nostalgic realism, producing not a perfect image of London as it was, but a mood of what has been. This "feeling" gets at their third dimension of their taxonomy, the "Extent of Presence" metaphor. Even if an image does not have high Reproduction Fidelity, it can still enact an intended metaphor when an audience views it and thus fulfill the rhetorical goal of the VR, MR, or AR application. The images used by the London Street Museum may be black and white, grainy, and thus not live up to our HDTV standards, but the sepia tones help enact the metaphor of a resurrected past spread before us in the present.

Of course, this taxonomy was created before the widespread use of smartphones and well before Apple introduced the iPhone in 2007. While the technological-premise of a smartphone's screen may be quite similar to viewing AR through a head-mount display, the logistics of how one interacts with reality changes drastically as one can move more freely about the world. However—while the dream (for now) of a lightweight head-mount display might not come from Google Glass's first iteration (as Layar's Dirk Groten and Ronald van der Lingen discussed in a June 25, 2013 blog post)—viewing an object while having the rest of the body unencumbered is much different from having to hold up a screen to view the augmentation. But besides providing a very useful starting point for describing and distinguishing AR, MR, and VR in 1993, the article also calls on scholars of AR and mixed media to continue to taxonomize and retaxonomize emerging technologies should it prove useful to do so.

While not as ambitious as Milgram and Kishino's taxonomy, Ronald T. Azuma offers a useful survey of AR to help consolidate the existing knowledge of AR at the time of the survey's publication. As Milgram and Kishino limit much of their taxonomy to technology and the technical aspects of AR production, Azuma also provides a survey of the various applications of AR, including medical uses, manufacturing applications, annotation, robotics, entertainment, and military. Azuma also does a better job teasing out the major modes of delivering AR at the time of the survey's publication, from Window on the World displays to head-mounted displays, and the various issues each of these has, such as the comparative safety issues of wearing a closed-view head-mount display versus a see-though head-mount display.

Azuma also discusses one of the major technical issues of AR, registration, which involves programming an AR-based image to appear where (and sometimes when) an author or designer intends. While objects in a totally immersive, virtual environment can be algorithmically synced to interact together, merging digital images with an analog world becomes more difficult. For instance, location-based AR installations may have a variance of many meters and thus not appear where intended every time. The other problem noted by Azuma is that of the AR sensor, particularly its input variety and bandwidth, accuracy, and range. While VR mainly needs a high device output to create an environment for the viewer, AR requires a high device input so that it can sense the images, videos, and 3D models it's meant to display and the world it displays upon. Such increased sensing power also requires increased bandwidth. The technical limitations that Azuma cites may seem outdated, for since his survey's publication in 1997, we've witnessed increases in broadband, miles of fiber optic cables, WiFi, 3G, and 4G wireless connectivity. Of course, any glance at a wireless carrier's coverage map will reveal that some areas are better connected than others, limiting the bandwidth, range, accuracy, and the full potential that authors of AR might achieve.

These two articles—written by computer engineers and scientists—provide much technical detail in attempting to define and classify the hardware and some of the applications of AR. Coming to grips with the hardware of AR—from the fast-moving cockpits of fighter jets to the innerspace first-person POV of Schwarzenegger's Terminator Model T-101—provides much of the intrigue about the AR experience. However, how we use the devices and technologies is as important as the devices themselves (for instance, the main purpose of the last two examples is for targeting and killing). Whether or not a particular application is a good idea usually falls to the humanities, and discussing these questions is one of our goals for putting together this collection.

Toward these questions, or prompting for these questions to be asked, Lev Manovich argues that we must develop a poetics for AR in his article "The Poetics of Augmented Space: Learning from Prada." In this work—which makes too many important points to be adequately summarized in this brief review—Manovich seeks to "re-conceptualize augmentation as an idea and cultural and aesthetic practice rather than as technology," a shift in focus away from the goals of Milgram, Kishino, and Azuma. Toward this shift, Manovich has to create his own taxonomy and makes an initially useful distinction between how spaces have been augmented in the past by previous forms of media and how this dynamic changes as the media itself becomes dynamic and often localized to an individual user as she carries around a portable device capable of filling any space with new information flows. For instance, although spaces have always been augmented by art, architecture, informational signs, or other visual elements to help one navigate or aesthetically enjoy a space, AR can provide continually shifting and individualized enhancements and augmentations not previously possible. Architects must now consider how cell reception and radio waves might bounce around their designs, and artists must consider more than just the space of the gallery for their artwork and also include outdoor areas.

Another important aspect that Manovich offers is that the user in an AR environment not only receives data (Azura's input problem), but becomes and transmits data through video and location-based surveillance, leading to his claim that "*augmented space is also monitored space*." In the current technology of individually-specific targeted ads, presented to us via Web robots that gather our user habits, this may not seem very shocking and we might conclude that, as Guy Debord states about the society of the spectacle, such self-surveillance is only indicative of a choice we've already made, something we do to ourselves. We hope that some of the articles in this collection help us ask if these practices are ones we really value, and if not, how to begin changing them. Manovich feels that unlike previous forms of architecture and art that dominate a society, ones that were more difficult for the average citizen to change (at least legally), then "today's electronic dynamic interactive displays make it possible for these messages to change continuously; making the information surface a potential space of contestation and dialog, which functions as the material manifestation of the often invisible public sphere." However, we might ask at what point does this contestation and dialog become commercialized and reterritorialized by the dominant paradigm? Can an AR of the public sphere by the public provide a space for critique?

Perhaps not in every case. As Manovich concludes, the fashion company Prada layers its stores with data, placing their product alongside images of glamour and beauty, making its intentions clear: they know they're selling an idea rather than a product, they short-circuit critique by displaying this openly, and they know the customer will purchase their products anyway. Prada, as Manovich explains, even reveals the technical specs and economic metrics of their worldwide retail, storage, and production spaces. The point Manovich attempts to make is that "all these spaces have to compete" with our smartphones, tablets, and future AR devices and so by overlaying their stores with data as all spaces become overlaid with data, Prada hopes something will catch the viewer's attention. Thus, ultimately Manovich argues that many of the questions associated with AR manifest in the interaction of data with the spaces through which data flows: "In short, I suggest that the design of electronically augmented space can be approached as an architectural problem. In other words, architects along with artists can take the next logical step to consider the 'invisible' space of electronic data flows as substance rather than just as void—something that needs a structure, a politics, and a poetics." While the taxonomies and surveys of AR technology certainly had to deal with space—for instance, head-tracking displays, GPS location, target acquisition, and registration itself—Manovich pushes these questions into the everyday spaces where we live, the public spaces filled with invisible data (and thus invisible space) that we increasingly take for granted.

Manovich's pioneering inquiry into the spatial implications of location-based technologies has initiated a trend among media theorists. Following the idea of augmented space, scholars have proposed similar concepts including *hybrid* space, *comprehensive* space, and *scripted* space—just to name a few. While none of these concepts strays substantially from Manovich's original notion, each proceeds by means of a different focal point and contributes important concerns for the humanistic study of AR. Whereas Manovich deals mainly with multimedia installations embedded on-site at public transportation hubs, cultural institutions, and commercial storefronts, Adriana de Souza e Silva centers on "the use of mobile technologies as social devices." Most notably, she posits that a crucial inversion occurs whenever online networks and computer games migrate toward physical spaces. Traditionally, in the guise of desktop PCs, the Web acted as a global village of remote communications, for which a user's location mattered little. As mobile devices enable (almost) anytime-anywhere access to online content and social networks, location is becoming increasingly important to the Web. In addition to instances of smartphone users turning to the Web for information anytime-anywhere—mobile search and GPS navigation have become cultural reflexes of sorts—designers of social networks and news websites have incorporated user location as a prominent variable that orients communication among users and/or organizes the content that each user receives. From Foursquare to Tapln, emerging mobile apps have reimagined the architecture of digital networks, paying homage to de Souza e Silva's theory in the process, by "emphasizing [users'] paths and connections to physical spaces instead of [virtual] nodes." Though de Souza e Silva does not comment on AR in detail, her discussion of the hybrid spaces created by mobile interfaces is foundational for its demonstrations of the ways in which spontaneous, location-based activities (re)shape digital networks and the various modes of communication they engender.

While spatial theories abound, surprisingly few humanities scholars have taken up the question of how to design and compose multimedia for AR platforms. Peter Anders, an architect by training, has outlined seven principles for this purpose. Creating AR or MR compositions, for Anders, is a matter of integrating "physical and virtual entities within a coherent design," to such an extent that, ideally, "action in one domain affects the other." Comparable to social networks that operate on a locative basis, extra-computational variables inhabit the user's sensory field alongside digital content; however, there is a noteworthy difference. Anders's AR compositions feature the perceived activities of physical, locative entities within their very frame, rather than just representing those activities at the level of computer code. That is, location-based apps *tell* us about location; AR compositions *show* place-based entities at work *within the work*. (In semiotic terms, the former is symbolic and the latter is indexical.) Because digital and geographic flows co-inhabit a shared space in AR compositions, Anders confers high priority to the principle of *reciprocity* in his design schema. He believes a "tighter coupling of material and cyber spaces" increases the likelihood that AR compositions will impart sensory extension (another of his seven principles), which denotes situations where a person's given sensorium becomes augmented to register otherwise imperceptible phenomena such as ultrasonic frequencies, exact temperatures of various objects, etc. Anders formulates his principles in distinctly architectural contexts, yet they provide a suggestive starting point for rhetoricians, designers, and compositionists looking to bring their expertise to bear on the unique opportunities and challenges that AR presents to digital creativity.

Researching urban living and digital aesthetics, Christian Ulrik Andersen and Søren Pold lend a useful historical perspective relevant to AR compositions. Highlighting the "written, coded quality of ubicomp," they align QR codes and AR apps with several public-discursive traditions quintessential to the rise of modern cities such as street signs, advertising, and graffiti. For Andersen and Pold, what distinguishes ubicomp from these other practices is the former's introduction of algorithmic scripts to urban spaces; hence their term for ubicomp's spatial quality: scripted space. In other words, modern cities have long been laced with texts, images, and audiovisual electronics; that this media and other parts of the street-level infrastructure can be managed through computation is a recent phenomenon.

Electric traffic lights provide an important albeit mundane example of the evolution of infrastructural media over the twentieth century. Invented in 1914, the first electric traffic lights were wired to switches that city employees operated manually from a control booth. Major cities began to computerize their traffic lights during the 1960s, and we have since witnessed a gradual transition from automated programs of "fixed-time signals" (e.g., timers that switch lights at regular intervals, sometimes in sync with nearby lights) to adaptive programmability of "semi-actuated signals" (e.g., sensor networks that switch lights via detecting the presence of vehicles and pedestrians). As we traverse scripted spaces, such as high-traffic intersections, we are experiencing the execution of computer scripts. Traffic light systems are visual media, situated at and responsive to crucial scenes of decision; at present, they constitute one of the most successful ways in which ubicomp has been integrated into the rhythms of everyday life, for the sake of enhancement. The system is very simple, of course. A column of three colors arbitrates the flow of traffic, effecting patterns of social organization that may rarely emerge spontaneously when drivers are left to their own devices. Traffic lights, emblematic of other mediums of scripted space, have been and remain a top-down, state-controlled production. The spread and democratization of AR, however, enables the bottom-up production of scripted spaces. One can create multimedia for ubicomp platforms—well beyond simple traffic lights—that resides at important scenes of decision and action, with the aim to effect new patterns of social becoming.

As Andersen and Pold suggest, rhetorical and aesthetic enterprises of this sort are precisely what need to be undertaken in urban spaces. Despite ubicomp's capacity to support scripted spaces, Andersen and Pold observe that much of the computing that people actually do in public—while moving among one another—remains personal or "predominantly exclusive." That is, engaging with mobile devices qua PCs, people move through scripted spaces as if they were "a setting for individual performative activities," and tend to neglect their potential as "a space for debate and knowledge dissemination." Digital participation in the former sense typically (though not always) competes with our ability to engage with the activities of the actants that surround us. Whereas embedded traffic lights prevent accidents, mobile text messaging contributes to them at an alarming rate. Rather than linking primarily to information pertaining to various remote contexts, a collectively engaged scripted space would harbor digital links that reaffirm and revitalize the urban space as a "basis of social encounter, communication, and debate." While people often read and add to the blogosphere and other virtual agoras as they inhabit an urban setting, Andersen and Pold claim "there has been little effort to actively promote the urban setting as a context for active participation." To do so requires us to invent "new forms of digital civic participation" while also creating "new ways of developing cultural interfaces in scripted spaces." In sum, the technical fact of bringing the virtuality of computation out into the physical world is not in-itself sufficient for creating a culture in which digital media become integrated with—for the sake of enriching—the extra-computational activities of everyday life.

To where, then, might we look for promising examples suggestive of this new technocultural paradigm? To art. That artists are pioneering much of the early innovative work with AR browsers should come as no surprise, especially when we recall McLuhan's observation that "it's always been the artist who perceives the alterations in man [sic] caused by a new medium, who recognizes that the future is the present, and uses his work to prepare the ground for it." Curator Simona Lodi chronicles the surge of AR works in Europe and North America starting in 2010, noting that AR has become an established medium in several major international art shows. Discussing public art interventions such as the MoMA Invasion by the Manifest.AR collective, Lodi locates the significance of these works in their capacity to transform our relationship with traditional cultural institutions, including museums but also any kind of public space. As a curator, she envisions a new breed of exhibits spawning in the wake of projects like the MoMA Invasion whereby "artists are invited specifically to use augmentation, information and immersion in a specific public or private space, with or without authorization." The city, the countryside—or wherever—act as an ad-hoc museum and a dynamic canvas. Here, the relationship between art, politics, and everyday life is perhaps more explicit and inseparable than ever. Aesthetic experience and social critique accrue on-location at the interstices of programmed media and live action—"it is the real object that activates the web." AR artworks provide the most concrete and fascinating indications of possible futures in which all the world's surfaces *link* to digital media. Collectively, in addition to their value as individual artworks, they model ways in which a variety of citizens might create AR projects and eventually supplement the Web as we now know it with—to borrow a phrase from John Craig Freeman—a thriving "world-wide public square."

Given the vitality of contemporary art and design practices and their capacity to illuminate the cultural and political affordances of the AR medium, Jay Bolter, Maria Engberg, and Blair MacIntyre call for new media scholarship to play a more *productive* role in relation to interaction design and media aesthetics. While cultural critics writing about emerging technologies commonly employ historical practices associated with traditional media as analogies for *interpreting* digital practices, Bolter et al. remind us that "these approaches look at media with a view to analysis and critique rather than creative production." In addition to posing analogies and contrasts for the sake of criticism, Bolter et al. assert that new media scholars should also provide useful frameworks for "develop[ing] a kind of media aesthetics that can guide designers as they explore new forms of digital media." These authors present the history of panoramas in parallel with their discussion of AR browsers, suggesting that critical awareness of the former might inspire design thinking relevant to the latter. After charting the emergence of panoramic paintings as a nineteenth century form of exhibition, Bolter et al. outline contemporary scenarios in which, for instance, museum professionals might design AR panoramas that overlay a displayed artifact and provide a visual representation of the artifact's original context. Their scholarly writing—coupled with their collaborative design projects in Georgia Tech's Augmented Environments Lab—marks a pioneering effort to reconfigure the humanities, computer science, interface design, and industry resources around the cultural development of emerging media technologies.

Following Bolter et al.'s approach—its insights and methodology—many of the scholarly essays in this collection aim to enrich AR production practices by examining contemporary projects in light of pertinent connections with historical traditions in philosophy, rhetoric, visual media, and science fiction. Just as artworks offer avant-garde models for thinking about AR compositions in various domains, the historical and theoretical resources unique to media studies can inform design thinking and project development outside of academia. Indeed, *Augmented Reality* is a product of crossing conventional boundaries to assemble contributions from scholars, artists, and industry leaders at an opportune moment in AR's development. Recently, media professionals have begun to proclaim that AR has hit the peak of its hype and will likely spend the next few years in the "trough of disillusionment" before it becomes widely adopted. Such periods of disillusionment, as suggested by Gartner's Hype Cycle for Emerging Technologies, in fact foster a desire for critical reflection on the value and potential of the medium and often push technologists toward more creative experimentation. Despite the waning hype—indeed because of it—there has never been a better time to cross-pollinate the discourse on AR.

Summary of Contributions

The contributions that make up this collection are divided into three parts: scholarly essays, interviews, and AR artworks. However, these divisions are arbitrary and we hope that the relationship between the essays, interviews, and artwork is much more fluid than what the medium of a book allows. This collection begins with Brett Oppegaard's article "Designing, Arranging, and Assessing Augmented Places through Mobile Media Alignment," in which he argues that while increased access and improvement of mobile technologies will provide more users to the data streams of AR, the "rhetorical resonance will come not from lining up pixels on screens but from aligning content in various forms that connect and contrast with the user's perceptions and needs, establishing an embodied and situated sense of place and time." Oppegaard offers that even the technical terms of AR themselves, such as "registration" and "calibration," should take on larger social meanings of human interaction to "transcend" the technological toward a better alignment with user needs and expectations. Toward this alignment, designers of AR content need to carefully take into account a user's needs within a particular location, the spatial surroundings themselves, and the context of the user and her actions in order to create a "thick" location-based AR experience.

Jason Helms turns to the integration of AR and comics in "Potential Panels: Toward a Theory of Augmented Comics" and offers that while the integration of AR into comics has been limited, it has the untapped potential to not only offer rich experiences for readers, but also change how we understand comics as a medium and genre. As Helms argues, most existing comics use AR to give their comics features that more resemble the bonus content of DVDs—such as superfluous 3D animations of characters stuck in an infinite loop, or interviews with the writers and artists—rather than augmentation that truly interacts and relates to the comic's story or rhetorical goals. Helms offers that Franco-Belgian comics such as *La Douce* make more sophisticated use of AR, but these publishers still only use AR to serve "as a gimmick to sell books and as a window into a historical machine." As such, "At their current state, AR comics are mainly marketing gimmicks with little art involved." Rather than positively augmenting comics, Helms argues that AR often hurts the reading experience of comics because it closes the meaning of a comic, or the addition of another layer through a third-party device becomes distracting. Because of this limited and undertheorized use of AR by mainstream comics publishers, Helms sees opportunity for innovation, especially by smaller independent comics, but this innovation may be more audible than visual.

Continuing along a comic theme in "'Sergey Brin Is Batman': Google Glass and the Rhetoric of Adoption in Popular Network Culture," Isabel Pedersen and Douglas Trueman argue that Sergey Brin is Batman. Of course, what they offer is much more complex than this, demonstrating that while science fiction narratives can offer us glimpses of non-existent (but potential) technologies, Google Glass is a "promise" that appears "as a new computer platform in the midst of prevailing discourses that had never before dealt with wearable computing in a mass communication milieu." In fact, depictions of AR in science fiction may actually hurt a widespread adoption of Google Glass as "most public discussion over eye displays stems from fictional portrayals, making Glass seem unbelievable or simply a trope of fiction or cinema." Even before Google Glass was released to the public, it was "desired, sensationalized, despised, and feared," offering a chance to look at the rhetorical positioning needed to gain acceptance of this new technology. Through an extensive review and discourse analysis of the marketing and conversations surrounding Google Glass, before it even existed as a physical device for general consumers, Pedersen and Trueman show that the persona developed of Brin—by himself and the general public, a persona that includes "human, inventor, entrepreneur, PhD, millionaire, Batman—provides the required credibility or ethos to make Google Glass and its augmenting abilities plausible." Thus, the authors conclude that "without Brin as the instigator, Glass would not be considered worthy of the kind of fame it enjoys."

What Brin has tried to offer through Google Glass is a personalized view of public spaces, and this increased personalization has cultural consequences. In "Life through the Screen: Location-Based Information and the Personalization of Space," Jordan Frith argues not that the development of location-based AR technologies is inherently good or bad, but that "we should be wary of utopian discourses of personalized search results, maps of friend's locations, and various location-based information filters." As users of AR make their location known to an AR app, space suddenly becomes very personalized, subject to the same user data that makes browsing the web unique for each user. By situating how such personalization may affect the larger "public space," followed by an analysis of the location-based AR app Foursquare, Frith concludes that "we need to critically examine the future ways in which AR may lead to an even more fractured experience of public space."

Moving back to the interplay between the realities of AR and how they appear in fiction, in his article "'Augpunk': Imagining Alternative Futures for Augmented Reality through Science Fiction," Joseph P. Weakland traces the development of "augpunk," a descendent of the science fiction "cyberpunk" genre that moves from cyberspace into augmented space, and explains what augpunk has to teach us about the present and future of AR, noting that AR and other emergent or potential technologies "often enter our cultural imagination through science fiction," Through readings of Tim Maughan's augpunk short stories "Paintwork," "Paparazzi," and "Havana Augmented," Weakland illustrates the ways that augpunk can criticize other mass media science fiction depictions of AR—depictions that often "carry with them the ideological residues of their development institutions"—and provide "glimpses of alternative futures for AR . . . that go beyond those accessible in more mainstream sf works." Ultimately, Weakland contends that augpunk "unsettles the economic, scientific, technological, institutional, and political dynamics that circumscribe our ability to imagine what AR can be or do."

While science fiction has long presented concepts of AR, the role of augmentation has long been held as a practice of memory. In "Gathering Memories with Augmented Reality," Jason Kalin situates AR within a longer history of memory augmentation. Noting that many traditional rhetorical practices of memory were already place-based, such as the Memory Palace, Kalin argues that as such "the art of memory was an early form and practice of augmented memory, which is . . . another way of saying augmented reality." Through a narrative describing his stroll about Chicago with Layar, HistoryPin, and other AR apps in hand, Kalin deftly considers how theories of digital network delivery and digital ambient delivery participate in the structure of "how a new media ecology introduces a new memory ecology" which ultimately determines "how memory is produced and how memory produces," especially as emerging practices of AR "disclose new modes of being with memory, and thus of being-in-the-world." These new modes of creating and being created by memory require "new aesthetics and rhetorics of memories appropriate to digital media culture" as our daily memory building via the constant integration and recording of memories through AR creates the possibility for the "monumentality of the mundane," a mundane reality out of which we may find "hidden memories full of wonder to discover a place from which we may build a future."

However, such a future may in the end be just part of a larger illusion, and in "The Dream Deferred: Augmented Reality as Rhetorical Realism," Scot Barnett argues that AR continues and perpetuates a "dream of a world in which things themselves speak, or more precisely in which things speak for themselves and in so doing bypass the whole (human) problem of reference and signification altogether." Many narratives and applications of AR devices offer this dream as they attempt to produce a transparent relationship between word and thing that becomes layered and conflated in real time. However, this attempt to bypass the ambiguity of language has been tried before, most notably through attempts to create universal languages, or through rejections of rhetoric as distortions of an external truth (realism). However, rather than reject realism outright and accept language as epistemological, Barnett returns to an ontological approach for how we might understand the layering of language within the larger complex made up by AR apps, designers, users, and the world in which they interact. Focusing on the AR app Tagwhat and turning to Heidegger and Thomas Rickert, Barnett offers that "the presence of language in many AR devices and applications opens up a wealth of possibilities for the rhetorical critic and theorist" so that "augmented reality has a great deal to teach us about rhetoric and much to contribute to rhetorical theory."

AR can also teach us about how we see, and not see, the "reals" within and around AR. In "SAZoo-AR, *Ethea*, and Computer Vision," Steve Holmes discusses the integration of AR into the experience of zoo spectatorship. A recent program by the San Antonio Zoo adds augmented displays and interactive content to zoo exhibits, seeking to better educate visiting children (including gamification through AR-based quizzes), spread a message of conservation, and give children a more "real" experience by including videos and other content of these animals in the natural ecosystems. To help achieve better education, Geomedia (the designer of the zoo's app) explicitly attempts to make the device disappear as an interface "to 'trick' students into learning." Of course, these institutions overlook the ways that AR can alter the viewing experience and learning of animals in unexpected or unintended ways. Through an analysis of SAZoo-AR via the postphenomenological interaction in SAZoo-AR, Holmes details the ways that embodied humans and computer vision interact through the zoo's AR app and argues that rather than provide a transparent experience in which the technology and viewing experience are ready-to-hand, "this content can be seen as part of an enactment of several overlapping and yet incommensurate reals that constitute the SAZoo-AR experience."

Continuing this conversation of creating new visualizations, Jason Farman pulls back the camera a bit and places AR within a larger discussion of the relation of mobile media technologies used for AR and how they create and change the ways we experience space. In his article "When Geolocation Meets Visualization," Farman discusses the dependent relationship between body and space in order to develop an understanding of what he describes as "mobile media space." Such spaces, created from embodied subjects in specific spaces, place a subject in a space multilayered with physical and virtual information. However, while older meanings of "virtual" used this term to refer to the non-physical, such uses did not discretely separate the "virtual" from the "real," instead overlaying the two in a way that both were always connected. With modern understandings of the virtual (through a transition into a "technological virtual"), "the virtual and the real continue to be discussed as opposites," which can provide blockages to our ability to critique their interaction. By examining practices of mapping as spatial practices (geographic mapping, concept mapping, biomapping, and mapping information through AR onto physical spaces), Farman explores "what 'space' means in our embodied practices of mobile technologies" as our "embodied relationship to these interfaces uniquely structures our experience (and thus conception) of the world around us."

Part 1: Scholarly Articles

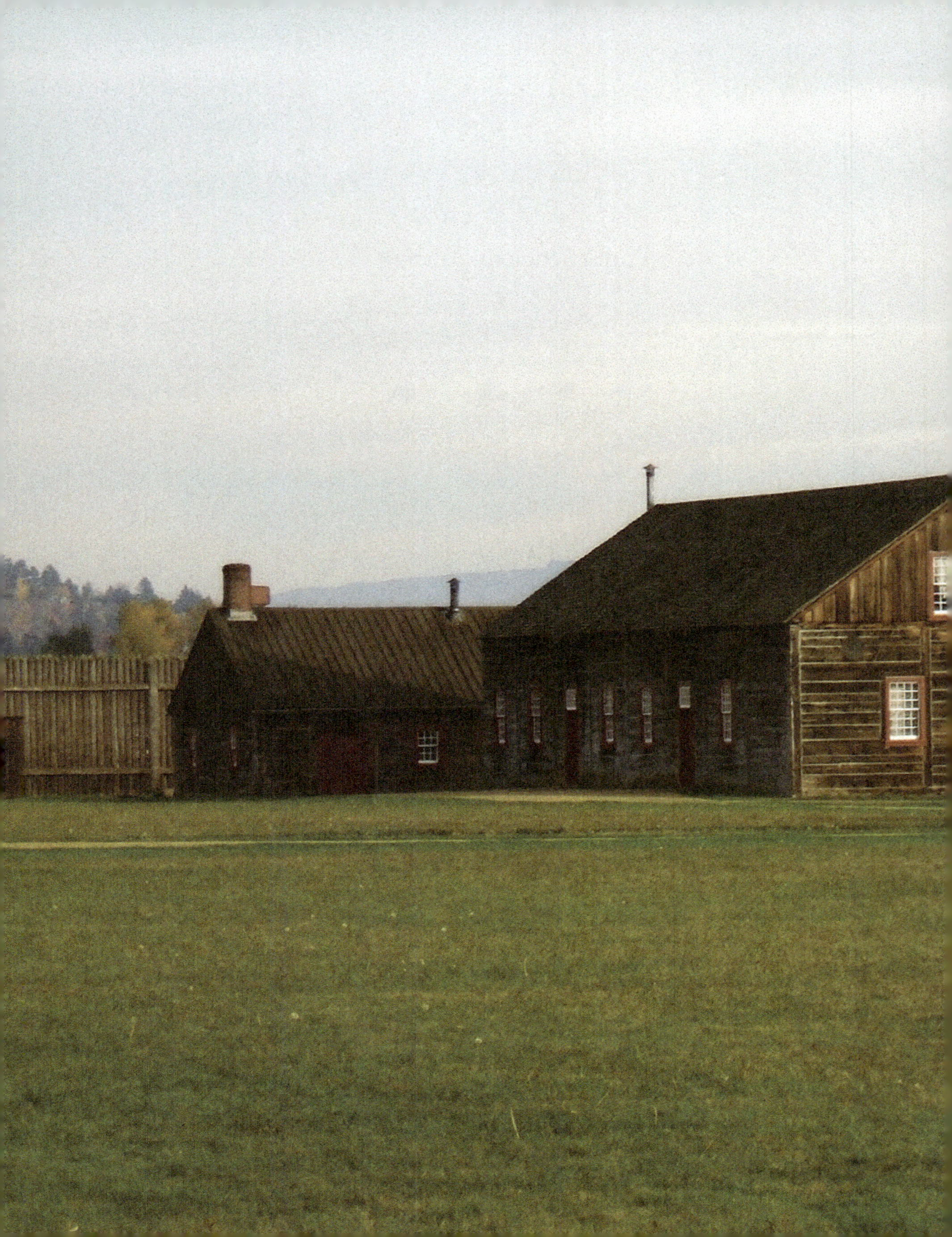

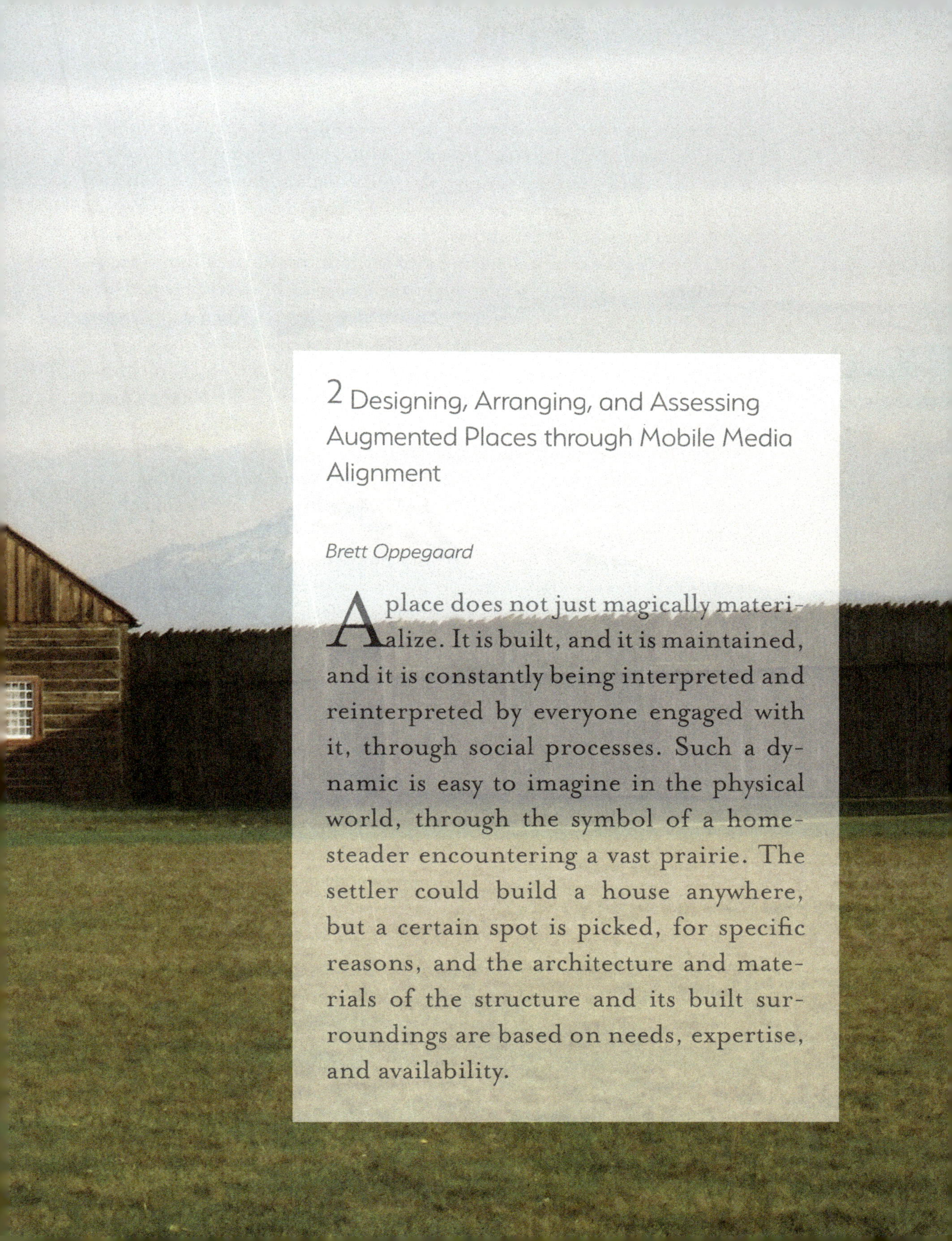

2 Designing, Arranging, and Assessing Augmented Places through Mobile Media Alignment

Brett Oppegaard

A place does not just magically materialize. It is built, and it is maintained, and it is constantly being interpreted and reinterpreted by everyone engaged with it, through social processes. Such a dynamic is easy to imagine in the physical world, through the symbol of a homesteader encountering a vast prairie. The settler could build a house anywhere, but a certain spot is picked, for specific reasons, and the architecture and materials of the structure and its built surroundings are based on needs, expertise, and availability.

If more people then come together in this bounded area, they invariably interact and socialize, and create meaning of the built environment together. A distinct culture emerges through the intermingling, the related activities, and the artifacts they construct, all of which helps to establish a context and a history of the place. What once was just a transitory space, an endless grassy field, then, has been inscribed and ascribed and transformed into a distinguishable physical place, which might even connect or overlap as part of a hub of places, as a great city might contain many locales. When digital space, though, also is considered as a part of this already complex transformation process, especially as inseparably blended with the physical space, such simplistic flat-world metaphors begin to disintegrate amid the entanglements that arise from the limitations of a physical example as an illustrative cognitive tool for understanding a mixed reality, or hybrid space.

How such space is represented and visualized has everything to do with how that space is embodied, fueling broader understandings of culture, identity, and agency, and how that space is embodied is how it transforms and becomes a place. Space today exists in a constant state of interplay between the physical and the digital, and people do not perceive a significant difference, in the sense that virtual sensations can feel just as "real," intimately linking space and embodiment. This perceptual shift—from human conceptualizations of embodiment within a physical world, with finite and distinguishable territory, to the openness and richness of a realm filled with endless hybrid space—changes how people regard materiality, space, and information in striking ways, especially generating new understandings of built environments. The rise of ubiquitous computing technologies, such as pervasive mobile devices, meanwhile keeps extending these perceptions and enriching these ideas, allowing people to see their surroundings as a layering of intertwined data, some of which they have access to, and some of which they do not, but all of which is there, as latent physical and digital sensations, seemingly just waiting for someone to free them from their dormant state and bring them to the accessible surfaces and interfaces.

"Rhetorical resonance will come not from lining up pixels on screens but from aligning content in various forms that connect and contrast with the user's perceptions and needs."

Improving technical precision and capabilities in our technologies will open up these environments for further explorations, but rhetorical resonance will come not from lining up pixels on screens but from aligning content in various forms that connect and contrast with the user's perceptions and needs, establishing an embodied and situated sense of place and time. With mobile technologies, the user is able to move fluidly while staying connected, allowing deft designers to curate and arrange digital information and generate useful interfaces to develop not just networks of proximity to the user's physical environment but also to the spatial and the conceptual. Such multifaceted and perceptive alignment of information could become the ultimate challenge of augmented design, and designers need new tools, methodologies, and theories to better understand and build these mixed reality environments to serve users and also to assess their effectiveness. This chapter therefore attempts to break some of that ground, by proposing a paradigm based on the theoretical construct of mobile media alignment.

Reductionism, of course, could be a path to allow researchers to see a part of this place-making design process in action, and many valuable research studies already have been conducted on the precise technical aspects of augmenting physical space with digital material in various ways. Yet generally left out of these discussions are the designers and the users of the places, in terms of their practical experiences in these processes of envisioning, making, maintaining, appreciating, and assessing places, which dictates the real-world value of these augmented places as social constructs, which is the focus in this piece. So what I extend in this chapter is not a purely theoretical discussion about this topic, nor a purely practical one, but a mesh, based on an evolving paradigm of mobile media alignment, which is intended to provide new ways to consider the design, arrangement, and assessment of augmented places. Such a social constructionist tool clearly is needed to allow designers and users of augmented places to precisely and holistically examine the effects of built and augmented places, created from digital material woven into, and integrated with, the physical environment. By focusing on the practicality and symbolic ideas that the term alignment can generate, especially in bringing together the experiences of designers and users in authentic situations and in physical places, what typically are considered technical terms, such as registration and calibration, can transcend their status as merely mechanical distinctions and instead become symbols of larger assessment ideals, as a way to ultimately judge whether a design works in its present form and delivery, or not.

Terminology and Context

I have already used a lot of terms with contentious histories, and the definitions of those words have been proposed and debated from many different perspectives. My intent here is not to initiate or revive linguistic debates. Instead, I attempt to make small and transparent adjustments to well-trodden terminology paths as a way to concentrate on the points I'm trying to establish, rather than to diverge into a discussion on definitions and semantics. While such debate is valuable and should continue, I focus elsewhere here on trying to develop a paradigm based on the user's experience in augmented reality and how designers can improve those experiences. That said, some discourse on the vocabulary of this work could be fruitful. But my hope is that rather than get sidetracked on debates about terms, we can establish the vocabulary, as used in this work, and then proceed to think more about alignment.

Distinguishing the word space from place, for example, and determining how those terms symbiotically coexist, has been a central topic of extensive discussion in various disciplines for many years. This chapter will build primarily from the definitions proposed by Tuan, who states that space is more abstract than place. In short, he writes, space is a realm without meaning, or a fluid zone of transition. When meaning is ascribed to a space, though, this zone gains its boundaries and its frameworks and transforms into a place. Conversely, when meaning of a place is lost, or that meaning dissipates, this zone reverts back into space, like the grassy plains that might eventually cover the remains of the homesteader's log cabin. Space, in turn, offers openness and freedom. Place, as a contrast, offers security and stability. One is needed to define the other. Space, from this perspective, therefore can be likened to movement, and place can be envisioned as the pauses, or stops along the way, in which people interpret the viewpoint and get to know a realm, however they define it, endowing it with value.

Developments of digital file sharing, mobile technologies, and ubiquitous computing have expanded such understandings of space and place in different ways, and from those foundations this chapter delves into the additional complexity created by the layering and interweaving of digital and physical spaces known broadly as augmented reality. Even that expansive umbrella label can be debatable, though, with de Souza e Silva noting the three distinct categorizations coexisting in recent scholarly literature, based on technology use, plus innumerable inconsistent variations pervading industry texts. Even this single book on augmented reality contains various author impressions of the term.

In this chapter, the base understanding of the concept comes from Milgram and Colquhoun's broad second categorization of augmented reality, or on cases in which any mixture of real and virtual environments overlap. The key to that categorization, from this perspective, is that the boundaries begin formation from the physical environment, as a place, and the augmentation element refers to digital layers applied to that place. That overlapping is where alignment occurs. An even broader third category of augmented reality also is proposed by those authors, called "mixed reality," and this chapter drifts toward that direction of even a more mingled physical and digital, attracted to de Souza e Silva's extension of the idea, with a merging of mixed reality, augmented spaces, mobility, and sociability that she calls "hybrid reality." Within hybrid reality are hybrid spaces, she writes, which are built by the connection of mobility and communication and materialized by social networks, developed simultaneously in both physical and digital spaces. This is a situation in which a real-world context is dynamically overlaid with "coherent" location or context-sensitive virtual information curated and arranged by designers and assessed by users. This is not a situation in which virtual experiences are enhanced by elements of the physical environment, which is a different concern, called augmented virtuality. This also is not a situation in which universal media is designed to appeal to users anywhere, which leans even more toward the virtual.

Within these hybrid spaces are the hybrid places, or physical locations that offer "embodied spatial" interactions blending the physical with the digital in specific ways that denote meaning of the place. While a place might be static long enough for examination, like a lava flow, the theoretical lens developing here includes the idea that as space becomes place, place also always is in a state of "becoming," as described by Pred. Place, therefore, needs to be understood as an embodied relationship with the world, constructed by people doing things, including designers curating and arranging built experiences, and understood in a never "finished," or even fixed, state. Yet, through this theoretical lens and the moment of pausing and examining a place, the transfiguration happens at such a pace, like grass growing, that observations can be relevant and accurate for extended enough periods for adequate evaluations to be made. Also, from this paradigm, there is no longer a homogeneous context for any given spatial area. Instead, pockets of different contexts exist within each place, open to differing interpretations, and any of these perspectives could be considered valid.

Making just a slight move sideways from these established positions on terms as a way to lessen the concentration on mobility and social networking, I also am using the label "augmented place" as an extension of augmented space, to bring the attention of the inquiry to the pausing point and to the mix of physical and digital sensations at a moment, from the user's perspective, starting from the foundation of the physical location but including the cognizance of digital layers as well, as part of a holistic understanding of a spot on this planet from the viewpoint of a ubiquitous computing user, such as someone equipped with a smart mobile device, at a particular point in time.

While these users certainly still could be classified as mobile, that overall fluidity of mobility pauses for a moment, with the user's mobility, in the process of creating the place and making connections to its augmentations. The social connections, if not related to the place-making, meanwhile are tangential to this place-oriented perspective. The mobility in this case, in a broad sense, could be visualized as a registration or calibration process, as the designer of the place curates and arranges the material in alignment with the augmented place, although not in the limited technical sense most often attributed to those terms. Instead, I envision the place coming into a sort of a momentary focus, through perceptions both digital and physical, and the user, at that point, being able to assess whether those perceptions are aligned with expectations and needs, or not.

Beyond Technical Issues

Augmented reality, as a concept, not a specific technology, has been under development for decades as part of the societal shift away from desktop computing and toward pervasive interactions with "smart" services, anytime and anywhere. It can be considered one of the core forms of ubiquitous computing, as envisioned by Weiser. Despite the many and diverse efforts expended to date, though, augmented reality arguably remains in its developmental infancy, especially in terms of satisfying users' expectations and providing positive user experiences, critical criteria for encouraging widespread adoption and acceptance. This stunted growth likely is because the most pressing of those needs is pragmatic relevance, including contextually relevant information easily available that allows for novel interactions with the physical world. Augmented reality systems, at this point, simply do not satisfy those needs very well. The major augmented reality systems—Layar (www.layar.com), Junaio (www.junaio.com), and Wikitude (www.wikitude.com)—all show great potential but also suffer from significant sensory inaccuracies and regularly misaligned content. Many perceptual issues have been identified in the application of current augmented reality technology as barriers affecting overall performance and thereby negatively swaying user perceptions. Those generally can be categorized as implementation errors (creating perceptual inaccuracies due to calibration errors), technological limitations (including static and dynamic registration mismatches), and "hard" problems (such as dealing with an expanded depth of field). Many of those technical issues can be fixed, and will be fixed, eventually. What cannot be simply addressed through better registration and calibration, though, are the bigger content and contextual issues; as in, when the novelty wears off, what will augmented reality truly offer the user, in terms of relevant and interactive information, that cannot be accessed in better ways in other technological forms, including even paper products, established and reliable, such as brochures. Augmented reality should consider itself in competition with every other mobile media technology, including paper, and focus on what it does best, and that is to dynamically align with augmented place.

Part of the current problems in the field are due to a combination of the various technical issues but also the attempt to rapidly increase in scale, as in trying to reach a large enough audience to make massive profits with a technology that has not really figured itself out yet, with augmented information not often enough adequately aligned with the user's location, spatial environment, and context. That overall dynamic is less technical, then, than theoretical, with a relative lack of focus on the user experiences and a lack of research on user-centered development in augmented reality, which helps to perpetuate that foggy view. In turn, user acceptance of augmented reality is equivalently low, based on perceptions about ease of use, value, and trust in the given technology, and it likely will remain low unless that primary paradigm of augmented reality is adjusted and aligned with user interests and common use-case scenarios.

Some researchers, in response, have focused upon improving registration and calibration from a practical viewpoint. Technical improvement, of course, would be beneficial in many ways, and is needed on many levels, but mobile augmented reality arguably has matured enough already to offer high-quality services. Audiences, though, still are not accepting and adopting augmented reality on the scale many suggest should be. Part of that disconnect seems to be caused by perception, or the recognition and interpretation of sensory stimuli, which is complex and multimodal, with each sense providing different information, simultaneously, which guides interpretations. The environment offers cues, both digital and physical, revealing affordances and constraints, and when those cues smoothly align, a positive user experience naturally materializes in satisfying ways. But when those cues are misaligned, or conflicting, as augmented reality systems today regularly confound a user's senses, this system creates noise that repels users rather than attracts them. From a user experience perspective, and on a theoretical level, both instrumental (utility and usability) and non-instrumental (joy and appeal) elements should be assessed, as subjective and holistic considerations of design, and augmented reality as a concept, should include not only the application and its functionalities but also the curation and arrangement of content, and that content's alignment in space and place.

In hybrid space, a person must pause and focus on a particular point of view related to the surroundings and layers of digital information, or simply flow onward. At that moment, through such crystallization of a perspective, distinctive attributes of the domain come into focus and others fade away as interpreters intuitively make sense of what the place means, to be right there, right at that moment, assessed from their diverse perspectives. Augmented places cannot be fully perceived at a distance, or remotely, since that would separate and mediate the experience from the physical world and filter out the sensations and unconscious tacit understandings that come only from sensory immersion in physical settings. Augmented places cannot be fully perceived on a physical level only, either, since the related digital information in the ether is as important to the engagement in the experience as air, whether the person accesses all of the information, or just a small sample of it, and regardless if the full potential of the situation is ever realized. This chapter will contend that a closer examination of such stabilized moments, by sustained concentration upon what can be understood about the physical-digital alignment of the situation, could lead not only to a better understanding of augmented places but to better user experiences within augmented realities and quicker development and adoption of the theoretical infrastructure needed for the growth of this field. To reach that level of sophistication, though, more grounding in the pragmatics of the idea is necessary.

From the design perspective, mobile media alignment can be thought of as a system of analysis and guidance. From the user perspective, it can serve as a system of assessment. In short, if the digital information is not aligned with the physical information in mindful ways, either the user is momentarily placeless or the information is momentarily lost in space. In a generic classroom context, Shaffer and Resnick envision authentic learning as meaning either: (a) materials and activities are aligned with the world outside the classroom, (b) assessment is aligned with (what students really should learn from) instruction, (c) topics of study are aligned with what learners want to know, and/or (d) methods of inquiry are aligned with the essential practices of a discipline. As an extension of that educational metaphor, if the users of ubiquitous computing technologies are understood and visualized by designers as situated and lifelong learners, they are not flowing through spaces, but pausing in places, educational settings needing alignment of materials and activities, designed to meet contextual lifelong learning needs of what users want to do and know, through methods tried and tested within the related disciplines.

Learning, from this perspective, does not happen at predetermined times in prespecified places. It happens whenever a person breaks from routine, reflects on the current situation, and resolves to address a problem, share an idea, or gain an understanding. These environments, in turn, dynamically are constructed in situ by mobile device users, as they interact with their surroundings. That description illustrates the natural alliance of learning as a contextual activity with mobile devices and the physical environment as complementary interfaces. The presence of a hidden reality, toward which our clues are pointing, and the discovery which terminates and satisfies a particular pursuit, is sustained by the same vision, that a small portion of reality has been contacted, and more of it exists. Physical and symbolic clues continually alert the minds of the open and the curious toward interactions within the global network, as points of immersion into humanity's collective intelligence and as reaching toward more contact. Even beyond the realm of explicitly documented and expressed knowledge, though, tacit knowledge also exists in ways that, as Polanyi stated, "We can know more than we can tell." One can envision this process as the mind reaching a pause of a place, opening its petals, and eagerly waiting for the intellectual dew. When flowing through space, the person finds a focus, and the personal participation of the knower in the knowledge that the person takes possession of, as it takes root within a flow of passion, as intellectual beauty, guides the discovery. When such a connection is made, alignment is evident and needs no further declarations. But augmented reality, in its present forms, rarely offers such clear payoffs. Designers of augmented places, for whatever reasons, generally are not regularly curating and arranging digital material in relationships with the physical environment of the user in the ways users crave to get it. Maybe a guidance system, like mobile media alignment, would help the focus remain on augmented reality's three greatest strengths, which start first with the knowledge of the user's location, then with knowledge of the user's spatial environment, and finally, and maybe most importantly, with knowledge of the user's context.

Tier 1 Alignment: Location

Ancient Greeks, forming the foundations of Western thought, first began describing place poetically, in recognizable patterns of expression, as a way to distinguish how one place was different than another, more than 2,500 years ago. Humans have been inscribing and ascribing their spaces and thereby transforming them into places for millennia. Those activities have included paintings on cave walls in France and carvings into stone in Egypt but also reenactments of historic battles, at places such as Gettysburg, and guided tours of the Stations of the Cross in Israel. Even early mobile delivery systems, such as papyrus scrolls, gained power not from their fluidity, or mobility, but from their eventual alignment with a particular location (such as providing prices in the local market), from their alignment with a specific spatial environment (such as the ways in which a map might flexibly inform an entire region), or from the alignment with a particular contextual situation (such as the news of the results of an important battle and what that might mean for the people during the rest of the war). So alignment of information, in a contextual lifelong learning sense, is not necessarily new, nor is it inherently digital.

Yet the importance of location, place, and alignment of information with augmented place shifted significantly in 2002 when the Federal Communications Commission began requiring GPS-locating hardware on every mobile device. That legislation meant that wireless carriers inherently were able to locate subscriber devices anywhere they happen to be, with great precision, and, in turn, data providers could know where the person was when they were receiving data. Since mobile devices, such as smartphones, have become like other appendage technologies, like shoes and clothes and eyeglasses, designers suddenly could know exactly where their audience was, what was around those people, likely what activities they had done, and through data analysis, also what they were probably most interested in doing in the future. Such information offered the potential for designers to more intricately and intimately arrange helpful services for users. From the user perspective, aside from the significant privacy concerns, the release of this information to designers meant that potentially their needs, whatever they were, no matter how individualistic, could be met more efficiently and effectively.

Location therefore became the foundational attribute of mobile apps, providing digital media that in many ways could respond to, and augment, place. Location literally creates the conditions under which interaction occurs, and it also provides the context from which information is interpreted and incorporated into use. No matter where you might be in cyberspace, there is not an alternative to being grounded in a location, and therefore, to be a part of a space that could be transformed into a place. So while a map, and other media technologies, has related place to a person's embodiment in a specific location before, mobile devices perform that orientation dynamically, and for the most part, autonomously, thereby becoming more an aspect of becoming cyborg than wielding a tool.

From the mobile media alignment perspective, then, an understanding of location starts in the physical environment. Since digital media is connected to place through GPS coordinates, or some other similar tracking and linking system, designers have the discretion to determine the radius of the tether to a place. Since much of my mobile media design work has been at heritage sites, I will use an example from that kind of situation. Imagine you visit a historic site, and you walk up to a historic house. Until you reach a place in which the designers of this built environment have arranged and programmed an interaction, you essentially are flowing through space, walking the paths, gathering tacit sensory data, seeking a focus. But once you reach the front porch of the house, for example, you logically might want to know more information, and the designers therefore would want to be in a position to give you some, since aligning an augmented place comes from a deep understanding of the user's needs, not from fulfilling a designer's whims. At this point, again imagine the petals of the user's mind fully opened, the most promising alignment potential would come from providing digital information about and related to either this front porch, the central element in the location, or whatever else can be perceived through the senses in this specific location. At probably no other time in the user's life is this front porch going to be more interesting than at the moment in which that person is there, in that location, communing with the place. So the mobile media alignment paradigm could be enacted by sharing in that place, at that moment, a video reconstruction of an important event that happened in that same spot, or an audio track giving voice to a letter written by someone who sat there once, or a still image of that same porch 50 or 100 years ago, showing other people from the past using the place, or an animation demonstrating the construction techniques used to make that kind of structure, or whatever. As long as the location, and what the user can perceive at that location, is in the forefront of the curated and designed and arranged experience, then alignment smoothly can happen; the more tailored to the location, the more aligned the experience could be. The more aligned the experience becomes, I theorize, the better the user experience will be. But tailoring information to the location is just the start of the design and arrangement process, an important but also limited part of creating alignment.

Tier 2 Alignment: Spatial

Location can be envisioned as the GPS-located spot on the map, and all of its surrounding perceptions, from the user's viewpoint when occupying that location and experiencing all of its sounds, sights, smells, etc. The spatial component of alignment is a recognition and awareness of everything physically nearby the user yet outside of the direct perceptions. Using the map comparison, again, imagine that the designer has the map and an understanding of the greater surroundings, while the user only can perceive what can be seen, heard, smelled, etc. To align on a spatial level is to not only curate, design, and arrange digital information to what the user can directly access through the senses, but also to be able to guide the user to even richer and broader connections just beyond perceptual reach, through such techniques as suggesting other locations to visit, importing information about nearby landmarks, attractions, and artifacts, and generally extending the senses of the user, thereby allowing a greater alignment to the augmented place through an expanded perspective of the location.

At the historic front porch, the user might be aligned to the location, per the example above, yet not be aligned at all to the larger space and what it offers. What if this particular porch could be used as an example of how people served and ate meals in the mid-1800s, before the widespread adoption of the formal dining room idea? The user might be able to learn that information and appreciate that perspective for its limited value, but if the designer of the augmented place also gave the user information about the old oak tree, just around the bend of the hill, where the village often came together to eat meals and build community instead of eating alone, the isolated information of just the location, while important and interesting, could grow even more in significance and rhetorical resonance, enlarging an example and transforming it into a theme.

Location can be considered the core of the alignment concerns, because without an augmented place there can be no expansion or abstraction of that central point. Without alignment of location, one might as well be sitting in a dark room, or a nondescript cubicle. Spatial awareness, though, is just the start of the superpowers that ubiquitous computing can bring to society. If designers can better align the spatial perspective with the needs of users, based on a location, an array of opportunities could present themselves to both, and contextual awareness then could create an unprecedented level of media alignment from those foundations.

Tier 3 Alignment: Contextual

Each of the three levels of alignment inherently increases in abstraction, yet because of the core tether to the physical location, and the augmented place, even contextual alignment remains grounded in practical concerns. In short, the more we use ubiquitous computing technologies, the better they get to know us, from the data we create, and the more predictive our needs

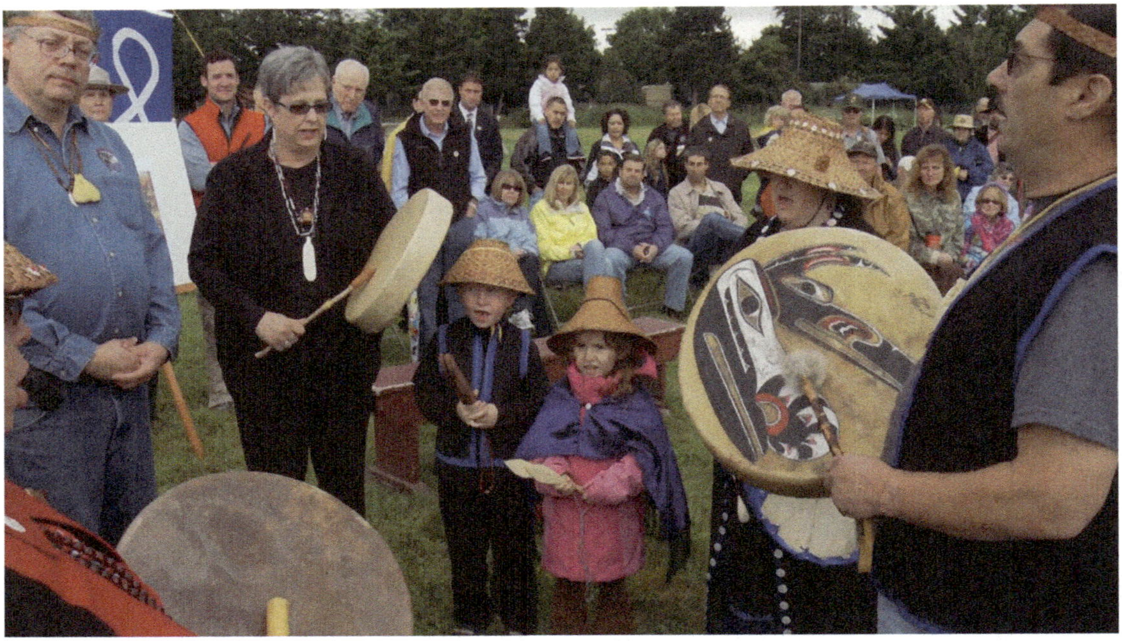

Figure 2.1: This Fort Vancouver Mobile video of Cowlitz Tribe drummers and chanters (www.fortvancouvermobile.com) has little meaning outside of its original context, as a ceremonial blessing for the opening of a reconstructed village at Fort Vancouver National Historic Site, in Vancouver, Washington. But when this video was embedded in the place, where it happened—through computer programming—and made available to visitors who could trigger the video to play on their mobile devices by entering the GPS-located push zone at the physical site, a novel sort of hybrid space was produced. This mixed-reality space can be embodied by the app user, and the mobile device can become the interface for the augmented place, not just a peephole through which to see information. In turn, the user can align the physical environment with that of the digital environment, to engage Tier 3 Mobile Media Alignment effect, and recreate the ceremony through a new kind of hybrid experience. © 2013 by Fort Vancouver.

AURASMA
Scan the image to view.

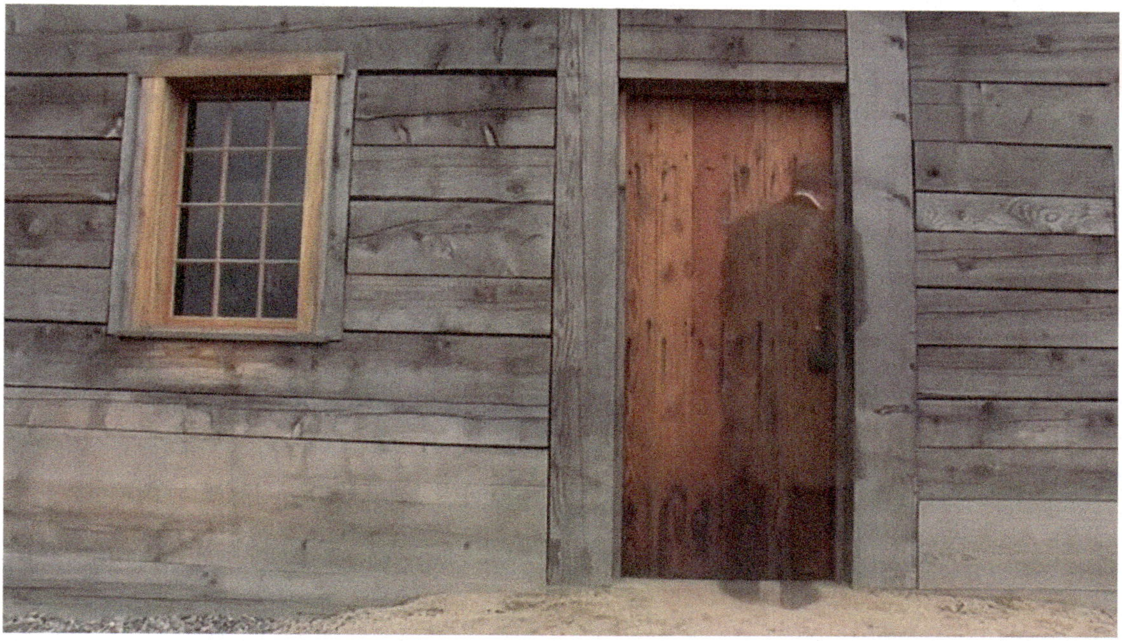

Figure 2.2: To further illustrate the potential of a Tier 3 Mobile Media Alignment strategy, of creating and distributing media in a particular place, this Fort Vancouver Mobile video reconstructs the arrival of the story's protagonist, William Kaulehelehe. His new home in the Pacific Northwest is much different than the one he left in Hawai'i. The period Hawaiian chant at the start of the video therefore transitions the context of the situation from a hopeful, new-day-is-dawning theme to the rigid English doxology, representing a dramatic change in culture for Kaulehelehe and foreshadowing troubles ahead. The mobile app user receives this video at the very doorway that Kaulehelehe enters, offering little in terms of expositional framing but instead allowing the user to create an immersive context-building experience through the augmentation of the physical scene. © 2012 by Fort Vancouver.

AURASMA
Scan the image to view.

can become. When many people use an augmented place, broad patterns of use emerge, and common actions repetitively appear, which can indicate to designers the richest opportunities for serving those users. When designers understand their audiences in great depth, or at least better, they can create more useful designs and more engaging experiences.

Contextual awareness, through such data gathering, provides virtually unlimited potential for contextual alignment or the precise matching of mobile media design to user's needs in place and in customized configurations. This type of alignment also is the most complex, dependent upon recognizing and serving needs that sometimes are motivated by desires not even conscious to the users. Related activities can be physical, psychological, social, etc., and they can tap into any number of technological resources in the vicinity and be accessible, connecting with mobile media that has been extracted, interpreted, and prepared for just that moment.

With mobile media, as with archaeology, context is essential, though, and an archaeological metaphor could be helpful for explaining this level of alignment, through envisioning the digital fragments that exist, signifying life past and present, and how those shards of people, places, objects, events, and activities—spanning space and time—can coalesce around a location through curation and imaginative design, and through precise arrangement become aligned with the user's specific needs. While any user can discover meaning in a mosaic, contextual alignment means a mindful and purposeful placement of these parts, based on location, embedded in an augmented place that begins with an understanding of the GPS-precise spot on earth being enhanced by mobile media, then recognizes the nearby affordances of the area, and finally, from the viewpoint of a designer serving a user, incorporates all of the data available about the user and the location to tailor contextually relevant and rhetorically resonant mobile media.

Conclusion

Looking through the augmented reality lenses of mobile devices, anyone can see that something, in a general sense, is slightly off-kilter. Beyond pixels not lining up just so, something deeper in this type of platform is out of registration and needs calibration. Many people have predicted that augmented mobile media will be great because it can present dynamic new ways to experience what is all around us, through elaborate sensory extensions, and that could be a powerful ability indeed. Embodied and present, mobile-device users inherently are immersed in dynamic juxtapositions of digital media and the physical sensations of the environment. They have fallen into an unpredictable and peripatetic swirl of information, technology, and haptics, gradually being understood as an augmented reality. Scholarly researchers, though, still are struggling to make sense of these complex mixed-reality situations, particularly from a theoretical perspective. Augmented reality is not a stabilized concept yet, either in terminology or technology. Compared to other platforms, such as social networks, it is not in widespread use. That novelty, at this point, might accentuate its effects and true potential and send researchers down wrong paths. Yet these paths need to be walked to discover what augmented reality will eventually deliver.

Mobile media alignment might be a way to positively affect a sense of emplacement, or an embodied and situated sense of place, and develop the sense of a "thick" authenticity to an augmented experience. Designers control such development directions through the curation of materials, the design of the experiences, and the arrangement of the pieces as they make them accessible through the interfaces they also create. But the users are the judges. They assess the augmentation and determine whether it works for them, or not, and in the hyper-competitive world of mobile apps, they vote with their fingers, every day, all of the time, by either using an app or swiping it away and discarding it.

Embodied and present, mobile-device users inherently immerse themselves into these mixed-reality environments, just by turning their devices on and experiencing what happens next. The unpredictable and peripatetic swirl of information, technology, and haptics can be disorienting and overwhelming. Scholarly researchers are struggling with how to make sense of such complex situations, particularly from a theoretical perspective. Mobile media alignment, at this stage, is an idea that could lead people, especially designers and users, toward a new perspective on augmented reality and the augmented places it can create. Such an initial framework, though, once extended as in this chapter, and, ideally, further refined through dialectical discourse afterward, needs to be put to the practical test.

If this idea creates an increased awareness of the importance of aligning mobile media with location, the spatial surroundings, and context, then that is a start. If this idea leads to an operationalization of the concepts, systematic interventions, and empirical data to establish the edges of its value (or lack of value), even better.

From the mobile media alignment perspective, designers should focus first on the user's needs in the location. The potential for users and fulfilling their needs in the spatial surroundings should be considered next, and then concern should be on the specific context of the user and how that context could create and predict needs, but also how it could fulfill those needs in dynamic and interesting ways, always tethered to the distinctive features of the location. The impression should not be made, though, that this is a linear process. Instead, the vision of mobile media alignment is of a design process that grows more complex, as it rises through the tiers, only to circle back around to location and continue through the process again and again for refinement. In short, if the designer does not have a great grasp of location, then any work on spatial or contextual issues would be flailing at the wind. Through each cycle of iteration, though, the designer should gain greater understandings of the place and the value of the augmentation, and get better and better bearings.

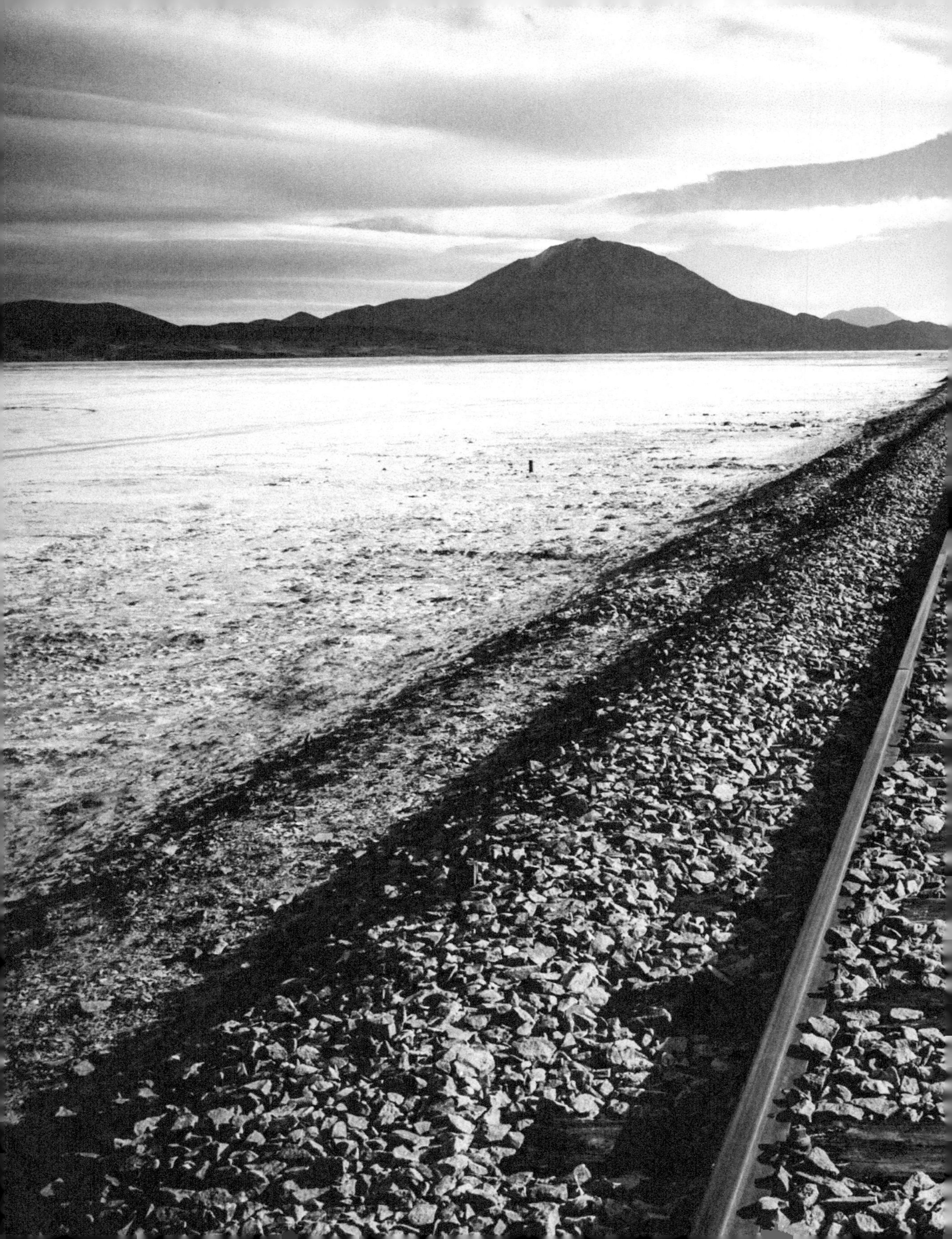

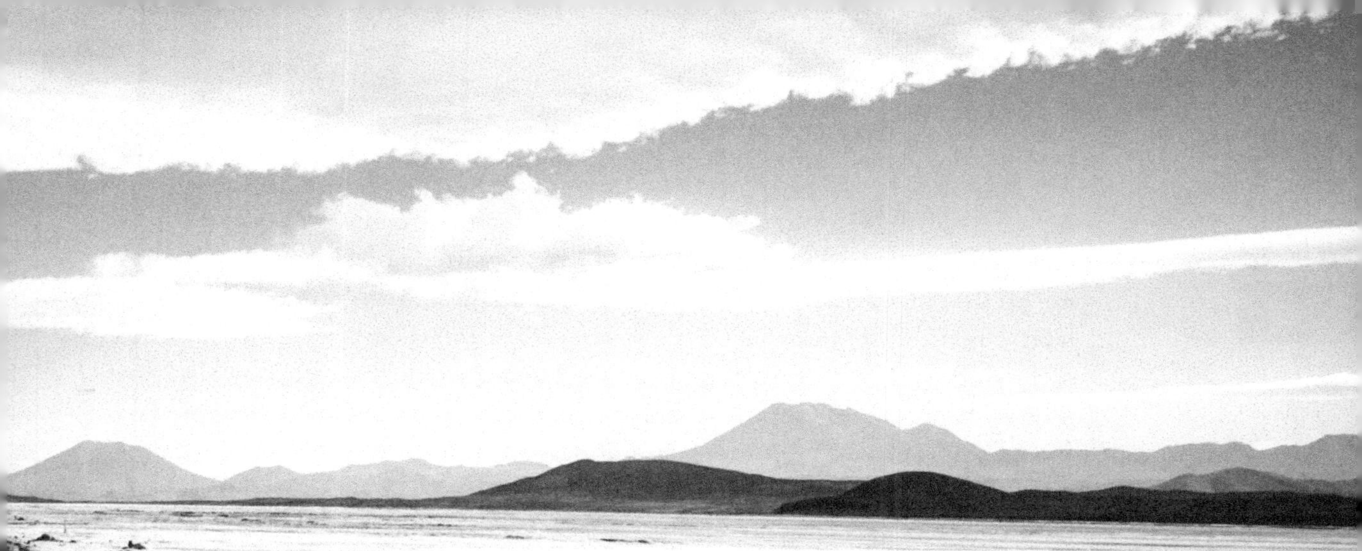

3 Potential Panels: Toward a Theory of Augmented Comics

Jason Helms

I remember the first time I saw *X-Men* #1 as a kid. Not the 1960s *Uncanny* #1—although the first time I saw a copy of that was a momentous occasion for a prepubescent comics fetishist—but the 1991 series written by Chris Claremont and illustrated by Jim Lee. Lee had drawn four different covers that, laid side by side, created a polyptic of super-powered mutants in Lycra battling each other over the fate of humanity. My best friend Grant laid them out on the floor for me to drool over.

The story inside was good, featuring a new threat from Magneto on his orbiting asteroid, but I returned again and again to the panorama created by the combined posters. This moment I fell in love with comics later signified for me all that was deceptive and manipulative about mainstream comics. Years later I realized this was just a marketing stunt to sell more comics. Instead of buying just one copy of a comic, collectors would have to buy all four, plus a fifth "deluxe" edition with a folding cover of the complete image. The flagrant money grab by Marvel should have portended to most collectors the imminent bursting of the comics collecting bubble. The interest of collectors led to a focus on elaborate covers for comics that would be boxed away like the Ark of the Covenant, never to be read by impressionable kids like myself. Comics became a sophistic: all appearance with no substance.

The comics industry survived the collecting bubble and is stronger than ever, producing big-budget films and garnering an ever more diverse readership. The big publishers are doing fine, but the market has made room for hundreds of independent titles. Amid all this prosperity, Marvel Comics has recently embraced augmented reality as a way to enhance comics and sales. Marvel AR is not the only example of augmented reality comics, but it is the most influential. When I see a three-dimensional Iron Man appear to burst out of an illustrated page and fly around, part of me cringes, fearing the inflation of yet another bubble around my favorite medium, filling until it bursts and the fickle fans find other fads.

I begin this chapter by investigating both comics and augmented reality through the ongoing debates of each medium's definition. I offer a brief history of augmented reality comics, exploring four examples in particular. These examples will provide a basis for theorizing what augmented reality comics have done and hypothesizing what they might be capable of. The last section will focus on the potential for augmented reality comics. Comic theorists have described the ways comics augment either text or image by supplying the latter. By adding an entirely new layer, augmented reality has the potential to complicate the current states of comics and comics theory. Independent artists might seem less likely to experiment with the capabilities of augmented reality comics due to economic obstacles. However, comic creators outside the American mainstream are already doing just that. These experiments can begin to show us what augmented reality and even comics themselves are capable of.

Defining Augmented Reality

While augmented reality's roots go back to the 1960s, it has recently moved to the forefront of the popular conscience and become a focus of academic attention. Unlike comics, augmented reality's definition is not under serious debate. In *Augmented Reality: An Emerging Technologies Guide to AR*, Gregory Kipper and Joseph Rampolla offer a threefold definition of augmented reality:

1. AR combines real and virtual information.
2. AR is interactive in real time.
3. AR is operated and used in a 3D environment.

Given this definition, a great deal of what is currently being marketed as AR would be excluded. Most Quick Response (QR) codes clearly fall short. QR codes typically link a real world object to a URL. Most QR codes stop there, simply connecting users to a website. However, if that URL then interacts with a real world object in 3D, then the experience would qualify as augmented reality. Many AR comics do just this, as will be seen below.

Another definitional hang-up is the question of medium. While augmented reality would seem to be a clear-cut medium—acting as a material connection between an author and a reader or user—it typically piggybacks along a pre-existing medium, augmenting both reality and the original artifact. Like much new media, augmented reality is difficult to pigeon-hole. AR acts as a container-medium much like computers and smartphones, but augmented reality's layering makes it unique. AR employs a medium to augment reality, to add a layer of information, functionality, or aesthetics. With AR, perhaps genre is more helpful than medium. While not all augmented reality experiences are in a similar genre, they typically act within the same genre as the original medium that they use to augment reality.

Defining Comics

Comics' definition has much less consensus. There have historically been two distinct formalist definitions of comics. Recently, scholars have entered the fray with radically new definitions. I have explored this conversation more fully elsewhere, but it will suffice to summarize it here.

Will Eisner, a major figure in comics theory and innovative artist and author, developed an early definition in his influential 1985 *Comics and Sequen-*

tial Art: "The fundamental function of comics art to communicate ideas and/or stories by means of words and pictures involves the movement of certain images (such as people and things) through space." Eisner's definition points in two directions simultaneously: the juxtaposition of words and pictures and implied movement through sequential images. This twofold definition later became a contentious divide for comics scholars.

In his 1993 *Understanding Comics*—a comics-format investigation of the medium—Scott McCloud stresses the importance of sequentiality for comics, borrowing Eisner's term *sequential art*. McCloud offers a robust exploration of the gutter, the space between two panels in a comic, repeating a simple two-panel comic throughout the book to explain what he calls *closure*. In the first panel we see a minimalist figure with his hand on his top hat. The second panel is identical to the first except that now the hat has been raised off of the figure's head. The reader participates by inferring movement between the panels—the figure is tipping his hat. McCloud makes much of the fact that all of this happens in the blank space between the panels. He calls this blank space *the gutter* and the inference *closure*. McCloud's formalist approach depends upon a definition that not only privileges movement but also excludes single-panel comics like *The Family Circus* and *The Far Side*. The fact that these examples are typically thought of as comics caused distress for many comics scholars, particular Robert Harvey.

Harvey finished his 1994 *The Art of The Funnies* before reading McCloud's book, but he offers a radically different definition of comics:

> The thing that comics do that no other graphic art does is to weave word and picture together to achieve a narrative purpose. Comics are a blend of word and picture—not a simple coupling of the verbal and the visual, but a blend, a true mixture. From the nature of the medium, then, we can draw up one criterion for critical evaluation: in the usual situation, in which both words and pictures are used, a measure of a comic strip's excellence is the extent to which the sense of the words is dependent on the pictures and vice versa.

Harvey privileges the juxtaposition of image and text rather than inferred movement across sequential panels. Just like McCloud, Harvey traces the critical consequences of his definition. The dependence of image and text on each other provides a measuring stick for critics. Here the reader is again a critical participant, completing the connection between words and text. If the text merely repeats the image, the comic fails as comic and the reader does not become involved in the comic.

Both Harvey and McCloud's definitions attempt to explain the participatory nature of comics, first noted by media theorist Marshall McLuhan. For McLuhan and McCloud, comics are a cool medium because of their low-definition cartoony art that users must complete and their high-participation closure across the gutter between panels. For Harvey, readers participate by completing the implied connection between image and text. Both McCloud and Harvey are comic creators: artists, not just theorists. This might explain their formalist tendencies. By the mid-nineties, two clear formalist camps had arisen in American comics studies hinging on comics' essential definition: sequential art or words and pictures. While there were certainly other approaches to comics during this time (psychoanalytic, auteur, feminist, new-historicist, genre, queer, post-colonial, etc.), these two camps dominated the conversation.

In 2007, Aaron Meskin weighed in with an influential article entitled simply "Defining Comics?" Meskin traced these conversations and their effect on art and aesthetic approaches to comics. He argued that despite their acceptance and dominance, both fail by excluding things that scholars typically consider comics and by including things they do not. The sequential art definition excludes single-panel strips. The words and pictures definition excludes wordless comics (of which there are numerous examples). Both definitions would include artifacts like the *Bayeux Tapestry*, *Trajan's Column*, and some hieroglyphics. For Meskin, this is a major issue. Meskin offered three possible solutions.

A historical definition would include everything scholars typically consider comics and exclude the others. Such a definition could also trace the influence of other media on comics and trace trajectories of the various media and genres in which comics have been created. Unfortunately, this definition could serve to exclude avant-garde comics as they buck the historical model rather than conforming to it.

Another solution could follow a similar crisis that art worked through in the twentieth century. Rather than defining art by formalist, essentialist, or historical features, George Dickie articulated an industrial theory of art based on the art world. In this definition, scholars do not debate what is and is not art so much as study any artifacts found in the art world. Not only would anything hanging in a gallery be fair game, but also preliminary sketches, letters, and interviews. Similarly, Meskin argues that thinking of comics as an industry, as a comics world, would side-step the definitional issue entirely while encouraging scholars to focus on traditional comics, exclude artifacts like the *Bayeux Tapestry*, and be ready for innovative avant-garde comics that push formal boundaries.

Meskin's last solution is even more evasive: we could give up the definitional project entirely. If that seems drastic, this last solution could easily be coupled with the second one for a more satisfying argument: we no longer care what is or is not a comic. Instead, scholars can investigate whatever part of the comics world they see fit. Meskin's comics world solution has been further investigated by Bart Beatty in his 2012 *Comics vs. Art*. Beatty traced the relationship of comics to the art world, one of attraction and repulsion, inclusion and exclusion. In doing so, he expanded Meskin's solution and offered a more complete theory of a comics world.

At present, then, comics studies has a formalist camp made up of two warring factions, sequential art and words and pictures, and a historical-industrial camp that attempts to side-step the definitional issue by theorizing a comics world or tracing historical roots. As we will see, augmented reality comics are especially problematic for the formalist camp. Which approach a scholar takes will greatly affect how the scholar looks at augmented reality comics.

A Brief History of Augmented Reality Comics

While augmented reality has been around since the sixties, augmented comics are of recent advent (beginning in 2010). Since little if anything has been written on them from a scholarly perspective, this history of augmented comics will be brief. In April of 2010, the first augmented reality comics debuted—two distinct works: Total Immersion's interactive Star Wars experience and *Retinex* by 3Satva (Michael Tres Satva). In early 2012, Marvel Comics, one of the two mainstream comics publishing houses, debuted Marvel AR, a smartphone and tablet app that would add a new layer of interactivity to its flagship titles. Later in 2012, French comic publisher Casterman partnered with Dassault Systèmes to enhance Francois Schuiten's *La Douce* with an augmented reality layer. After investigating each of these examples, we can begin to form some idea of the current state of augmented reality comics and sketch potential futures.

In 2010, Total Immersion, an international augmented reality company, created an augmented reality layer that interacts with existing *Star Wars* comic books. In a video posted to YouTube, a man sits at a desk in front of two vintage *Star Wars* comics (issues four and eight) and a computer monitor. When he puts issue eight in view of the webcam, the monitor displays a three-dimensional Luke Skywalker standing on the comic cover. Luke practices idly with his lightsaber, swinging it back and forth as the dull droning of the lightsaber fills the speakers. As the man manipulates the comic, we can see a 360 degree view of Luke in motion. When issue eight is put in front of the monitor, Darth Vader appears and goes through a similar routine. When issue four is brought alongside issue eight, Luke and Vader engage in realistic duel, lightsabers clanging off of each other. The man rotates the comics to demonstrate the three-dimensionality.

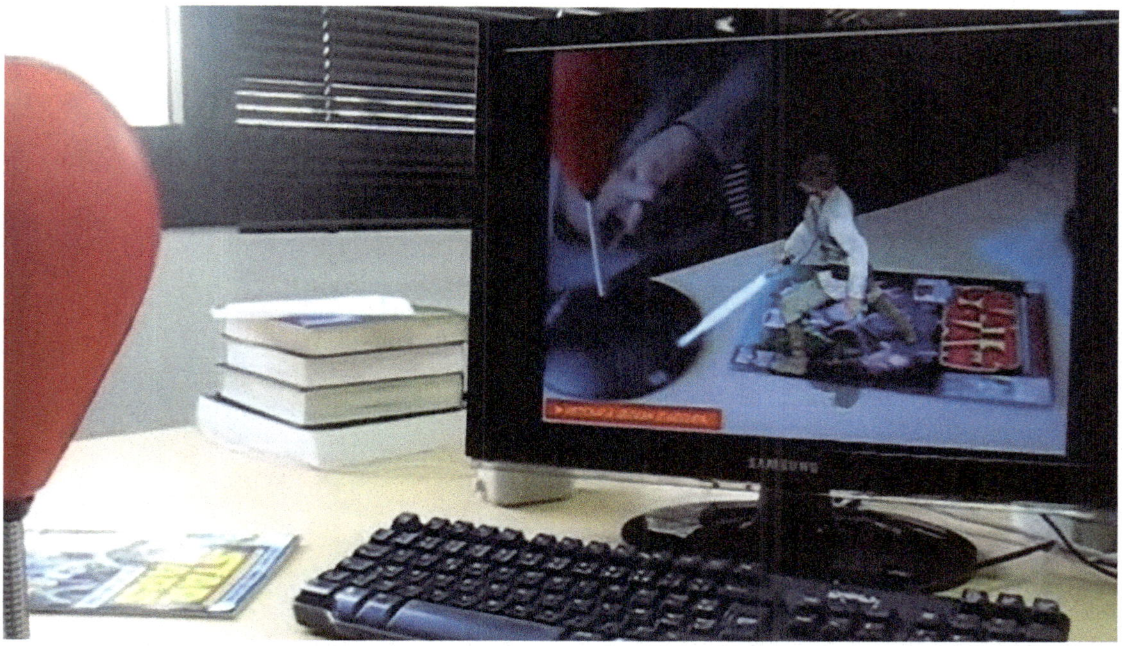

Figure 3.1: Star Wars Comics featuring Augmented Reality Experience with Luke Skywalker and Darth Vader. © 2010 by Total Immersion.

AURASMA
Scan the image to view.

As one of the earliest entries into augmented reality comics, this example stays truest to other flashy examples of augmented reality. The reader can seemingly manipulate the characters in three dimensions (the illusion appearing on a monitor). Distinct iterations interact with each other in simulated battle. The layer is added to pre-existing artifacts (1970s era comic books). Each of these factors makes the Total Immersion's project unique and interesting.

However, a number of factors weaken this example's rhetorical power. First, the augmented reality does not clearly connect to the content of the comic. While it includes characters from the comics, the fight between Luke and Vader could be attached to any of the comics as a loose metonymy signifying nothing more than Star Wars itself. Second, this seems to be an in-house project used to promote Total Immersion but never entering the public market. The video and techblogger references to it are all that seem to remain of the project. The embedded URL no longer connects to any particular page on Total Immersion's website, and a variety of searches failed to turn up any evidence that the project has been pushed forward.

If Total Immersion's Star Wars comic project is all flash with no substance, then 3Satva's *Retinex* occupies a position directly opposite. Independent comic artist 3Satva partnered with SpiralConcepts to create a comic with an augmented reality layer. Unlike Total Immersion, *Retinex* was not a pre-existing comic to which an augmented reality layer was added but designed as a hybrid artifact from the start. *Retinex* depicts a dystopian future Los Angeles in which technology has run rampant and privacy is at a premium. A mysterious figure, Seek, steals information from the surveillance obsessed DJ-CEO-dominatrix-mafiosa Daunt. Daunt responds by unleashing Retinex, a cybernetic surveillance program on the unwitting Fade, a Rasta graffiti artist. Since only one issue was ever created, we get no further in the story. Augmented reality icons appear on about a third of the pages connecting readers to a now defunct Web app. The experience appears to have been fairly rudimentary: short animations, a three-dimensional image, and simple interactive images (as a reader manipulates the book, the color changes). However, the augmented reality layer was tied closely to the story, offering new perspectives and information on the comic. 3Satva created a much more complex reading experience than Total Immersion, but his augmented reality layer is not as snazzy as three-dimensional figures in combat. As will be seen below, the complex reading experience of *Retinex* makes it difficult to classify it as a comic in either of the formalist comic definitions.

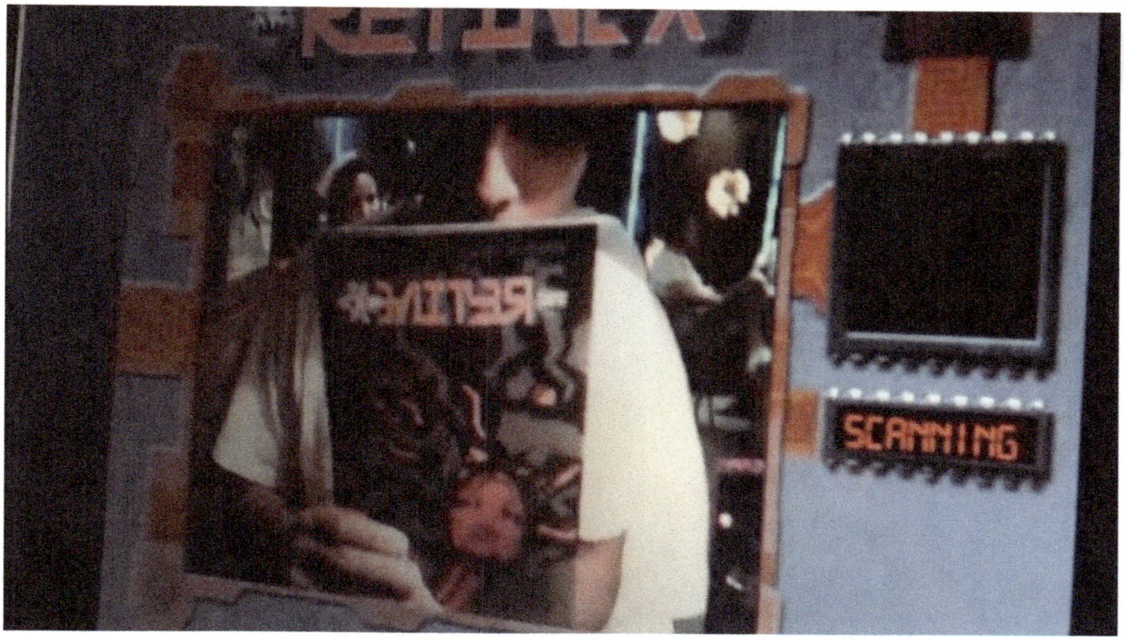

Figure 3.2: *Retinex*. © 2010 by Damon Hernandez.

AURASMA

Scan the image to view.

In early 2012, Marvel Comics partnered with Aurasma to add an augmented reality layer to its flagship comics, beginning with a crossover of its two most popular franchises in the *Avengers vs. X-men* (*AvX*) miniseries. The most impressive example from Marvel AR was the earliest promotional art for *AvX*. Illustrator Adi Granov's image of Iron Man (the most recognizable Avenger) fighting Magneto (the long-time villain and now member of the X-Men) foreground's a simple two-word slogan: "It's coming . . ." When users open the Marvel AR app on their smartphones or tablets, their device's screen shows the camera's view of the poster. On the screen, a three-dimensional animation of Iron Man appears to walk off the poster and hover in mid-air. Iron Man idly warms up his equipment and flies into the air before dropping hard onto an implied surface and standing up to warm up his equipment, repeating the exercise infinitely. The user can move the device around to get different angles on the action, always keeping the cover in view of the camera. The effect is impressive. Like Total Immersion's Star Wars project, the three-dimensional Iron

Man is all flash. He does not attack Magneto on the new layer or offer new information, but the intent of the promotional poster is to impress, not to provide a coherent reading experience.

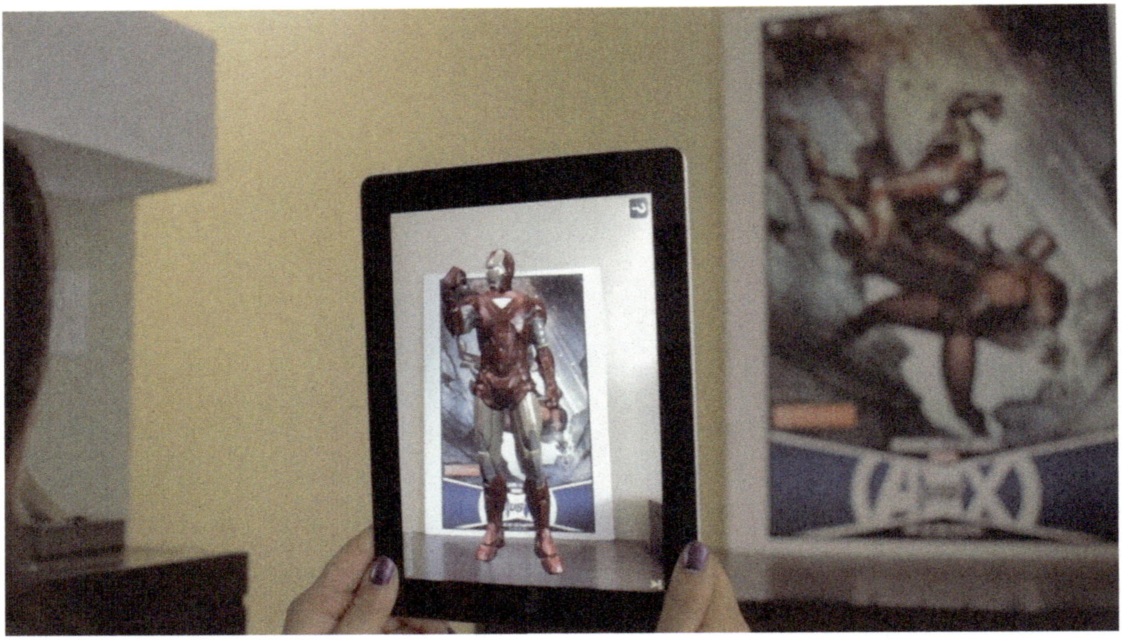

Figure 3.3: Marvel Aurasma Ironman Demo. © 2012 by Aurasma.

AURASMA
Scan the image to view.

When *AvX* was released a few months later, readers found numerous opportunities to use their new Marvel AR app, roughly three to four per episode. In the earliest examples, editors, staffers, and creators offer background information on characters, writing, and art. Editor-in-chief Axel Alonso appears to step off the page to introduce the series to new readers, walking around on the comic on screen. Individual panels are analyzed for the reader with an animated art layer that depicts the original pencil art dissolving into the inked version and finally the color version they see before them. In each of these early examples, the new layer remains a clear example of augmented reality. By the end of the series, these augmented reality layers have gotten more tenuous with the Marvel AR logo seeming to burst from the surface of the page before filling the screen and dissolving into a video. It is debatable whether this is truly augmented reality. Instead, in these later examples the Marvel AR app operates more like a QR code reader that links readers to a video. In more recent comics, Marvel AR has settled into a predictable pattern: the cover can be scanned to provide an introduction to the comic, acting like a "previously on" segment of a television show, bringing in new readers. Two or three of the interior pages offer AR logos that link readers to videos of editors giving somewhat schlocky interviews about the characters, staff-created in-world animations (*Robot Chicken* style stop-motion animations depicting the characters' action figures in silly situations, mock advertisements for companies that exist within the comic's world), or more commonly the familiar pencils-ink-color visual history of the page.

In a recent conversation with Marvel Comics writer Jonathan Hickman, I asked how much input creators have on the AR content. While Hickman was clear that Marvel allows creators to give input on the AR, it by no means requires it. Hickman has so far not been very involved in the process because of the time constraints involved in writing multiple monthly books for multiple publishers. As most Marvel creators are under similar constraints, it is unlikely that they have much time for AR either. Marvel AR's examples are closer to DVD extras than to the immersive reading experience of *Retinex*. They are impressive, but offer little after the initial experience. For the most part, they do not substantially augment the reading experience. Subsequently, they do not endanger the resulting experience's definition as comic. Instead, there are really two experiences: reading a comic and watching a video. The two have only a tenuous link and the comic remains pure in a formalist sense.

The final example comes from French comics publisher Casterman and Belgian comic artist Francois Schuiten. Schuiten has been a major figure in the Franco-Belgian comics world for three decades, teaming up with Benoit Peeters to create the critically acclaimed *Les Cités Obscures* series.

For scholars unfamiliar with the Franco-Belgian comics tradition, it is important to note that French language comics are not the juvenilia of their American counterparts. Their comics offer adult themes with nuanced stories and complex visuals. Even their children's comics blow away American mainstream comics in terms of art, prose, storytelling, and style. Hergé's (Georges Remi) *Tintin* occupies a sacred space in the Franco-Belgian comics canon with his *ligne claire* style influencing dozens of artists over much of the last century. Mœbius (Jean Girard) created erotic, surrealist art influencing not just comics artists worldwide but many major films as well. Schuiten's work with Peeters has more in common with Italo Calvino than with Spiderman.

La Douce is Schuiten's first solo comic, but it is clearly influenced by his work with Peeters. Like *Les Cités Obscures*, *La Douce* depicts a parallel reality full of steampunk inventions and modernist design. The story follows an engineer who is in love with his train, often referring to it as a woman. He fights against the industrialists who want to forsake the railroad in favor of a network of trams. He is caught attempting to steal his beloved train, the historical SCNB type 12—the book's title works on a pun between *douze* (twelve) and *douce* (sweet). When he is released from prison years later, he finds his timeline has diverged from our own and a net of towers loom over the landscape carrying cable cars to and fro. Attempting to find the railroad graveyard that houses the 12, he hitches a ride on a cablecar. A young mute woman smuggles herself along with him and the two become friends. After a series of adventures she finds the train and the two of them ride off into the sunset, shoveling coal into the 12 and laughing.

As the book seems to preach against the relentless march of technological progress, the augmented reality layer is caught in ironic tension. When readers open a Web app and put the inside cover in front of a webcam, the screen appears to show a three-dimensional version of the SCNB type 12 rolling out onto the tracks on the surface of the book. The reader can manipulate the book to get other views or lean it left or right to adjust the speed of the train as it flies through the countryside. When the train appears to be going uphill it slows, when the book is tilted to make the train go downhill it speeds up. As the train pulls into a stop, the image dissolves into a video of Schuiten inking an original page from *La Douce*. Schuiten's masterful pen strokes provide enthusiasts with a more enticing experience than the slightly mechanical cross-dissolve panels of Marvel AR. Schuiten loves trains and modernist design—having designed metro stations in Brussels and Paris—and the streamlined SCNB type 12 provides a template for exploring both passions. The animation of the augmented reality layer fills readers with an appreciation for an eighty-year old train that looks like a Buck Rogers space ship.

La Douce also foregrounds a tension between the past and the future in both content and form. The plot operates not as a strictly antitechnology fable, but perhaps as a conservative technological fable. The lead character's fear of new technologies mirrors his fetishistic obsession with older technologies. Similarly, the new-fangled augmented reality layer provides an *objet petit a* for fetishists of both old and new technologies. Because AR comics do not currently threaten to replace traditional comics, the irony does not threaten the stability of the book. Instead, the AR serves as a gimmick to sell books and as a window into a historical machine. That it relies on a new machine does not seem to bother its creators.

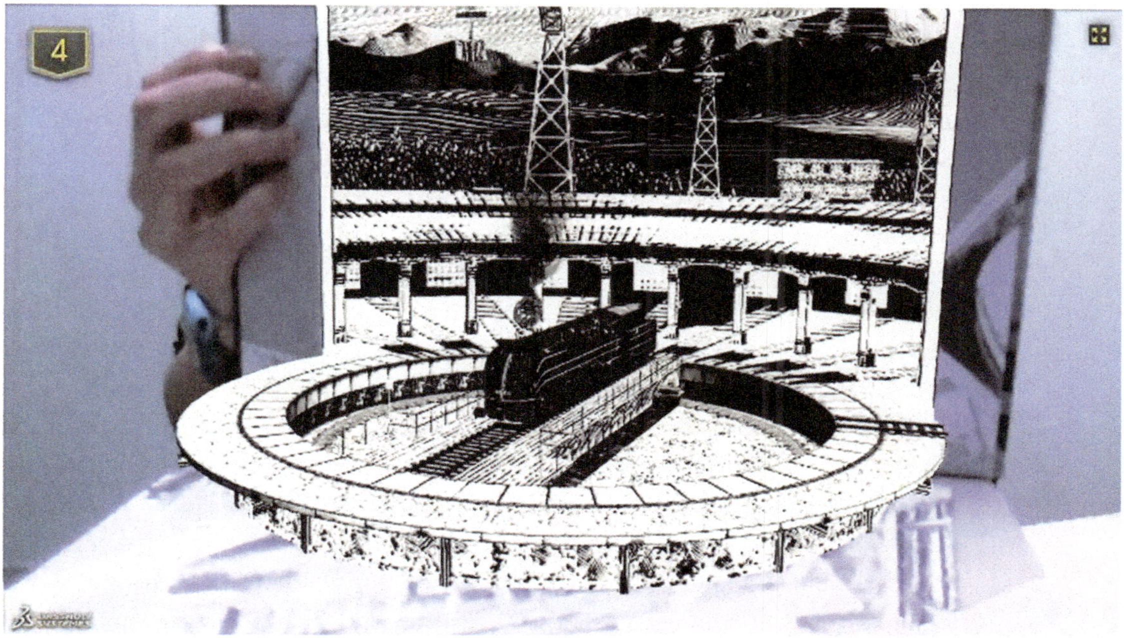

Figure 3.4: *La Douce*. © 2012 by Casterman/Schuiten.

AURASMA
Scan the image to view.

Augmented reality has not yet made itself at home in comics. Holding a smartphone over a comic or putting a comic in front of a webcam rips the reader out of the reading experience. The jarring interruption does not fit the comics reading context: alone or with friends immersing oneself in a story, reflecting on its pictures. A fetishistic comics collector who puts alternate covers in mylar bags would be unlikely to press the pages firmly on a table to get a proper registration of the AR app. I recently asked the manager of my local comic shop what she thought of Marvel AR, a technology that has been available for over a year. She had never heard of it. When such a minority of readership is viewing AR content, it will probably not demand many resources from creators and publishers.

Potential Futures

Augmented reality comics do not make much economic sense for mainstream publishers unless they continue to devote a bare minimum of time and money to them. However, experiments by independent creators offer more potential. 3Satva's *Retinex* provides a salient example of how AR could substantially augment the comic reading experience. However, it also complicates that experience from a formalist point of view. The two industrial/historical critical comics approaches would likely have no trouble calling *Retinex* a comic or at least including it in the field of artifacts worthy of study for comics scholars. Both formalist positions run into snags when trying to define *Retinex* as a comic.

From the classic sequential art point of view, augmented reality does not augment the comics reading experience, but weakens it. For such scholars, closure signifies the core experience of reading comics. By mentally filling in the gaps between panels, the comics reader becomes involved in a way that is distinct from other reading experiences. AR comics fill in that gap for the reader, reducing the reader to a less-participatory viewer.

From an image-text point of view, again, augmented reality falls short of the comics reading experience. Here, the close juxtaposition of image and text is supplemented with a third layer, but that third layer is not organically integrated with the other two layers. Instead, the AR layer requires a clunky interface that distances the reader from the comic. While traditional comics allow for multiple interpretations of the relationship between image and text, AR comics reduce the openness of the text.

We can look at the *AvX* teaser poster to offer an example of how this works. In the cover art we see Iron Man and Magneto locked in combat, juxtaposed with the simple phrase "It's coming . . ." and the title *Avengers vs. X-men*. David Carrier has argued that even a single panel can provide a space for a sequential interpretation. Rather than a gutter between panels, a single panel comic has a gutter on each side. The viewer participates by closing this very open text. We might wonder how these two allies have become enemies: has Magneto returned to his evil ways? No, that wouldn't explain why it says X-men unless he has persuaded other X-Men to join him. Perhaps Iron Man's close ties to the US military industrial complex have pitted him and the other Avengers against the counter-cultural X-men. The quoted phrase leads me to think I should have seen it coming. Perhaps there have been hints.

Unfortunately, an augmented reality layer does not enhance this open text. It could offer answers to the viewer's questions, but that would effectively close the text—not an effective use of a teaser. Instead, it offers a non sequitur: a three dimensional Iron Man warming up his suit, hovering for a moment, then returning to the ground, on endless repeat. Rather than augmenting the teaser, it offers another unrelated teaser, this one with nothing to do with the actual product being advertised.

Comics operate as syntagmatic artifacts resting on a paradigmatic structure. The vast range of potential linguistic and extra-linguistic signifiers that can occupy a single comic page offer a great deal of flexibility and specificity for comics creators. However, the high degree of technological know-how required in creating a sophisticated augmented reality layer like the three-dimensional Iron Man animation reduces the potential signifiers available. In other words, it took a lot of time for someone to create that three-dimensional Iron Man so it could be applied to any teaser trailer that might include Iron Man. That relationship is too open, and it would be difficult to close it given the specific image we have on the poster (Is this Iron Man warming up for his big fight with Magneto or Iron Man warming up to get pizza?).

> *"Imagine reading Bill Sienkiewicz's* Stray Toasters *while the voice of a comics scholar explains the multiple media involved in a single page, or looking at* Krazy Kat *strips augmented with a visual commentary layer that highlights the cat's ever changing gender, the romantic tensions between the three main characters, or the important social and racial background."*

That is not to say that there are not possibilities for augmented reality to actually augment comics. To do so, though, the AR layer would need to be created hand-in-hand with the comic's creator if not by the comic's creator. The partnerships currently common between tech companies and creators make more economic than creative sense. The experience would need to be better integrated, perhaps via Google Glass or a similar, more organic interface. If that is the case, then we will need to either wait for such an interface to become more widespread or look to art installations as a possibility for AR comics. The advantage of an installation would be that the artist could provide the interface. If this solution were implemented immediately, what kind of reading experience could we hope for?

An AR layer needs to either be integrated seamlessly into the comics reading experience or offer a reflection on the distance the interface produces. If the former, the AR could provide a three-dimensional rendering of historical artifacts (like *La Douce*) or a HUD style commentary on individual panels. There are certainly other possibilities, but I think that animating what already occurs in the panels is not a promising avenue. While most AR examples are visual, the AR layer could just as easily augment the comics reading experience with audio: background music, voices, or sound effects. We might envision a wordless comic that syncs its audio channel to the current page or a commentary track synced to a worded comic. A commentary provided either by audio or visual means could augment an existing comic, acting as a docent for a museum-worthy comic. Imagine reading Bill Sienkiewicz's *Stray Toasters* while the voice of a comics scholar explains the multiple media involved in a single page, or looking at *Krazy Kat* strips augmented with a visual commentary layer that highlights the cat's ever changing gender, the romantic tensions between the three main characters, or the important social and racial background. As an educational tool, AR could introduce non-comics readers to the material and contextual complexities of a given page. An AR layer could also serve to alienate a viewer from a comic. Alternative comics artists have used alienation to great effect already and the added layer could increase that alienation, allowing artists to include smartphones as part of their medium.

Of course, these are merely two suggestions for where augmented reality comics could find fruitful footing. At their current state, AR comics are mainly marketing gimmicks with little art involved. Augmented reality is being used to sell books, but it has much greater potential. When I look at that three-dimensional floating Iron Man, I cringe just like I do when I look at the five *X-Men* #1 covers, worrying that perhaps we are seeing another bubble waiting to burst—if not an economic bubble then at least a credibility bubble. But that cringe isn't my sole response. I also remember back to comics spread on the floor of Grant's room in 1991, and I think, that's so cool. I wonder what they'll do next.

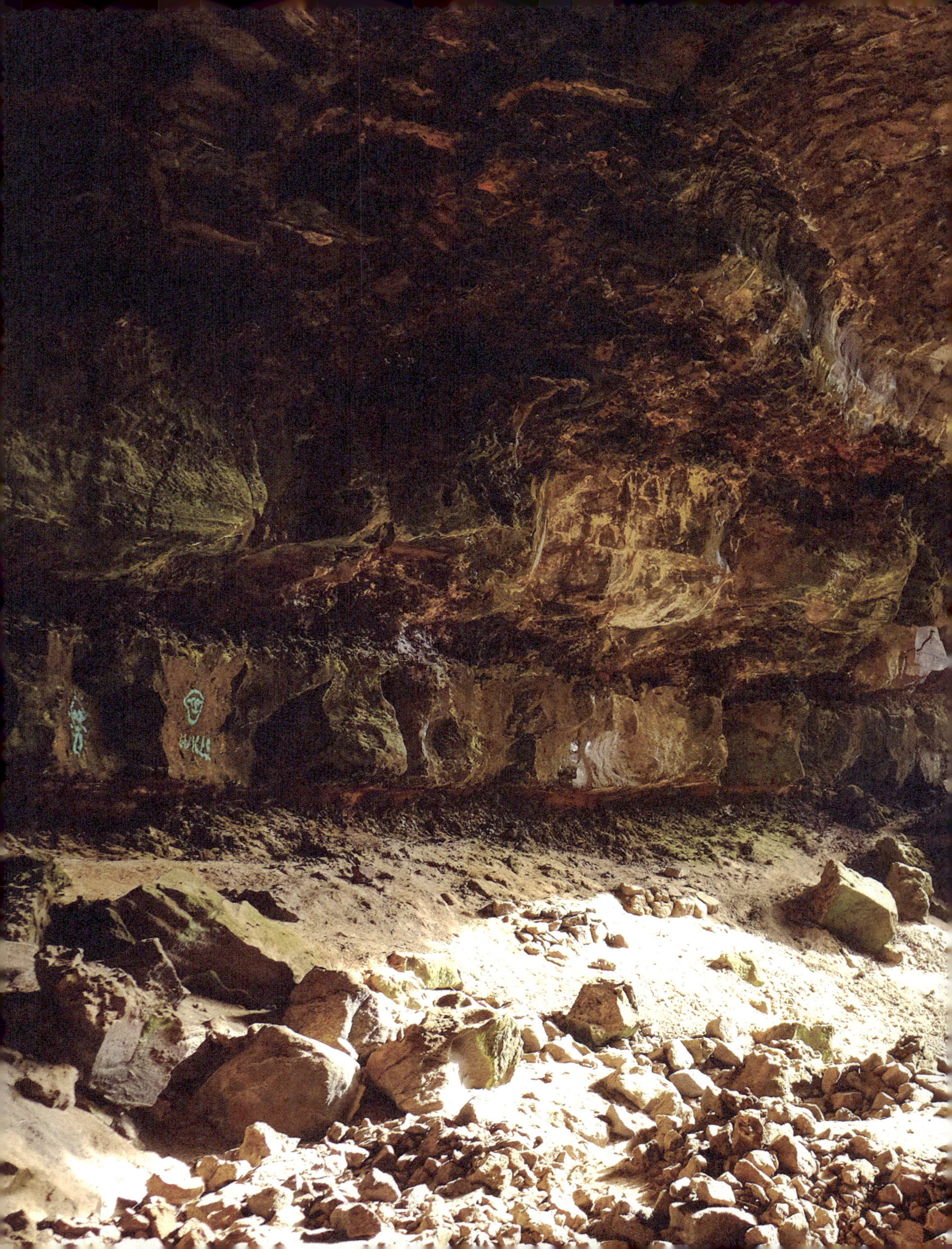

4 "Sergey Brin Is Batman": Google Glass and the Rhetoric of Adoption in Popular Networked Culture

Isabel Pedersen and Douglas Trueman

> *"Sergey Brin Finally Lets Someone Else Wear Google Glass"*
>
> —*Gizmodo*, May 30, 2012

The emergence, anticipation, and celebration of Google Glass are cause for reflection. Google proclaims that it is instigating a new era in human-computer interaction or what some are calling our *digital life*. On one level, Glass is a prototype for a transparent computer display worn over one eye that offers an augmented reality viewpoint, made available in 2013 to consumers not part of the initial launch. On another level, Glass is a promise, one that plays out in the context of numerous social media and real-world events, leveraging the claim that Glass will become a new computer platform.

Glass is framed in news media as the brainchild of Sergey Brin, the American computer scientist of Russian descent who co-founded Google. Brin is also mythologized in online articles as a real life "Batman" who is developing a secret facility resembling the "Batcave," adding fuel to the fire behind Glass. Glass has also graced the face of legendary clothing designer Diane von Fürstenberg who wore it at New York Fashion Week 2012, illustrating Google's strategically planned photo opportunities which play on the public's zeal for device fetishism. Yet, Google's persuasive tactics have a broader reach than simply product placement. Chronologically, Glass's first public instantiation was through a YouTube concept video titled "Project Glass: One Day..." (released April 4, 2012, 2:31 minutes in length) that frames it as the first mainstream augmented reality wearable eye display, and for the sake of simplicity, we will refer to this video simply as One Day.

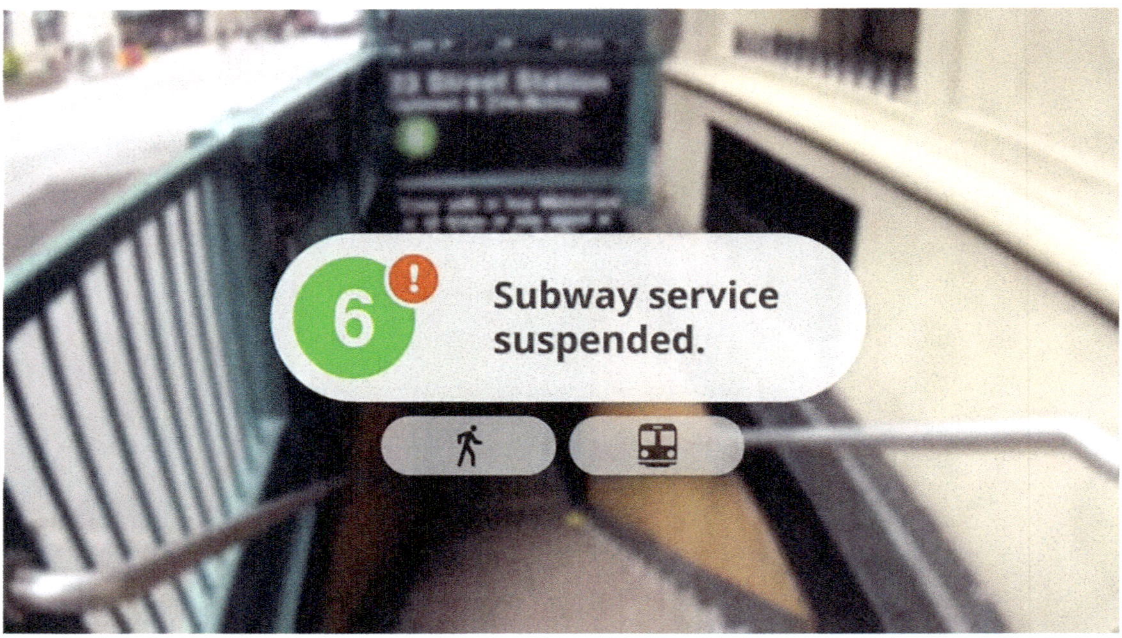

Figure 4.1: Project Glass: One day . . . © 2012 by Google.

AURASMA
Scan the image to view.

Having been viewed more than 20 million times, One Day has morphed into a viral marketing campaign. In the video, Google promises that Glass will comprise a fleet of features that will enable us to take videos, interact with personal contacts, and navigate maps, amongst other things, all without the cumbersome use of a hand-held smartphone. More so, it promises a lifestyle. In one blog post, Google states that "A team within our Google X group started Project Glass to build this kind of technology, one that helps you explore and share your world, putting you back in the moment." Nearly a year after its first public mention, Google launched a massive social media campaign called #ifIhadglass in conjunction with its Google Explorer Program. Running for only a week in February 2013, thousands of Internet users sent tweets and blog posts using the hashtag #ifIhadglass, competing for the chance to purchase the device in a pre-release scenario. Each person was encouraged to disclose a personal reason for wanting Google Glass; eight thousand hopefuls "won" the opportunity to buy the device before everyone else. Glass just recently allowed general consumers to purchase the product, and even more recently shut down their initial Glass Explorer program in order to develop future models. Still, its reach remains significant. As authors, we are interested in the early or pre-2013 impact of Glass when the sensationalized public revealed so many motives about technology and the future that Glass seemingly creates for us.

Above all other categories, Google Glass is a computer that features a "*H*eads-*U*p" eye *D*isplay (HUD) that does not require one's hands for most interactions. The computer graphics appear over the wearer's field of vision. It might also be termed a *H*ead-*M*ounted *D*isplay (HMD) because it rests on the head, literally using the ears to keep it up like a regular pair of glasses. For most of its processes, it requires a connection to the Internet. It is classified as augmented reality because of the computer-generated graphics that it produces using a transparent screen, which does not occlude one's view of the real world. Google promotes Glass as an extension of the current smartphone, meaning that it offers the basic functionality of the iPhone—for example: texting, recording videos, browsing the Internet, etc.—from a first-person viewpoint. For most people, eye displays are not considered "everyday" technology. This is the major conceptual hurdle that Google faces.

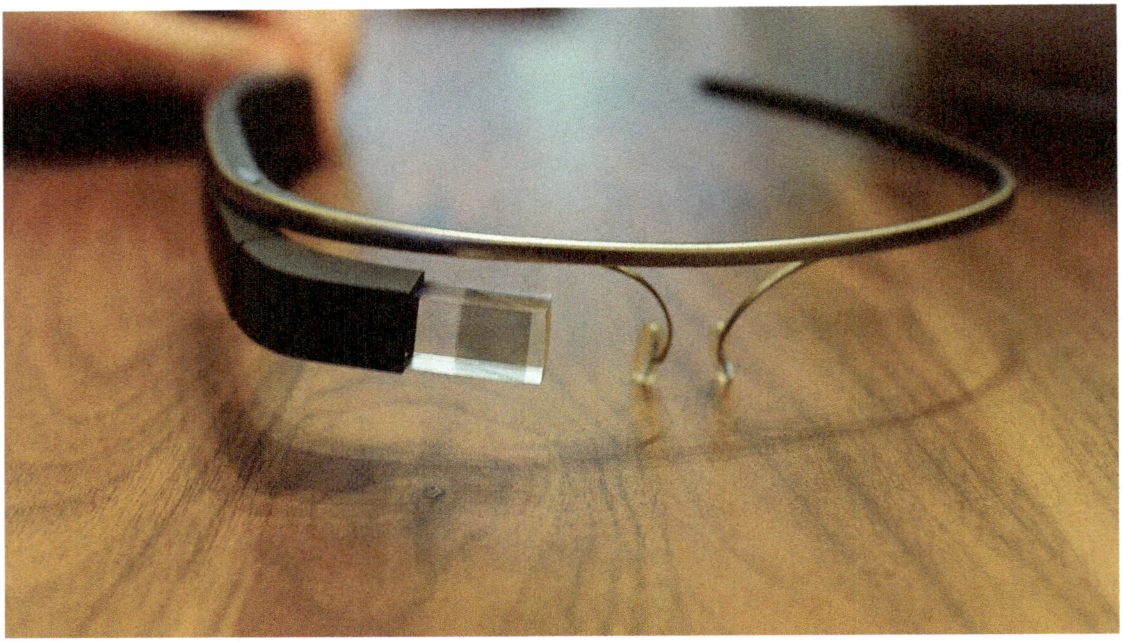

Figure 4.2: Google Glass Explorer Edition: Google's augmented reality head-mounted display as glass form. © 2012 by Google. This file is licensed under the Creative Commons Attribution-Share Alike 2.0 Generic license.

The first appearance of Glass was on Sergey Brin, who wore it to an April 5, 2012, public event in San Francisco. Provocative headlines emerged such as "Google 'Project Glass' Replaces the Smartphone with Glasses" and "Google X Labs: First Project Glass, next space elevators?" We argue that Glass's birth signifies not only a marketing phenomenon heralding a technological prototype, it also suggests and speculates that Glass's popularization is a rhetorical instigator for the adoption of a new paradigm in Human-Computer Interaction (HCI), the wearable eye display. Glass's process of adoption operates in the context of mainstream and popular culture discourses, a phenomenon that transforms over time as the idea accrues a greater audience. More, we argue that most salient of all during this span of time is the way Google Glass is framed in media as the brainchild of Sergey Brin. The promise of Glass, the rhetorical strategy that Google uses in these first months to persuade the public to embrace the eye display platform, relies upon the ethos of Sergey Brin.

Glenn Stillar writes that "Rhetoric deals with language's role in identification and division among social agents; it focuses on the exchange of discourse as a central mode through which social orders are constructed and transformed through addressed symbolic action." Our methodology is to concentrate on the first emergence of Glass in mainstream discourses. We treat it as a media phenomenon through three text clusters that play out in a quasi-linear way (see figure 4.3).

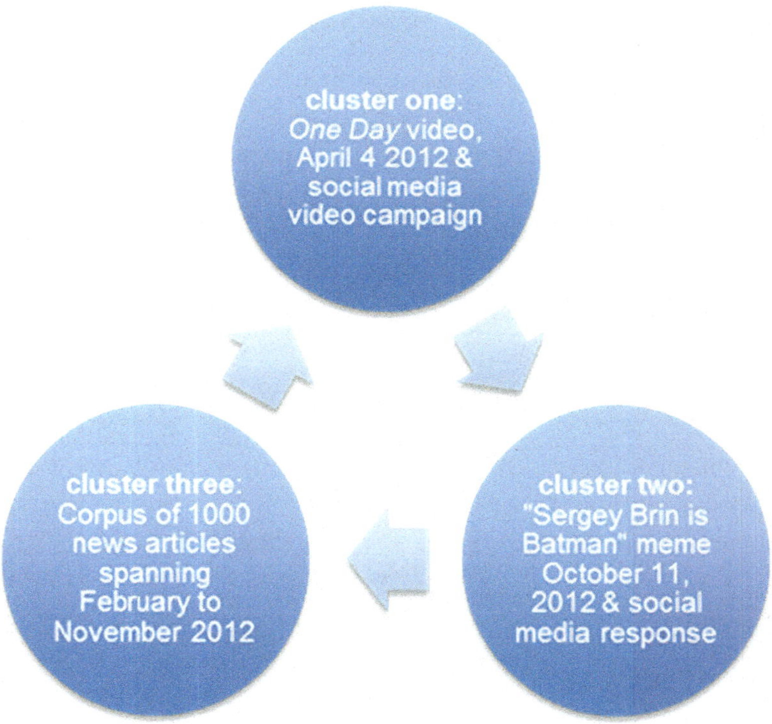

Figure 4.3: Discourse Analysis Model for Three Text Clusters. © 2015 by the authors.

For the first cluster, we also observed and collected the content of Google's YouTube social media campaign and sampled several videos produced by Google that announce and celebrate the coming of Glass. Here we offer a basic reading of the One Day video released on April 4, 2012, and analyze it using Burke's codicil concerning "perfection." The second cluster analyzes how Sergey Brin's character is framed in public responses as a larger-than-life persona, a modern day Batman amid an ideology that promotes perfectionist, transhuman values. To chart this rhetoric, we moved backward in time to the fall of 2011 in order to understand the rhetorical grounds upon which Glass emerges before April 4, 2012. For the third cluster, our study draws on the discourse analysis of a corpus of 1,000 mainstream print news articles and online media pieces spanning February 2012 to November 2012 that mention Google Glass. During this time, and surrounding the release of the promotional video, Glass was celebrated and hyped extensively in mainstream print media. All three clusters of texts signify the impact of Google Glass before Glass existed as a material consumer artifact for the public. We see this particular span of time as an opportunity to study the rhetorical and tactical performance led by Google to cast Glass as a new computer platform in the midst of prevailing discourses that had never before dealt with wearable computing in a mass communication milieu.

Previous work grounds some of the claims made in this chapter. Pedersen's *Ready to Wear: A Rhetoric of Wearable Computers and Reality-Shifting Media* makes the argument that discourses of augmented reality and specifically those associated with wearables are vulnerable to rhetoric that frames an imminent technological future for society without exploration or even appropriate definition. By embracing new inventions like Glass, through the language of announcement without attending to embedded (mis)assumptions about humans and nonhumans, we pave a future for ourselves that might be detrimental. In other relevant work, Encheva and Pedersen consider the Google Glass One Day marketing video by identifying it as an instance of *predictive advertising*. Arguing for predictive advertising as a hybrid form using Baudrillard's "integral reality," they argue that Google capitalizes both on the futuristic techno-fantasy of the narrative as well as the realism of it as a cinematic construct, simultaneously framing it as a fact as well as fiction. Finally, Pedersen and Simcoe argue that the Iron Man phenomenon is an exemplar to reveal how popular culture films and their surrounding discursive vocabularies generate not only a fan

> *"To understand Glass as an augmented reality consumer device being thrust upon us, we need to attend to how it is framed amid value-systems, ideologies, and culture."*

following, but also motivate amateur augmented reality inventors. Many other writers take a critical humanities approach to new media including Paul Virilio (*Information Bomb*), Mark Andrejevic (*iSpy*), and Janon Lanier (*You Are Not a Gadget*). Working on the ontological and metaphysical plane are philosophers who treat this friction not as a binary between human and nonhuman media devices; rather, following Bruno Latour they understand the associative or networked relationship amongst entities. In this vein, Katherine Hayles writes, "contemporary technogenesis implies continuous reciprocal causality between human bodies and technics."

This chapter takes a much broader view of the Glass phenomenon arguing that Glass's emergence needs to be contextualized according to the constructed persona of Sergey Brin both before and during Google's promotional campaign. In simple terms, without Brin as the instigator, Glass would not be considered worthy of the kind of fame it enjoys. Nor would augmented reality itself be seen as a viable new medium of communication for everyday people. However, in more complex terms, the rhetorical positioning of Brin is a by-product not only of planned media events; it is also due to social media response and online memes that amount to provocative rumors. To understand Glass as an augmented reality consumer device being thrust upon us, we need to attend to how it is framed amid value-systems, ideologies, and culture.

One Day and Augmented Reality

In a sense, One Day serves as a definition for augmented reality authored by Google. Realizing that augmented reality had labored under the weight of awkward definitions for decades, Google chose to offer a simplified version of the technology, a *day in the life of* video featuring a young urban *flâneur* who we could admire. In the course of the video, Google's character wakes, has breakfast, wanders the city, visits a bookshop, admires street art, drinks coffee, meets a friend, and shares an intimate moment with a girlfriend at sunset. Even before one confronts his augmented or virtual life, one desires his lackadaisical existence and his short perfect little day. He is decadent, cultured, and indulged.

The portrait of augmented reality is quite specific. Google's character yawns, stretches, and waits as an array of fourteen virtual icons appear before him that signify a calendar, voice commands, Google search, time, weather, friend chat, camera, and several other recognizable smartphone features. Over the rest of the video, we observe him using these icons to make his pedestrian trip around his neighborhood easier (e.g., first-person viewpoint), more delightful (e.g., locate a friend in a store), and free of any hindrance (e.g. alternative map routes when the subway fails). What is innovative is the feeling that over his field of vision pops up his virtual friend, his *Jeeves*. And the overwhelming message is that *Glass as Jeeves* will stroll around with this character, augmenting his reality in a manner that makes it even more serendipitous than before.

The One Day video functions to normalize what augmented reality as a platform is for, the tasks it can fulfill, and the potentials it reveals. It offers us a way to live that seems more perfect than the way we live now. Burke argues that humans are goaded by a perfection principle. Basing his "definition of human" partly on the Aristotelian notion of *entelechy* ("possession of *telos* within" or having its own end within itself), Burke defines humans as always striving for a state of completion or full actuality. He ironically labels us "Rotten with Perfection." Humans attach this sense of entelechy onto logonomic systems and work to attain perfection in a way that is as destructive as it is constructive. Also influenced by Burke, Michael Hyde calls it "both a benefit and a burden" in his book *Perfection: Coming to Terms with Being Human*. These Glass videos narrate a utopian future where life is ordered by a pre-*scriptive* personal computer, a Jeeves who will always be there. The character in One Day lives a mediated life whereby no task such as building his calendar, navigating a bookstore, or meeting friends suffers any interruption. Augmented reality translates to a life of seamless bliss. Reminiscent of both the augmented life of *Star Trek: The Next Generation* and the saccharin sweet utopia of the film *Pleasantville*, One Day promotes a perfect world and perfected digital lifestyle that is hard to resist.

Google planned the April 4, 2012 release of the One Day video as an event motivated to enact more than the announcement of a new product, which in weeks quickly garnered 18,762,646 views. The release also coincided with the start of Sergey Brin's scheduled media appearances wearing Glass which began on April 5. Over the spring and summer of 2012, several other concept videos emerged introducing the public to Google Glass and the fascinating potential for this new computer platform. Most salient are "Project Glass: Trampoline Video" (May 24, 2012: 716,460 views) and "Project

Glass: Live Demo At Google I/O" (June 27, 2012: 1,092,418 views). A "media event" has been defined as a live, televised event that marks or changes history. It usually implies that everyday people anticipate such a live event, plan to watch it, and remember it in a personal way (e.g., the inauguration of President Barack Obama on January 29, 2009). However, the rise of a networked Internet society has morphed the notion of "media event" considerably given that news is accessible to people constantly across myriad digital communication channels. Tweets interrupt one's breakfast with information that one would never have experienced until the six o'clock news hour on television. Manuel Castells conceptualizes the network society as "the social structure resulting from the interaction between the new technological paradigm and social organization at large." Our notions of what is newsworthy have morphed due to networked access to news. However, what has not morphed is the impact and affective reaction that people experience personally in response to news events.

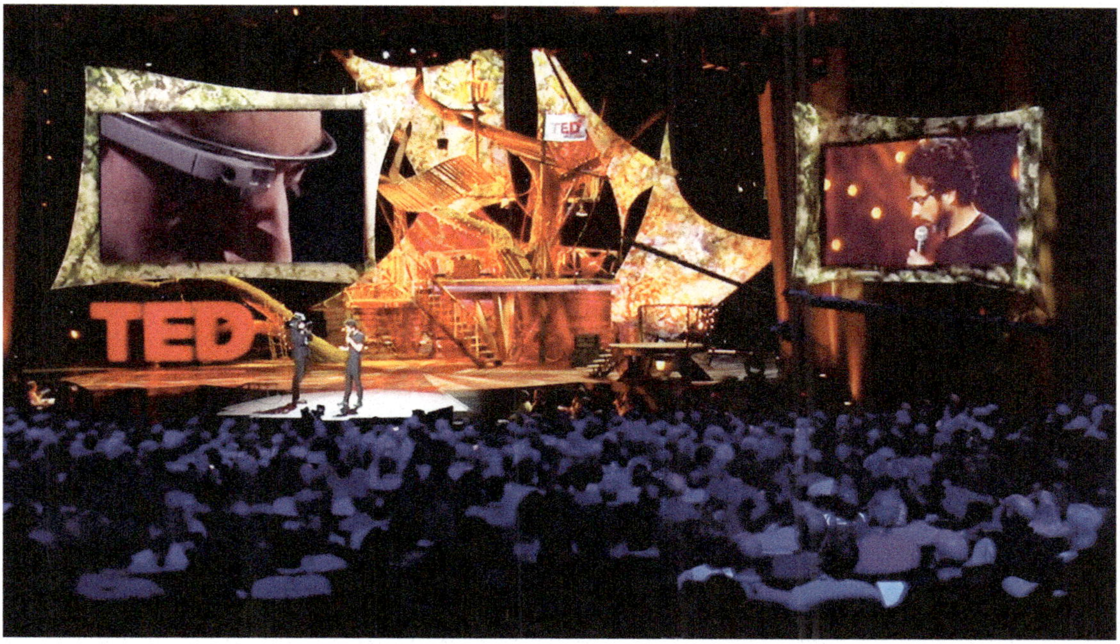

Figure 4.4: Sergey Brin: Why Google Glass? © 2013 by TED.

AURASMA
Scan the image to view.

From here, this chapter moves outward from One Day in order to explain Glass amid a broader rhetorical landscape, one that takes into account its fame within the context that precedes it.

Augmented Reality Eye Displays

The first chapter of Everett M. Rogers's work *The Diffusion of Innovations* opens by pinpointing the crux of the issue for most new technology:

> Getting a new idea adopted, even when it has obvious advantages, is difficult. Many innovations require a lengthy period of many years from the time when they become available to the time when they are widely adopted. Therefore, a common problem for many individuals and organizations is how to speed up the rate of diffusion of an innovation.

The urgency in Google Glass lies in the fact most public discussion over eye displays stems from fictional portrayals, making Glass seem unbelievable or simply a trope of fiction or cinema. Science fiction and popular references to the eye display are almost too numerous to list, but most are featured in military uses: Arnold Schwarzenegger's *Terminator* from the 1984 film had implanted eye technology that let him identify possible targets using augmented reality vision. Tom Cruise's Maverick in *Top Gun* had a rudimentary display to indicate an enemy plane's target acquisition and current G-forces. Many first-person shooter video games, including Bungie's landmark series *Halo*, feature eye displays that give the player real-time status updates on player enemy locations, shield levels, remaining ammunition, and waypoint information. Indeed, gamers will have no trouble understanding what Google Glass hopes to contribute to their real lives, as the experience of a virtual HUD laid over top of a virtual world is commonplace. Interestingly, while many film and television shows are adding HUDs to their storytelling to add a science fiction or futuristic feel, there is a movement in game development away from the very HUD that Google proposes as many gamers consider them to be "screen clutter" and block a player's view of a created world. The video game series *Dead Space* by Electronic Arts is an exemplar of this new style: traditional game information such as health and ammunition has been woven into character design, allowing for an unobstructed view. Game developers and Google developers, ironically, are advancing their respective technologies in opposing directions. While Google seeks to enhance real life with augmented reality, game developers are trying to streamline from their fictional worlds any and all visual distractions.

Real heads-up eye displays are not new either, but they are also geared to specific audiences rather than the general public. The *Land Warrior* system, developed by the US army over the past decade, for example, includes a heads-up eye display with an augmented reality visual overlay for soldier communication. Many well-known inventors have contributed eye display technology, research, or applications over the past two decades including Steve Mann (Visual Memory Prosthetic), Thad Starner (Remembrance Agent), and Rob Spence (Eyeborg). Commercially, Vuzix is a company that currently manufactures transparent eye displays for entertainment.

Significant to this chapter is the fact that wearable eye displays and augmented reality have not been embraced in the mainstream as a legitimate computer platform in the league of the smartphone or the laptop that emerged as remediations of traditional phones and desktop computers. This chapter charts the curious mainstreaming of augmented reality and the persuasive tactics that accompany it.

"Sergey Brin Is Batman"

On October 25, 2011, *Business Insider* published an article called "Googlers Are Passing Around A Crazy Rumor About Sergey Brin Working On Architecture" that opened with a provocative claim:

> 'Sergey Brin Is Batman.' That's the meme flying around the Google office, several sources within the company have told us. While Brin has a number of pet projects, the most interesting one is a potential project involving architecture.

This article frames Brin as Batman and it paves the way for much press on the Google X Lab, the real-life secret lab that is touted to be developing a space elevator, a self-driving car, and now Google Glass. In subsequent articles by the same writer, there is mention of a rumor that Brin is creating an architectural blueprint for a "Batcave." We also sampled blog posts by nonprofessional individuals who circulated this meme as blog-worthy news. "Sergey Brin is Batman" operates as social capital amongst those who are genuinely interested in what Google is inventing as well as those who are simply sensationalized by the idea. The circulation of the "Sergey Brin is Batman" meme is significant on several fronts. First, it was never promoted by Google itself; enthusiasts framed Brin in this manner as a humorous response to the flood of futuristic inventions coming out of Google. Second, the notion of Sergey Brin being Batman was established before Glass was announced. His fictional framing as a superhero, a cyborg identity, was established grounds upon which Glass enters the discourse. In a sense, the meme functions through what Kenneth Burke terms *familial substance,* which is rhetoric that is concerned with the network of relations to other things, an ancestry of sorts. By naming the substance, the *whatness* of a thing in the world, one can name what is intrinsic to it (what it is) as well as what is extrinsic (what it is not). In more simple terms, no one really believes Brin is Batman; the rhetorical act frames Google as an entity that can produce a superhuman/transhuman future for us using familial terms. The emergence of Glass, a dream for an augmented reality future, sits on the same persuasive substance established by a public following.

Further to our ongoing study, we identified a trend in our second cluster in print and online news articles. The name "Sergey Brin" appears 713 times in the corpus of 1,000 print and online news articles about Google Glass. Often the story concentrates on Brin's activities, comments, whereabouts, and future expectations amid news of Glass as a technology that only exists as an artifact of the press for the public. The overwhelming appearance of his name, more so than any other Google employee, led to the realization that Brin's larger-than-life persona functioned as rhetorically significant. Rupert Till explains the definition of how an individual must amass popular fame in order to form a "cult of personality":

> A celebrity is someone who is well known for being famous, and whose name alone is recognizable, associated with their image, and is capable of generating money . . . For a star to progress to a point where they are described as a popular icon requires their achievement of a level of fame at which they are treated with the sort of respect traditionally reserved for religious figures. In order to be described as a popular icon, a star has to become a religious figure, to develop their own personality cult and recruit followers.

While it would be a stretch to call Brin a pop cult icon, the point is that Google Glass and the constructed *character* of Sergey Brin co-create each other, generating the kind of popularity often reserved for celebrities like Bill Gates, the late Steve Jobs, and Mark Zuckerberg. However, no computer platform has been popularized and sensationalized at such an early stage and so uniquely. Brin—human, inventor, entrepreneur, PhD, millionaire, Batman—provides the required credibility or ethos to make Google Glass and its augmenting abilities plausible. According to Aristotle:

> Persuasion is achieved by the speaker's personal character when the speech is so spoken as to make us think him credible. We believe good men more fully and more readily than others: this is true generally whatever the question is, and absolutely true where exact certainty is impossible and opinions are divided . . . his character may almost be called the most effective means of persuasion he possesses.

Ethos is a highly contested term which has been explored extensively by philosophers and rhetoricians and this chapter is not the site for a new discussion. However, Craig Smith emphasizes how Aristotle meant for ethos to be taken as the public manifestation of a character:

> For Aristotle, it is a given: everyone has *ethos* whether it be noble or ignoble. Before one even speaks, that *ethos* has an ontological dimension because it emerges from the way one makes decisions, the way one lives on a day-to-day basis, the way one dwells. Those decisions are informed by one's values, one's practical wisdom, and one's goodwill all of which are addressed in detail by Aristotle. Thus, Aristotle *assumes* the knowledge of the Athenian fore-structure of *ethos* as a dwelling place and then reformulates the notion of dwelling place to present a rhetorical understanding of *ethos*. As an empiricist, he examines not what is given in the culture, but the notion of *ethos* as the *public* manifestation of a person.

Smith makes the point that ethos is not simply the portrait of a speaker *being good*; he accounts for the situated and embodied dimension of ethos that is akin to the notion of dwelling within or through a culture instantiated in public forums in a manner that is commensurate with public desires. By dubbing Sergey Brin "Batman," technology enthusiasts heroize his persona according to a common or recognizable and desired value system.

Fascination with the Batman Myth

What does it mean for public discourse to yoke Brin and ultimately the emergence of Google's innovations to the fictional persona of Batman? And how does the metaphor operate rhetorically as a marker of ethos?

Created by comic artist Bob Kane and writer Bill Finger, Batman first appeared in Detective Comics #27 in May of 1939. In the 70 years since, Batman has achieved iconic status in comic books, film, television, animation, and video games. Batman's tale of billionaire playboy Bruce Wayne, who fights crime from the shadows by night, runs counter to almost all other superhero archetypes, aside from Tony Stark's Iron Man. Whereas almost all other superheroes have been bestowed with superpowers from cosmic radiation, genetic mutation, or laboratory accidents, Bruce Wayne is an everyman who defeats his foes with guile, fear, and technological genius. Batman's moral code prohibits him from killing his enemies, and this restriction on his behavior has led to the creation of many devices to subdue, defeat, and restrain opponents in non-lethal fashion.

While British agent James Bond also featured many of his own gadgets that have now come to fruition (cameras the size of credit cards, radio receivers that slip in one's ear canal), the fact that 007 was given his technology from the British government does not grant the secret agent the level of ethos that Batman and Brin have obtained. While Bond's many gizmos have often saved the day, 007 himself has no respect for technology. He often is frequently admonished by lab advisor Q to treat his gear with care, but then destroys it in the pursuit of his mission. Indeed, the recent Bond film *SkyFall* (2012) features a Bond so frustrated with his inability to cope with modern technology used by his enemies that his solution to protect the life of MI6 leader M is to take her "back in time" and hide her at an abandoned farmhouse using nothing more than an ancient shotgun, booby-traps, and his wits.

A more comparable character to Brin than 007 would be Marvel Comics' Spider-Man's alternate ego Peter Parker who invented his wearable webshooters in the bedroom of his uncle's house. Like Spider-Man, Batman's wearable technology was created out of one man's necessity, and it is this archetype of the lone scientist working in domestic isolation for the common good that fueled much of today's modern technology: one only has to look at the early years of Steve Jobs, Bill Gates, and Sergey Brin to see the real-life equivalent of a genius who ignores social convention in dogged pursuit of a vision.

As the mythology of Batman evolved past ink strokes on comic paper, so too did Batman's means of procuring his technology. While Tony Stark of Iron Man is internationally famous for being a genius inventor, Bruce Wayne is seen more as a savvy investor and playboy than having any great technological prowess. The invention of the microchip in 1959 ultimately destined Batman's gear to become increasingly computerized, and his mythology evolved to suit the then modern era. Rather than add computer programming and hardware development to Batman's long list of world caliber skills, the comics saw the introduction of a character named Lucius Fox. Played by Morgan Freeman in the Christopher Nolan trilogy, Fox works as the research head of Wayne Enterprises' Applied Science Division and supplies Batman with much of his portable technology. This evolution of the Batman mythos runs the Caped Crusader parallel to James Bond in that both figures have access to cutting edge technology developed not in isolation, but by teams of highly skilled professionals working with near limitless financial and technological resources—much like the modern day equivalent of Google.

While the original Batman was able to toil away in the solitude of the Batcave to serve the greater good, the evolved Batman makes use of a team, which remains unaware of its technology's ultimate usage.

The Batcave can also be construed as a metaphor for the allure generated by "Google X," which appears in the corpus of our study 273 times under several descriptors, such as "laboratory," "team," "project," "research group," and set of "engineers." The word "secret" occurs 206 times, emphasizing Google X's positioning as a mysterious location where innovation occurs. The corpus exudes unwavering confidence surrounding Google X. Most significant of all, the word "future" occurs 735 times suggesting that Google is creating the future that we will all ultimately fulfill. By clinging to the mystery surrounding Google X, and fantasizing it in fictional terms, the discourse betrays a utopic future.

Interestingly, modern science fiction must intrigue readers with its portrayal of what might be, and the development of the smartphone made much of Batman and James Bond's once-futuristic technology obsolete. A child who has grown up with an iPad would not be impressed with Batman's older technology, and so both Batman's mythology and his tech must evolve to stay relevant for his audience. While it's difficult to see the practical commercial application of Batman's portable shark repellent from the 1960s, the eventual transformation from low-tech camp to a high-tech wizardry is profound. The high-tech display that lets Batman see otherwise invisible objects through visual depictions of sonar waves in *The Dark Knight* has almost limitless applications, be they military, medical, or civilian. Celebrating the future, (super)heroes march onward, shunning technological obsolescence, and cloaking innovation in secrecy as value-systems function in fiction and they are very much mirrored in the discourse surrounding Google Glass.

Conclusion

There will come a day when Google Glass is considered obsolete and will only be available for viewing in a museum, when wearable computers using augmented reality are as ubiquitous as people, and when fiber optic transfer speeds seem sluggish. Google's approach is to bring Glass into public social networks before it emerges, minimizing consumer's struggle with adopting the device and thus maximizing its potential. Google generates a culture and a mass mainstream following for Glass as a new computer platform by mediating how it is introduced to the public. Media emergence now operates at a speed that makes analyzing models of adoption difficult. While applicable research has been conducted on the adoption of "hyped technologies," we live in a world now where the consumption, celebration, and entertainment of proposed technologies (or technology proposals) run rampant. Google Glass—desired, sensationalized, despised, and feared, before one can even buy it—is bound up in popular and public culture and it affords us the opportunity to study this rhetorical process on a mass scale.

Acknowledgements

This research was undertaken, in part, thanks to funding from the Canada Research Chairs program and the Social Sciences and Humanities Research Council of Canada.

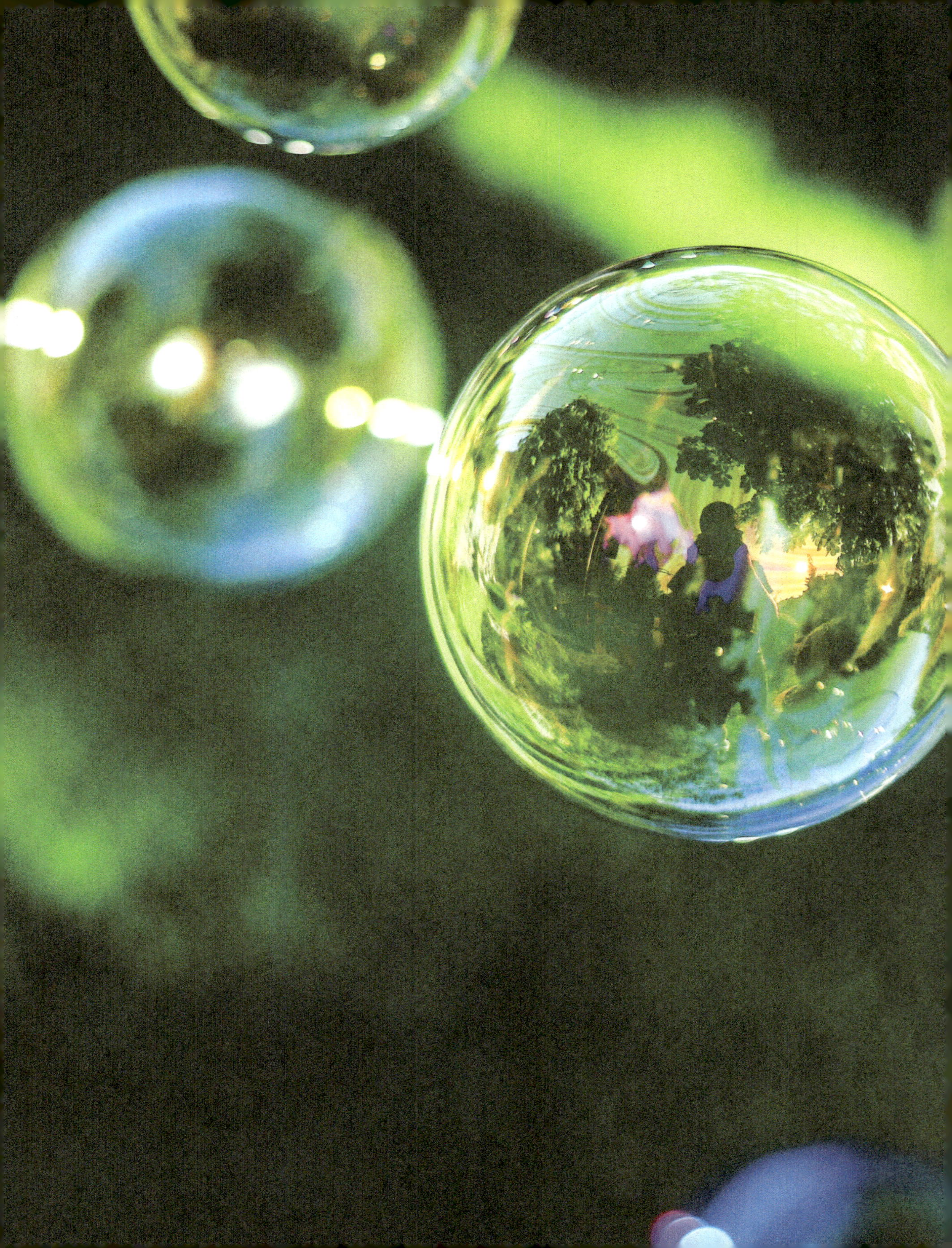

5 Life through the Screen: Location-Based Information and the Personalization of Space

Jordan Frith

I spend a lot of time on the Internet. As I write this chapter, I go back and forth between working on this text and jumping from site to site online. Undoubtedly, some people reading this chapter will not make it all the way through without killing some time online. Some readers may even search for the same things I search for and go to the same pages I go. However, I will not be browsing an identical Internet as any of my readers. The search results might be similar, the sites may look close to the same, but they will likely not be the same.

To illustrate my point, I want to touch on a few sites I visited today. First, I went to my Facebook page, which is obviously personalized and different than anyone else's Facebook page. Then I went to Reddit's front page, but the front page I saw was personalized for me because I choose to follow certain Subreddits. Then I went to Slate.com, where I likely saw a similar, though not identical, page as anyone else would. The page I went to had a prominent ad for a credit card that featured a cute picture of a pit bull-type dog. I cannot be certain, but I imagine that the ad was personalized based on my previous browsing history related to pit bull rescue organizations. Throughout the day, I also perform many Google searches, and the results I get are based on my previous searches and previous browsing history. It may seem like a minor point, but the Internet I experience has been personalized just for me, often in ways I do not even realize.

One of the major concerns about these forms of personalization is that people are increasingly presented with information that confirms their preexisting beliefs. In other words, if I consistently browse liberal news sites, I will be more likely to be presented with links tailored to a liberal audience. This concern has been called the "filter bubble," and it is important to keep this criticism in mind in the face of the utopian arguments about personalized browsing and convenience. Another important point to note is that, while this personalization is now more technologically possibly than ever before, the ultimate goal is nothing new. In the mid 1990s, Negroponte famously wrote about the "Daily Me," which was a plan for a customizable daily newspaper personalized for each reader. Now, in our current moment, we have come close to the point Negroponte predicted almost twenty years ago.

Recognizing that many of us live in a personalized, fractured information environment is nothing new. However, what is relatively new is that these forms of personalization have begun to move out into the physical world. As researchers have noted, digital information is increasingly organized around physical location. We map restaurants, gas stations, photos, Wikipedia pages, and tweets. We use smartphones to manipulate the digital data we access about locations, in a sense using our mobile in-

"We need to critically examine the future ways in which augmented reality may lead to an even more fractured experience of public space."

terfaces to exert some control over our experience of public space. Just as our Facebook pages, our search results, and many of our favorite online sites are personalized for us, our experience of space has now become more and more dynamic and personalized depending on the geotagged information we access through our mobile devices.

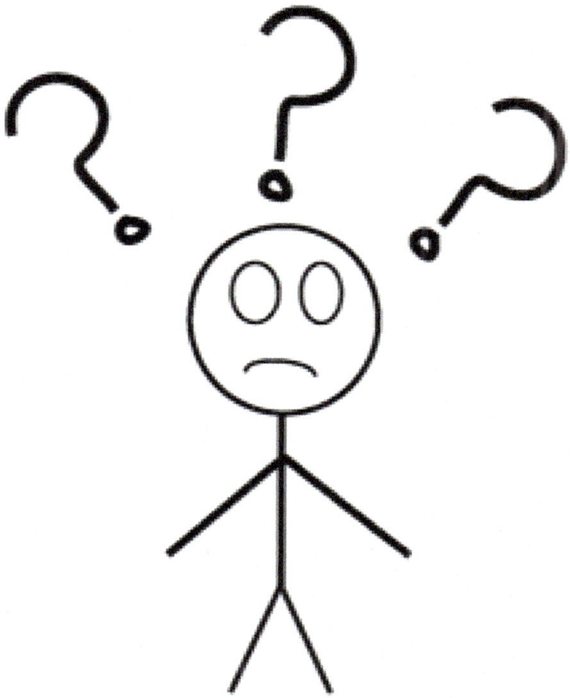

AURASMA
Scan the image to view.

Figure 5.1: The "Filter Bubble." © 2013 by You Loop.

This chapter examines those issues of spatial personalization in more detail and critically examines the potential consequences. My ultimate goal is to discuss a possible future for augmented reality (AR) in which people's mobility becomes its own sort of "filter bubble," with the spatial information people access being partially determined by their personal preferences and past behaviors. To situate my analysis, I begin by engaging with seminal theories on the constitution of public space to show why these types of personalization may contrast with an idealized view of what it means to engage with public space. I then use a few examples of popular location-based services such as Foursquare to examine the novel ways in which we "filter" our experiences of space through mobile applications. I choose to examine commercial location-based services rather than more experimental AR applications because I believe these location-based services show how AR will likely be shaped as it becomes more and more commercially viable. After discussing existing location-based services such as Foursquare, I then conclude with a speculative section arguing that we need to critically examine the future ways in which augmented reality may lead to an even more fractured experience of public space.

An Idealized Public Space

AR cannot be separated from the spaces in which it is used. Applications like Layar or projects such as Phillyhistory.org encourage people to move through public spaces and access information through the interface of their mobile phone. The same is true of location-based services such as Wikime, Foursquare, and Yelp. Fundamentally, these applications are designed to help people manage their experience of the public. Consequently, to fully conceptualize the potential social impacts of AR and location-based services, it is crucial to develop an understanding of what we mean by "public space."

"Public" is a term we use frequently but rarely define. As Weintraub points out, scholars should define what they mean by the term because there are at least four common, and sometimes contrasting, meanings, including different meanings in economics and feminist thought. One of the most influential conceptualizations of the public, and likely the most important for understanding the social impacts of mobile technologies, is the "sociability model." The sociability model is most closely linked to thinkers such as Sennett (*The Fall of Public Man*), Jacobs, and Whyte, and views public spaces as spaces in which strangers and difference coexist. As Sennett writes, urban public spaces are "a milieu in which strangers are likely to meet." Jane Jacobs, in her seminal book *The Death and Life of Great American Cities,* writes something similar about the meaning of the urban:

> Great cities are not like towns, only larger. They are not like suburbs, only denser. They differ from towns and suburbs in basic ways, and one

> of these is that cities are, by definition, full of strangers. To any one person, strangers are far more common in big cities than acquaintances.

As Jacobs's and Sennett's quotes suggest, the public spaces of the city are spaces of heterogeneity; they are spaces of difference. Moving through these public spaces, we confront strangers and we confront newness in the forms of restaurants we may not be familiar with, organizations that hold different views, and sites that portray alternative memories of a place. The difference we confront while in the public spaces of a city matters because, as Sennett argues, "A city isn't just a place to live, to shop, to go out and have kids play. It's a place that implicates how one derives one's ethics, how one develops a sense of justice, how one learns to talk with and learn from people who are unlike oneself, which is how a human being becomes human."

What Sennett and Jacobs are ultimately arguing for is an embrace of the heterogeneity of the public. However, while heterogeneity may be the ideal, people often exhibit homophilic tendencies that focus on sameness rather than difference. Homophily can be best understood using the old aphorism that "birds of a feather flock together." In other words, people tend to seek out others who are like them and go to new places that are similar to the places they already frequent. One of the most well know examples of how homophily can shape physical space is the "white flight" of the 1950s in which white people in the United States fled the more heterogeneous spaces of the city for the more homogenous spaces of the suburbs. These forms of homophily also shape online spaces. For example, boyd details how in the late 2000s white teenagers fled Myspace for Facebook, and Myspace became a social networking site that featured a disproportionate number of minority users.

While homophily has always been a part of human behavior, we are seeing new ways in which homophily is enabled through digital technology. One way is the informational homophily I discussed in the introduction. Rather than engaging with differing opinions, people can spend their time online confirming their preexisting beliefs. Online social networking sites also show how new forms of homophily are possible in the digital age. Sites like Facebook provide a new form of public space in which people interact in the view of others and test out social norms. However, sites like Facebook are a more homogenous public space than a typical urban space. We do interact there in a modified public, but our audience is sorted and personalized based on the friend networks we actively cultivate.

These examples of both offline and online homophily show that the desire to interact more with the similar than the different is widespread, and importantly, not determined by any technology. My argument in this chapter is not that technologies *cause* homophilic behaviors, but rather that they enable new behaviors. People in the 1950s would have likely preferred to receive a *NY Times* that was personalized for them or choose from hundreds of news sources to find ones that agreed with their world view; however, they often did not have that option. People also would have likely preferred to interact with a personally cultivated social network rather than more geographically determined community. With the rise of the digital, information of all kinds is able to be sorted, filtered, and manipulated to match people's preferences. Importantly, the same is true of many of the mobile applications that have become popular with the widespread adoption of smartphone technology.

Location, Mobile Technologies, and Homophily

As I discussed in the previous sections, many online sites allow people to sort information to match their preferences. Location-based services now, in a sense, bring the ability to self-sort information out into physical space. These forms of informational filtering and sorting are key to the development of location-based services, and as de Souza e Silva and I argue, mobile applications are often desirable because of the control they enable people to exert over their experience of physical space. In this section, I want to examine how that control over one's experience of movement and physical space relates to location-based services, a discussion I will then link to the potential social impacts of the widespread adoption of augmented reality.

Manovich famously argued that, with the growth of digital technologies, we have moved from the narrative to the database as the dominant symbolic form of contemporary society. Gordon argues that contemporary urban places have begun to replicate the shift identified by Manovich. Urban spaces are often now designed to allow people to choose from pieces of urban information to actively construct meaning. Gordon refers specifically to urban spaces, but his analysis of the city as a database provides a useful framework for understanding the control people can exert over spatial experiences using mobile technologies. People now actively choose much of the spatial information they engage with, allowing increased power to construct individual experiences of public space.

Location-based services shape the experience of the city as a database because these applications are built around the importance of physical location. They allow people to do things such as map nearby restaurants, map Wikipedia articles, or locate their friends. Importantly, many of these applications, such as Yelp and Foursquare, allow people to "search" physical space and return information that matches their term, and this information is of course drawn from a multitude of different databases; consequently, these applications allow for the form of "database city" Gordon discusses. As de Souza e Silva and Sutko argue, people who use location-based services receive a unique set of results that depends on their search terms, preferences, and precise physical location. The different results returned by location-based services matter because these forms of spatial searches will have a significant impact on how people "read" physical space. People rarely move past the second page of search results on Google; if a website does not appear on the first page of results, it might as well not exist for many people. As smartphones become increasingly popular and people use their mobile screen more and more to "read" their space, we can expect something similar to happen. If a physical location does not show up on a list of recommendations, for some people it may as well not exist.

Recognizing that the ways information is displayed on mobile interfaces will increasingly shape experiences of public space shows why it is important to analyze how these applications work. These developments also show why it is necessary to critically examine how mobile applications may also contribute to new forms of what de Souza e Silva and I call "differential space." Our concept of differential space is adapted from the concept of differential mobilities, which is a key concept in the growing field of mobilities studies. Differential mobility refers to groups' unequal access to the ability to move. For example, mobility is experienced differently for someone riding in a private limo compared to someone riding a city bus even if those two individuals may travel down the exact same streets. The personalization enabled by various mobile applications, and increasingly AR, will likely contribute to new forms of differential space in which two people may move through the same physical space but experience it differently. For example, someone using an AR application like Layar or a location-based service like

Foursquare moves through a physical space dense with digital information. This information can be personalized so that even people using the same applications move through a form of differential space in which information is presented to them differently. Whereas physical informational markers are available to everyone, the digital information presented through mobile interfaces is only available to the person using certain applications with certain search terms.

To deepen my discussion of mobile personalization, I now want to turn to a deeper analysis of the popular mobile application Foursquare. The point of my case study is not just to analyze the design of Foursquare; instead, I want to discuss the application to examine how current, popular location-based services relate to the issues of personalization I discussed above.

Foursquare and a Possible Future of Personalization

Foursquare was released in March, 2009 at the SxSW festival in Austin, Texas. The application was designed to be both a social networking application and a mobile game. Users form networks of their friends and then go to locations and check in. Their check-ins are shared with their Foursquare friends, allowing people to use the application to coordinate with others and show off to others through the sharing of location information. They also score points and earn badges for going to locations, and they can compete with others over mayorships by checking into a location the most times.

Foursquare has changed significantly in the years since its release. People still check into locations and can earn badges and mayorships for going to certain locations, but the application has begun to focus much more on mobile search through its Explore feature. The Explore feature is a recommendation-based spatial search engine that draws from Foursquare's vast database of check-ins to show locations that meet certain criteria. For the purposes of this discussion, I want to focus on only two elements of Foursquare: the ability to locate friends and the ability to search through locations based on previous behaviors.

Foursquare's location-based social networking function is nothing new. Other mobile services, such as Loopt, Facebook, and Latitude, also allow people to share their location with friends. The first such service in North America was likely Dodgeball, which was founded in 2000. Dodgeball did not use GPS to locate people; instead, people texted their location to the

Dodgeball server, which then sent out their location to the user's Dodgeball friends. While Dodgeball's design is a far cry from today's more advanced location-based services and AR applications, it is an important predecessor that shares many of the fundamental design goals of location-based services like Foursquare. Namely, Dodgeball focused on making people's space more legible by mapping the location of friends, a capability that will likely be prominent in future AR applications.

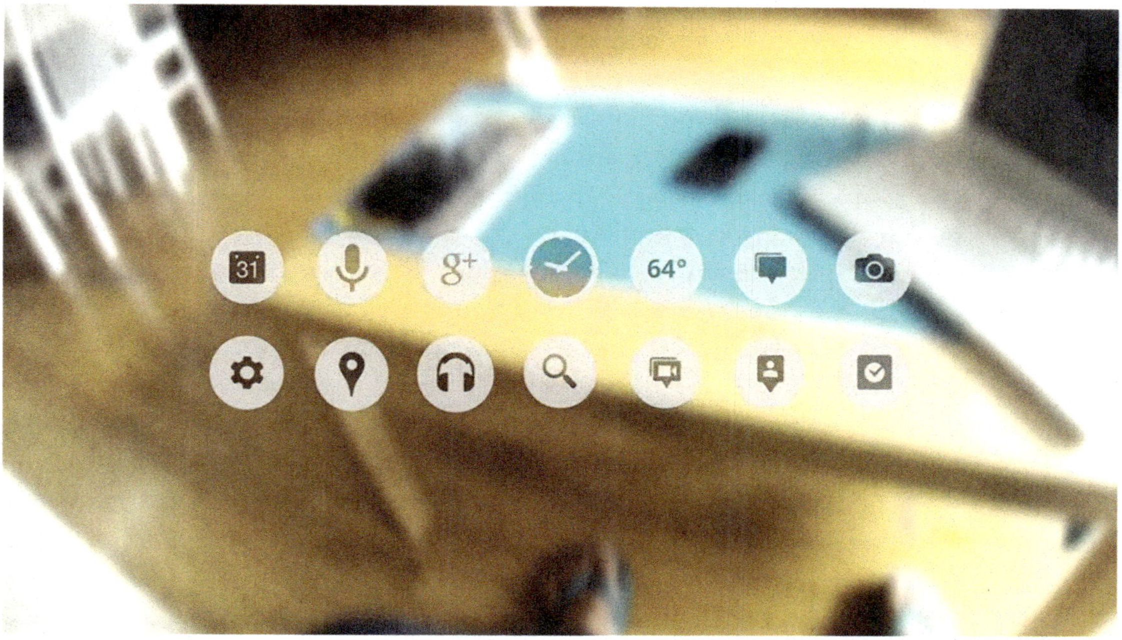

Figure 5.2: Project Glass: One day. . . . The person in the promotional video http://bit.ly/2ggZIBF) receives an alert through Glass that tells him his friend is nearby. He then uses that alert to find the friend, which represents a more advanced form of spatial sorting than the check-in lists displayed through applications like Foursquare. © 2012 by Google.

AURASMA
Scan the image to view.

While Dodgeball was an influential predecessor to today's more technologically advanced location-based social networks, it did meet with some criticism in academic literature. The most scathing criticism came from Crawford, whose main criticism is that applications like Dodgeball harm the heterogeneity of urban public spaces. They do promote serendipitous encounters in a way ("oh look . . . my friend just checked in down the street!"), but that serendipity is a controlled form of chance encounter dictated by the design of the software. Unlike ideal public spaces in which people may encounter otherness at any moment, mobile software like Dodgeball "is all about matches: about finding sameness in a sea of otherness and connecting like with like—or the friend of like with like." Crawford's statement was also supported by empirical work Humphreys performed with Dodgeball users. Humphreys found that Dodgeball contributes to the "illusion of 'looser' sociality despite reinforcing homophilous tendencies" and that while "Dodgeball informants did meet new people when using the service, the kinds of people they met were friends of friends and tended to be similar to themselves in terms of demographics such as age and education."

The discussion of mobile social software and homophily is closely related to the types of informational homophily discussed in online spaces. In fact, Gordon and de Souza e Silva point out that, in some ways, location-based mobile technologies can bring the worst of the self-sorting of online spaces (for example, the ability to interact only with one's network in networked publics) into the streets of the city. We can see that clearly in the design of Foursquare, which can be thought of as the evolution of earlier software like Dodgeball. Foursquare allows people to log in to the application and see exactly where their friends are located, a technological capability that will likely move in to AR applications that locate different pieces of digital information through mobile interfaces. Other mobile applications, such as Grindr, focus more on finding strangers than friends. However, these applications also raise issues of homophily because they alert people when someone nearby matches a set of predetermined preferences. For example, Grindr may find nearby men who match certain physical characteristics. As Farman writes, these types of mobile applications demonstrate "a desire to engage with an other that fits within the self's pre-established frame of otherness." The point I am making here is not to say that applications like Foursquare, Dodgeball, or Grindr *cause* people to seek out homophily in public spaces. Research shows that people often choose the similar over the different. However, recognizing that homophily is a common human behavior does not mean that we should not remain critical of how new mobile applications enable people to engage in new ways of filtering their encounters through mobile interfaces.

Of course, finding friends will likely only be a small part of future AR applications. A more common use will likely be the ability to search through physical space to find pieces of disparate information, and Foursquare's Explore feature works as an interesting example of the types of AR applications we will likely see in the future. Here it helps to discuss how Explore works. First off, the feature is designed to help people find new places, which is seen most obviously in the Explore name. People log in to Foursquare and then are encouraged to search for places nearby (e.g. search for 'bars' or 'tacos'). The spatial search does encourage exploration and, in a way, can be thought of as fighting back against homophily and repetition. However, as we will see, the exploration the feature encourages is not quite as adventurous as it seems.

Explore works through an interesting algorithm that draws from the billions of Foursquare check-ins and provides personalized recommendations to show people where members of their social network, and other people who check in to the locations they like, check in. Explore also shows people where their friends tend to check-in to recommend new locations (see Figure 5.3). This is important because, as the Foursquare engineers explained in a presentation on Explore, over 60 percent of people's check-ins are to locations that someone in their Foursquare social circle has already been.

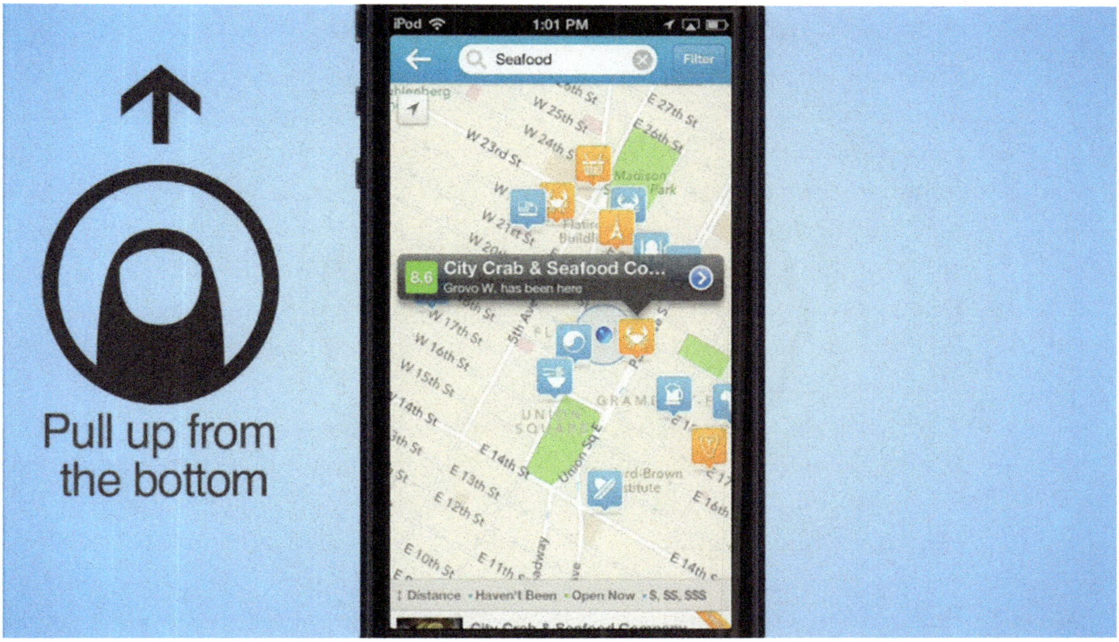

Figure 5.3: "Explore Places Near You Now on Foursquare." © 2013 by Grovo.

To use Explore, the Foursquare user goes to the Explore tab and chooses a distance to filter recommendations (ranging from a one-half mile to ten mile radius). The feature then tells them where

AURASMA
Scan the image to view.

to go, but even more importantly, it tells them why they should go there. So if I click on the Explore tab from my house and search "bars" within a ten mile radius, I receive recommendations and explanations that say things like "people who go to the RipRocks and Oak Street Drafthouse [bars I have checked in to] also go here." The feature also tells people which locations they have checked in to are similar to that bar based on check-ins (for example, "Busy Bee is similar to Raleigh Times and Foundation").

While the Explore feature was not released until 2011, Foursquare and other similar applications emphasized exploration long before that. Foursquare, for example, used "Foursquare on your phone gives you & your friends new ways of exploring your city" as its tagline as far back as 2009. However, understanding the algorithm behind personalized spatial search features like Explore shows why we need to critically examine the types of encouragement that are built into the design of these applications. It is true that many mobile applications encourage people to go to new places and find new things. However, the results returned on these searches are personalized for each user and based on data designed to suggest places that are not truly different; rather, they suggest places that are "just different enough." The assumption built into the algorithm is that if someone has a favorite bar or restaurant, they will also like bars or restaurants popular with people who go to the person's favorite bar or restaurant. People may be engaging with others and finding new locations to visit, but just how different they are is debatable. Features like Explore do a good job of providing personalized spatial results based on someone's past behavior, but they also filter space in a way that can encourage them to find the "sameness in a sea of otherness" that Crawford feared.

Personalized spatial search engines like Explore and friend locator features show how smartphones and other Internet-enabled mobile devices enable us to bring the filtering of online spaces into the physical world. The information environment we operate in is increasingly personalized based on our past behavior, and now our experiences of physical space, filtered through various mobile interfaces, will likely be personalized as well. In the final section of this chapter, I extend this discussion to future AR applications to examine how issues of personalization will continue to play out in various mobile applications.

AR and the Future of Personalization

As many of the chapters in this book detail, the future of AR is still in a great deal of flux. For all the hype that goes back to the 1990s, AR applications like Layar are still not nearly as popular as more traditional-looking mobile applications like Yelp, Foursquare, or UrbanSpoon. However, with the release of Google Glass, we can now see that AR is possibly entering the mainstream, which makes this the perfect moment to critically examine how future AR applications will impact how we navigate urban spaces.

This chapter has focused on how mobile applications contribute to new forms of personalization in public space. To do so, I began by discussing online information seeking before moving on to location-based services such as Foursquare. I did so because both online behavior and popular location-based services like Foursquare will likely shape the future development of commercial AR applications. To discuss how this will work, I want to briefly touch on what is likely the most popular current AR application: Layar.

Layar draws from nearby location-based information just like location-based services such as Socialight, Yelp, or Foursquare. Where Layar and other AR applications differ from today's location-based services is in how information is displayed. Whereas Foursquare or Yelp display location-based information in a fairly typical list form, Layar has people look at their surrounding space through the interface of their mobile phone. While the display of an AR application like Layar does differ from popular location-based services, the information that is displayed and how the information is organized are not fundamentally different. Pieces of digital information are still uploaded with locational metadata that enables them to be located in physical space. The mobile device then uses GPS and wireless triangulation to show where those pieces of information are located in comparison to the mobile device. Consequently, because future AR applications will likely focus more on new ways of displaying information rather than entirely new ways of understanding digital information, we can expect to see many of the issues of personalization I discussed with the example of Foursquare play out in future AR applications.

An AR application like Layar already provides options to filter the information one accesses based on the different "layers" one chooses to display. We will likely see those forms of filtering become more advanced in the mold of something like Foursquare's Explore feature, allowing users to only see information that may match their preferences, previous places they went, or the preferences of their social network. We can also expect AR applications to introduce more advanced ways to locate friends and find "sameness in a sea of otherness." (As mentioned earlier, the ability to locate friends was highlighted in one of the first YouTube advertisements Google released for Glass.)

As a thought experiment, I want to think through how this may look in actual practice. Imagine you are standing next to a forty-five year old man on a street corner in downtown New York City. You both look down the street and see the same oncoming taxi cabs, the same hurried crowds moving toward and away from you, and the same set of shop displays lining the street. Then, however, you both stop and hold up your phones or tablets running the same AR application. The space becomes different for each of you. Your phone may show you that two of your friends are part of the approaching crowd. It may place a marker above a certain coffee shop, telling you that your friends go there or that it's similar to a coffee shop you already frequent. You may see an alert at a store that is 500 meters away and offering a closeout special for a product in which you had expressed interest. The possibilities are endless, but what existing spatial search engines like Explore suggest is that what you see will not be the same as what the man next to you sees. He will look out on a space that features different information, different highlights. In a sense, it will be as if certain signposts are available only to him.

The example described above represents exactly what de Souza e Silva and I discussed in our concept of differential space. Even more so than with today's current location-based services, commercial AR applications will be able to display a physical space differently to two people depending on their preferences and past behaviors. Many of the practices of self-sorting and informational homophily that have been detailed about online spaces will likely be brought out into physical space. My argument is not that this will be inherently bad or lead to the destruction of public space, a criticism that has been made about mobile technologies going back at least as far as the Sony Walkman. Instead, I raise these issues because they are important to consider at this point in the development of AR applications. As humanities scholars and designers, we should remain cognizant of the ways these forms of personalization may lead to a fractured spatial informational landscape and move us further away from an idealized public space filled with heterogeneity and difference.

Conclusion

For all the hype going back over a decade, we are still in the relatively early stages of AR development. We can expect that, as AR continues to grow, we will see more and more mobile apps that draw from some form of augmented reality. This chapter examined a possible consequence of the growth of AR: the personalization of space. As I detailed, many of us already operate in a fairly personalized informational environment. We customize webpages, form personal networks, and receive personalized search results. These forms of personalization have also begun to affect our experiences of physical space through the popularization of location-based services. The next wave of the forms of differential space enabled by mobile technologies will possibly come in the form of augmented reality. As scholars, we should be wary of utopian discourses of personalized search results, maps of friend's locations, and various location-based information filters. None of these technological capabilities are inherently good or bad, but as I hope I made clear in this chapter, they do raise interesting questions for us all to consider.

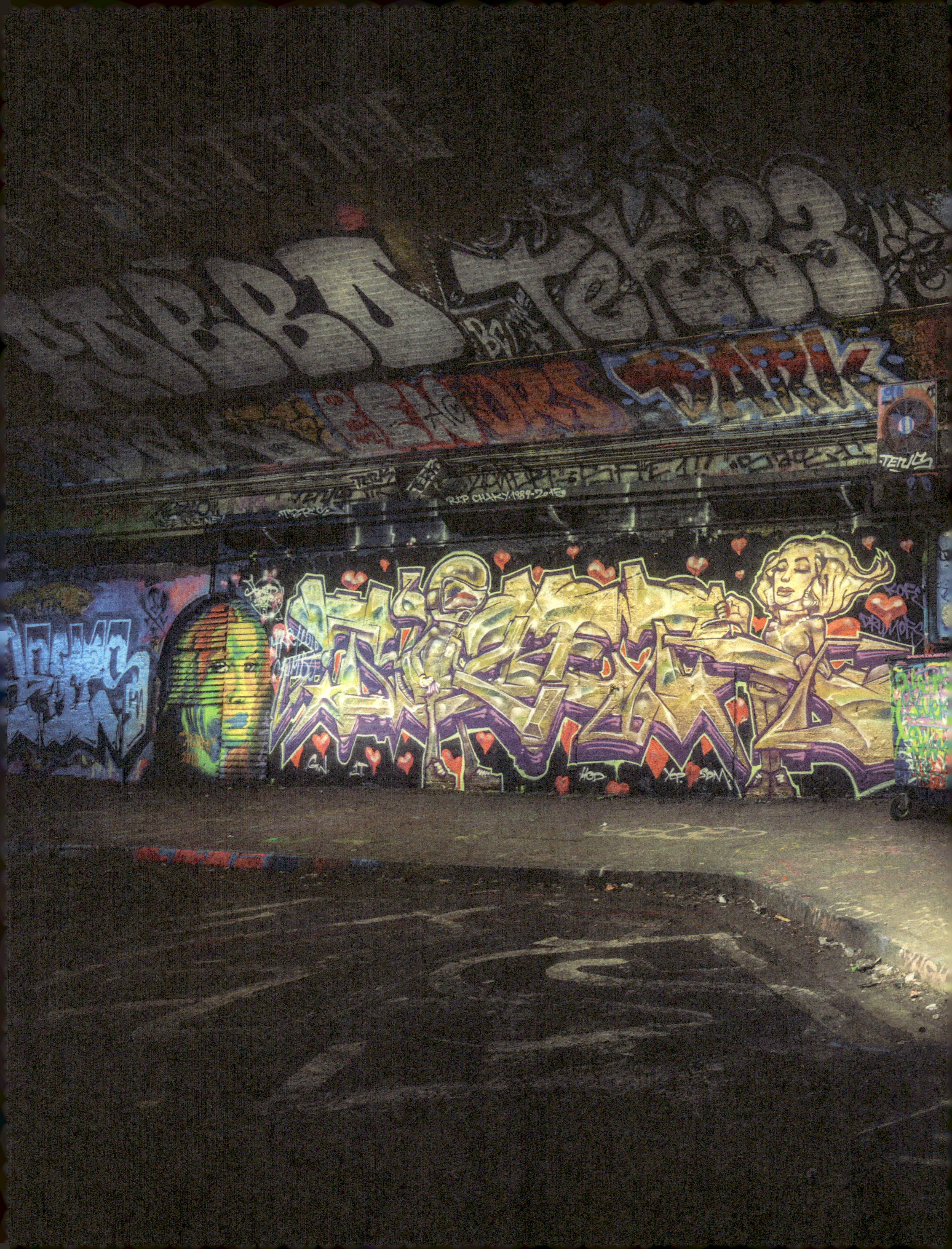

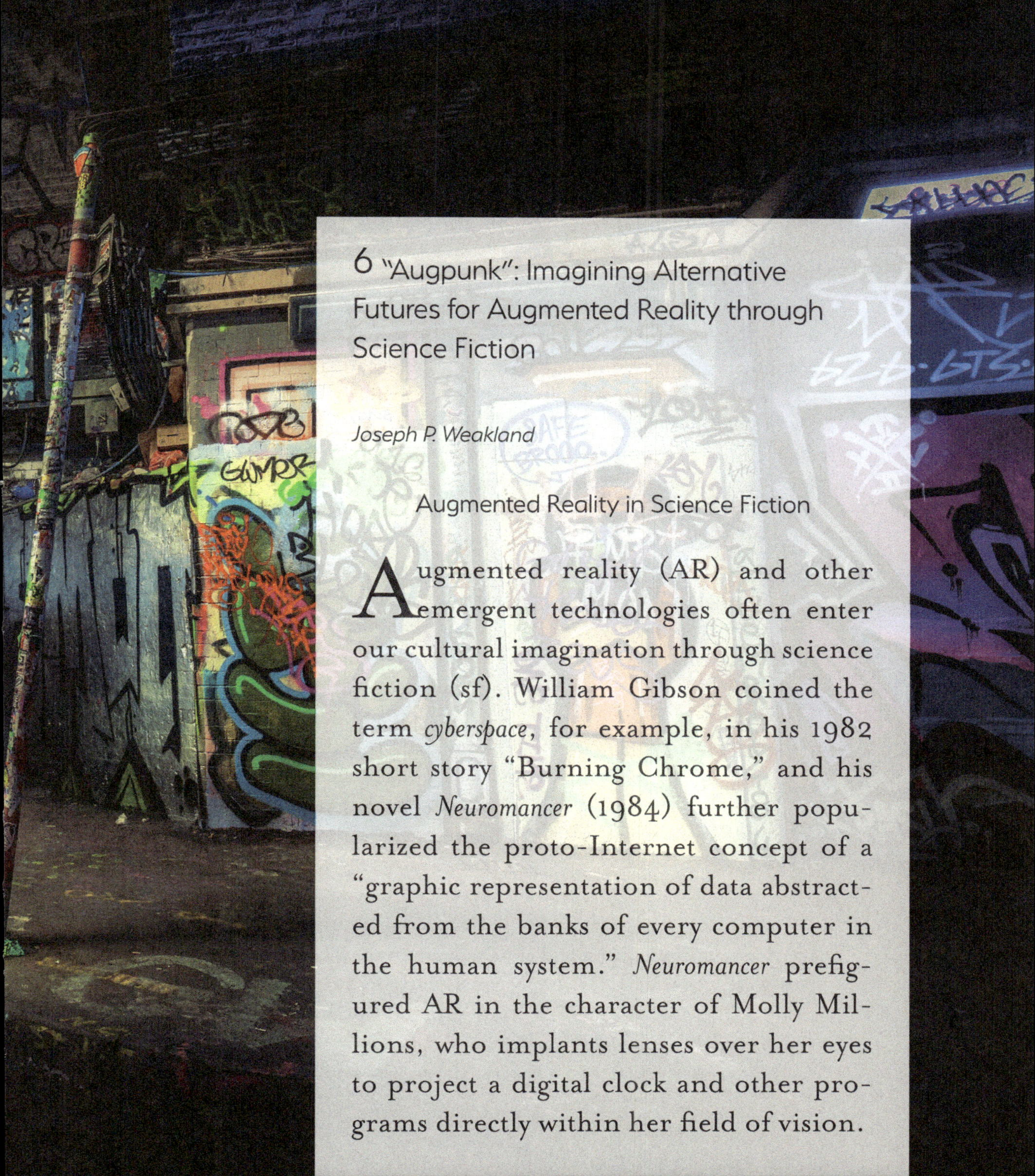

6 "Augpunk": Imagining Alternative Futures for Augmented Reality through Science Fiction

Joseph P. Weakland

Augmented Reality in Science Fiction

Augmented reality (AR) and other emergent technologies often enter our cultural imagination through science fiction (sf). William Gibson coined the term *cyberspace*, for example, in his 1982 short story "Burning Chrome," and his novel *Neuromancer* (1984) further popularized the proto-Internet concept of a "graphic representation of data abstracted from the banks of every computer in the human system." *Neuromancer* prefigured AR in the character of Molly Millions, who implants lenses over her eyes to project a digital clock and other programs directly within her field of vision.

Many other print sf works also imagine augmented reality. David Brin's novel *Earth* (1990) features "Tru-Vu" lenses which enhance the wearer's vision and broadcast video information to surveillance authorities. In Gibson's *Virtual Light* (1994), a pair of glasses transmits visual sensations to the user's optic nerve. The 2000s saw AR become the subject of several more novels, including M.T. Anderson's *Feed* (2002), a dystopia in which a ubiquitous brain-computer interface allows companies to spam costumers' vision with pop-up advertisements. Vernor Vinge's *Rainbows End* (2006) is arguably the most fully realized treatment of how pervasive computing and AR might transform all areas of human life, including culture, education, commerce, and national security. Vinge imagines that in the near future we will wear computers imprinted on smart clothes and access the Web through AR contact lenses. Communities of users form "belief circles" and construct their own mixed-reality worlds through sharing a common AR-overlay. In 2007, characters in Gibson's novel *Spook Country* declared that "cyberspace is everting," turning itself inside out with the advent of "spatially-tagged hypermedia," with "the artist annotating every centimeter of a place [and] every physical thing" with locative media viewable through mobile phones and headsets.

While sf's print tradition has explored AR for at least the last thirty years, it is big-budget science fiction films that provide the most iconic images of augmented reality. In *Terminator* (1984) and its sequels, we see in first-person perspective how the cyborg's vision is augmented with targeting overlays, facial recognition programs, mechanical diagrams, and other tactical information. Similarly, the alien in the *Predator* series wields an AR helmet with thermal vision and targeting systems. The most recent popular films to represent AR are *The Avengers* (2012) and *Ironman* (2008) series. In action sequences featuring Tony Stark's armored suit, the films cut between external shots of the suit itself and close-ups of Stark's face inside the helmet overlaid with visual data. Through consistently linking AR with supremacy in combat, these films should remind us of AR's origins in military hardware; armies widely deployed the technology in heads-up displays (HUDs) for aircraft and other vehicles well before AR entered popular culture.

"Science fiction plays a significant role in conditioning the public's attitude toward new media technologies, including augmented reality. "

Indeed, popular representations of technology don't enter culture newly formed, but instead carry with them the ideological residues of their development in institutions like militaries, corporations, universities, and governments. Science fiction then becomes one crucial arena in which emergent technologies (re)acquire meaning and value. According to Istvan Csicsery-Ronay, sf "embeds scientific-technical concepts in the broad sphere of human interests and actions, explaining them, mythologizing them, and explicitly attributing social value to them." Presently, science fiction plays a significant role in conditioning the public's attitude toward new media technologies, including augmented reality. Across the entire array of extant media, sf speculations allow the public to imagine what new media devices might be possible or desirable. A recent Internet meme shows how the television series *Star Trek* imagined inventions like the mobile phone, tablet computer, video conferencing, and Google Glass far in advance of their entry into the real-world. Science fiction also bleeds into advertising for mobile devices: Google's "Nexus" (a reference to the replicants in the 1982 film *Blade Runner*) and Motorola's "Droid" series of smart phones play on the sf android's ability to evoke *cool* and *cutting-edge* with an element of titillating danger. Finally, sf's visual depictions of an ever-more technologized future function to secure the public's consent to continual scientific and technological innovation, as well as the larger culture of economic expansionism that enables these processes.

Mass media science fiction representations of AR thus overshadow the smaller number of provocative sf works that examine this technology more critically. In order to support this claim, however, it's first necessary to identify some (and not all) of the closely-related imaginative and representational properties that give sf this critical capacity. For many scholars of science fiction, these properties allow us to distinguish between sf proper and what they term "sci-fi," a style of fantasy in which "almost anything can exist if it is made to appear to interact with setting and protagonists." By contrast, sf is "a zone of playful game-rules that constrain the imaginary world-construction in sophisticated ways." The recent short film "Sight," for example, explores how universal AR might transform activities like cooking and dating. This science fiction attempts to think rigorously and systematically about how new scientific and technological developments unfold across the full spectrum of human—and frequently non-human—activities. Works like David Brin's *Earth* and M.T. Anderson's *Feed* extend their consideration of new technologies toward the environmental cost of perpetual economic growth—a cost that includes the ecological footprint of electronics manufacturing.

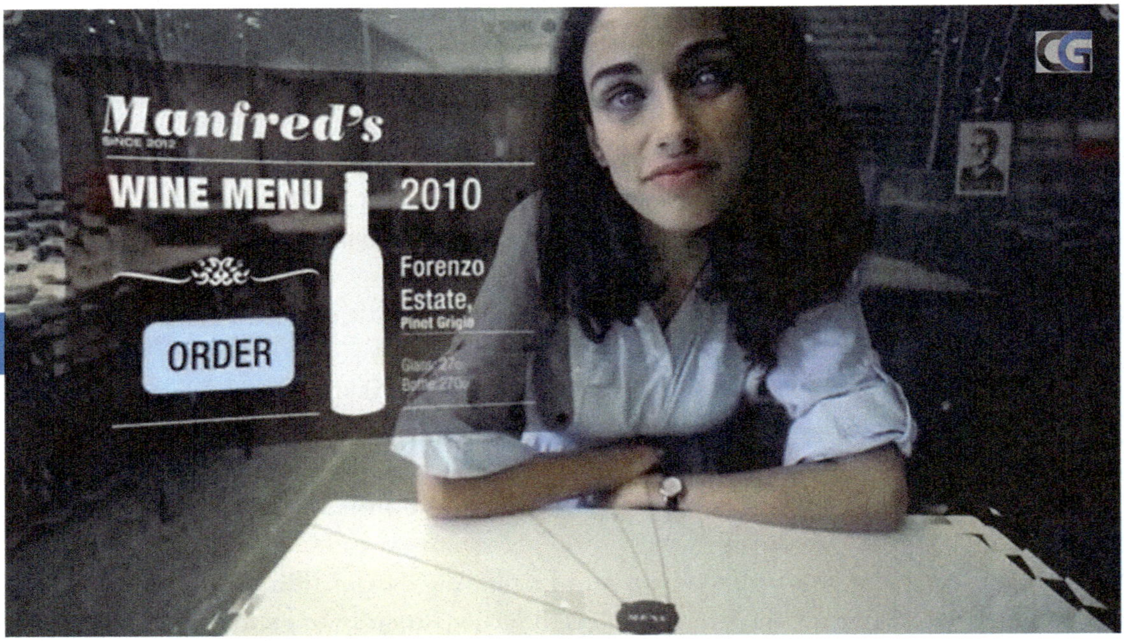

Figure 6.1: Sight. © 2012 by Eran May-raz and Daniel Lazo.

AURASMA
Scan the image to view.

Following scholar Darko Suvin's influential theory, sf also creates "cognitive estrangement" in readers through producing strange worlds that diverge from our empirical environment, wresting mundane elements from their ordinary contexts so that we might consider them anew. The skyscrapers of stacked garbage in the film *WALL-E* (2008) confront the viewer with the massive amounts of trash humans produce. Suvin draws on Berthold Brecht's definition of *estrangement* as "a representation . . . which allows us to recognize its subject, but at the same time makes it seem unfamiliar." While myth and fantasy also estrange their audiences from the world, science fiction is *cognitive* estrangement because it is "organized by extrapolating the variable and future bearing elements from the [reader's] empirical environment," i.e., sf is always an estrangement built from forces already at play within the present. In *WALL-E* these "variable and future bearing elements" are the ecological consequences of present economic activities; these elements are variable because—as proponents of sustainability argue—we have the power to change them. This leads us to the idea that sf is more than simply a genre of *scientific* and *technological* extrapolation. Instead, sf insists on the malleability of *social* institutions and attempts to imagine viable utopian alternatives—or at least imagines what dystopias might come into existence if present trends continue unabated.

Cyberpunk Rebooted

In distinguishing between "sci-fi" and "sf," I don't wish to create a false opposition between "sci-fi" as mass culture and "sf" as high culture; these styles mutually influence and bleed into one another. I do, however, wish to identify a set of cultural texts in which sf's critical capacities are most powerfully concentrated on augmented reality. In 2009, AR blogger and sf author Thomas K. Carpenter coined the term "augpunk" to describe cyberpunk godfather William Gibson's novel *Spook Country* and other AR fictions. This chapter further develops what this neologism might mean. I take "augpunk" to refer to works that draw on the conventions of cyberpunk science fiction to represent AR and locative media technologies. It is my central claim that augpunk provides readers with glimpses of alternative futures for AR and other mobile technologies, futures that go beyond those accessible in more mainstream sf works, as well as those disseminated by industries and technology developers themselves. Augpunk unsettles the economic, scientific, technological, institutional, and political dynamics that circumscribe our ability to imagine what AR can *be* or *do*. In addition, augpunk may also catalyze new ideas for deploying AR within our world, just as cyberpunk influenced generations of computer scientists and programmers.

Cyberpunk's history makes it particularly appealing as a candidate for disrupting popular AR imaginings. Cyberpunk emerged as an sf movement in the 1980s largely in response to the increasing availability of personal computers and the rise of hacker culture. Cyberpunk men and women occupy the social fringes and consist of loose associations of hackers, outlaws, artists, the poor, deviant subcultures, drug addicts, and other marginalized groups. Cyberpunk worlds feature shadowy, gritty urban environments inspired by the hardboiled detective fiction and film noir of the early twentieth-century. These stories contain a ubiquitous information network, "cyberspace," and imagine the consequences and possibilities of virtual (and later augmented) reality, genetic engineering, artificial intelligence, robotics, nanotechnology, pharmaceuticals, and body modification. Cyberpunks struggle for freedom, and freedom of information, in a world dominated by corporate conglomerates and surveillance states. Although the term "cyberpunk" was originally coined by author Bruce Bethke in his 1983 short story of the same name, most scholars recognize William Gibson's 1984 novel *Neuromancer* as the subgenre's archetypal literary manifestation.

For cyberpunk ringleader and longtime AR booster Bruce Sterling, cyberpunk captures "a new kind of integration," "the overlapping of worlds that were formerly separate: the realm of high tech, and the modern pop underground." In his preface to the 1986 cyberpunk anthology *Mirrorshades*, Sterling writes, "Cyberpunk comes from the realm where the computer hacker and the [punk] rocker overlap, a cultural Petri dish where writhing gene lines splice. Some find the results bizarre, even monstrous; for others, this integration is a powerful source of hope." Mirrored sunglasses were a recurring icon for the 80s movement, and their augpunk descendants now wear AR-shades or smart contact lenses that anticipate (or derive from) real-world devices like Google Glass. Similarly, augpunks no longer desire to jack into cyberspace in order to escape meatspace, as cyberspace has now completely "colonized the physical." Artist Anthony Antonellis captures this new confusion through an AR tattoo transmitted by an RFID implanted under his skin.

Cyberpunk 1.0's influence on both sf and popular culture has waned over the years, and the genre has been roundly criticized for failing to live up to many of its utopian ambitions. However, its persistence comes from its ability to imagine how powerful new technologies might exert force within the world once they move out of laboratories and onto the streets. Cyberpunk draws on punk music's DIY (Do-It-Yourself) ethic, envisioning how, in Gibson's words, "the street finds its own use for things." This DIY ethic helps explain the interest in new techno-punk sub-genres like "biopunk" (DIY genetic engineering), "nanopunk" (DIY nano-technology), and "steampunk" (DIY Victorian-era technology). *Augpunk* works transpose this vision to AR devices, imagining how people might use AR outside of (and in opposition to) cultural institutions such as the corporation, the university, the government, and the military. In the next section, I read British sf author Tim Maughan's *Paintwork* as an augpunk reboot of cyberpunk. The value of augpunk lies in its ability to help readers imagine uses for AR and locative media technologies that disrupt the visions afforded by mainstream, massively-disseminated science fictions—including those science fictions promulgated by the technological and industrial elite.

"Paintwork"

Tim Maughan's self-published collection of short stories, *Paintwork* (2011), presents a near-future in which AR devices like Google Glass have saturated most parts of the globe. The collection's title story begins with a street artist working under the pseudonym "3Cube." 3Cube is a young ambitious "writer" of QR code graffiti in the street art scene in Maughan's hometown of Bristol, England ("writer" is slang for graffiti artist). 3Cube's pseudonym evokes the tradition of local writers like Bristol-born graffiti artist and musician Robert Del Naja, who worked under the name "3D" in the mid-1980s. Today, Bristol's street art scene is globally recognized for the work of secretive writer "Banksy." Banksy's admirers note the "humorous and subversive nature of his artwork," while his detractors regard him as "simply [a] criminal," willful vandal, and prankster.

For the augpunks depicted in "Paintwork," Banksy is the perfect role model; his pieces incorporate anti-authoritarian messages, and he describes his work with a sense of menace when he says, "A wall is a very big weapon. It's one of the nastiest things you can hit someone with." To those who would label his graffiti and that of other street artists as vandalism, he responds,

> Imagine a city where graffiti wasn't illegal, a city where everybody could draw whatever they liked. Where every street was awash with a million colours and little phrases. Where standing at a bus stop was never boring. A city that felt like a party where everyone was invited, not just the estate agents and barons of big business. Imagine a city like that and stop leaning against the wall—it's wet.

Maughan pays direct homage to Banksy when an aspiring writer in his story gazes "at the few, still-remaining Banksy works" in future Bristol. However, in Maughan's vision of urban life in years to come, Banksy's utopian vision has not yet been realized.

In "Paintwork," several related cultural and technological developments threaten Bristol's tradition of street art and the artists who practice it: new surveillance techniques that allow the police to nab would-be artists in the act rewriting public space, the widespread deployment of "smart" surfaces that absorb and erase graffiti (a speculation that first appears in William Gisbon's 1999 novel *All Tomorrow's Parties*), and the uncertain place of street art itself in a new world of AR-overlays and locative media—a world in which the artist's audiences may simply decide to ignore his or her work in favor of their own preferred augmented reality layers.

The augpunk writer 3Cube overcomes these obstacles and carries on the writer's tradition with newly-invented urban tactics. In order to retain his anonymity and avoid the authorities, 3Cube wears "shoes [two] sizes too small for him," introducing randomness into the "gait-tracking software" that would link him to his work by patterning his movements around the city's streets. This surveillance software is programmed into unmanned aerial vehicles (UAVs) turned away from threats abroad and toward Bristol's own population. 3Cube receives real-time support while unleashing his "bomb" (the graffiti artist's term for a large work) from the computer hacker Tera—a former writer now confined to a wheelchair who uploads real-time data on police traffic to 3Cube's AR "spex," *Paintwork*'s futuristic equivalent of Google Glass. "Between disgruntled pensioners posting the precise loitering patterns of bored teenagers to the legit wikis, and the dealers and look-outs reporting squad car and UAV movements to the illegal ones," Tera assembles a "real-time model of police activity across South Bristol," allowing 3Cube to avoid detection while working at his craft. In a database culture in which movement in both physical space and cyberspace is amenable to data mining, the augpunk exploits both sides of the dialectic between pattern and randomness in order to disrupt the system.

3Cube's target is an unblemished Coca-Cola billboard protected by a nearly impenetrable layer of "nano-gloss," a fictional neologism Maughan invents to name a surface engineered with nano-scale manufacturing techniques. The nano-gloss protection makes the billboard impervious to vandalism—particularly graffiti—and allows transnational advertisers to reassert their dominance over the local visual culture of Bristol. Against this defense, the artist's traditional spray-paint can is useless. 3Cube instead bombs his target with so-called "bug-juice," an aerosol of nano-scale machines capable of penetrating and marking the nano-gloss. Alongside his nano-upgraded spray-paint can, the writer totes another invention that disrupts the reader's expectations of the traditional graffiti artist: a hand-made stencil for a large-sized QR code. 3Cube uses the stencil to paint the QR code over the

Coca-Cola billboard's own advertisement code. When people on the street view the code's link through their AR spex, they are surprised to discover the generic Cola-Cola advertisement replaced by 3Cube's own graffiti animation. The graffiti writer thus takes Coca-Cola's advertising space for his own and swaps the corporation's placeless vision of product enjoyment with a vision rooted in the streets and culture of Bristol itself.

While graffiti artists have always been concerned with how their work occupies, appropriates, and reconfigures urban space, 3Cube in particular "thinks about depth a lot. Depth, perspective. How to force and manipulate both. It is what he is best known for." This is because 3Cube's medium allows him different expressive affordances than the writers who preceded him. Whereas earlier writers didn't incorporate digital elements directly into their final pieces, 3Cube takes full advantage of the digital potential of QR code bombing. 3Cube's first piece, "painstakingly calculated from Google Maps and Street View," makes the billboard appear transparent, "as though someone has punched a hole through a sheet of paper." Through this widening breach, the work opens across

> the skyline of Bristol . . . across the sea of warehouses and industrial units toward the seventy year old towers of the Barton Hill Estate that he calls home . . . But the illusion doesn't stay set for long. After precisely two seconds the sun starts to burst out from the dark clouds above the towers, banishing the drizzle and turning the Bristol night sky to day. The view turns from monochrome to electric, vivid colour; and where the sunlight—so warm-looking he can almost feel it—hits the structures below they start to transform, huge exotic plants and flowers erupting from the post-war industrial landscape, until the whole scene has become fields of organic, inviting nature.

3Cube's effort is part of a trilogy to be released over three consecutive nights. He views the piece as a "statement about how he feels his city—his home—can unleash its vibrancy through defiance of those that would attempt to control and regulate space." 3Cube's bombs on two other Coca-Cola billboards render visions of a city reclaimed by a Jurassic-era jungle and an inrushing urban ocean.

3Cube's trilogy estranges viewers from their present world for the purpose of contemplating alternative worlds, blurring the boundary between graffiti and science fiction. His work allows his audience to experience the dissolution of urban space controlled, regulated, and surveilled by police and corporations, as well as to experience Bristol as a collective site of renewal and possibility. For 3Cube, the aesthetic experience is rooted in the street: "This is street art and his real audience is the street." Accordingly, he prefers a "first-hand wry smile or a confused glance over the re-posted echoes of a gushing thousand-word review or a sarcastic hundred-and-forty character Tweet." Finally, while the narrative doesn't emphasize the ecological content of 3Cube's work, his pieces foreground the natural systems that make city life possible: oceans, plants, and other organisms.

The central irony at play within "Paintwork," however, is that *no one sees* 3Cube's trilogy. An anonymous writer—later revealed to be the hacker Tera in the story's *denouement*—"burns" each of 3Cube's installments, overwriting the artist's QR pieces using the billboard's built-in repair system. Instead of using QR codes himself, Tera bombs the entire billboard in 2D black and white. Each burn is a direct, tonally-inverted response to 3Cube's pieces, "morbid and full of futility, as if declaring with nihilistic glee that Bristol and its decades old street art movement were finally dead." They variously depict Bristol's Barton Hill skyline as "[the] lifeless fossils of a long dead dinosaur," "crumbling Towers" onto which "fizzy-drink can bombs" rain down, and finally as "disintegrating silhouettes against a blindingly white blast [and] black mushroom cloud."

Tera's 2D burns on 3Cube's 3D work represent the leading edge of an aesthetic backlash against AR technologies within the Bristol street art scene. The writer "Artefackt," for example, tells 3Cube he's "getting back into 2D" because "3D is dead. Augmented is over. It's just fucking background noise. It's just fucking TV and Twitter and all . . . this [shit]. Disposable, infinitely fucking copyable noise. Mass produced and instantly forgotten." Likewise, Tera tells 3Cube, "everybody just walks around with their spex on, looking at their own content." 3Cube eventually comes to recognize these artists' inchoate desire to "make something permanent and handcrafted, but with machines." Artefackt and Tera seek to restore some sense of authenticity to street art, and, as Walter Benjamin reminds us, "the whole sphere of authenticity is outside of technical—and, of course, not only technical—reproducibility." Contrary to their rhetoric, both Artefackt and Tera "sell out" their work to advertisers, and it remains unclear what role machines will play in defining a new 2D aesthetic. 3Cube is left alone to carry this avant-garde forward, and he begins by turning an old-fashioned spray-can against the "Bristol City Council regulation-issue magnolia paint" on his bedroom wall. Perhaps even the story's hardline 2D artists would be content to have their work QR coded as locative media for posterity's sake: in 2010, the Berlin-based artist "Sweza" photographed several graffiti pieces that were later effaced. Sweza restored them as locative media using QR codes installed at each piece's original location.

Thus, with the conclusion of "Paintwork," Maughan imagines augpunk's eventual demise—at least among the street artists who may choose to embrace it for a time. In a June 2013 interview, Maughan acknowledges the transience of his vision, saying,

> I get the impression that QR [Quick Response] Codes are already going out of fashion, [but] I don't mind that because when I was writing about them, they were a fairly new thing. . . . That's what *Paintwork* is all about. I like the idea that you can look back at science fiction from the '60s, '70s, '80s, now, and go, 'well, that's wrong about the future, but that doesn't matter because it was reflecting the values and concerns of the time it was written.' . . . It makes science fiction an important and historical document.

To this I would add that augpunk science fiction can also function as more than a historical record, but also as a shaping force in the continued development of augmented reality and locative media in our contemporary moment and beyond. Maughan's work allows readers to experience a vision of how these emergent technologies are transforming both the present and the future. "Paintwork," in particular, explores an augpunk strategy for reclaiming urban space and forming communities through locative art. Through situating new inventions within concrete narratives, these sf visions also allow readers to imagine new uses for AR within their own local contexts.

"Havana Augmented"

Maughan's short stories "Paparazzi" and "Havana Augmented" speculate as to how gamers might participate in augpunk culture through reconfiguring one of cyberpunk's long-running tropes. *Neuromancer* and other cyberpunk works in the 1980s imagined transnational corporations displacing nation states as the dominant global force, with corporate workers pledging loyalty to their employers in a kind of neo-feudalism. For Frederic Jameson, this element of cyberpunk was less speculative and more "an expression of transnational corporate realities." In "Paparazzi" and "Havana Augmented," however, Maughan replaces cyberpunk's traditional corporate antagonist with a new one: the online gaming guild. He speculates that in the near future, online gaming guilds—communities of gamers who play and collaborate within the same game(s)—will come to wield enormous power. These stories extrapolate trends present today: namely, the complex interactions between real economies and virtual economies already taking place within MMORPGs (Massively Multiplayer Online Role-Playing Games) like *World of Warcraft*, where so-called "gold farmers" labor within the game's economy to amass valuable in-game items. The gold farmers sell these items to players who use "real" money to purchase them, most often through the farmer's third-party website. Even for those players not in the gold farming business, "their game play might be more stressful and demanding than their actual jobs . . . MMORPG players pay game companies on a monthly basis (between US$10 and US$15) to work and get burned out." In Maughan's story "Paparazzi," powerful gaming guilds assimilate the function of gold farmers and employ gamers as wage-laborers. An unlucky film maker ends up on the wrong side of Sakura Guild and is forced to work as a sweatshop laborer in the virtual reality game *A Wind of Blades*. Modeled on a simulacrum of Feudal Japan, the Sakura Guild exerts such control on its many members that it becomes a major cultural force with the ability to influence both the game industry and nation states.

"Havana Augmented" takes place in the same world as "Paintwork," but changes locations from Bristol, England, to Havana, Cuba. In "Havana Augmented," the Sakura Guild approaches the Cuban government in order to open up economic relations. Because of sanctions and trade restrictions, Cuba largely missed the AR revolution that swept other parts of the globe. The country drew the Sakura Guild's attention with the viral release of *Street Iron*, an AR game designed by Havana hackers and gamers. *Street Iron* is played through AR spex with a built-in brain-computer interface (called a "focus interface" in the text) that functions through correlating patterns in brain activity with in-game commands. *Street Iron* players control towering robots modeled on Japanese mecha anime and the US *Mechwarrior* series of games. *Street Iron* is a heavy modification (or "mod," in gamer slang) of the game *Roll-*

ing Iron, the latter of which could only be played in cyberspace through a stationary focus interface. The hacker and gamer Marcus creates *Street Iron* with materials from *Rolling Iron*, adapting it for play in the augmented urban space of Havana. In the more robust definition of the locative media interface developed by Jason Farman, *Street Iron* creates an interface not simply between the player's brain activity and his or her mech avatar, but "between technologies, landscapes, and characters" all enlisted by the game in the "embodied production of social space."

The result is an instant success not only for Marcus's local group of gamers, but for those who choose to play *Street Iron* outside of Cuba. Marcus whets the international gaming community's appetite with YouTube clips of "giant mechs stomping around real-world Havana, exchanging chain gun fire and rocket attacks, [and] clashing in ground shaking hand-to-hand combat," which "spread like viral wild-fire around the game sites, blogs, and video sharing sites." Once Marcus leaks the full (and free) version of *Street Iron* onto the net,

> videos came flooding back; clips of giant mechs clashing in the streets of London, Paris, Tokyo, Tehran, LA, Beijing, Mumbai—the major cities of the world on augmented fire as secret, unseen wars were fought. AR gaming wasn't new to the outside world; however, doing it on this kind of scale in these busy, built-up areas was usually restricted by those that provided and monitored the spex-spaces. Due to its built-from-the-ground-up, home-brew design, *Street Iron* existed outside of those rules, it became something rebellious and anarchic, drawing in players desperate for a thrill in the way no official, legitimate product ever could.

Like "Paintwork," "Havana Augmented" is centrally concerned with how augpunks might resist prevailing power structures through reclaiming urban space and producing new, subversive spaces, such as those *Street Iron*'s players create through bypassing restrictions on the possibilities for augmented reality play.

Havana's gamers similarly repurpose the content of *Street Iron* in order to imbue it with elements of their local culture. The gamer Paul's mech, named "Alphonso," sports

> an over-waxed, gleaming green and white paintjob that mimicked the famous restrosheens Cuba's petrol-heads proudly gave to their seventy year old US muscle cars. In a similar way to how their love and care in maintaining their antique rides was both a nod towards and a snub of their US designers in the face of decades of trade embargo, the finish that Marcus had given Alphonso was aimed squarely at the Japanese artist that had come up with the original hellcat design. It sort of said, 'Yeah. We like your work, but look what we've done with it now.'

Alphonso's paint job also signifies the longevity of *Street Iron* and the ingenuity of the hackers and gamers who allowed it to far outlive its *Rolling Iron* source material. Marcus's constant updates firmly embed *Street Iron* within Havana's gamer culture, giving it a much longer shelf-life than the typical commercially-developed game. His work resists the logic of planned obsolescence characteristic of mainstream games, predicated as they are on franchise strategies of yearly title releases and even more frequent expansion pack releases. Both of these commercial techniques fragment the player community between those who purchase the new content and those who don't. Likewise, *Street Iron* features no in-game economy to stratify players based on their purchasing power or turn them into wage laborers; instead, a cybernetic economy of skill requires players to manage their mech's internal systems, movement, and weaponry in order to win.

The Sakura Guild seeks to co-opt Marcus's augpunk game and turn it into a vehicle for opening up Cuba to commercial investment and guild recruitment. The Guild floods Havana with "free, dumbed down" spex ahead of an exhibition match between Leo Kim, celebrity gamer and Sakura Guild leader, and Havana native and *Street Iron* player Paul. Paul is under pressure from the Cuban government to cooperate with Sakura, but he experiences a crisis of conscience when he sees firsthand the Guild's plan to colonize Havana's mixed real and virtual urban spaces: "Virtual billboards hung in the air down the street, covering the fascias of some of the buildings, or hanging across the street like banners. They were advertising games like *Rolling Iron* and *A Wind of Blades*, soft drinks and fast food, Nike shoes and other clothes. Stuff you couldn't even buy in Cuba." Paul challenges Leo Kim to single combat, under the condition that the Sakura Guild leaves Cuba should Paul win. Paul's challenge comes after Leo Kim defeats his team in the exhibition match using an updated version of *Street Iron* to equip his mech with evasive jump jets—a move that for Paul is tantamount to cheating. It's only fair, then, that Marcus rolls back the *Street Iron* client to the pre-update version during their duel—which Paul wins. The Havana youths thus expel Sakura by reclaiming communal ownership of their game, breaking it away from Sakura's aims to commercialize *Street Iron* and Havana's augmented cityspace.

By insisting on the creative autonomy of the AR gamer, Maughan provides a narrative illustration of what Farman believes should be the "ultimate goal" of locative media games: "engaging users in the production of spaces and [examining] how these spaces can either reinforce or resist the dominant power structures." "Havana Augmented" and other augpunk stories provide many figurations of a key actor within this project: the *bricoleur*, or one who transforms techno-cultural artifacts "into something they were never initially designed for but in which they find their significance." The French word *bricoleur* refers to one who practices *bricolage*, translated as "tinkering" or "DIY." The augpunk *bricoleur* engages in "creative misuse" of emergent AR and locative media so as to resist dominant power structures, as well as to ensure the diversity of our physical, digital, and imaginative ecologies.

From Augury to Augpunk

My elaboration of augpunk is also a form of creative misuse; I have extended Carpenter's term far beyond his original usage. In taking the central conceit of my essay from a weblog, I am also guilty of punking the boundaries between academic and non-academic discourse. Indeed, the question of what value augpunk may have in the ongoing scholarly conversation concerning cyberpunk fictions and their legacy must be left to others. I will instead conclude by reflecting further on what the neologism augpunk can mean for those concerned with the future of AR and other emergent mobile media technologies. The word *augmented* (as in augmented reality) contains within it the root word *aug-*, for "increase." Cosmetic surgery discourses use the word *augmentation* to refer to the practice of enlarging organs or regions of the body, as in breast augmentation, for example. This poses no irony for augpunk, as cyberpunk frequently explores how surgery and biotechnology can modify and enhance the human body. Cyberpunks augment themselves not to pursue a commercial image of beauty, but for classic punk shock value: in

Neuromancer, a punk replaces his face with "a simple graft grown on collagen and shark-cartilage polysaccharides, smooth and hideous."

More interesting for our purposes may be the ancient Roman ritual of "taking the auspices," a duty performed by an "augur," defined as:

> A religious official among the Romans, whose duty it was to predict future events and advise upon the course of public business, in accordance with omens derived from the flight, singing, and feeding of birds, the appearance of the entrails of sacrificial victims, celestial phenomena, and other portents.

The augur did not predict the future, but determined whether a course of action already underway met with divine approval. In much the same way, AR fictions invoke possible futures as a way of drawing our critical attention to forces at play within the present. In Tim Maughan's augpunk stories "Paintwork" and "Havana Augmented," the street artists 3Cube and Tera, the hacker Marcus, and the gamer Paul interpret signs within their worlds and engage in public life through intervening within collective visions of the future. 3Cube and Tera ask their respective publics to consider new possibilities for locative media and augmented space in urban life. The artists present two possible futures: 3Cube's image of a reclaimed Bristol cityspace, and Tera's grim challenge to commercial culture and what he perceives as AR's banalizing aesthetics. Marcus and Paul create a new way for gamers to use augmented urban space, and intervene in public life by untying the future of their game and their city from the influence of the Sakura Guild. Each character examines the viscera of his world, recombining its elements so as to intervene within a system. The augpunk's interventions are "a practical contribution to a media system (e.g. some product, tool, or method) intended to challenge underlying assumptions or reveal new ways of proceeding."

Unlike the ancient augur, of course, none of these characters attach themselves to a priestly order or its contemporary institutional equivalent. Instead, the augpunk works outside of established institutions, and his or her public visions often run counter to the will of their leaders. This isn't to sketch too neat a historical parallel between these figures. However, companies such as Microsoft, Intel, Apple, and Google employ futurists like Ray Kurzweil, currently Google's Director of Engineering. Kurzweil's visions of "spiritual machines" and a "post-biological future" surely indicate that a mystical, prophetic impulse resides even at the heart of today's most rational, technocratic institutions. The augpunk as augur, then, seeks to give the prophetic/futurist impulse a DIY character, acting as heretic to the technocratic dogma of the corporate futurist.

The success of the ancient augur's ability to predict future events could only be judged in retrospect. An augur's failed predictions would indicate his lack of skill in taking the auspices. The augpunk's failed predictions mean something else. They are, as Maughan suggests, a historical record, a window into society's hopes and anxieties at a particular cultural moment. But the presence of such visions within public discourse also enlarges and enriches our possibilities for action and intervention in the present. AR fictions, like Maughan's and those of the authors whom I cite in my introduction, may introduce readers (especially those outside of AR's insider communities) to possibilities for AR and locative media technologies that they might not have otherwise imagined. In addition, these visions allow us to contemplate how these devices interact with the larger sphere of human activities beyond the microcosms presented in AR's "market discourse," which, as John Tinnell writes, "constantly summarizes [AR's] function as simply augmenting the real with virtual overlays." Further, sf is a powerful vehicle for exploring how "ubiquitous networks of interactive, graphical overlays *transform*—not (only) augment—the very ontological categories/relations by which we come to advance claims about realities."

Nonetheless, popular media frequently depict these technologies as struggling to transition from the realm of speculation into that of scientific fact and "real-world" practice. Within this formulation, emergent technologies strive to become "reality" and deliver on the promises of techno-hype. This implies that in order to reach maturity, AR must leave science fiction behind. Interestingly, cyberpunk author Bruce Sterling, who delivered a keynote address at the 2013 Augmented World Expo, may have played into this mentality. When asked whether he reads any AR fiction, he replied:

> I'm not sure it makes a lot of sense to write fiction nowadays 'about ar,' because it's no longer a fictional topic. It's become like writing fiction 'about cinema': you can write good fiction about someone who works in cinema, but not fiction about cinema itself. AR is not sci-fi "Augment-

> ed Reality" anymore. It's become a real-world phenomenon, a new industry of real augmentation.

Sterling would do well to remember Donna Haraway's dictum that the "boundary between science fiction and social reality is an optical illusion." AR should embrace its science-fictional status and resist as long as possible the ossification and "taken-for-grantedness" that affects technologies that achieve cultural ubiquity. Accordingly, we should continue to geotag AR within critical science fiction's imaginative space of virtual possibility. Science fiction assumes a virtual set of scientific, technological, social, political, environmental, and institutional coordinates that extend outward from our contemporary moment. This sf epistemology reveals the present as only one contingent, shifting manifestation of these virtual coordinates. In this way, sf itself can function as augmented reality, enlarging and enhancing our understanding of these technologies within a metaverse of critical futures.

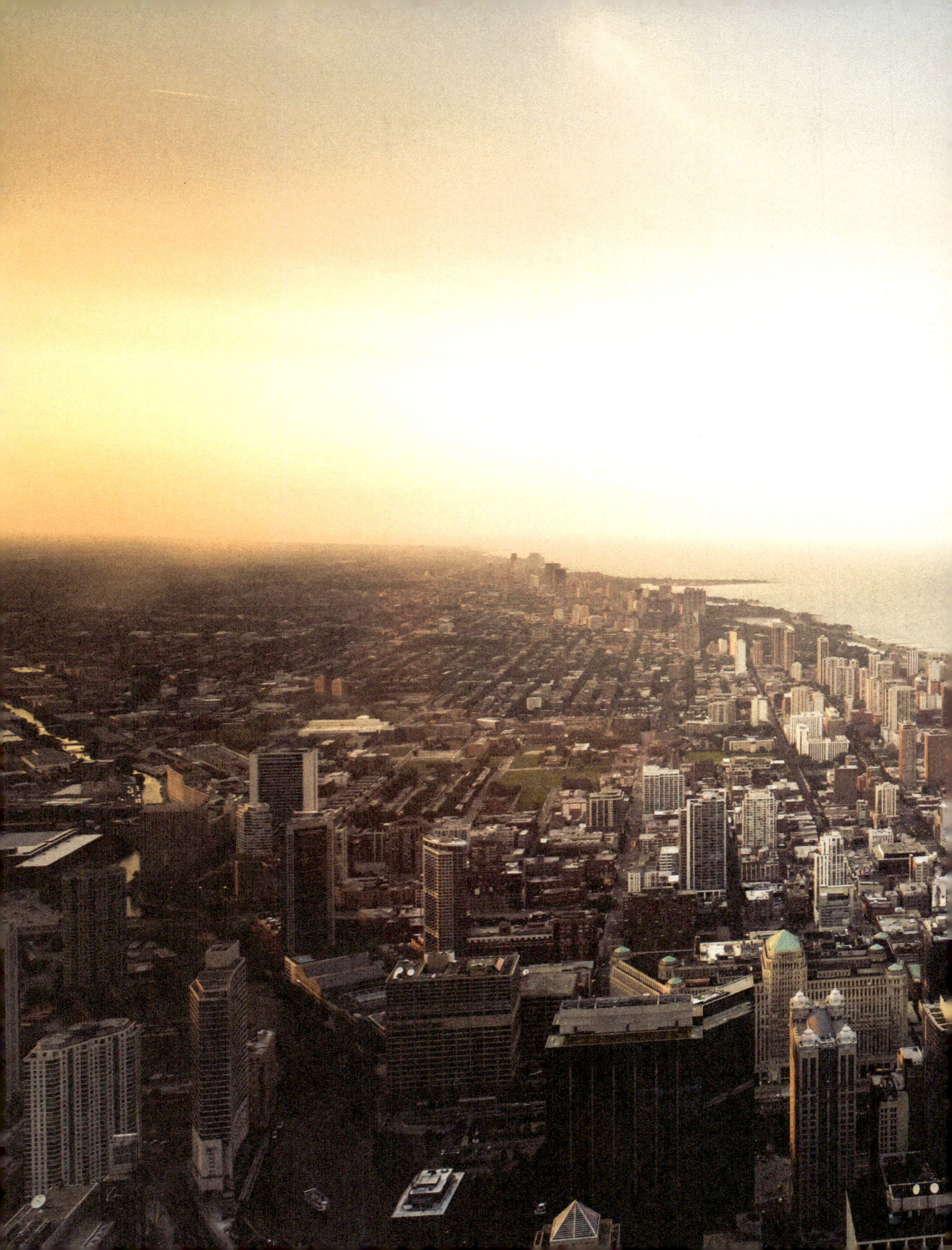

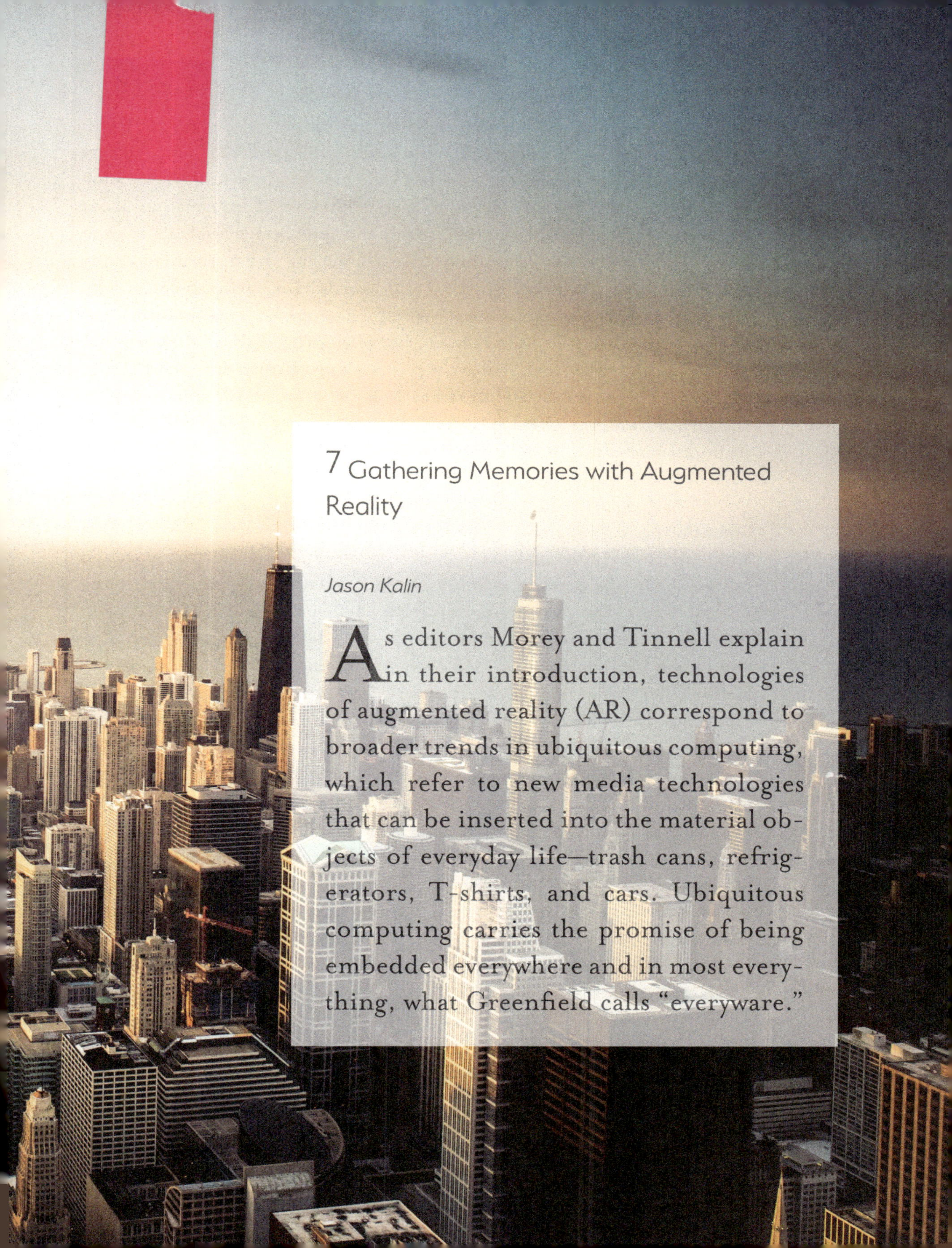

7 Gathering Memories with Augmented Reality

Jason Kalin

As editors Morey and Tinnell explain in their introduction, technologies of augmented reality (AR) correspond to broader trends in ubiquitous computing, which refer to new media technologies that can be inserted into the material objects of everyday life—trash cans, refrigerators, T-shirts, and cars. Ubiquitous computing carries the promise of being embedded everywhere and in most everything, what Greenfield calls "everyware."

In this vision, ubiquitous computing does not simply recede into the background, but rather constitutes the very conditions of everyday life: "Things as fundamental as the way we wake up in the morning, get to work, or shop for our groceries—are remade as an intricate dance of information about ourselves, the state of the external world, and the options available to us at any given moment." As such, ubiquitous computing and augmented reality have the capacity to transform the world into "a rich environment of hidden information and capabilities, waiting to be made available to us, and responding to our needs, both hidden and obvious." Indeed, Fuller and Matos explain that what mattered most to John Seely Brown and Mark Weiser was "not technology in itself but rather its capacities to continuously recreate our relation with the world at large." Ubiquitous computing and augmented reality are embedded in and generative of material cultures; they are aesthetic and rhetorical world-making, world-building technologies.

As forms and practices of aesthetic and rhetorical world-making, ubiquitous computing and augmented reality have been connected to forms and practices of individual and collective memory. This development should not be surprising because memory has long been connected to new technologies—from Plato to the present, from poetic performances to writing to Evernote (a desktop and cloud-computing note-taking application) to Layar and Junaio (AR applications). Given the intertwined history of memory and technology, it is apt that developers of AR applications are exploring ways to create new experiences of memory. Furthermore, memory—along with rhetorical practices of memory—is a world-building activity in which how we remember is as important as what we remember. For example, the rhetorical art of memory, as articulated in *Rhetorica ad Herennium*, Cicero's *On the Orator*, and Quintilian's *Institutes of Oratory*, developed memory as a technique for delivering speeches. The art of memory relied upon a system of *topoi* or *loci* whereby the rhetor would imprint vivid and distinctive images of what was to be remembered onto specific places within a known architectural space. Visually and imaginatively walking through this architectural space would allow the rhetor to recall information as needed to deliver the most appropriate speech for the occasion. In this way, the art of memory—as techne, as technique, as technology—offered a particular way of being in and relating to the larger world. Uricchio, for instance, argues that the art of memory enacted a social practice for "manipulat[ing] and understand[ing] an accreted visual history and evolving present." AR applications that overlay dynamic digital information onto physical space share much with the rhetorical art of memory and its orientation to "an accreted visual history and evolving present." Put differently, the art of memory was an early form and practice of augmented memory, which is, as I argue, another way of saying augmented reality: memory itself and the art of memory—and by extension new technologies of memory and their corresponding sociotechnical practices—gather together a copia of mnemonic objects and things that offer the rhetor a place from which to speak so that she may build, augment, and transform her reality marked by ever-shifting exigencies. Indeed, memory and technologies of memory help disclose new exigencies in and of reality, thus creating the possibility of new worlds to inhabit. Memory manifests the rhetor's place and time in a world; therefore, changes in the technologies of memory will transform that world and how she comes to dwell within it.

In this chapter, I explore augmented reality as a sociotechnical practice to animate memory as a central persuasive force for the future of digital rhetoric. In her study of ubiquitous computing, including wearable technologies and augmented reality, Pedersen addresses the concept of augmented memory, specifically arguing "that inventors' discourses justify augmented memory according to a dehumanizing rhetoric of need (i.e., we need better memories so we need an augmented memory), leading to a machine-centricity embedded within these justifications." Whereas Pedersen focuses on the dehumanizing aspects of this rhetoric, I attend to how forms and practices of augmented reality disclose new modes of being with memory, and thus of being-in-the-world. In doing so, I do not attempt to contradict Pedersen's insights, but rather try to intensify the connections among technologies and memory that she identifies: "Through this complex process of discursive friction, rhetorical manipulation, and media ecological vying, augmented memory emerges." Like Pedersen, I attend to the rhetorical assumptions and motivations of augmented memory by following and advancing two prevailing metaphors of memory—network and ambience—to show not only how memory has always already been augmented, but also how augmented

"Augmented reality technologies generate forms and practices of rhetorical world-building by which we may not only preserve our memories, but also inhabit them."

reality introduces potential new aesthetics and rhetorics of memory appropriate to digital media culture. Finally, I connect these concepts to an orientation in digital media culture that I refer to as the monumentality of the mundane through which every moment becomes fit for memory and through which we practice our everyday lives. Put differently, AR technologies and the aesthetics and rhetorics of augmented memory create worlds wherein we may dwell, or as the headline for Google Glass announces, "Welcome to a world through Glass." AR technologies generate forms and practices of rhetorical world-building by which we may not only preserve our memories but also inhabit them. As such, the material-digital things of augmented reality and augmented memory become essential building materials of everyday life.

Media, Mediations, and Metaphors of Memory: A New Memory Ecology

By superimposing digital objects onto the real world, AR technologies and applications, such as Layar and Junaio, change the embodied experience users have with their surroundings. AR smartphone apps are referred to as "reality browsers," or in Tinnell's apt description, "world browsers." And as technologies of memory, we may call them "memory browsers," for they allow users to access and browse various forms of memory, from Wikipedia articles to Yelp reviews to Instagram photos. World browsing thus becomes a practice of memory browsing, and vice versa. In commenting on the influence of world browsers, Tinnell writes, '"World browsing is already initiating changes in the presentation of cultural archives that will have changed the way we build, exhibit, and experiences histories." Augmented reality transforms the ontology of memory because memory, especially collective and public memory, always requires material supports. For instance, Zelizer explains that collective memory is material, relying upon texts and artifacts, monuments and memorials. Dickinson, Blair, and Ott similarly note that public memory needs material support for its ongoing performance. Olick refers to the materiality of memory as the problematic of representation: there can be no directly mimetic, no pre-representational experience of memory. As such, media and their materiality are integral to expressions and performances of memory. Indeed, Olick stipulates that the media of memory "are everything, and even if there is some ultimate truth of events, representational media clearly shape its delivery to us." The materiality of media actively shapes memory and its mediation: "The media of memory decisively shape not only specific memories but also memory's mediating functions." Changing the material supports changes what we experience as memory. Most studies, especially in the field of rhetoric, have been interested in conventional forms of media and mediation, such as monuments, memorials, and museums. Nevertheless, recent scholarship has begun to argue more explicitly that new media technologies oblige scholars to rethink memory by "changing what we consider to be the past" along with the acts of remembering and forgetting.

Given the "amorphous" qualities of memory, metaphors have long been used to understand what memory is and how it works. Among the most common metaphors of memory have been technologies because technologies, Draaisma suggests, are the means of developing artificial memories. Here, I turn to metaphors used to describe and interpret the contemporary intermediation of technologies and memory: "Our relationship with memory, the metaphors we use to understand it and the cultural constructs that surround our conceptualization of it, must be central to any digital interpretation of memory." For instance, Garde-Hansen, Hoskins, and Reading argue that metaphors of memory based upon more traditional "broadcast era" media have become outmoded in a "digital media ecology" that facilitates the "accessibility, transferability and circulation of digital content." They thus advocate "a concept of digital memory as one that rethinks time as linear and move toward a concept time and memory as spatial and involving organic participation with inorganic structures." In short, a new media ecology introduces a new memory ecology, affecting both the media and mediations of memory. Therefore, we ought to consider the production of memory—both how memory is produced and how memory produces—so that we may begin to understand how we are situated within this new memory ecology. To do so, I focus on network and ambience as metaphors to show how they help us invent and understand the sociotechnical forms and practices of augmented reality as augmented memory.

Augmented Reality and Digital Network Memory

To foreground this new memory ecology, Hoskins proposes the metaphor of the network and the concept of digital network memory to show how individual and collective memories are bound together with networked technologies. The concept of digital network memory emphasizes "the dynamics of mediated memory as something created when needed, driven by the connectivities of digital technologies and media, and inextricably forged through and constitutive of digital social networks." Hoskins argues that digital network memory emerges through "on-the-fly" constructions. In so doing, digital network memory temporally and temporarily connects moments to moments, memories to memories—what he refers to as "another next first time," which is "a recognizable and sequentially located new moment, a patterned new moment that can be understood because of its similarity to previous moments and because of its place in the joint unfolding of biography and history." Such temporal and temporary connections enact a shift from media content to sociotechnical practices—not so much what individuals or groups are remembering but rather how they are remembering.

As an example of digital network memory and augmented reality, we may consider the AR smartphone app Layar, one of the more popular AR platforms. For the Layar platform, developers and contributors may create layers that merge the physical environment with digital information, and the app includes a section, for instance, of "Recommended Layers," which allows the user to choose among Instagram photos or Twitter posts that have been geotagged with nearby locations, or Wikipedia articles of local attractions, or neighboring places to eat and drink. Drawing upon my own experience as a brief example to emphasize the ordinary, everyday quality of these AR interfaces, choosing the Instagram layer reveals thirteen points of interest, or Instagram photos, with each appearing as a small dot on a radial map. Spinning and walking around causes the photos to pop up displaying the people, places, and things around me. Not surprising, given the kinds of photos typical of Instagram, my neighbors seem to love their pets. Similarly, the Twitter layer shows twenty-four points of interest with each tweet displayed as I move myself and my smartphone in the direction of the tweets' geotagged location. I read that many of my fellow Chicagoans seem to either have slept in or have been out enjoying the beautiful weather along the lakeshore, perhaps taking in the air and water show, sounds of which I can hear echoing all around me as I walk down my otherwise quiet street. Here, we begin to see how Hoskins's concept of digital network memory informs this experience of augmented reality, and vice versa. Layar connects me temporally and spatially to others as they go about making their lives. Digital network memory works within a culture of connectivity—a new media ecology—wherein sociality has become thoroughly mediated and technical: "Making the web social means 'making sociality technical.'" With each Instagram photo and tweet I am connected, temporally and temporarily, to a memorable moment, however mundane, of my neighbors and fellow Chicagoans. And these shared memories are constructed on-the-fly with each step I take, obliging me to consider how my experience of this present time and place connects to another's.

Continuing to walk down the street, I switch to the layer for WikipediaWorld, which connects Wikipedia articles to local points of interests, in this case primarily historical buildings. Doing so I learn about the Francis J. Dewes House built in 1896 in the Second Empire architectural style with influences of the neo-Baroque. The mansion was designated as a Chicago landmark on June 12, 1974. According to Wikipedia, Francis J. Dewes immigrated to the United States in 1868, began his career as a bookkeeper for local breweries, and founded his own brewery in 1882. I have often strolled by this mansion, attracted to its opulence but not realizing its history and connection to Lincoln Park. Following the WikipediaWorld layer, I also encounter the Brewster Apartments, the Theurer-Wrigley House, and the Reebie Storage Warehouse, which has the distinction of being one of the finest examples of Egyptian Revival architecture in Chicago. The Theurer-Wrigley House was built in 1894, and the mansion and coach house have over 20,000 square feet of living space. Originally, the mansion was owned by the brewer Joseph Theurer, who sold it to chewing gum magnate William Wrigley, Jr., and later occupied by his son Philip K. Wrigley. Two brewers were building mansions in Lincoln Park in the late-1890s, and I am left wondering how these layered memories of brewing affect Chicago to this day as a thriving scene of craft brewing. These buildings, as connected within the WikipediaWorld layer and as connected to me in the moment of interaction, register as important parts of this neighborhood's collective and public memory—now a part of my own memory that I may pass on to others.

I continue to explore the layered memories around me by switching from Layar to HistoryPin, a smartphone application that allows users to upload archival photographs and to pin them to a Google Maps map. Opening HistoryPin, I see several Lincoln Park photos awaiting me. The HistoryPin app allows the user to make an image that layers an old photograph of a place onto the present-day place so that past and present appear on the same screen, in the same image-space, thus creating a new form and practice of augmented memory. Like the Layar app, HistoryPin combines experience and memory, and in so doing adds mnemonic and memorial depth to the surface of the streets. As I stand in the street, aligning the archival photograph and my physical surroundings, I am brought to regard the past in the present. As a form of digital network memory, I make a temporal and temporary connection with the photographer of the archival photograph. The material networked assemblage of AR app, smartphone, archival photograph, GPS, and LTE bring me into the point of view of the past. Farman writes, "By utilizing technologies that draw on a person's location through GPS, a user is understood as being situated in relationship to technology and thus experiences the world as a collaboration between digital and material interfaces." My experience and memory of these multiple, simultaneous places and times becomes such a collaboration. As I stand in the street, cars come and go into the present and buildings rise into the past: fewer cars in 1934, and maybe quieter than the 72 decibels (there is an app for that) of the current scene. HistoryPin juxtaposes experience and memory in "the beauty of participation." Passers-by look askance at what I am doing, and we become connected to one another, if only for a moment.

Such encounters are possible because city streets already are factories and depositories of experience and memory. Or as Solnit comments, "A city is many worlds in the same place." AR smartphone apps, like Layar and HistoryPin, taken into the streets, provoke a bodily engagement with the everyday material of the street, of reality. Farman refers to this mode of embodiment as the "sensory-inscribed body" which he defines as both "a sensory engagement across material and digital landscapes" and the incorporation of "sociocultural inscriptions of the body in these emerging spaces." Importantly, the sensory-inscribed body "is always implicated as a sensory-inscribing body." Being connected to the AR app and its mnemonic database, my memory, as augmented, is inscribed and goes on inscribing as I connect with others in the neighborhood, in what Hoskins calls "interactional trajectories."

Digital network memory regards the moment of connection as the moment of memory: "Memory is not in this way a product of individual or collective remembrances, but is instead generated through the flux of contacts between people and digital technologies and media." According to Hoskins, remembering becomes a process of temporal and spatial navigation, and navigation enacts "interactional trajectories," which refer to the experiences of individuals and groups connecting and disconnecting "to a melee of networks over time, in addition to their experiences of and orientations to non-networked objects, places, and people."

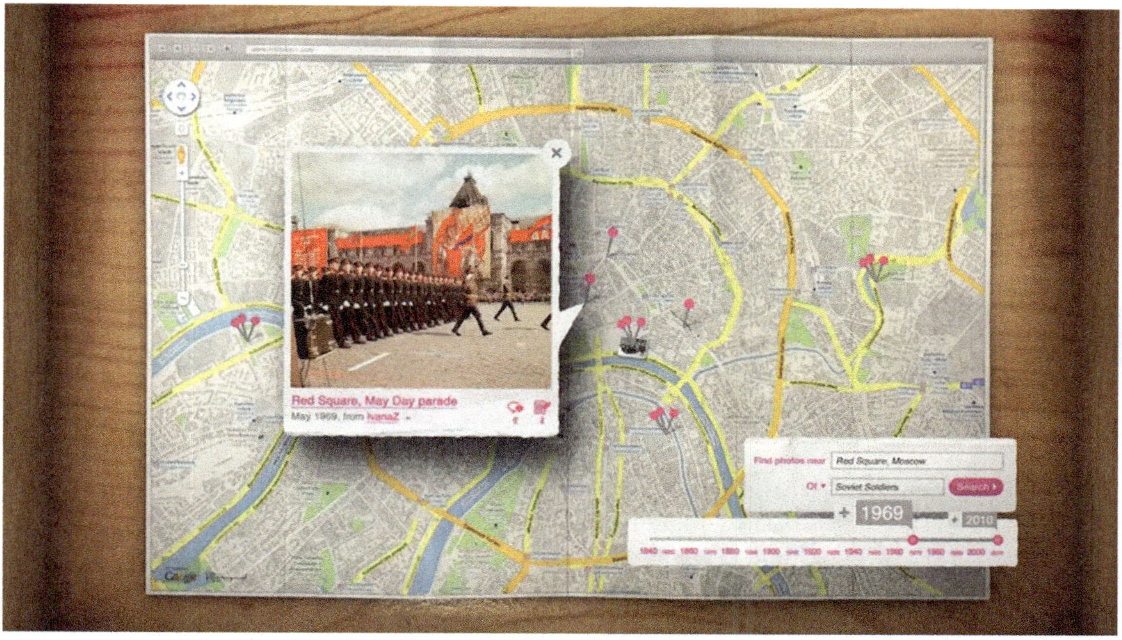

Figure 7.1: Historypin. © 2010 by Historypin.

As I and other Layar and HistoryPin users incorporate and become incorporated by these technologies as the material-digital interfaces of everyday life, we interact with a "melee of networks" as we connect and disconnect to different mnemonic and memorial objects. We each produce a different interactional trajectory that informs—indeed, brings into form, gives shape to—a collected, collective memory of our neighborhood, of Chicago. Together, Hoskins's interrelated concepts of digital network memory and interactional trajectories show how a new media ecology introduces a new memory ecology. Within this new memory ecology, memory performs the moment of connection that both is inscribed and inscribes—memory as world and memory as world building. And world building requires something more than connection; it requires a world in which we already dwell.

AURASMA
Scan the image to view.

Augmented Reality and Digital Ambient Memory

Digital network memory and interactional trajectories demonstrate how digital media technologies, including augmented reality, engender "a radical diffusion of memory." That is, memory, as I show through my own experience above, has become radically diffused across networks of individuals, collectives, and publics along with new media technologies so that memory must be assembled across those networks. I argue, however, that this radical diffusion has consequences for memory that are not made visible by the metaphor of the network. Therefore, to complement the metaphor of the network, I propose that we attend to ambience and to what I will call—following Hoskins—digital ambient memory, to suggest how the production of memory, including technologies of (augmented) memory, is the environment in which we live and practice our daily lives within contemporary digital media culture. Drawing upon the work of Rickert, I suggest that the metaphor of the network, though helpful, does not account for how memory itself is more than connective or connection.

In his reading of Heidegger, Rickert argues that language and thought—I include memory as a fundamental capacity of rhetoric—are principles of Being in which we abide. Rickert thus advances the concept of ambience "to push against the metaphors of connection to, first, metaphors of environment, place, surroundings, and second, metaphors of meshing, osmosis, blending." Following the metaphor of ambience, the production of memory would be open to "forms of 'connection' that are not solely link-driven." Here, ambience implies an enmeshing of memory with digital media technologies and their sociotechnical forms and practices:

> Like the metaphor of the network, ambience connotes distribution, co-adaption, and emergence, but it adds an emphasis to the constitutive role of the overall, blended environment that the network does not. The ambient is immersive in that it is post-conscious and auratic, being keyed to various levels of attention that are nevertheless always in play at a given moment; and it is blended in that no element can be singled out as decisive, for they are all integral to its singular emergence.

An ambient rhetoric highlights how, for example, an environment produces its subject: "Music becomes ambient when the environs become part of the music—or . . . when the environs 'play' the music." As such, ambience signals a "dissolution of the subject-object relation . . . and the incorporation of the material world as integral to human action and interaction." A digital ambient memory similarly emphasizes how memory is enmeshed in digital media technologies and sociotechnical practices, creating an environment that helps to produce memory, to make memories appear in public.

As Rickert suggests, "If the network metaphor captures the logic of the hardware of emerging network culture, ambience captures the 'software' logics of being and doing that arise from the network." A digital ambient memory better acknowledges the sociotechnical practices of the "technological unconscious" that produce, capture, store, and display the proliferation of digital network memory. Furthermore, digital ambient memory connotes how memory itself gathers and is gathered by things, including technologies. Put differently, mnemotechnics, like the art of memory and AR technologies, are technics for building memory as world and world as memory. Digital ambient memory makes visible the ongoing disclosure of a memory-world, a world in which we already dwell. Rickert employs the concept of dwelling "to mean how people come together to flourish (or try to flourish) in a place, or better, how they come together in the continual making of a place." Dwelling, then, is a mode of gathering and thriving manifested by a dynamic attunement to the world.

The previous examples show how digital ambient memory illuminates the mnemonic and memorial activities of augmented reality in a new metaphorical light. Whereas digital network memory foregrounds the temporal and temporary connections made through an AR application, digital ambient memory shows how, and to what extent, the total enveloping material-digital assemblage brings about the production of memory. When I view the Instagram photos and tweets that surround me, an enveloping memory-as-world emerges that is not limited to those momentary connections; rather, those connections are another disclosure, another folding of digital ambient memory in which I already find myself and through which I may inhabit this memory-as-world differently. Similarly, when HistoryPin compels me to stand in the street to align the past and present, I am brought into its regard as a subject of not only the AR application but also the digital ambient memory it affords: a subject "will be what comes to the point of view, or rather what remains in the points of view." Augmented reality as digital ambient memory produces the subject capable of experiencing and interpreting its rhetoric, its meaning. In this way, digital ambient memory better accounts for what Fuller calls "medial will to power," which recognizes the capacities of media to invent new material, physical, and psychical compositions.

Medial will to power is not a networked intention, but an ambient force "composed by the mutual intermeshing of various other forces that might be technical, aesthetic, economic, chemical—that might have to do with capacities of human bodies as affordances—and which pass between all such bodies and are composed through and among them." Medial will to power is the force that "moves things across thresholds." And moving things across thresholds invents the subject-object relation of digital ambient memory: "The subject is a case of perspectival position rather than a categorical a priori condition of knowledge." In his explication of ambient rhetoric, Rickert posits, "An environment is always a situation, and that situation, in its absolute singularity, calls a subject into being—or, put differently, carries out the panoply of actions possible in real time engagement." In this sense, then, we do not push the buttons on AR apps to connect with memory; rather AR apps push our buttons, inventing us in their situations of memory and pushing us into their regard. Consequently, augmented reality as digital ambient memory cannot only be that which links or connects us to a past, present, and future; it is also the environment in which we live and from which we may gather and are gathered by past, present, and future worlds. We dwell with digital ambient memory as it brings us into being, and in so doing, offers possibilities of inventing new experiences of memory. In the case above, Instagram photos, tweets, and WikipediaWorld entries help gather a sense of emplacement in a world of digital-material things in which I have always dwelled but have never known before. Put differently, digital ambient memory constitutes the present from which I may act upon the digital-material things that are being remembered. Here, the present refers to "a way of occupying time, not a specific moment." Whereas digital network memory enacts the specific moment as the moment of connection, digital ambient memory connotes a holding together in time, a gesture toward how to live life inside time. When enmeshed in digital ambient memory, every memory is not only an evanescent moment of connection but also a potentially kairotic encounter with the world in an ongoing moment.

To glimpse again the potential of augmented reality as digital ambient memory, I turn to the admittedly speculative reality of Google Glass. (But in this case, speculation can be productive because digital ambient memory always occurs just before us, or out in front of us, as it brings us into being. Digital ambient memory is a speculative metaphor of the shape of memory to come.) To promote Project Glass in April 2012, Google published a concept video titled "One Day." As viewers, we watch the video from the first-person perspective, that is, from the perspective of the wearer of Google Glass. For example, we stretch with the wearer of Glass as he awakes from an afternoon nap, pours a cup of coffee, and then looks out a window where time and temperature are digitally displayed above the city skyline. We then watch as he noshes on a ham sandwich while also receiving and responding to a pop-up text message from his friend asking to meet up later that day. Once he ventures outside, a digital pop-up alerts him that the subway station is out-of-service, but a map appears showing him the location of the nearest in-service station. He follows the route as displayed to him with digital directional arrows, stops in front of a poster for a concert and speaks aloud a reminder to buy tickets, and meets up with his friend for coffee at a food truck to which he checks in. Soon after, he encounters graffiti of which he makes a photo to share with his Google+ circles. Realizing he might be late, he runs up to a rooftop just in time to connect via a video chat with his girlfriend Jessica, whose face is displayed in a small window. He brandishes his ukulele, strums a few notes, and looks out as the sun sets beyond the horizon—a view he now shares with Jessica, who says, "It's beautiful." A memorable moment to close a (un)memorable day.

In a second video for Glass's official release, titled "How It Feels," we again look out from the first-person perspectives of multiple Glass users (or perhaps, one very active user). One user takes in the sunrise aboard a hot air balloon; another climbs up to a trapeze swing; another prepares to go on stage; another flies an aircraft while creating a group video chat with his pilot club; another plays with his dog; another spins a child by her arms; another holds snakes while sharing the video with his children. Throughout, Glass wearers take pictures, record videos, and share both synchronously and asynchronously with family and friends. And again the video ends with a memorable moment. Floating in a hot air balloon, Baxter receives a text message from Jessica, "How's the view up there?" Calling upon Glass, he takes a picture, shares it with Jessica, and says, "It's beautiful." Both videos end with "It's beautiful," and in both the videos begin to fade out during the

"It's beautiful" moment. So, the "It's beautiful" could refer to not only the view that is being shared, but also the Google Glass experience itself.

I offer a detailed account of both videos to highlight the ordinary activities that are being shown, especially in the first video, "One Day." The title "One Day" may refer to the future—one day this technology will be real—and the present day being shown—just one day among many, but no less memorable for this ordinariness (a reminder that "one in a million" may refer to both the singularly special and the familiar commonplace). Though many of these activities are ostensibly ordinary and mundane, the Glass videos portray them as worthy of memory, and thus the impetus for connecting with others—a form and practice of digital network memory. Similarly, "How It Feels" points to how Glass, and by extension AR technologies, include an affective dimension: how do these technologies feel and how do they make us feel? AR fundamentally alters our affect and what will feel as memorable by building a world of memory. Therefore, in their mundaneness, these videos also evoke a digital ambient memory wherein the enveloping world becomes involved in the production of memory—again, both how memory is produced and how memory produces. Google Glass—augmented reality as digital ambient memory—transforms the world in which we dwell by gathering things and being gathered by things. Google Glass users have the potential to not only be attuned by the world, but also care for the world in which they find themselves by drawing upon memory as world building. Together, the concepts of digital ambient memory and dwelling point toward an emergence of what I call a monumentality of the mundane that signals a culture of memory and a digital rhetoric that is newly and fundamentally mnemonic and memorial.

Conclusion: Monumentality of the Mundane and the Muddle of Memory

As I advance the concept, the monumentality of the mundane refers to a physical and psychical orientation to the contemporary new media-memory ecology. Influenced by endless quotidian Facebook status updates and Twitter posts, and as we see in the Google Glass videos, the monumentality of the mundane orients us to every moment as one ripe with and for memory, for recording and sharing and remembering with and for others. Every moment is ephemeral and so must be made to endure. Digital network memory shows us how we connect to these ephemeral memories; digital ambient memory reveals how we are emplaced with an enduring mnemonic and memorial media environment. Chun argues that this dynamic between the ephemeral and the enduring exists within software itself and has become transcoded, to use Manovich's concept, into cultural practices. Chun suggests that the enduring ephemeral marks both the fleeting and the repetitive processes of digital media culture: "Internet content may be available 24/7, but 24/7 on what day?" And we may add, "for whom?" The enduring ephemeral enacts a "nonsimultaneous new" that demands a response over and over again. When every moment demands a response, memory becomes the mundane, ambient recording of the everyday. As such, augmented reality not only links us to memory but also enmeshes us in it, thus creating a desire to gather and to be gathered by ordinary experiences and to gather others around those experiences as memories. In this way, augmented reality produces and contributes to an endless enduring ephemeral of our current new media-memory ecology. Ernst writes, "There is no ending online. There's no closure, no linear basis. It's about bringing it in, checking it out, constantly evaluating." Hoskins suggests that this unending digital archive de-monumentalizes memory; however, I suggest that it monumentalizes differently, appearing as digital ambient memory and the monumentality of the mundane. The mundane becomes memorable: we Instagram our meals and share with whomever may come into its view. Though there may be no closure, there is enclosure within a memory world.

A digital ambient memory acknowledges that every digital memory leaves a trace beyond the initial contact or connection. Andrejevic refers to this as the "digital enclosure," which he defines as "the creation of an interactive realm wherein every action and transaction generates information about itself." Lacey suggests that the digital enclosure allows digital memories to "both retain information about personally relevant events while at the same time adding to the existing body of knowledge by creating new information in which others will participate." Augmented reality produces a digital memory enclosure that draws us in. As I show with the examples of Layar and HistoryPin, along with the Google Glass videos, augmented reality gathers an environment of digital memories that calls us into being as a subject capable of acting in that environment. Whereas the metaphor of the network implies links and linking, nodes and connections, streams of information, the ambient implies a muddle, not a middle, that "continually scrambles middle and pole, interior and exterior, recursively refolding them one into the other." With augmented reality, we may find ourselves in the ambient muddle of memory.

I have drawn upon my own experiences to emphasize the pedestrian (in both senses of that word) forms and practices of augmented reality and to show that most of us already are implicated within a new media-memory ecology of augmented reality and augmented memory. Augmented reality encloses the material of everyday life—mediated memories—as building blocks. The street photographer Garry Winogrand once said that "he photographed in order to see what the things that interested him looked like as photographs." Bogost interprets this to mean that Winogrand "makes photographs not to capture what he sees, but to see what he will have captured." Winogrand photographs "things just because they were there." Similarly, I argue that augmented reality returns us to material reality, to a world we already inhabit but in such a way that we might dwell differently; that is, to see things just because they were already there and to be allured by their presence as mnemonic, wondering objects.

Bogost argues that wonder "demands pause for its own sake." Wonder is a way to orient to objects as objects, to respect objects as objects in themselves. In this sense, the monumentality of the mundane does not have to be a mindless, habitual response to everyday life; rather, it could be a way of dwelling with mundane things as wonder-full. Wonder is asking not, "How may I use or master this thing?" but rather "What am I to this thing?" Wonder is asking, "What else is there, here, anywhere right now?" Augmented reality, as aesthetic and rhetorical practice, may allow us to encounter our mundane reality as a world of hidden memories; to see memories as things in the world in which we may dwell with wonder; to feel that every thing has a shadow appended.

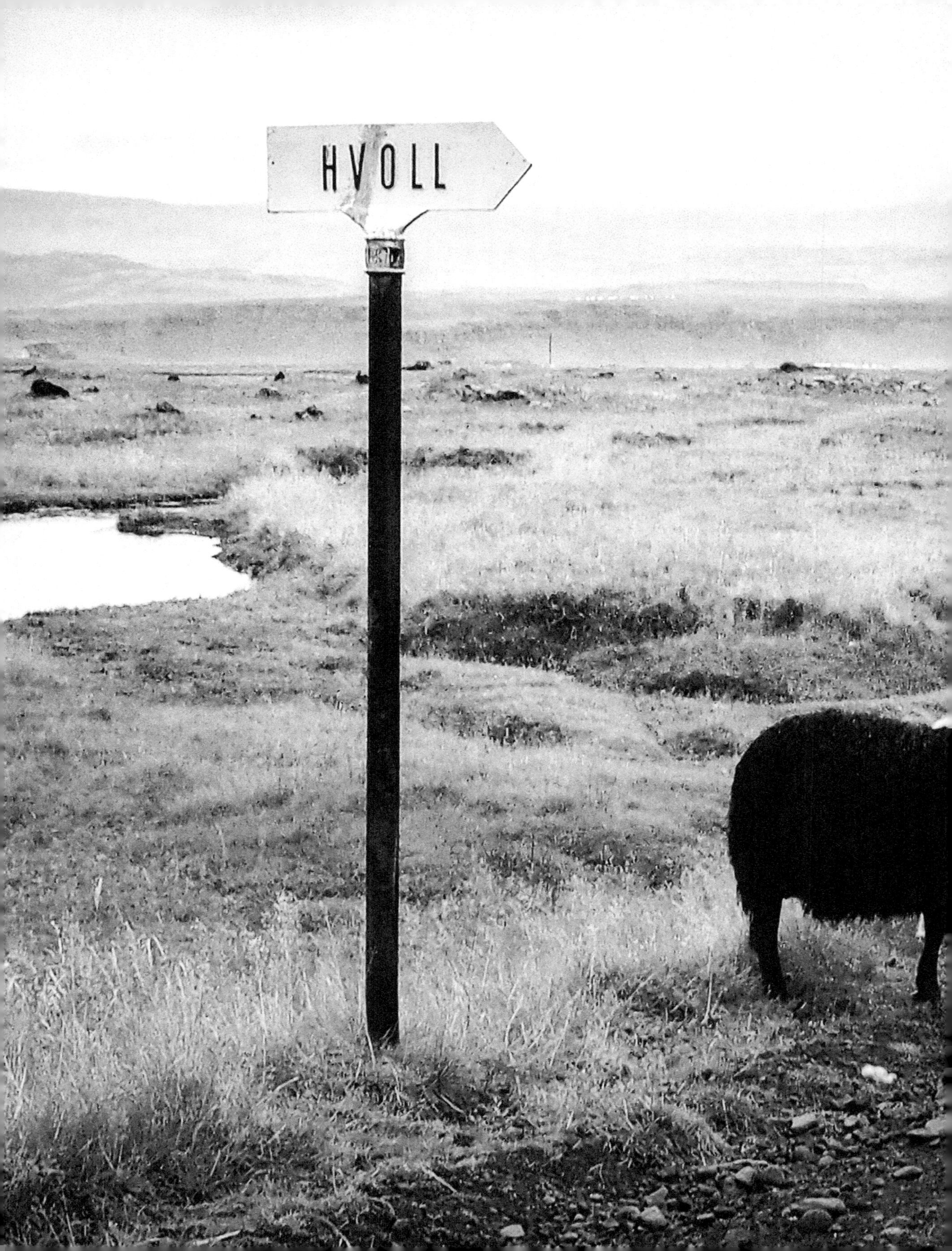
HVOLL

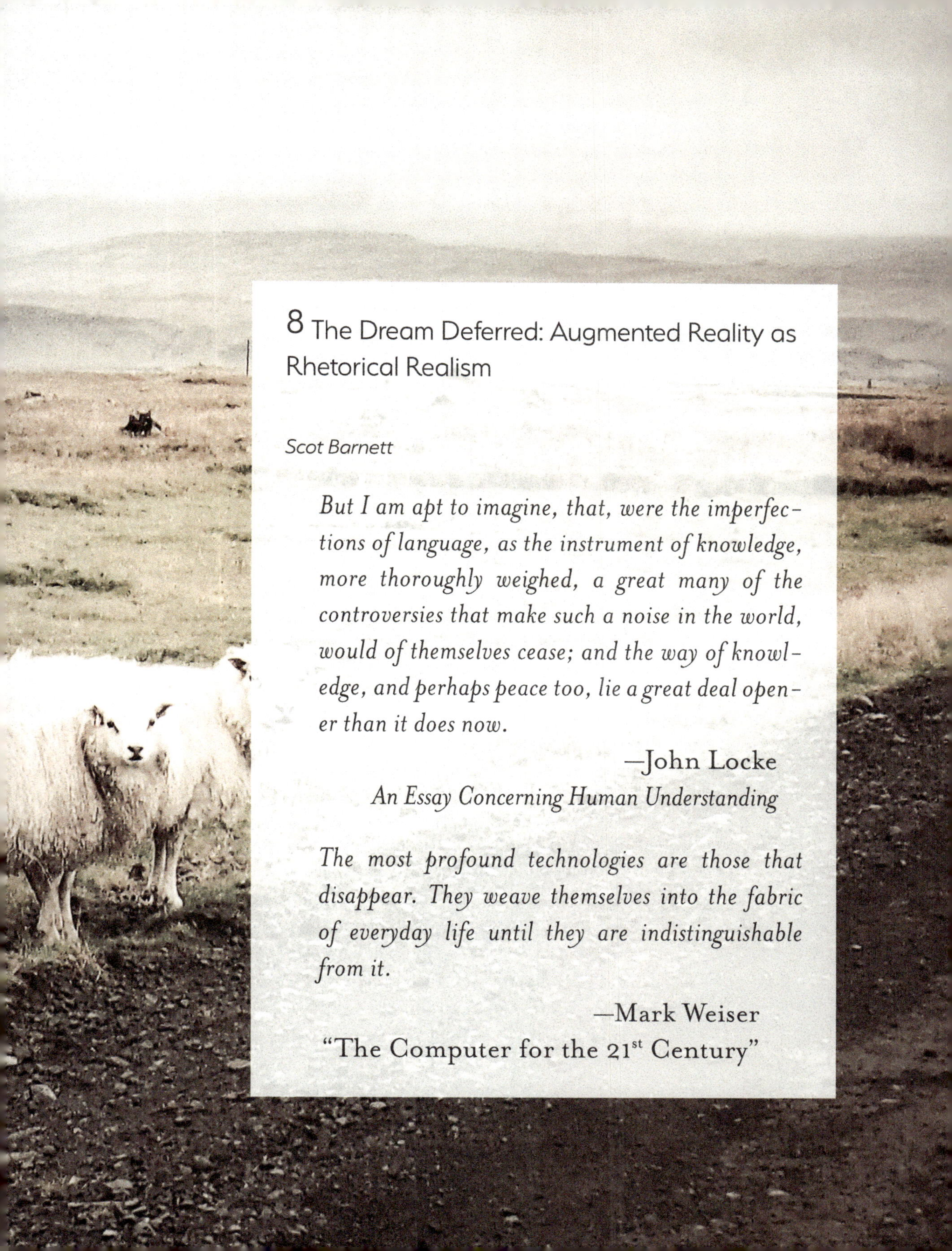

8 The Dream Deferred: Augmented Reality as Rhetorical Realism

Scot Barnett

> *But I am apt to imagine, that, were the imperfections of language, as the instrument of knowledge, more thoroughly weighed, a great many of the controversies that make such a noise in the world, would of themselves cease; and the way of knowledge, and perhaps peace too, lie a great deal opener than it does now.*
>
> —John Locke
>
> *An Essay Concerning Human Understanding*

> *The most profound technologies are those that disappear. They weave themselves into the fabric of everyday life until they are indistinguishable from it.*
>
> —Mark Weiser
>
> "The Computer for the 21st Century"

> *We human beings, in order to be who we are, remain within the essence of language to which we have been granted entry. We can therefore never step outside it in order to look it over circumspectly from some alternative position. Because of this, we catch a glimpse of the essence of language only to the extent that we ourselves are envisaged by it, remanded to it.*
>
> —Martin Heidegger, "The Way to Language"

In a well-known episode in Book III of *Gulliver's Travels,* Gulliver finds himself at the Grand Academy of Lagado on the island of Balnibarbi where scientists are performing a series of strange and comical experiments. In one laboratory, a chemist is attempting to extract sunlight from cucumbers; in another, an "ingenious architect" is celebrating his new way to build houses beginning with the roof and working down to the foundation. When Gulliver enters the School of Languages, he finds three professors of differing nationalities working to correct the "imperfections" (to use Locke's term) of natural language. Swift describes their first experiment as attempting to "shorten discourse, by cutting polysyllables into one, and leaving out verbs and participles." Their second project, however, is considerably more ambitious, both in scope and presumption. Rather than work within the structures of existing discourse, the three language professors have devised "a scheme for entirely abolishing all words whatsoever." Since words are only names for things, the professors reason it would make more sense—and would help alleviate misunderstandings brought about as a result of natural language—if people simply expressed themselves through things:

> many of the most learned and wise adhere to the new scheme of expressing themselves by things; which has only this inconvenience attending it, that if a man's business be very great, and of various kinds, he must be obliged, in proportion, to carry a greater bundle of things upon his back, unless he can afford one or two strong servants to attend him. I have often beheld two of those sages almost sinking under the weight of their packs, like pedlars among us, who, when they met in the street, would lay down their loads, open their sacks, and hold conversation for an hour together; then put up their implements, help each other to resume their burdens, and take their leave.

While this new method makes longer discourses more difficult and less practical, the professors argue that it is well suited for shorter conversations, particularly in one's home where one "cannot be at a loss." "The room where company meet who practise this art, is full of all things, ready at hand, requisite to furnish matter for this kind of artificial converse." As I discuss below, among Swift's targets in this satirical episode is the seventeenth-century London Royal Society, specifically, efforts by Society members such as Bishop John Wilkins to invent entirely new language systems as a way to resolve the ambiguities and indeterminacies inherent in natural languages. If Swift were writing today, however, he might as well have chosen to satirize researchers in augmented reality and ubiquitous computing. For instance, one can easily imagine Swift's Gulliver coming ashore not at Balnibarbi but at the similarly fantastical PARC or MIT Media Lab, wandering among the laboratories and marveling at the researchers' attempts, in Mark Weiser's terms, to "weave" computer technologies "into the fabric of everyday life." Strolling past the Ambient Research Room and Wearable Eye Display Lab, we can imagine Gulliver stumbling into the Tangible Media Center, where three professors, led by Durrell Bishop, are putting the finishing touches on what they call the Marble Answering Machine. As opposed to standard digital answering machines that can sometimes be hard to use and control, the Marble Answering Machine promises to capitalize on users' intuitive abilities to associate physical things with virtual information.

> Bishop's answering machine has a stock of marbles. Whenever a caller leaves a message on the answering machine, it associates that message with a marble from the stock, and the marble rolls down a track to the bottom, where it sits along with the marbles representing previous messages. When the owner of the machine comes home, a glance at the track shows . . . how many messages are waiting: the number of marbles arrayed at the bottom of the track. To play a message, the owner picks up one of the marbles and drops it in a depression at the top of the answering machine; because each marble is associated with a particular message, it knows which message to play. Once the message has been played, the owner can decide what to do: either return the marble to the common stock for reuse (so deleting the message) or returning it to the track (saving it to play again later).

As Paul Dourish notes, the goal behind augmented reality projects such as the Marble Answering Machine is to "use physical reality to model the virtual or electronic world" so that the problem of interacting exclusively with virtual information is now translated into "interacting with the physical." Much like the invented language lab in Swift's fictional Academy, the dream for researchers in the areas of augmented reality and ubiquitous computing is to bring information and reality into better agreement and harmony with one another. While the prospect of filling our pockets with innumerable physical referents may seem impractical or far-fetched, as research in augmented reality demonstrates, we nevertheless continue to dream of a world in which *things themselves speak*, or more precisely in which *things speak for themselves* and in so doing bypass the whole (human) problem of reference and signification altogether.

As I argue in this chapter, efforts such as these to bring language and information into correspondence with external reality suggest at least two forms of realism evident in, and traceable across, both rhetoric and augmented reality research. The first of these, epistemological in nature, conceives of language and its relationship to reality in terms of truth, correctness, or, in Martin Heidegger's terms, "adequation." The second form of realism evident in augmented reality research and rhetorical theory understands and situates language ontologically as a suasive force in its own right that is not necessarily reducible to truth claims or representational accounts of reality. Together, these two forms of realism constitute a large part of the rhetoricity of augmented reality just as they have informed perceptions of rhetoric from antiquity to the present. Thus, I argue, rhetoric and augmented reality are best understood as mutually informative research areas, with developments in augmented reality providing the exigence for rhetorical theorists and critics to reconsider how various versions of realism have informed rhetorical theory and helped shaped rhetoric's long and contentious history.

Though realism has become something of a devil term in modern rhetorical theory—due in large part to its perceived opposition to more contemporary constructivist views of knowledge and sociality—its persistence in the rhetorical tradition is hard ignore, whether as a foundation for rhetorical theory or as a boogey man used by rhetoricians to advocate alternative ways of viewing the world. As I demonstrate in what follows, however, there are many shapes realism can take, not all of them wedded to the tenets of metaphysical or "naïve realism." Given the entrenched nature of our human-centric understanding of language and reality, attuning ourselves to these other realisms will require, among other things, a shift in how we view language and the kinds of questions we ask about language. It is my wager that developments in augmented reality can help us achieve such a shift by enabling us to rethink the question that has long been at the fore of rhetorical theory: What is language, and what is language's relationship to reality? Rhetorician and media theorist Isabel Pedersen has already begun to explore the role language plays in augmented reality research, most recently in her book *Ready to Wear: A Rhetorical of Wearable Computers and Reality-Shifting Media*. As the subtitle of book suggests, however, Pedersen's emphasis is on the *rhetoric of* augmented reality. Building on her work, I believe we should also consider what place language itself has in augmented reality. That is, we should also use the occasion of these new developments in augmented reality to, in Heidegger's words, "bring language as language to language," and to explore what this shift in our thinking about language reveals about the *rhetoricity of* augmented reality, and conversely, what augmented reality reveals about rhetorical theory.

Putting the World Back Together: Epistemological Realism

As its name suggest, augmented reality aims to *augment* one's experiences of reality. Unlike the rhetorics of disembodiment that frequently accompanied visions of virtual reality in the 1980s and 90s, augmented reality tools and devices offer users digital information "*in addition to* the real-world reality that they currently experience." Augmented reality devices such as Google's new wearable eye display computer Glass, for example, work by layering digital information (most prominently actualized in the form of *language*) over physical reality as perceived by the device's human user. To one outfitted with such a device, any appropriately tagged object, building, or landmark can appear visually synchronized with information, such as the object's definition in the OED or the landmark's Wikipedia entry. A number of more common (and thus far more readily accessible) smartphone and tablet applications capitalize on this idea. Apps such as Tagwhat, Acrossair, Layar, and Wikitude World Browser, for example, allow smartphone users to tag and visually overlay information about physical locations in one's vicinity, including restaurants, hotels, monuments, cinemas, and other geotagged places. Whereas virtual reality programs favor interactions that take place in a fictional, computer-generated world, where the user moves into another world through some form of mediated immersion (think, for example, of *Second Life* or films such as *Tron* or *The Lawnmower Man*), augmented reality platforms such as Google Glass and the Google Goggles app shift the location of computing and interaction into the user's world and lived experience. As Paul Dourish explains, in augmented reality, "The site of interaction is the world of the user, not that of the system. That world, in the augmented reality vision, may be imbued with computation, but the computer itself takes a back seat." Put somewhat differently, the key innovation behind augmented reality "is to allow the physical and the informational realms to *seamlessly merge and mingle*."

As Dourish and Clark's descriptions indicate, one of the assumptions informing augmented reality research is that the world itself is not only capable of being "imbued with computation," but is in fact already awash in its own intrinsic information, much of it concealed from our naked perception. Indeed, as Dourish, Weiser, Donald Norman, and numerous other proponents of augmented reality and ubiquitous computing argue, it is the computer itself—that bulky, obstinate, and oftentimes conspicuous machine—that is standing between us and a clearer, more transparent, and less mediated view of reality. As Jay Bolter and Richard Grusin have argued, the desire for "transparent immediacy" expressed in new media such augmented reality is an old one; the same desire to position a viewer "in an immediate relationship to the contents of that medium," they observe, is evident as well in Renaissance perspective painting and in modern photography. With respect to language, the desire for transparent immediacy has an equally long history and, as in the visual arts, has had tremendous influence in shaping our expectations of and attitudes toward language. Indeed, one of the most common accusations leveled against rhetoric—that rhetoric is inherently deceptive, manipulative, and dissembling—grows out of the desire to see the world as it really is and to let the world as such speak for itself. And just as assumptions about reality and mediation have transformed the world within which rhetoric and rhetorical theory take shape, modern assumptions about reality and mediation are not only guiding the discursive debates over augmented reality; they are in fact constitutive of the environment within which this thing we call "augmented reality" is currently taking place.

Using the tools and apps described above as a reference point, we can begin to explore the rhetoricity of augmented reality by considering how rhetoricians themselves have tarried with a comparable realist worldview rooted in language and language's abilities to offer us an immediate and transparent window on the world. In as much as rhetoric has been closely associated with language throughout most of its history—with all of language's advantages and imperfections falling under the jurisdiction of rhetoric at one point or another—rhetoricians have repeatedly found themselves on the front lines of debates over language's epistemological and representational capacities. That rhetors seem to offer listeners what is most pleasing rather than what is best for their souls is, of course, one of Plato's main objections to rhetoric, and it's the one that in various forms has continued to haunt rhetoric as both a practice and an object of theoretical inquiry. But it's in the late Renaissance and Enlightenment when the intellectual climate, rather a few powerful but individual voices, began to truly change perceptions of rhetoric. With the rise of modern scientific epistemology and its accompanying assumptions that knowledge is no relevant matter but rather something fixed, stable, and discoverable through rational methods of inquiry, rhetoric once again came under fire, though this time with detractors raising similar concerns about language as a whole. The legacy of Ramism embodies these suspicions in as much as Ramus's widely influential diminution of rhetoric to "mere" style is rooted in a decidedly *epistemological* form of realism. Such a realism assumes: 1) the existence of a mind independent of reality; 2) that truth inheres in objects and therefore constitutes a correspondence between language and reality; and 3) that as a result of 1 and 2, there can be one and only one way to capture truth accurately. For Ramus, language is the issue standing in the way of true knowledge, and thus it is language that needs to be corrected and hammered into shape so that truth can be communicated as transparently as possible. Though Ramus leaves a small role for rhetoric to play in the transmission and dissemination of knowledge acquired through other means and other styles (most notably the plain style), his perfect rhetoric, as Walter Ong suggests, is ultimately to have no rhetoric at all. The "plaine delivery of the Word without painted eloquence," as the Puritan ideal for preaching puts it—this is the dream of Ramist rhetoric as well.

Diagnosing and attempting to transcend the ambiguities of language was something of a rhetorical pastime for scholars in the late Renaissance and Enlightenment. Though he distances himself from Platonic and Ramist views of rhetoric, Bacon nevertheless shares his processors' suspicions about language. Most notably, his Idols of the Market-Place emphasize how words, being arbitrary symbolic representations of things, tend to "obstruct the understanding." Words, he says, "plainly force and overrule the understanding, and throw all into confusion, and lead men away into numberless empty controversies and idle fancies." Almost a century later, Locke throws these concerns into even sharper relief, arguing that when addressing epistemological matters practitioners should employ clear language and perspicuity so as to avoid the "doubtfulness and imperfection" of words. In particular, words that do not have clear referents in reality—words such as "murder" or "sacrilege," which Locke dubs "mixed modes"—pose the greatest challenge to perspicuity. As does the art of rhetoric, which according to Locke embodies "all the artificial and figurative application of words eloquence hath invented." Rhetoric, he laments, is that "powerful instrument of error and deceit" that appeals to our desires to be deceived and leads us astray from "the preservation and improvement of truth and knowledge." Against the realist standard beginning to inform work in philosophy and the natural sciences, rhetoric seems to fall short in almost every way in that it reputedly colors or embellishes reality rather than allowing us to access things as they really are.

Other than avoid rhetoric altogether or relegate it what Richard Lanham calls the "weak defense" in which "good" and "bad" forms of rhetoric exist in tension along side one another, scholars in the late Renaissance and Enlightenment don't appear to have many solutions to the problems they identify. If words, language, and rhetoric really are distorting lenses, then what are we to do? How can we find ways to communicate and represent the world that cut through all of the noise and ambiguity associated with human discursive action? How do we put the world (back) together again? Enter Bishop John Wilkins. A member of the London Royal Society and collaborator with a number of fellow members, including Robert Boyle and John Ray, Wilkins authored an important treatise on preaching that celebrated the plain style favored by the Royal Society and that also helped transition rhetorical theory away from Ciceronianism. These explicit contributions to rhetorical theory not withstanding, Wilkins is best known today for his 1668 work *An Essay Toward a Real Character and a Philosophical Language* in which he formally presents (and describes in elaborate detail) a new universal language intended to "represent things by such peculiar signs and names as should express their natures." Nothing short of ambitious, Wilkins hoped his newly invented universal language would eventually replace existing natural languages, with all of their ambiguity and imprecision.

Wilkins was not the first to attempt such a feat. According to Arika Okrent, "language invention was something of a seventeenth-century fad." What distinguished Wilkins from the pack of language inventors, however, was his ability to capture not only language's symbolic aspects (something other language inventors of the time had learned), but also to incorporate language's relational and conceptual dynamics into his new linguistic system. Wilkins understood, well before Saussure and the Structuralists, that meaning in language emerges from relationships among concepts, and that these relationships are what also enable ambiguities to proliferate in natural languages. Thus a universal language must, according to Wilkins, find ways to approximate language's relational dynamic while at the same time ensuring that the meanings produced through these relations are consistent for all language users. Wilkins's solution to this problem was to organize concepts (which he problematically viewed as universal) into numerous hierarchical structures. For example, if you wanted to know the word for "dog," you would simply follow a line down from category XVIII (Beasts) to subcategory V (oblong-headed) and, finally, to sub-subcategory 1 (Bigger Kind). There, you would find the symbol for dog, which consists of four discrete lines that vaguely approximate the image of a dog. In contrast to other invented languages of the time, Wilkins's hierarchical schema did not simply offer symbolic substitutions for existing words; much like our modern thesauruses, it also emphasized the meanings of concepts insofar as they emerge relationally by way of contiguity and differentiation. Like every other invented language, however, Wilkins's universal language ultimately failed to catch on. Despite some early admirers, including the mathematician John Wallis, by the time Wilkins died in 1672 his invented language had become merely the stuff of history—just another failed attempt to find a cure for Babel.

In claiming that the best way to ensure understandability is to speak with things themselves, Swift's language professors are, of course, poking fun at the Royal Society and Wilkins in particular. But there's more going on in Swift's satire than its lampooning of Wilkins's hubris at first indicates. As Stanley Fish suggests in a discussion of Wilkins and his dream of a universal language:

> The idea [behind Wilkins's project] is that such a language, purged of ambiguity, redundancy, and indirection, will be an appropriate instrument for the registering of an independent reality, and that if men will only submit themselves to that language and remain within the structure of its stipulated definitions and exclusions, they will be incapable of formulating and expressing wayward, subjective thoughts and will cease to be a danger either to themselves or to those who hearken to them. In this way, says Wilkins, they will be returned to that original state in which the language spoken was the language God gave Adam, a language in which every word perfectly expressed its referent.

In Fish's view, Wilkins's desire to return to some originary state by putting language, body, and world back together again epitomizes an *anti-rhetorical* bias widespread among philosophers and natural scientists. What Fish fails to consider, however, is how the form of epistemological realism expressed in Wilkins's project retains at the same time an important (if much maligned) place in rhetorical history and theory. Realism, in other words, is not at all anti-rhetorical but rather constitutive—historically and theoretically—of particular ways of thinking about rhetoric and rhetoric's place in the world. When augmented reality specialists and researchers in distributed cognition argue for the importance of "putting brain, body, and world together again," they are therefore following a long line of rhetorical realists who, like Ramus, Locke, and Wilkins, have dreamed of a world in which transparency and immediacy reign and things speak for themselves.

On the Way to Language: Ontological Realism

At this point, it would easy to shift the preceding discussion of rhetoric, augmented reality, and realism into a critique of the many problematic assumptions that constitute realism as a rhetorical and philosophical worldview. Truth does not inhere in things, and that's that. Moreover, language is never a mere passive conduit for information, and the dream of transparent immediacy is, and always will be, a dream deferred. Richard Rorty offers a succinct and representative example of how easy it is today to critique realist views of language and truth:

> Truth cannot be out there—cannot exist independently of the human mind—because sentences cannot so exist, or be out there. The world is

> out there, but descriptions of the world are not. Only descriptions of the world can be true or false. The world on its own—unaided by the describing activities of human beings—cannot.

Statements such as this, which are commonplace in the wake of the linguistic and social turns, appear to put the final nail in the coffin of epistemological realism. Indeed, Rorty's constructivist conception of language seems in many ways the better model for thinking about how language is theorized and actualized in augmented reality devices and applications. While the world may be "out there," descriptions of the world—such as a pop-up Wikipedia entry—are not. Or are they? As I argue in this section, how we answer this question depends greatly on the worldview we bring to it. Most discussions of language, including Rorty's, build from an epistemological foundation. As we saw above, epistemological examinations of language tend to focus on issues of truth, correctness, and representation, with the realist concluding that truth lies external to human being and the idealist or constructivist concluding that truth is precisely what is produced through social discursive action. From an epistemological perspective, in other words, realism is always going to come up short. But what if we began elsewhere? What if, for example, we began from an *ontological* rather than *epistemological* foundation?

As I alluded to above, there are many different versions of realism available to us, including a number of ontological realisms that bypass many of the problems associated with epistemological realism. Broadly speaking, the difference between *epistemological* realism and *ontological* realism hinges on their respective presumptions about human beings and the degree to which human beings are responsible for reality being what it is. Whereas epistemological realism argues that "our representations and language are accurate mirrors of the world as it actually is," ontological realism displaces the human's privileged status by refusing to "treat objects as constructions of humans." According to Levi Bryant, ontological realism, in fact, "thoroughly refutes epistemological realism or what ordinarily goes by the pejorative title of 'naïve realism.'" Assuming this is the case, what might an ontological approach to realism reveal about language and our relationship to it? Again, I believe augmented reality sets us on the way to thinking about this possibility insofar as augmented reality dramatizes other forms of realism and other ways realism might productively engage and inform work in rhetorical theory going forward. To explore this possibility, let's return to one of my opening examples of augmented reality applications.

The Tagwhat application epitomizes many of the aesthetic and practical goals of the mobile augmented reality applications described above. The app enables smartphone and tablet users to access information about their surroundings by leveraging and synchronizing their device's built-in camera, GPS, and Web-enabled software. Here is how the developers of Tagwhat describe their program to prospective users:

> Tagwhat is the most comprehensive feed of hyperlocal content in the world. Its award-winning mobile apps instantly find and deliver actionable content about the places around you. Tagwhat delivers the right content to the right people at the right time so that you never miss what's happening nearby again . . . To deliver the right content at the right place and time, the Tagwhat team leverages crowdsourcing, publishing partnerships, open sources like Wikipedia, and proprietary algorithms that scour the Web and social feeds to find actionable hyperlocal and hyper-relevant content.

In offering users "actionable content" about their surroundings, Tagwhat aims both to augment users' lived experiences (hey, that band I like is playing at this club tonight) and to cut through the noise of possible information by tailoring content specifically to users' identified interests and preferences. Despite its attempt to bring language and information into better correspondence with physical reality, however, there's little in Tagwhat to indicate that the application is attempting to actualize some version of epistemological realism. For the Tagwhat user, the principle concern isn't knowledge as such; that comes later if at all. The more immediate and pressing question on the minds of Tagwhat users is ontological in nature: What *is* this place? What distinguishes the application rhetorically, therefore, and what helps put us on the way to an ontological rhetorical realism, is that language itself is involved in the unveiling of hyperlocal content. Language constitutes and emplaces users in specific, unexpected, and even surprising ways (I am a fan of this band who is now waiting in line to see them).

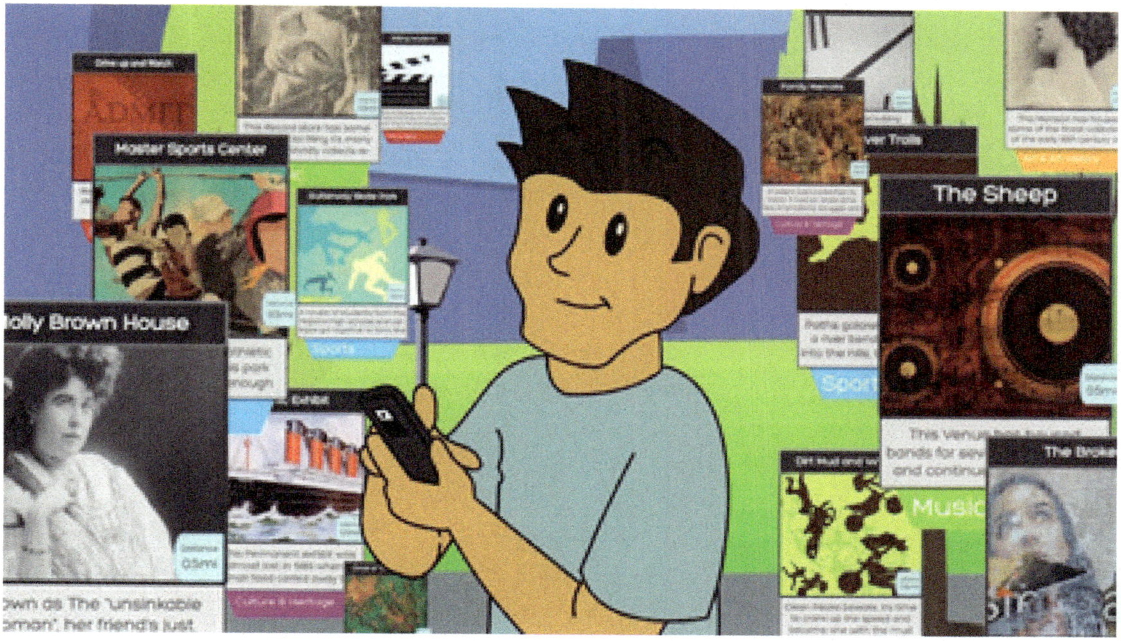

Figure 8.1: Tagwhat. © 2011 by Tagwhat.

AURASMA
Scan the image to view.

If we try to project epistemological assumptions onto Tagwhat rather than attempt to understand the app's rhetoricity on its own terms, we are instantly presented with a problem. In contrast to most situations we recognize as rhetorical, there doesn't appear to be an identifiable rhetor in Tagwhat (Is it the app's developers? The user's Facebook friends? The places themselves?). Nor is there an easy way to conceptualize audience, exigence, or appropriateness (*kairos*). The constituents of this particular situation are fluid and dispersed, as is their control over what information appears for a given person in a given time and place. What we encounter with apps like Tagwhat is thus another form of the rhetorical situation altogether, one that seems to place a greater emphasis on immersion and responsiveness to the world than on the intentional production of persuasive speech. In *Ambient Rhetoric*, Thomas Rickert draws attention to these aspects of rhetoric along with rhetoric's connectedness to place, specifically to the ways rhetoric is always already "enmeshed in and within its surroundings." Building on Martin Heidegger's ontology of language as well as recent developments in augmented reality, Rickert argues for new ontological ways of imagining rhetoric that resist the lure of the subject-object dichotomy which tends to emphasize human mastery or control over the materiel of persuasion. He suggests that to appreciate the rhetoricity at play in ambient or augmented reality environments we need to dramatically rethink how we have traditionally imagined rhetoric. Faced with applications such as Tagwhat and the Tangible Media Group's "ambientROOM" project, epistemological rhetorics that privilege the individual rhetor's control and understanding of discourse seem increasingly less relevant. In their place, Rickert proposes an ontological rhetoric that effectively distributes control throughout the environs, meaning that rhetoricity is not solely the responsibility of human rhetors but is rather what already inheres in the world as a condition of possibility.

This shift toward ontology poses a number of challenges to rhetoric, of course. But it also deeply troubles many of our assumptions about language, most of which presume that meaning, suasion, and expression emerge on only one side of the subject-object divide. As Rickert documents in impressive depth, Heidegger offers a valuable alternative to this view of language, one that prepares us to rethink the age-old question of language's relationship to world just as language itself is being dramatically re-imagined through new computing technologies. In keeping with his understanding of human being or *Dasein* (literally, being-there) as situated in a world, with *world* referring both to what *Dasein* has and to what constitutes *Dasein* as a particular being-in-the-world, Heidegger sees language not simply as an instrument for human speech but, more primordially, as the way in which world itself is revealed to *Dasein* as something we are concerned about and attend to in our everyday dealings with things and others in the world. In *Being and Time*, for example, Heidegger characterizes language as an intentional activity as well as a way of revealing world *as world*: "Discoursing or talking is the way in which we articulate 'significantly' the intelligibility of Being-in-the-world." As Rickert suggests, passages such as this indicate that for Heidegger "language emerges from a background of holistic meanings and tacit coping" (rather than solely from an autonomous and individual speaker or writer) and, further, "that meaning already permeates the world around us, even if it is not yet linguistic meaning." According to Heidegger, language precedes us. Thus, language is itself already infused with meanings and possibilities that are not necessarily the direct results of human rhetorical actions. Language is our means of engaging world, including others in the world, but prior to these activities language opens us to the world as an "a priori relationship and exposure to world."

Heidegger's best known, but least understood, statement on language—that "Language is the house of Being"—attempts to capture the complex ontological conditions that enable *Dasein* to come into relation with Being as such. As Rickert points out, readers sometimes view this statement as anticipating more recent constructivist claims about language and knowledge, such as the one cited above from Richard Rorty. Paraphrasing Heidegger, Rickert argues against such interpretations, rightly insisting that Heidegger's notorious statement must be understood within the scope of his overall thought, which consistently resists idealism in favor of a more holistic—that is, ontological—conception of Being:

> Language does not grant things their being. Rather, language stems from world, understood as a composite of meaning and matter. On this account, the world comes to speaking in language and gives bearings to being, human beings included, but cannot be understood to issue solely from human being; the world is the largely assumed and relied-on background stitchwork of relations emergent with our everyday doing and making.

Again, the issue for Heidegger is control. Whereas traditional views grant human beings mastery and control over language, Heidegger's fundamental ontology gives a great deal of agency back over to language. "It is *language* that speaks," Heidegger boldly proclaims in "The Way to Language." He continues:

> We not only *speak* language, we speak *from out of* it. We are capable of doing so only because in each case we have already listened to language. What do we hear there? We hear language speaking.

Not simply the property right of autonomous human agents, language for Heidegger is what speaks by saying (*die Sage*), that is, by showing. Out of unspokeness or the unsaid (what has not yet been shown) emerges the possibility of a kind of saying that precedes signs and that puts us on the way to speech and that lets what is coming to presence shine forth. This is *language*, and language is what

"Augmented reality has a great deal to teach us about rhetoric and much to contribute to rhetorical theory."

"delivers us human beings over to releasement toward unconstrained hearing."

Though he resists the tradition of realism, as his conception of language makes clear, Heidegger nevertheless retains some realist positions within his fundamental ontology, most notably the first thesis of realism regarding the existence of mind-independent realities. Far from constituting a critical blindness or liability in Heidegger's work, these kernels of realism, rethought as they are through ontology, are critical for helping us understand the ways language is functioning in augmented reality devices and applications. How language emerges in Tagwhat, Heidegger helps us to see, needs to be understood through all of the worldly complexities that the application references and discloses to users as possible subjects of concern, from the physical spaces one encounters to the social networks that reveal some of the relational factors informing our being-in-the-world. For the Tagwhat user, language is no mere intentional or representational act (it is not only epistemological, in other words); it is, instead, what is *speaking* at a given time and place, what stems from world and is the composite of meaning and matter. Thus when the Tagwhat user responds to language's call—when she accepts the disclosive potential given over to her through language—she confirms her primordial relationship to language, which is not to master language but to listen "in such a away that we let it tell us its saying" and, in response, to speak from out of language.

Toward Rhetorical Realism

Language, of course, is only one aspect of augmented reality. Nevertheless, as I have tried to illustrate in this chapter, the presence of language in many augmented reality devices and applications opens up a wealth of possibilities for the rhetorical critic and theorist. When we approach augmented reality *as rhetorical*—when we see it as possessing some form of rhetoricity that may or may not equate with the *rhetoric of* augmented reality—we find that augmented reality has a great deal to teach us about rhetoric and much to contribute to rhetorical theory.

With respect to language, augmented reality offers a valuable window into the history of rhetorical theory, helping reveal some of the realist commitments that have informed our field's development as well as some of the differing forms realism has taken through the years. Whether epistemological or ontological, realism has long been a framework for thinking about (and against) rhetoric. This isn't to suggest, however, that epistemological realism and ontological realism are fundamentally at odds with one another, and that one of these realisms is therefore "more rhetorical" than the other. Indeed, Wilkins's failed attempt to create a universal language illustrates some of the ways epistemological and ontological rhetorical realisms can overlap and mutually inform one another. Though it falls short on the basis of epistemology, from an ontological perspective Wilkins may have been on to something. For example, he recognized that language is not merely an instrument for symbolically representing concepts in the world but has a material dimension of its own that precedes understanding and that establishes the conditions of possibility for rhetorical action. Where Wilkins fell short in his ontology, however, was in presuming that one can master and control language. He failed, in other words, to see that language is *a thing of the world* and as such possesses its own ontological weight and rhetorical agency. And like all things in the world, language cannot be easily reduced to human commands or interventions. As augmented reality apps such as Tagwhat dramatize, language resists us at times, it withdraws from our consideration, and it occasionally acts in ways we can't always predict or control. These are not imperfections to be corrected or avoided, but are what define language as such and that consequently shape our relationship to language as beings in the world. A multi-faceted realist approach to rhetoric can help further attune us to the rhetoricity at work in language and world, so long as we're willing to listen to what language—to what rhetoric—is saying to us.

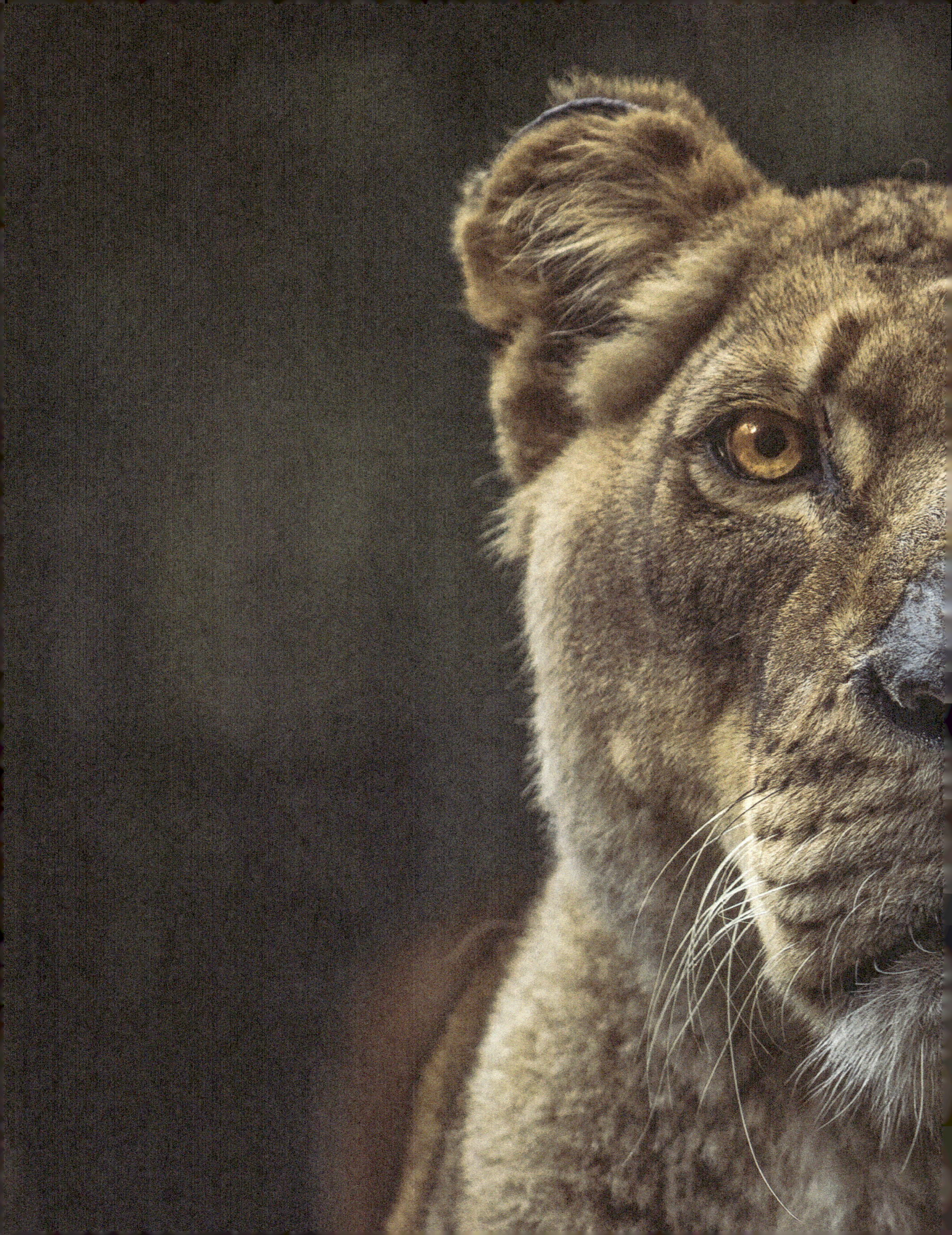

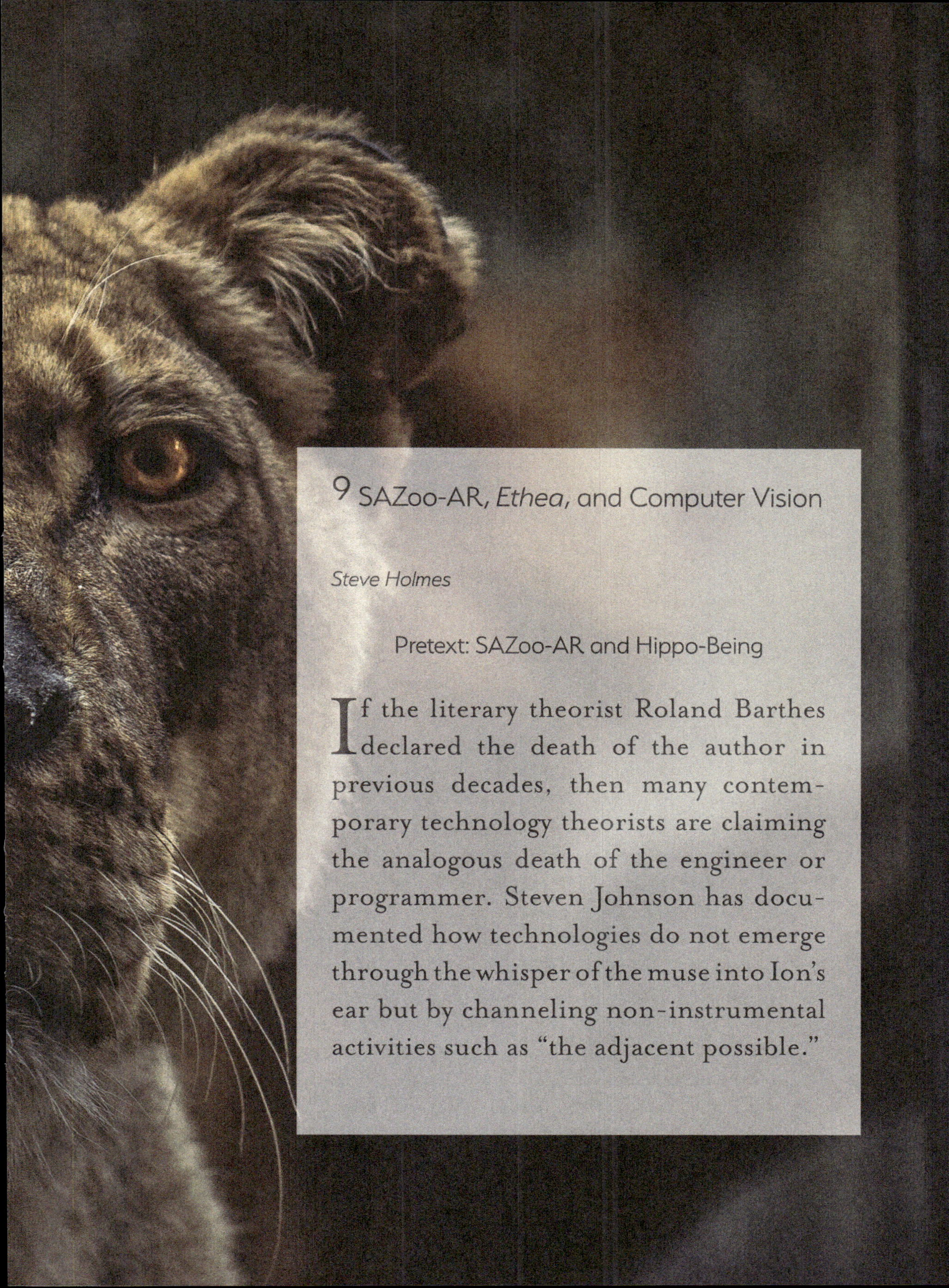

9 SAZoo-AR, *Ethea*, and Computer Vision

Steve Holmes

Pretext: SAZoo-AR and Hippo-Being

If the literary theorist Roland Barthes declared the death of the author in previous decades, then many contemporary technology theorists are claiming the analogous death of the engineer or programmer. Steven Johnson has documented how technologies do not emerge through the whisper of the muse into Ion's ear but by channeling non-instrumental activities such as "the adjacent possible."

Rather than being entirely planned and executed by an isolated individual, Gutenberg's printing press actually borrowed design elements from existing winemaking technologies—a historical coincidence that more conservative Protestants surely must have loathed. Johnson also describes how Gutenberg never could have anticipated the far-reaching consequences of his invention, such as enabling the rise of the modern nation-state. In the German philosopher Martin Heidegger's famous tool-analysis, humans tend to render technology invisible (*Zuhandenheit*; readiness-to-hand) through habitual and instrumental use. When a smart phone suddenly refuses to unlock, the smart phone becomes what Heidegger calls a broken tool (*Vorhandenheit*; presence-at-hand). The user cannot avoid a consideration of the vast technological constellation of actors that sustained the smart phone's functionality. Technology's "enframing" (*Gestell*) designates how humans and technologies co-produce a manner of being-in-the-world that is irreducible to a human's intentional aims. These are no mere metaphysical speculations as Heidegger's claims are now empirically verifiable. Embodied cognition and technology theorists like Paul Dourish have demonstrated technologies concretely impact our neural networks. Even the simple act of using a computer keyboard forms "an unconscious but accessible background to our activity . . . [and is] essential to our mode of being."

Despite their pervasiveness among media theorists, such complex views of technological agency are seldom reflected with the commercial or popular discourses that accompany a given commercial augmented reality (AR) platform or app. The world's most popular developer of AR apps for handheld mobile devices, Layar, focuses much of its discourse on readiness-to-hand features such as usability, monetization, and commercial and creative development. Many AR app developers understandably market their products by appealing to content developers and users' respective abilities to instrumentalize the superior ways in which AR apps create interactive and multimodal content. I want to introduce my purpose for this essay by briefly describing one specific example of this type of discourse: the SAZoo-AR app produced by Geomedia's Zoo-AR division for the San Antonio Zoo in 2012. An early news release on Geomedia's blog firmly stated the company's belief that Zoo-AR technology could create a more "authentic" educational experience for children and teens: "How can we change the 30 seconds kids spend at a zoo exhibit into 10 minutes? Better yet—how can we make them walk away with a *real* impression." Geomedia placed numerous AR "targets" at over ten exhibits in the San Antonio Zoo including Japanese Giant Salamanders, Komodo Dragons, and Hippopotami. They enabled children with smart phones and tablet devices to interact with SAZoo-AR's multimodal installations.

A brief examination of Geomedia's Zoo-AR website details the way in which Geomedia promises to deliver this "*real* impression." If the hippopotami are sleeping or inert, as is often the case when one visits the zoo, then SAZoo-AR offers children the ability to interact with a virtual 3D hippopotamus in the same physical proximity. Geomedia utilizes *gamification* to create added incentive for learning by allowing children to earn coins by answering quiz questions as they progress through AR targets. In one promotional video, "What Is Zoo-AR?," project leader Jeremy Kenisky argues that "computer vision" coupled with AR's 3D interactivity offers an unprecedented educational experience.

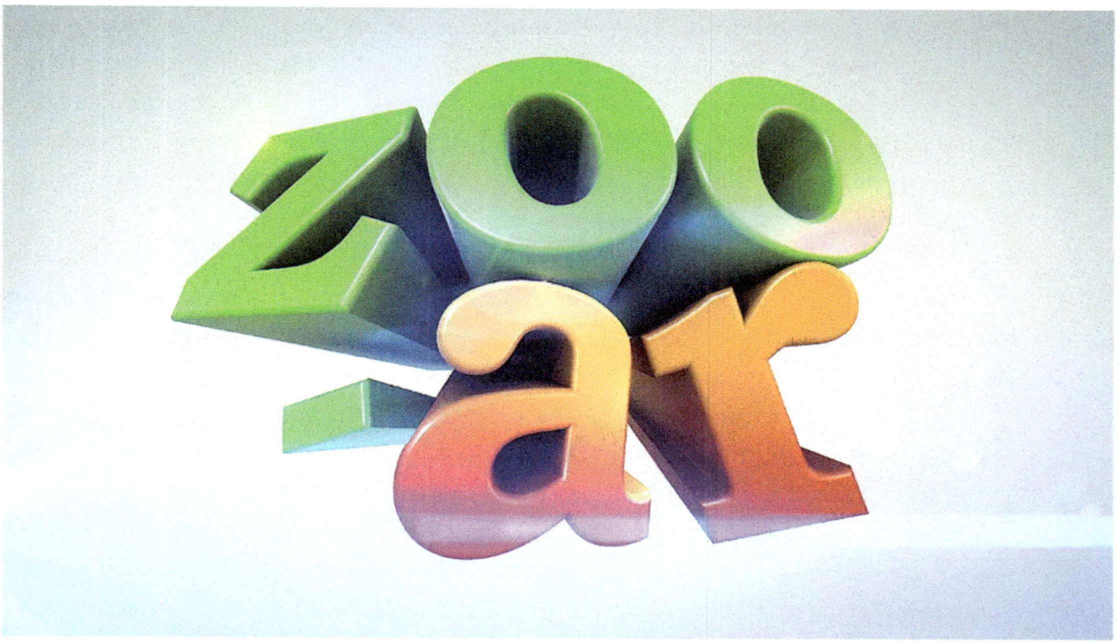

Figure 9.1: Zoo-AR Teaser. © 2012 by Geomedia.

Unlike the imprecise vision technology of geotagging, computer vision's increased accuracy guarantees better educational success. The video features Marybeth Green (PhD), a graduate advisor in instructional technology from Texas A&M University-Greenville, who

AURASMA
Scan the image to view.

comments that traditional zoo-based communication has been flat and lacks the "Third [interactive] dimension [of AR]." Geomedia also ties this learning to an explicit conservation message. The company maintains that this message tends to be ignored by patrons given the zoo's traditional non-interactive textual placards that often adorn each cage. Donald Hawkins, a PhD candidate from Education Service Center (Region 20) confirms that Zoo-AR's goal is to better present the reality of the zoo: "Obviously, having some type of augmented reality app that includes the real world is going to provide students with more hands-on manipulativeness [sic] that really pushes their learning to the next level."

In another promotional video entitled "AR Education," Hawkins cites the ways in which AR technology specifically addresses the popular "multiple intelligences" theory posited by Harvard University developmental psychologist Howard Gardner. Gardner's discussion of spatial, tactile, and auditory learning styles serves as the primary justification for the importance of AR's 3D objects in relationship to grasping the educational "real" of the zoo animal. Given the successful implementation of all of these factors, Geomedia concludes with a utopian claim: "Not only are we totally increasing the value of a zoo attendance, we're changing learning. *Forever*." "*Forever*" epitomizes the company's belief that increased interactivity through AR apps can lead to better and longer-lasting educational experiences.

Even from a cursory outline of SAZoo-AR, cultural theorists would likely raise numerous challenges. The digital divide is worth keeping in mind. SAZoo-AR's educational benefits presuppose a (largely white) middle- to upper-class family with disposable income. Some might also question the assumption that interactivity is more conducive to learning than a "lack" of interactivity inherent in non-AR and non-3D environments. It is true that many textbooks and popular novels tend to minimize text's visual interactivity through homogenous font styles, sizes, and colors, but a recent *Chronicle of Higher Education* article documented a study where using non-homogenous fonts ("visual disfluency" or, simply, Heidegger's broken tool) produced better memory retention for the reader. Simply put, text-in-itself does not lack interactivity. Along different lines, Gardner's "multiple intelligences" theory—Geomedia's sole scholarly ground for the interactivity/education pairing—has been specifically criticized for a lack of empirical evidence and the use of overly general categories. An assumption of a productive relationship between gamification and education is contentious as well. Media theorist Ian Bogost has repeatedly suggested that gamification impoverishes the actual potential of videogames and games with AR apps to produce learning.

At a more ontological level, Plato would point us to the problem of whether the thing-in-itself of the animal can actually be given to the senses at all regardless of the technology employed. Plato complains that all actual zebras in the world are merely impoverished copies of the ideal form of zebra-ness. The "real" zebra never appears in perceptible form. Captured and decontextualized from "nature," zoo animals in SAZoo-AR are already "mediated" by artificial environments, tanks, and fences. Echoing Donna Haraway, Bruno Latour suggests that the presumption to better capture and display the thing-in-itself—Kantian *noumena*—is linked to Enlightenment, Western, and masculinist fantasies of the domination of (feminine) nature:

> But if you missed the galloping freedom of the zebras in the savannah this morning, then so much the worse for you; the zebras will not be sorry that you were not there, and in any case you would have tamed, killed, photographed, or studied them. Things-in-themselves lack nothing, just as Africa did not lack whites before their arrival.

Despite their commendable conservation narrative, Geomedia ultimately avoids addressing the politics of spectatorship at the zoo in the first place. From these perspectives, SAZoo-AR could be said to place additional layers of digital mediation between the viewer and the "real" of the hippopotamus as it exists in nature.

Conjecture: Animal Appearance

I have raised these concerns not to reject Geomedia's claims about the potential effectiveness of the crucially important project of improving education through new interactive and mobile technologies. Given that Geomedia's Zoo-AR division is attracting new customers such as the Witte Museum's Dinosaur exhibit in San Antonio, it is safe to assume that the alliance between education and AR has been successful and is only going to expand in the near future. It is more the case that SAZoo-AR's educational discourse provides an occasion to theorize an accurate accounting of SAZoo-AR's relationship to the objects that it strives to render "more real" through layered 3D digital interactivity over physical environments.

I believe that SAZoo-AR's "real" can be productively examined by turning to contemporary work on phenomenology. Phenomenology is a philosophical approach started primarily by Edmund Hussurl and carried on through Heidegger, Alphonso Lingis, Emmanuel Levinas, Maurice Merleau-Ponty, and many others. Phenomenologists are concerned with what appears to humans in our experience of the world. Contemporary "postphenomenologists" like Don Ihde and Ingrid Richardson add a more nuanced focus on empiricism and technology to this previous body of thought. Postphenomenologists avoid (at first) value judgments about a given technology, that is, a claim about whether SAZoo-AR offers a better or worse educational experience and conservation message than a zoo without any AR apps. Postphenomenologists primarily seek to describe an experience (appearance) as a complex enactment of the real. This real is co-produced through our complex material relations as embodied beings with technological relations that cannot be reduced to human perception, representation, and intentionality alone.

SAZoo-AR's instrumental aims correspondingly must be situated as affective but not entirely determining differentials within a much larger mind-body-technology-environment meshwork. Postphenomenologists in the tradition of Ihde possess the broad premise that each unique human-technology relation cannot be reduced to any other, and each relation produces unique ways of knowing, interacting, and being-in-the-world. In other words, SAZoo-AR is quite correct in that AR apps create unique experiential affordances through haptic and tactile interactivity. However, postphenomenology additionally investigates the invisible "readiness-to-hand" features that contribute to our mode of being-on-the-SAZoo-AR-app alongside its presence-at-hand features, and thereby provides a complex manner of describing its range of affectivity and potentiality for education.

In what follows, I explore several, but by no means comprehensive, aspects of postphenomenological interactions in SAZoo-AR. Geomedia figures the SAZoo-AR user as "disembodied," and I consider how a fully *embodied* user interacts with SAZoo-AR through co-productive processes of *infolding* by examining corporeal elements such as facial expression, the publicness of looking at mobile media screens, zones of attention and inattention, and the role of the animals as embodied participants. Since Geomedia's educational claims are also grounded in larger AR industry shifts from geotagging to computer vision, it is also necessary to consider the camera's perception in itself as it is enabled by computer vision—technological embodiment. In a common *topoi* across the AR app industry, computer vision promises to simulate the human eye in the way that it examines objects, thereby decreasing the distance between human and machinic visual "reals" when it comes to perception. Yet, despite its simulation of the human eye, computer vision engenders much more complex and nonhuman perceptions of zoo animals. I examine both the camera lens of my iPhone 5 that I employed when I visited the SAZoo-AR installation in June of 2013, and certain features of the real-time processing software for computer vision. Both embodied human interaction and computer vision offer viable methods to challenge the conflation of the appearance of the real with the content that the user interacts with. Rather, this content can be seen as part of an enactment of several overlapping and yet incommensurate reals that constitute the SAZoo-AR experience.

From Disembodied Interface to Corporeal Infoldings

From Geomedia's ontological presuppositions, a disembodied user floats free of his or her body and physical relationships with technology and can focus on—be persuaded by—an AR app's procedures, protocol, and content. A Cartesian brain-in-vat confronts the bare life of the Turing Machine (the discrete interface). By contrast, a postphenomenological view of the user always requires a materially embodied individual—body, brain, and environment—that is simultaneously subject to and co-productive of a variety of affective events with a diverse array of actors—human and nonhuman. It is not just within Geomedia's promotional literature that we find this tension between embodiment and disembodiment for AR. In his essay "The Poetics of Augmented space," one of the first to employ the concept of digital augmentation in relationship to physical space, Lev Manovich makes a strong move to argue that AR must constitute a unified phenomenological experience at the level of code. In AR's blending of the physical and digital means of perception, he asks "[D]o we end up with a new experience in which the spatial and information layers are equally important? In this case, do these layers add up to a single phenomenological gestalt or are they processed as separate layers?" Manovich unfortunately maintains AR as an "other" space from "natural" human perception, making us "goddesses" as Haraway maintains, before we are cyborgs. Postphenomenology perceives these multiple layers—content, perception, and code—as creative and unique encounters both for the human and for the computer.

Hyperimmersion and the "window" metaphor for AR viewing are two major tropes of disembodiment that occur throughout Geomedia's website. The more that SAZoo-AR can make the handheld device "disappear," the more that learning can occur. Consequently, Zoo-AR offers statements such as "The animals in Zoo-AR are not just 3D models. You can interact with them, learn how they move, hear what they sound like and discover how they interact with their environment. Because Zoo-AR users 'learn by doing' they feel more engaged." Supported by Gardner's educational theory ("learn by doing"), the "real" can be manipulated and effectively grasped. One local newspaper report of the beta release of SAZoo-AR reflects this common claim in that one can "pinch" a "real" hippopotamus, providing an *im*-mediate (e.g., with minimal mediation) access to the thing-in-itself.

"No technology is neutral—each transforms human perception, from the printing press to the smartphone."

Such ontological assumptions produce corresponding beliefs about the educational potential of SAZoo-AR. Geomedia argues that the invisibility of the device's protocols and sense of technological mediation correspond to the novel ability to "trick" students into learning:

> The same people who were creating the most beautiful toy labels yesterday that kids couldn't help but have, are now teaching those same kids about conservation and educating them on how they can change the world . . . We tell kids they're playing a game and looking at animals. But in reality we're teaching them more than any sign or plaque ever could, and we're building into them a true understanding of conservation, and in ways they can help . . . Not only do you have their full attention, you have their inquiry and their passion too. It really boils down to a simple question—when was the last time you saw kids reacting to their school books the way they do to our technology?

Plato famously compared rhetoric to an "adulterated wine" that innately good people (Geomedia) might employ to move students to virtuous ends while morally corrupt people (non-educational toymakers and sophists) employ rhetoric for immoral ends. This coercive vision of persuasion converts children (audience) to empty containers who are deprived of the ability to make autonomous or creative responses.

Geomedia is not incorrect to suggest that perception is substantively different in digital interactions with a virtual recreation of an animal's habitat. However, additional embodied relations also produce the ways in which educational literacy takes form. Anne Friedberg writes: "the metaphor of the window has retained a key stake in the technological framing of the visual field. The Windows interface is a postcinematic visual system, but the viewer-turned-user remains in front of (*verstellen*) a perpendicular frame." As embodied subjects, there are no windows through technologies. No technology is neutral—each transforms human perception from the printing press to the smart phone. Aristotle calls rhetoric, for example, a *techne*: a teachable craft and art. Ihde elaborates in *Technics and Praxis* that *techne* is not reducible to human instrumental aims. *Techne* is more akin to nonconscious embodiment and affect. Later in *Technology and Lifeworld*, he extends Heidegger's concept of "world" (*gert*) to describe a complex of meanings manifested through practice. However, unlike Heidegger who inexplicably distrusted modern technologies and who held out hope for a God to intervene and save us, Ihde is a resolute empiricist. Our technological mediation means that we were never in a pre-technological Garden of Eden in the first place. *All technologies* co-produce vision. It is not a simple matter that some do (AR apps) while others (textual placards in zoo exhibits) do not. In *Existential Technics*, Ihde declares "Insofar as I use or employ a technology, I am used by and employed by that technology as well. . . . We are bodies in technologies."

From the perspective of postphenomenology, Gardner's interactive and sensory educational literacies are not specific to AR apps, although AR apps certainly intensify certain aspects of haptic and sensory interactivity in unique ways. Every human-technology relation is simultaneously a body-tool relation. Postphenomenology thereby eliminates metaphors of disembodiment such as "mediation" and "interface" because they presuppose a "natural" (Edenic) way of viewing that is somehow accessible independent of technologies of the body and the nonhuman. Haraway suggests that we should use the term *infolding* after Merleau-Ponty. Infolding more accurately describes the cognitive, haptic, somatic, and perceptual affects—products of *physis* and *nomos* alike—which constitute the "real" as an enactment of these different forces. In the context of mobile media studies, Richardson illustrates infolding through her concept of: "*technosomatic involvement.*" This approach retains the medium-specific ways in which an AR app can produce a different reality than a television screen, while also factoring in the experience of embodied interplay. Simply put, for earlier technological determinists such as Marshall McLuhan and Harold Innis, the technological object determines the subject. Richardson instead articulates a space of co-production—the emergence of *quasi-subjects* and *quasi-objects* (Latour's terms)—"in which the body-media relation is also moored by sedimented cultural habits, body-metaphors and tropes surrounding our engagement with screens, and the impact of the situated or built environment upon that engagement . . . Tools are not merely perceptual extensions, but cause concrete and corporeal reactions and dilations."

Face

Infolding calls our attention to concrete points of relationality and embodiment that are bound up with the use of SAZoo-AR. Many of these factors are not strictly technological or individual, but social. Geomedia's promotional videos feature numerous users' exited reaction shots ostensibly as evidence of SAZoo-AR's inculcation of a genuine positive experience. Yet, the face for an embodied user obtains differently with the same screen, content, and software protocols depending on whether the user is in public (with friends or in a crowd at the zoo) or in private. Many researchers point to the empirical studies of Ting-Toomey and Kurogi who have demonstrated that self-performance of the embodied user in front of a screen is culturally specific—further evidence that cultural dispositions impact technological perception. For example, Americans may be more used to opening themselves to public forms of learning on phones, while Japanese tend to retain a distinction between *honne* (true feelings) and *tatemae* (public face). Koreans value *nunchi*, "the ability to 'read' and interpret others' faces and social cues." All of these practices are at once produced and conditioned by SAZoo-AR's specific manifestation, but in forms that are irreducible micropractices that no amount of excellent AR app design can account for or entirely produce.

One might begin to wonder how non-traditional English speakers or non-normative bodies relate to SAZoo-AR. To emphasize my purpose again, I raise this speculation not as criticism in any remote sense. Simply put, there is no normative body in SAZoo-AR, regardless of the intention of the design, without rendering technology back to a window or an instrumental design. Such a view would be to place the "real" of appearance back within the device alone. Consequently, an "educational experience" in SAZoo-AR must be greatly expanded to include various somatic responses. The AR app user in front of parents, peers, animals, and alone is dramatically different, and it is in these complex folds and technosomatic involvements that something akin to the "real" appears. The unique way that SAZoo-AR infolds us is our unique *technosoma*. To take an analogy, it may alternately deviate from or mirror what we recognize as a mode of "being-on-the-phone": "[activities] such as stopping, bowing the head to conceal the face and reduce audibility, shielding one's mouth with the hand to define a provisional private space, or deliberately not altering one's trajectory or visual/facial orientation, and directing one's gaze into the middle distance, as is the case with the more blatant Bluetooth pedestrian." I was struck when watching the promotional videos that the chief comments of featured users related to novelty and surprise but seldom reflected the gain of any new educational content. Users were invariably posed in pairs and groups. They likely enacted what Erving Goffman has called *gestural prefigurement*: "various public postures that may reflect cultured/learned performances *of* interactivity" rather than serving as a sign of a direct correlation between interactivity and learning.

Zones of Inattention

Interactivity and augmented perception are core elements of SAZoo-AR. In the Blue Fish AR installation, one can start a video while taking an educational quiz about how ocean pollution relates to the survival of the Blue Fish. However, interactivity exists at multiple corporeal or infolded levels. As has been well-documented by mobile media theorists, our engagement with the mobile device involves a different body position than traditional televisions (we "lean back" not "lean forward") and face the screen in a proximal manner, with corresponding changes in the immersive investments of our other body parts. SAZoo-AR engages this dimension as "leaning in" (immersion) is equated to "active" (more genuine) learning. Laura Singer has pointed to the variance of zones of attention and inattention that obtain through any media device. However, active and passive in this context are relatively unimportant distinctions for postphenomenology, particularly when they are tied to pre-constituted value judgments. All media involve "activity" or what Manovich calls *viewing regimes*, a term that references the body's frontal relationship with any technological device. In a movie theater, all other dimensions are "back," with a full frontal centering on the screen. Optimally, screen size, lighting, and surround sound work to dissolve the perception of boundaries between technology and body (one no longer feels "in front of" but "within"). By contrast, television viewers often flip between channels, cook, chat, or mute the content, making for larger degrees of inattention.

Given the vast number of non-digital stimuli at the San Antonio Zoo, one immediately wonders what type of attention SAZoo-AR may command at a given installation site. The burden on Geomedia's promotional literature lies in the demonstration of the ability to effectively limit zones of inattention while creating lasting zones of attention. SAZoo-AR targets designate a point of concern for the screen. They indicate what is relevant and what is not in a much more directed manner than a mere "placard," which is only part of the entire sensory experience of viewing a cage. Indeed, for larger exhibits like the hippopotamus, where one walks around the entire cage from multiple viewing points, it is even more difficult for textual placards to create some sort of sustained message. Screens and AR targets can better direct users' attention. However, this involvement-in-the-world offers no direct relationship between learning and the content of the screen. The screen creates a specific sense of involvement in the world when one clicks the "Start Zoo Adventure" button and we "sit down, quit—physically or cognitively—other activities we may have been performing, and watch the screen"—our "screen-ness."

We are "mobile bodies," as Manovich argues, but mobile devices in themselves are also "fractured" and layered, creating what Ihde calls a "pluriviusal" mode of being in the world composed of gaming, the animals themselves, AR targets, and others. "Surround sound" for SAZoo-AR includes not only the one-way sound—which strives to place the user in the "front" of the smart phone or tablet—but also the surround sound of other children and parents interacting with the physical space as well as the vast cacophony of animal noises (especially bird noises) from the park itself. Postphenomenology "calls for a certain kind of *inattention*—a persistent openness to the world, a subsidiary awareness that is different from reflection as such. Inattention is not the same thing as distraction—a scattering or absence of attention—rather, it refers to the different distances at which we hold the rest of the perceptual field, including the body. To offer purely anecdotal evidence, I visited the SAZoo-AR exhibit in June 2013. While the SAZoo-AR videos are short in length, whether I watched a video to full-length generally corresponded to how noisy the environment was.

These observations are in keeping with Harper and Richardson's conclusions that all mobile interaction is hardly ever a "dedicated practice." Rather, its usability presupposes the ecology of other objects and activities within the built environment. Introna and Ilharco note that despite the lack of surround sound and the fully frontal relationship of the screen, *mobile media screens* cannot discipline the body in the same way as traditional media or computer desktop monitors. As copious research has demonstrated, the relationship between screen and perception is less one of "being in front," and more of a momentary "turning towards." Thus, Geomedia's goal of converting a thirty-second experience at the San Antonio Zoo into fifteen minutes is already complicated by its medium. A user's activities are interrupted through checking texts and missed calls, email and software updates, and "Push Button" notifications. Not in the context of AR apps but mobile media in general, Richardson calls these interruptions part of the "variable ontology" of mobile media that show how subjects, tools, and objects emerge relationally in any interaction. Sensory dedication and immersion—a core component of Zoo-AR's AR pedagogy—varies *not* in relationship to the interactivity of the device alone or its content, but in relationship to its fully and emergent technosomatic complex.

Animals

As a final consideration, the animals—the subjects of the user's gaze—must also be seen to co-produce the real. Even sleeping hippos do not sit as passive receptacles within a cage for an AR app's digital version of Barthes "empire of signs." Geomedia often tries to supplement a sense of ecological immersion—a seamless digital representation of a Blue Fish's ecology—through independently accessible video-content shot from the "perspective" of the natural ocean habitat of the animal. An analogy can be found in Haraway's discussion of National Geographic's CritterCam program: "Indeed, the visual structuring of the TV episodes emphasizes bodies, things, parts, substances, sensory experience, timing, emotions—everything that is the thick stuff of crittercam's lifeworld. The cuts are fast; the visual fields, littered; the size scales of things and critters in relation to the human body, rapidly switched so that the viewer never gets comfortable with the illusion that anything much can be physically taken for granted in relation to oneself." For the Blue Fish installation's video, the cuts and scales are similar. However, Haraway suggests that these perspectives are misleading: "Insofar as I (and my machines) use an animal, I am used by an animal (with its attached machine). I must adapt to the specific animals even as I work for years learning how to induce them to adapt to me and my artifacts in particular kinds of knowledge projects. Specific sorts of animals in specific ecologies and histories make me adapt to them even as their life doings become the meaning-making generator of my work."

Animals as well as AR app users are disembodied when they are merely presented as passive objects for data-gathering subjects (humans) that machines neutrally present. This is an extremely valid criticism not of AR apps writ large, but in the specific ways that SAZoo-AR utilizes the technology. Animals are not preserved as symmetrical actors with a sense of their own agency and intentionality. Attaching a camera to an animal makes us part of the animal: "If those animals are wearing something of my making, our mutual but nonidentical co-adaptation will be different. The animals, humans, and machines are all enmeshed in hermeneutic labor (and play) by the material-semiotic requirements of getting on together in specific lifeworlds." Rather than affixing a camera to the Blue Fish or hippo, SAZoo-AR tries to make us seem like we are in the ocean or cage with them. SAZoo-AR offers the seductive sense of sensory participation (digital overlay) without physical alteration—an opportunity, to be overly cynical, to simulate being a colonizer without actually causing any distress to the animal. In this larger postphenomenological sense, we can see then that a "tacit" conservation message also comes with a much more explicit tactile sense of Western mastery of the animal world—maintaining animals (and technology) as a permanent "out there"—a pristine Wordsworthian reserve distinct from the human and zoological space.

Computer Vision

"Flesh," as Merleau-Ponty observes, means that the world itself is an agent that alters in response to the human user's and the animal's flexible corporeality. A smart phone's camera itself also is not a fixed object/entity, but a thing. Haraway writes, "[T]he infolding of *others to each other* is what makes up the knots we call beings or, perhaps better, following Bruno Latour, things. Things are material, specific, non-self-identical, and semiotically active." Mark B. Hansen argues that any digital image is processual: "the digital image demarcates an embodied processing of information." Computer vision for SAZoo-AR's real-time processing is also embodied, but AR discourse tends to elide these concerns with a narcissistic focus on anthropomorphism. "Computer vision is about enabling the computer or mobile device to make sense of a 3-D image the way humans do," media analyst Frank Gillett commented to *Wired*. Postphenomenology does not strive to compare human and nonhumans as striving to be "equal" perceiving entities of the same object. Nor does postphenomenology require conscious reflection as part of a thing's "experience" of reality. The point is not to ask why digital cameras for SAZoo-AR continually fail—and they have to this point in history—to perceive experience in the same way as humans, but to explore what instead characterizes the digital camera's unique infolded experience, particularly those that are not immediately visible to the user.

Imagine that I am standing in front of the San Antonio Zoo's Rhinoceros exhibit with the stock 8-megapixel Facetime HD camera on my iPhone 5. Similar to conventional cameras, all digital cameras possess lenses designed to focus light and to produce some sort of image of a rhinoceros. My camera does not focus light on a film (or a retina and neural networks), but onto a semiconductor that converts light into electronic records which in turn are as processed into data. The iPhone in particular employs a complementary metal oxide semiconduction (CMOS) that converts light into electrons. Each cell in the image takes on an accumulated charge or value that can be read. Some cameras employ CCD modes, using an analogue-to-digital conversion unit. This unit converts each pixel to a digital value by measuring individual charges at each photosite and in turn morphing charges into binary forms that can be read by the computer. By contrast, CMOS devices possess transistors and a system of wires that do not digitalize, but amplify and move the charge through wires.

This technological information is *not* merely an engineer's denominative description of processes for two primary reasons. First, the camera's experience—its "flesh"—has everything to do with the energy that it takes for the computer to encounter itself. Having several transistors next to each pixel on the CMOS sensor lowers the light sensitivity. Chemically, an increased number of photons strike the transistors rather than the photodiode. Thus, they consume over 100 times less power than a CCD. Thus, a higher quality of pixel in the CCD comes with the impossibility of employing CCD for handheld mobile devices because they would drain the battery too quickly. Secondly, the photosites on the sensor are actually colorblind. Unlike human eyes, an intensity is recorded, and a filter is relied upon to examine light in its three primary colors. Again, there are relational differences. Some filters employ beam splitters, where input light is divided into three different strands, where each individual sensor has an identical perception of the object, while responding only to one primary color. However, this latter method would require a device that was too large to transport around the zoo. iPhones employ a color filter array over each individual photosite—that is, they apply multiple filters to a single sensor.

Quite distinct from the digital's or computational's associations with cold logical precision and the inability to act in the absence of direct input and accounting, the camera never experiences or encounters the "full" image. Each sensor is broken up into red, green, and blue patterns, wherein the computer "guesses" based upon the information within the general vicinity of the sensor. Critical theorists familiar with Louis Althusser might be amused to find that this process is called "interpolation," where the "lack" of direct input produces the image. Despite computer vision's better grasp of an object than the previous AR standard of Geotagging, it is not true—with regard to the better functional access to the object—that computer vision better reveals the "real" of the object.

Common filters for iPhones include the "Bayer filter." In *Alien Phenomenology*, the object-oriented ontologist Ian Bogost offers us a way to conceive of the phenomenology of the CMOS, by contrasting the Bayer filter pattern to a less common one: the Foveon sensor. The Foveon sensor, like the first model I discussed, measures each wavelength at each photocell. Yet, rather than resulting in better pictures, users quickly discovered that the object—the rhinoceros—shifted in response to any slight change in light sensitivity or ISO. Bogost writes, "Because the Bayer sensor's method of amplifying light sensitivity is analogous to that of the film emulsion, while the Foveon sensor's method of amplifying light sensitivity is not. Higher speed films are more light sensitive because the grains of silver halide on the emulsion are larger than in slower speed film. When photons strike the crystals, they cause a chemical reaction that creates a small covering of silver on the film. The size and distribution of these coverings vary in proportion to the size of the grain." The Bayer algorithm was specifically designed to "mimic" non-digital cameras whereas the Foveon operated by a literally nonhuman way of assembling images. The key point, Bogost argues, is that no camera possesses agency over, for example, the color green on the filter any more or any less than a human. Yet, it is nevertheless true that each camera has a genuine phenomenological experience that, in a sense, is no different (ontologically) from the human eye's perception. In fact, Foveon sensors are similar to our "mesopic vision" or the conditions under which our eyes become confused in dim light and oscillate constantly between rods and cones, color and monochrome. Bogost offers a parallel to a bat's vision: "Just as the bat's experience of perception differs from our understanding of the bat's experience of perception, so the camera's experience of seeing differs from our understanding of its experience. But unlike the bat, the Foveon-equipped Sigma DP provides us with exhaust from which we can derive a phenomenal metaphor to chronicle that experience." Bogost concludes, "Irrespective of the underlying electro-optical mechanisms that make it behave, the sensor's perception as a whole is metaphorized as mesopicism. As light sensitivity is adjusted up on the sensor, it is as if the sensor had been shrouded in increasing levels of dusk. Such is what it is like to be a Foveon digital image sensor, even if this is not what it is to be one." I could go on at length detailing the various technological components of the camera's vision filters, but each would only work toward an overall postphenomenological perspective regarding how these various elements tell us about the camera's encounter with the rhinoceros. The point is not that the camera ultimately simulates yet falls short of the way that the human eye processes vision. The point is more that its reactions are subtle and worthy of documentation in terms of how they perceive and store images in unique ways—subtleties that our eyes cannot directly perceive but which—as any vinyl record purist will observe in relationship to .mp4 compression—will have definite technosomatic consequences and create more infoldings at broader structural levels and micropractices.

Digital Traces

While Geomedia obviously relies on the camera hardware on smart phones and tablet devices, they do not publicize their software systems for proprietary reasons. To consider the software component for computer vision, I have selected what I believe to be a close approximation: Open Source Computer Vision Library (OpenCV), which specializes in real-time computer vision development. A camera's software actually has to locate real world coordinates from camera images while actually bypassing the camera entirely in a process called "image registration"—a form of computer vision derived from video tracking. The first goal of most computer vision software programs is to locate some sort of marker. The names of these markers are intriguing and give us a metaphorical glimpse of the phenomenological realities that they create across various AR platforms. For example, Layar's official blogger Adrienne Goetz describes how "The Layar browser can tell which objects in the real world are augmented because the visual *fingerprints* of the objects are preloaded into the application based upon the user's layer selection. When a user aims their device at an object that matches the fingerprint, the app instantaneously returns the associated AR experience."

OpenCV analogously calls these fingerprint elements "features." Barthes, in *Camera Lucida*, writes of being stung by a "punctum"—an emotional wounding—while contemplating a belt buckle in the photograph of a cowboy. A punctum is not consciously composed or intended by the photographer, but instead designates his unconscious yet subjective experience of an element of the photograph. Amazingly, Barthes's process is quite analogous to how features in OpenCV operate: features are a group of pixels that possesses some "unique" attribute such as an edge, a corner, a certain motion, points, or color contrast. Analogous to the guesswork of the Bayer filter, OpenCV's basic building block algorithm possesses templates that hunt for close approximations of features such as a face template, line detection, or face detection. OpenCV employs templates because they are faster methods of organizing otherwise heterogeneous and discontinuous features. Human visual recognition requires reductions of visual complexity to aid in pattern recognition. Funes the Memorius, Borges's fictional character who cannot forget, becomes literally incapable of thinking. Templates similarly allow feature detectors to establish repeatability to determine if a given feature can be located in two or more successive images of the same object. However, unlike human eyes, computer vision also can employ high-level algorithms to aim the camera at certain parts of an image to be searched rather than trying to process the entire image at once.

Motion detection is a core algorithmic component of OpenCV. Unlike a static photographic image, AR apps have to track, fix, and process multiple series of features in order to know when to generate the appropriate software content. Like a normal video camera, OpenCV tells the camera to take "frames" per second, using a method called "frame subtraction" (or background subtraction). The software converts an image to grayscale, and subtracts the current frame from each previous frame, enabling the software to search for a change. OpenCV regulates the update speed and encourages image accumulators within the software to "forget" earlier images. Edges are detected in monochrome with a lighter image next to a darker image, trying to find where a sufficient number of contrasts assemble. By use of the Hough transform algorithm, Open CV (like most computer vision programs) offers a way to locate straight lines that define the boundaries of an image. The program actually gains "knowledge" of the object by what the rhetorical theorist Kenneth Burke calls "perspective by incongruity." Not unlike a baby's gestalt vision, computers have to be trained offline. Computers are shown the "learning algorithm" which consists of a series of positive images (with a face) and negative images (without a face). This learning results in a file that produces a range of semblances of a given object to tell the camera what to detect. Each sensor in each program will be different depending on which images it has been shown. The radical postphenomenological implication is that *each* sensor will perceive reality *differently*. Such training is no easy feat given that a 24X24 pixel face can have over 40,000 possible combinations or scales. Image training turns cameras into Aristotelians. In search of an ideal order and weight number for pixels detected, they themselves do not perceive "objects" (substance), but use object-tracking, depending on features (*qualia*) to predict where objects can appear next in the frame. Computer vision perceives a number of potential object realities that never actually come to pass.

The real-time imaging, in a sense, mimics the Bayer filter's perception of the objects. Consider the "blobs" (interest points) detector function. This detector works on vision gestalt as well. If a corner detector can easily pick out straight lines, then blog detectors have to work on areas that are too smooth—like the Hippo's bulbous stomach. Unlike line or straight edge detectors, blobs do not work on a point system but in terms of regions and overall image structures. Their perception is distinct from the way that a corner detector can grasp the accidental features of the object. Size and perspective to the object—the object itself and the user co-produce the act of seeing for the camera—matter. If an image is too small or too far away, then what appears to be smooth close up will become a point, and the camera's image signal processor will misread it and fail to generate the appropriate content that corresponds to the detection of the Hippo.

Conclusion

The postphenomenological point of computer vision is that each of these technological processes is not simply a change in a fixed protocol of a computer program. Code is "hypocritical," Wendy Chun writes: "Code does not always or automatically do what it says . . . it carries with it the possibility of deviousness . . . execution, and a whole series of executions, belatedly makes some piece of code a source, which is again why source code was initially called pseudo code." Similarly, computer vision and object-tracking do not do what they say, and instead offer unique ways for us to consider the ways in which the camera experiences its object in real-time. Computer vision and other processes of interactivity with SAZoo-AR form new object moments. Both events place SAZoo-AR's users into embodied assemblages that produce subjectivities, relations, and processes. Each swipe of a touchscreen enacts new "reals" in terms of establishing unique body-tool relations. Echoing Latour, granting AR apps potentiality and "agency" in this sense means that technological black boxes have to be pried apart by cultural studies theorists and exhumed to locate the ways in which mobile media technologies radically restructure experience at multiple affective levels.

In considering a range of postphenomenological perspectives on SAZoo-AR, I have sought to ask what an embodied user and an embodied technology can tell us about the "real" that appears within the San Antonio Zoo's educational learning space. The significance of my argument lies appropriately enough in an animal allegory. As defined by Aristotle, the ancient Greek concept of *ethos* referred to an artistic proof (*pistis*) (as distinct from a logical proof), whereby the speaker attempted manufacture a credible persona to be believed by an audience. For example, Geomedia musters PhD researchers in its promotional videos to establish the educational value of its product. Drawing on Heidegger, Charles E. Scott offers a more primordial inflection of *ethos* by considering its etymological root in the term *ethea*: dwelling-places or "haunts" of humans. In Homer, this term referred to a domesticated horse—an ostensible zoo animal despite the zoo's attempts to simulate its natural ecology—who breaks free and returns to its "*ethea*" in the wild. *Ethos* is the disciplined/instrumentalized identity that is carved out against the "natureculture" space of *ethea* that postphenomenology seeks to trace. In the context of education, Sophocles's *Ajax* notes "the proper time for influencing the *ethos* is childhood." I agree that SAZoo-AR does attempt to gesture toward the *ethea* of animals. However, Geomedia's own discourse betrays its inability to theorize its own technosomatic *ethea* for modern technology as well as the animals that it aims to use to create a "*real* impression." By contrast, *ethea*, embodiment, and computer vision are what ultimately enable researchers to grasp a sense not of the real, but of the variable ontologies that produce the *real* of the zoo.

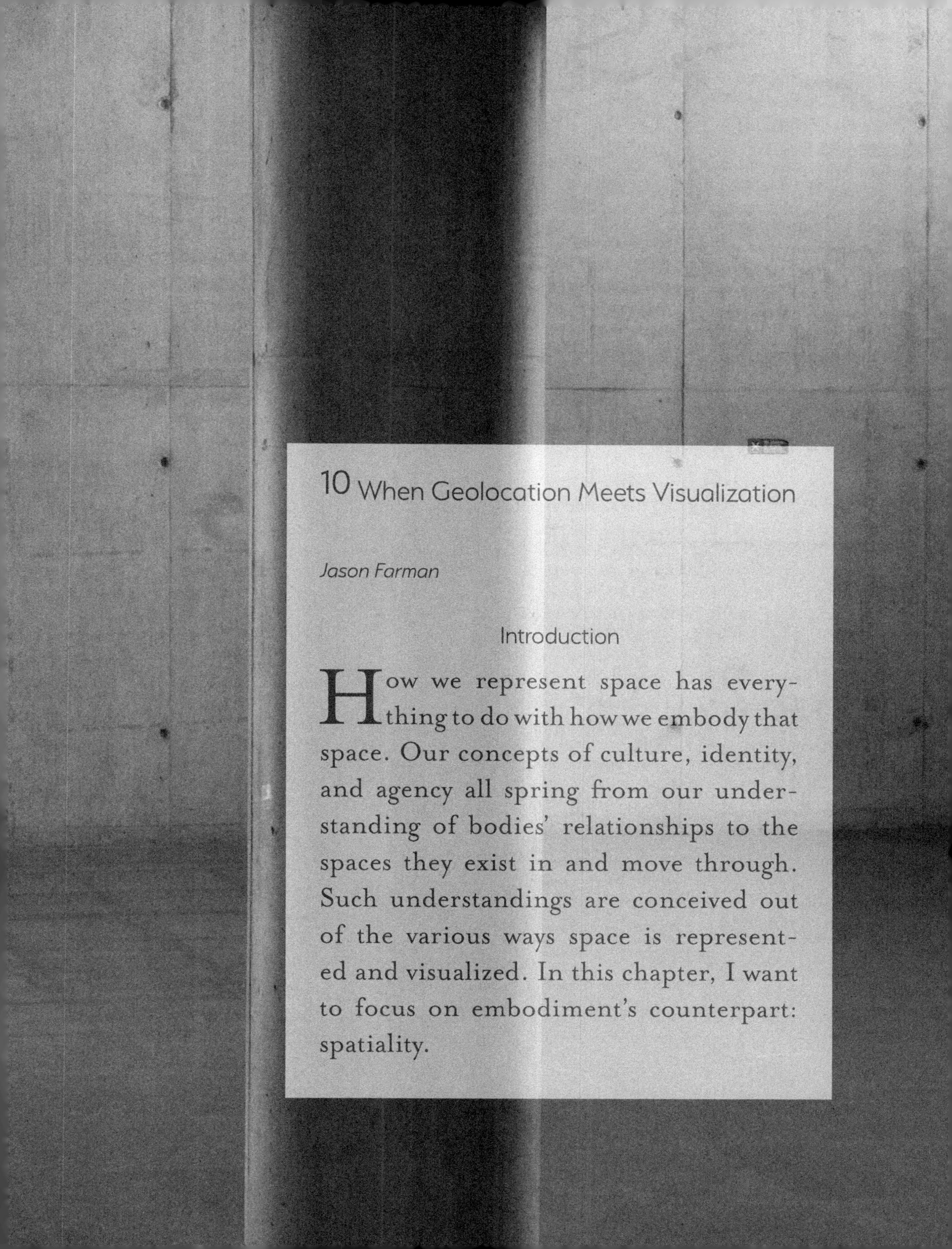

10 When Geolocation Meets Visualization

Jason Farman

Introduction

How we represent space has everything to do with how we embody that space. Our concepts of culture, identity, and agency all spring from our understanding of bodies' relationships to the spaces they exist in and move through. Such understandings are conceived out of the various ways space is represented and visualized. In this chapter, I want to focus on embodiment's counterpart: spatiality.

Since embodiment and space are indelibly linked together, it is important to develop a strong understanding of our usage of the term "mobile media space." Such an understanding is undoubtedly linked to the various ways space is represented on mobile devices, representations that a community comes to rely on to interact with pervasive computing space. In order to define the various ways space is produced in our mobile media era, I will draw on several examples that demonstrate the various ways we embody and practice space. These examples are primarily rooted in ideas of mapping: from mapping geographic regions to mapping ideas and concepts in word clouds, from mapping information and visualizations onto landscapes through augmented reality applications to mapping disaster zones through site-specific text messages. Mapping, as a means of representing and practicing space (and the cultural capital that is so intimately connected to this concept), serves as a key example in the exploration of what "space" means in our embodied practices of mobile technologies.

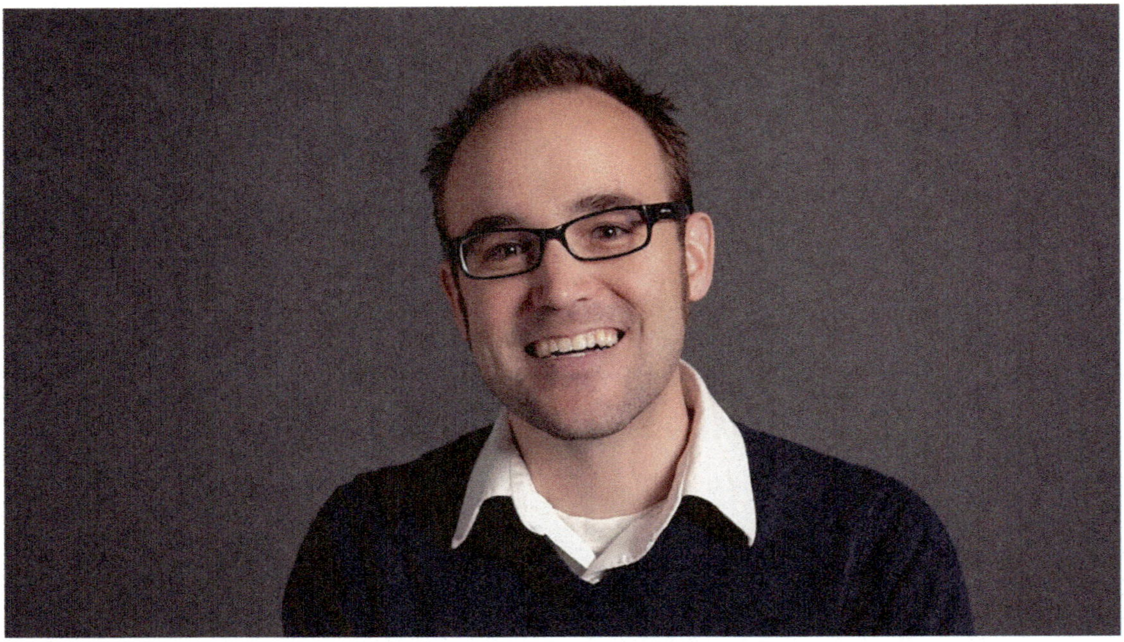

Figure 10.1: Jason Farman on "Community and Mobile Technology. http://bit.ly/2gi0xdF © 2013 by University of Maryland College of Arts and Humanities.

AURASMA
Scan this page to watch

The Space of Virtuality

On a recent trip to Boston, after being dropped off at my hotel by a taxi, I placed my luggage in my room and stepped outside to find a restaurant. I loaded a map on my phone, hit the button that would request my location, and noticed the blue dot that located me at an intersection. I looked at the nearby street corner signs, which did not match the place that the map located me. I knew the map was representing my location incorrectly. I also knew the name of the nearest intersection. But, I had no idea where I was! Though I had barely taken a few steps outside of the hotel, I was already lost. With no one nearby to help clarify the discrepancy, I tried a few techniques to get the map to show my correct location so I could find out which restaurants were within walking distance. I did a search for my hotel and discovered that the map was placing me about a half-mile from my current location. What struck me most about this situation was the feeling of displacement I had until the map lined up with my physical location. I had an odd anxiety about being lost but couldn't quite figure out why. It dawned on me that as I typically move through a new place, I use my mobile device to inform me of the context of my location. The "virtual" world of the mobile interface deeply affects the way I move through my everyday life. I savor the context-aware information my mobile device provides me and, when the representation of my environment on my device does not match up with the material space around me, I feel that one of my lenses to the world has been broken.

Increasingly, our experiences of virtual space are dissolving into the practices of our everyday lives. In fact, by tracing the history of the term "virtuality," we immediately see that the intimate relationship between the virtual and the "actual" has always been historically assumed. For Elizabeth Grosz, this dissolve takes place at the level of the perceptual, noting that the most striking transformation heralded in by digital technologies is the "change in our perceptions of materiality, space, and information, which is bound directly or indirectly to affect how we understand architecture, habitation, and the built environment." Though Grosz continues to utilize the dichotomy between "virtual" and "real" space (as exemplified in her book's title: *Architecture from the Outside: Essays on Virtual and Real Space*), her ultimate goal is quite aligned with my approach to pervasive computing space (as actualized through mobile technologies). By interrogating whether or not the "computer screen [can] act as the clear-cut barrier separating cyberspace from real space," my chapter parallels Grosz's argument that "virtual objects are now capable of generating the same perceptual effects as 'real' objects." Ultimately, an updated approach is needed for our conceptions of how virtual and material spaces interact. Here, we must complicate "our notions of real, of body, and of the physical or historical city . . . [and] what they seem to oppose."

While pervasive computing space often prompts a comparison between the "real" and the "virtual," such dichotomies do little to inform our embodied experience of this kind of space, especially in an age when the perceptive interaction with the digital environment offers a significant embodied experience. We might even ask, what distinguishes the "real" space when a virtual interaction offers a very "real" experience. Instead, by understanding the space of the digital and the space of the material to have constant interplay and permeability between one another, distinguishing the space of the virtual from the space of the real does not inform a nuanced understanding of pervasive computing space, mobile media space, or space broadly conceived.

The term *virtual* is drawn from the Latin word *virtus*, which has had many meanings over the years including "virtue," "force," "power," and then, in 1959, it began to be used in computing terms as that which is "[n]ot physically existing as such but made by software to appear to do so from the point of view of the program or the user." This use of the virtual as that which is not physical but emulates the physical (such as *virtual memory* or *virtual machine*) gestures back to the 1600s, when people used it to refer to metaphysical ideas related to Christianity, especially in distinguishing between the physical practices of faith—such as taking communion or getting baptized—and the metaphysical/"virtual" components of faith—such as the inward belief and connection to God. Connecting the virtual to the spiritual illuminates the historic idea that virtuality is non-physical and largely about potential or a process of becoming. However, this definition of the virtual had never been opposed to that which is real. For people of faith, sometimes that which is "virtual" and metaphysical is even *more real* than the physical world in which they live.

This definition is only one approach to the virtual. Accompanying this approach to the virtual is the idea of the virtual as simulation. The extended history of using the virtual to stand in for ideas of simulation is traced by Adriana de Souza e Silva and Daniel Sutko and is what they term the *technological virtual*. They write, "Because the Internet was mostly accessed through fixed interfaces (e.g., personal computers) that were physically attached to a home or office space, physical spaces were perceived as independent from digital spaces. Accordingly, digital worlds, such as chat rooms and multiuser environments, were considered 'virtual' because they allowed people to meet in nonphysical, simulated spaces." The emergence of the relationship between virtuality and simulation is linked to a shift in computing from a "culture of calculations to a culture of simulations." De Souza e Silva and Sutko note, "In the culture of simulations, everything is taken at interface value." The simulation as a screen representation that stood in for physical spaces has since caused a significant amount of cultural anxiety due to the potentials present in these forms of representation (from fears of children committing acts of violence after playing a violent videogame to people being so distracted by their devices that they no longer pay adequate attention to the physical space around them). De Souza e Silva and Sutko rightly trace this anxiety back to Plato's anxiety over art as a representational form that would draw us away from the "real" world. This fear has extended into contemporary discussions of digital interfaces as spaces that threaten to become more important—and will thus eventually subsume—"actual" space. As Umberto Eco has argued, once there is a 1:1 relationship between the representation and the thing it represents (such as a map that is the exact size of the space it represents), the former will destroy the latter. They are unable to coexist.

These theories of virtuality and simulation fail us in important ways: they do not take into account the sensory-inscribed experience of virtuality as a multiplicity and tend to ignore the materiality of the virtual. The virtual has been experienced throughout history as not a privileging or erasing of one space over another. The virtual is instead an experience of multiplicity. It is an experience of layering, and the constant interplay that bonds the virtual and the actual together is the pleasure of virtuality. As John Rajchman writes, citing Proust: "The virtual is 'real without being actual, ideal without being abstract.'" This constant interplay—without a full dissolution of one space into another—is the key to the success of virtuality. Rajchman continues: "The actual is then what manifests and effectuates the virtual, but the actual never *completely* shows or activates all that the virtual implies. Something always remains."

Virtuality is experienced as a multiplicity that "can never be reduced to a set of discrete elements or to the different parts of a closed or organic whole. (This is what Bergson called 'qualitative' rather than 'quantitative' multiplicity.)" Thus, as we experience the virtual through our mobile interfaces, it is vital to note that virtual space always implies a counterpart, such as Gilles Deleuze's coupling of the virtual with the actual. For Deleuze, these are not oppositional terms; instead, they serve as counterparts indelibly linked to one another. In this view, the virtual would never fully dissolve into the actual because it is already an integral part of the ways we have always experienced the actual. From our interfaces to our imaginations, the virtual and the "realized" have historically been tandem and complementary elements of our experiences of everyday life.

Yet, the virtual and the real continue to be discussed as opposites. One reason we are so drawn to discussing space in such bifurcated terms is largely due to a significant shift in our experience of space with the advent of mobile computing, especially with Internet-capable devices. The move from personal computing to pervasive computing, a shift characterized by the move from immobility to mobility, has allowed for online space to interact with material space in unprecedented ways. Smartphones allow us to go online from any place with an Internet connection, a fact that is quite amazing after connecting online for years while attached to non-mobile places. By having a device (one we carry with us wherever we go) that is able to interface with the world in a way that transforms our everyday experience of space into an experience of multiplicity, the production of virtual space is with us on seemingly unprecedented levels. This experience of virtuality, it must be noted, extends Deleuze's (and later the work of N. Katherine Hayles) idea that the virtual is a "process of becoming." Instead, the virtual better represents "being-as-becoming." Mobile technologies' impact on the production of space demonstrates how the virtual is always understood as a state of being that is intertwined with a state of becoming. This being-as-becoming is a present-tense experience of embodied space informed by past and future potentials. Essential to this experience of virtual space is the way that the practice of materiality is informed by various modes of representation. Examples from mobile and locative media will demonstrate how the production of embodied space is enacted.

Augmented Reality and Embodied Implacement

One key feature of locative media is the ways in which data can be organized and accessed with site specificity. This site specificity affords users a new window into the meaning of complex data and ideas. The transformation of complex information into manageable visual layouts is the ultimate goal of practitioners of "information visualization." Information visualization is important to the ways that locative media utilize the convergence of material and virtual spaces. One key technology that allows for this organization and display of spatial data is augmented reality (AR). This technology, in essence, superimposes data onto an object (or person) through a mobile device. Whether the interface is eyewear, a vehicle's windshield, or simply holding a smartphone up to a building to gather information about the site, the meanings of places are augmented by data overlays. This can be utilized for commercial purposes (as is largely the case now with mobile phone AR applications, which are still in their infancy), as seen in the Layar application for the iPhone. Layar activates the phone's camera and, by holding it up to the surrounding space, users are able to gather information about the stores, activities, real estate, and other site-specific points of interest in the immediate vicinity. These forms of visualization, according to artist Tom Corby, are able to "capitalize on humans' natural ability to spot patterns and relationships in visual fields (cognition). This enables an intuitive identification of structures, which would not be available if presented in purely numeric form."

AR on mobile devices is also being utilized in the arts and the preservation of histories. In 2010, the Museum of London released an iPhone application called Streetmuseum, in which users go to a variety of places around the city that correspond to one of the many historical photographs and paintings in the museum's collection. Users are able to utilize the phone to overlay the historical photographs onto the material landscape. Based on location and the direction you are facing, you are able to juxtapose images from the past with current surroundings. Additionally, users can access information about the image and the historical context. For example, a user can go to the gates of Buckingham Palace and bring up a photo taken in 1914 of the arrest of Emmeline Pankhurst. Holding the phone up toward the gates will position the photograph on top of the live image of the space captured through the phone's camera. Tapping on the image offers a caption for the photograph, this one saying, "Emmeline Pankhurst arrested outside Buckingham Palace. Carried past reporters to be taken to Holloway prison, Emmeline shouted 'Arrested at the gates of the Palace. Tell the King'. The arresting officer died two weeks later of heart failure." Pankhurst, one of the leaders of the British suffragette movement, who was arrested on several occasions during protests for the right of women to vote, is here juxtaposed with our present-day context. Similarly, if a user of the Streetmuseum application stands at 23 Queen Victoria Street, the application will bring up an image of the Salvation Army International Headquarters tumbling to the ground soon after the night raid on May 10, 1941, "the most severe attack London had sustained throughout the Blitz," as described by the caption in the application. While the Streetmuseum application has been well received, AR in general at the time of this writing has often been deemed gimmickry. However, AR applications like Streetmusuem demonstrate the ways that mobile technologies are able to imbue space with meaning, thus transforming a space by giving it a sense of place. Additionally, beyond the ability to implace people, mobile technologies are able to offer users new ways of visualizing information.

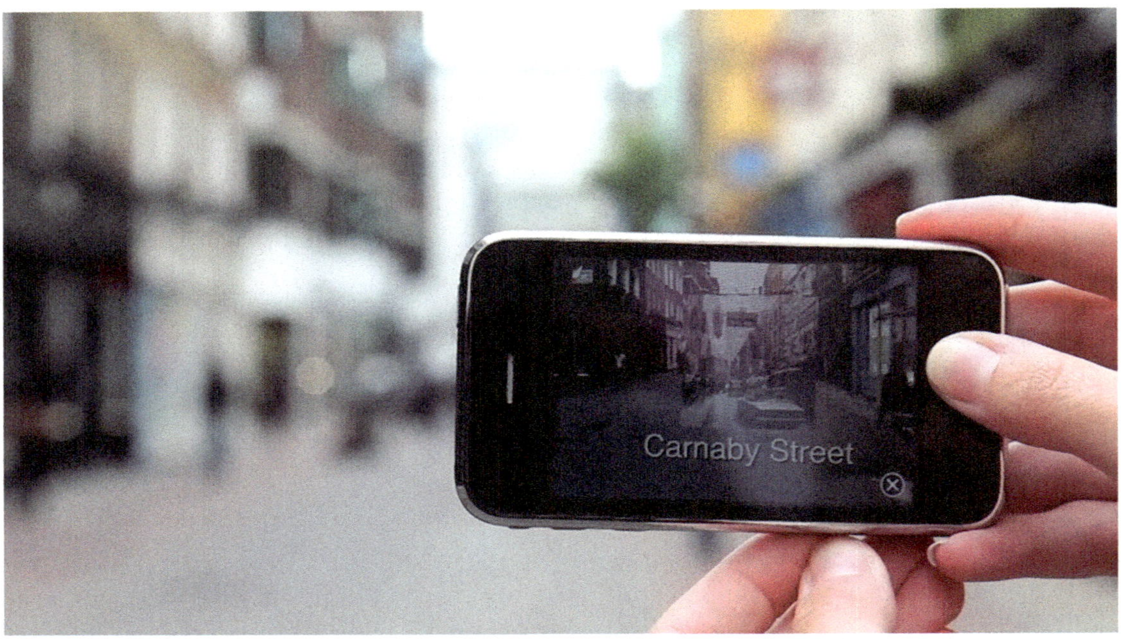

Figure 10.2: Museum of London Streetmuseum App. © 2010 by Museum of London.

AURASMA
Scan the image to view.

The transformation of space into place is linked to what Edward Casey calls "implacement." Related to Heidegger's *Dasein* (roughly understood as "being-in-the-world"), implacement locates our situated nature and our sense of proprioception with others and with objects in a space. Implacement serves as the counterpoint to displacement, which "represents the loss of particular places in which their lives were formerly at home." This loss of place is "tantamount to losing one's existence" for many. Embodied implacement gives us the sense of direction in a particular place—direction not only in movement but also in purpose. Implacement gives us a sense of embodied integrity in a particular locale and also answers the questions "Which way am I going?" and "What am I doing here?" Implacement offers context for embodied being-in-the-world: "What is my history with this place?" For emerging generations, such questions no longer prioritize between material space and digital space since these spaces simultaneously inform our experience of implacement. Our lived conception of space, especially the online realm, is very much a situated experience always contextually informed.

When we use technologies as a way of developing implacement, the media specificity and materiality of the technology must be a central concern in our analysis. Here, it is important to note that *embodied content* is non-transferable across media and across situations; instead, as we are implaced, we give context to the information we interact with. This information characterizes our environment and our embodied engagement with that space. In other words, accessing information on Wikipedia while at your desk is quite a different experience from accessing the exact same information from a site-specific interaction with a mobile device. One example that remains memorable for me was reading a bit of history about the Oxford martyrs before one of my trips to the UK. I had read some background about Thomas Cranmer, the Archbishop of Canterbury, his work to push through Henry VIII's divorce, and his eventual renunciation of the Pope leading to being burned at the stake. I took a tour of the University Church where Cranmer gave his last sermon and loaded up some of this history on my phone's GeoPedia application. This app detected my location and I was able to read a bit about what happened during Cranmer's last sermon. The article mentioned that a portion of a pillar had been cut out to create a ledge for a stage on which Cranmer stood. With my phone in hand, I hunted for the cut pillar and located it. Standing where Cranmer stood, I read again about his sermon in which he took back his signed confession that recanted his "heresies" against the Catholic Church. At this spot, he renounced the Pope and said that his hand would be the first to burn for signing the confession that recanted his Protestant beliefs. He was pulled from the pulpit and dragged to Broad Street, where he was burned. While I had read about these events prior to my trip, standing at this spot and making the walk to Broad Street while reading the details on my mobile interface transformed the content. Though the content was identical to what I had encountered at home in the United States, the medium it was delivered through and the site-specificity of the application I was using made the meaning of what I was reading completely different. Both my situation and the medium that informed that situation altered the ultimate meaning of the content. The power of site-specificity to engage us with information in an embodied way has led to a growing interest in finding ways to transform the landscapes around us into information interfaces.

"The landscape around us can serve as a type of interface where data of all types can reside, from the quotidian rankings of various restaurants to the mobile mapping of crisis zones after a major natural disaster."

Landscapes as Information Interfaces

In recent years, there has been a major transition in digital culture toward a focus on the importance of location. From location-aware technologies to a renewed interest in the role of proximity in online social interactions, site-specificity has gained a new foothold in the cultural and scholarly imaginary. Landscapes, it can be said, have become information interfaces much like the graphical user interface of a computer screen. The landscape around us can serve as a type of interface where data of all types can reside, from the quotidian rankings of various restaurants to the mobile mapping of crisis zones after a major natural disaster. This notion has recently been literalized in the creation of the N Building in Tokyo. The façade of the 24-story building is a large Quick Response (QR) code, which allows mobile devices to scan the side of the building and gain detailed information about what's going on inside in real time. The QR codes on the building, which can contain larger and more varied characters than a standard UPC barcode, are able to connect to URLs and AR information. When users scan the façade of the N Building, they are able to connect with people's Twitter feeds that are geotagged within the building. Also, stores within the building offer real time information over an AR interface. Here, the notion of a hardscape that is an interface for information is literalized.

Our locale—which should be distinguished from "location" much in the same way that place can be distinguished from space as that which is practiced and specifically contextualized—has always served as a type of information interface long before the advent of digital technologies. Information is communicated about a space in a variety of ways, most of which are not digital. From street signs to graffiti and from statues to billboards, cities have used the urban landscape as a site of information. Our embodied interaction with a locale offers insights to the meaning of the place and our situatedness there. However, a locale's context is limitedly known and much may remain unknown to us during our interactions with that place. As Derrida has argued,

> But are the conditions of a context ever absolutely determinable? . . . Stating it in the most summary manner possible, I shall try to demonstrate why a context is never absolutely determinable, or rather, why its determination can never be entirely certain or saturated. This structural non-saturation would . . . mark the theoretical inadequacy *of the current concept of context*.

For example, people can often spend most of their lives in a particular place without knowing certain significant facts about that location. Even the events that are known are understood in a limited way. Context, it must also be understood, is ongoing and never settled.

Many site-specific and location-aware technologies are addressing both the desire for further context and the engagement with ongoing contexts so that we may transform locations into locales. Therefore, while AR interfaces may not do anything revolutionary in regards to historicizing a place (people could, for example, simply take the 1914 photograph of Emmeline Pankhurst and hold it up to the gates of Buckingham Palace instead of using a smartphone to do it for them), the major shift here is the implication of the user in the act of defining the site. By utilizing technologies that draw on a person's location through GPS, a user is understood as being situated in relationship to technology and thus experiences the world as a collaboration between digital and material interfaces. While this notion harkens back to many discussions held over the last fifteen years about "what's *new* about new media," my brief reply, especially in connection to mobile interfaces, is that our embodied relationship to these interfaces uniquely structures our experience (and thus conception) of the world around us. Therefore, while holding a photograph of Pankhurst up to Buckingham Palace is one experience of that place, using the exact same photograph in the exact same place but on a digital interface like an iPhone will be an altogether different embodied experience. The same is true of reading a print newspaper and the exact same content but on a mobile device. To reiterate, the embodied experience of content is non-transferable across media. Instead, by investigating the media specificity of our engagement with cultural objects, we can see that interfaces shape our embodied engagement with space and the ways we practice space as a lived place. This extends Lev Manovich's distinction between media and "new" media: "All existing media are translated into numerical data accessible for the computer. The result: graphics, moving images, sounds, shapes, spaces, and texts become computable, that is, simply sets of computer data. In short, media become new media." Thus, the transformation of our cultural objects into binary data, such as a photograph of a significant event in front of Buckingham Palace, also transforms our embodied engagement with these objects. Here, the "sensory-inscribed" mode of embodiment developed in the previous chapter again becomes significant. Our experience of place through mobile technologies is at once a phenomenological engagement with this particular medium and a mode of reading the significance of that mode of engagement. Our bodies sense the world as a collaboration between material and digital spaces while simultaneously interacting with the cultural inscriptions written into the experience, such as the privacy implications of disclosing your location to businesses and other users.

Maps and Mobile Media Space

The correspondence between the material world and digital media indeed has many predecessors. An extensively practiced form of this mode of engagement is navigating a place using a map. From print media representations of place, to words scrawled on a scrap piece of paper noting landmarks, to GPS navigation systems, our traversal of space has long been understood as the correspondence between the material world and the ways we represent that world. We rely on maps to offer us an external visualization of our internal sense of proprioception. Maps give us a sense of where we are in relationship to the places around us. As Paul Jahshan notes in his book *Cybermapping and the Writing of Myth*, while cyberspace is a place people inhabit, we must still contend with bearings and thus "the problem of mapping is unavoidable." Such a problem becomes unavoidable because our ability to traverse space in a meaningful way is inherently tied to the mode of representation that constructs that space. The mobile map in its many instantiations is thus a key example of how representations of space in mobile technologies inform conceptions of—and interactions with—pervasive computing space.

Mobile maps, however, are very culturally situated and various maps of the same location offer us a very different sense of implacement. A famous example of this type of relationship between representation of space and conception of space is seen in the difference between Mercator's 1569 map of the globe and the Gall-Peters Projection Map published in 1973. In the Mercator projection, used for nautical navigation, continents like Africa appear smaller in landmass than those closer to the poles, like Greenland. The Gall-Peters map sought to address this discrepancy by making a map that better visualized the landmass of each of the continents. The Gall-Peters map sought to amend the ideologies that were inherent in the representation of global space in the Mercator map. Mercator's map projection came to be a visualization of Western supremacy by emphasizing the size and location of Europe. An everyday example for the mobile age is seen in the distinction between the overhead/aerial view of a map and the street view offered in maps such as Google and Bing. The point of view offered by these maps engages the user along a spectrum from "disembodied voyeur" to "situated subject." Taken one step further, location-aware devices that can pinpoint a user's location on a map and trace his or her movements through space offer a unique representation of being in a space. By distinguishing between the ideologies behind the disembodied voyeurism of the satellite view and the situated nature of the street view, both maps offer a very particular ideological stake in the status of bodies in the digital age.

The interface of each of these maps is indeed mobile—they are each designed to be portable and to function while moving through space. While print maps may have not confused the distinction between material space and its representation, the mobile interface offers us a distinctly fluid relationship between space and representations of space. In other words, we are living in a time in which the two realms of the realized and the realizing (or the actual and the virtual) do not signify themselves as exclusive spaces; instead, the interaction between these spaces continues to become mutually constructive. The reason for this transition is that the media specificity of mobile devices embodies us in a very particular way in space. The very practice of embodied space is becoming entirely reliant on the seamless interaction between our devices and our landscapes. The representation of space is not outside of the lived experience of that space. It is instead entirely incorporated into the production of embodied space. We have thus moved beyond the theorization of our mobile devices as a type of prosthetic to our bodies—an extension of ourselves out into the material world—but instead have to conceive of our devices as absolutely integral to the very foundations of embodied space in the digital age. As Jean Baudrillard noted, "The territory no longer precedes the map, nor does it survive it."

Yet, our interactions with maps often avoid the critique that we typically give other forms of representation. This is especially true with mobile maps since, as representations, they so closely mirror the material landscape we are navigating in real time. As Raymond B. Craib argues, drawing from Baudrillard's quote above, "Jean Baudrillard's choice of the map as an example is highly appropriate—no other image has enjoyed such prestige of neutrality and objectivity . . . The most oppressive and dangerous of all cultural artifacts may be the ones so naturalized and presumably commonsensical as to avoid critique." Thus, we tend to interact with our mobile maps without interrogating their mode of representation and the consequences. Users of maps employ them because they are reliable and only when they fail us does their interrogation come to the fore.

Another key distinction between pre-digital maps and current mobile maps is the ways in which users are able to contribute to and alter maps. User-generated content is one of the defining features of Web 2.0, and maps have also incorporated user data, imagery, and information to create new notions of spatial mapping. This is especially seen in many locative art projects that investigate this relationship between space and cartography. As Drew Hemment notes, "Digital mapping is at the core of many locative projects," in which artists explore modes of representing embodied movements through cartography. He specifically draws on examples like Esther Polak's *Amsterdam Realtime*, in which "participants roamed the streets of Amsterdam equipped with networked GPS devices, and traces of their movements were relayed to a projection screen in an exhibition space." The project demonstrates collaborative cartography that is deeply connected to users' bodies and their movements through everyday space. Here, mobile devices show the lived space of the city through the bodies navigating through space. Such a map can serve to represent the lived and embodied nature of that space. Another key example of this mode of mobile cartography is Christian Nold's *Biomapping* project. *Biomapping* offers a perfect example of the representation of space working in collaboration with mobile technologies and information visualization. The project, which began in 2004 and has thus far taken place in four cities including San Francisco, Paris, Greenwich, and Stockport, equips participants with a mobile device similar to the technology used on a polygraph machine that tracks their galvanic skin response (GSR), logs their GPS coordinates, and allows them to annotate their locations as they navigate the city on foot. As they walk, their stress is visualized on a map, with each person represented by a different color wall that traces their movement and shows the spikes when they experience heightened physical encounters. In his article on the uses of information visualization in the arts, Tom Corby nicely summarizes the procedures behind *Biomapping*:

> As part of the University of Westminster exhibition, self-selecting student volunteers were introduced to the project in a workshop situation. Each was fitted with a device and sent out on an hour-long walk of the university and its immediate environs, which includes a hospital and a densely built-up urban environment. While this was happening each student's changing location and level of arousal were sampled every 4 seconds by the device and the data downloaded to a memory chip. This information was then fed into Google Earth and visualized as three-dimensional forms to produce, what Nold calls, an "emotion map" of the area.

As they moved (and even after the fact upon reviewing their map) participants were able to tag certain locations they note as high stress or high stimulation areas. In San Francisco, for example, a participant tagged an area with, "Noticed an ambulance and decided to follow," which is then followed by the tag, "Could see the guy on the stretcher." As Chris Perkins writes about the project, "There is a relationship between GSR response and emotional arousal: anger, being startled, fear and sexual feelings can all produce similar responses. Using this system it is possible to construct individual tracks and display the ridges and troughs of emotion on a map. Results can be merged into composite maps reflecting wider social responses." Corby develops the consequences of user-generated mapping and annotations in *Biomapping*:

> These conversations allowed a number of interesting outputs to accrue. For example, consensual interpretive processes allow participants a deeper purchase on ownership of their data. By taking analysis and information-gathering out of the hands of experts, persons normally considered as "subjects" of study are enabled to construct understanding of results in any way they see fit. Thus, the work provides an alternative to institutionally directed visualization practices that is rooted in what Nold has described as social or "bottom-up" data gathering.

In *Biomapping*, the stark contrast between the aerial map and the visualizations of the participants' emotions demonstrates the equally harsh juxtaposition between the indexicality of the map (especially one that utilizes satellite or aerial photographs) and the notion that maps are ultimately lived and changing representations. Returning to Craib's argument that maps are so commonsensical that they avoid critique, the notion that a photograph, particularly a map that utilizes a photograph, could be wrong is easily dismissed by many. Here, satellite imagery, since it is removed from a human agent that takes the photograph, is often deemed as an accurate representation of a place at a particular moment in time. As I have argued elsewhere, though photographs have undergone scrutiny in the digital age, and their reliability as indices of reality is continually questioned (since photographs can be so easily manipulated with digital technologies), the satellite map has not undergone equal scrutiny. Instead, maps are seen as static representations of reality. One key reason for this is that the technologies used to capture map images like these are disembodied technologies, such as the satellite which does its work silently in our orbit without being manned or without a hand snapping the shutter closed. Because of the satellite's automation, there is no human subject implicated in the act of taking the photograph. The disembodiment associated with this mode of representation makes it seem more reliable, since human error or manipulation isn't woven into the process of creation. This false imaginary associated with satellite mapping is undone in Nold's *Biomapping*. What we are given in conjunction with the satellite map is a visualization of human movement throughout the mapped space, thus demonstrating that the space itself is constructed by human movement, not by disembodied technologies.

Our sensory-inscribed experiences of geographic space are always informed by the ways we represent that space. Here, *Biomapping* gives a representation of what it means to be a pedestrian in a crowded urban environment. We can immediately associate the city with the process of being embodied by the space. The map in Nold's project represents a lived locale, the practice of space that transforms it into lived place. These representations go far in dismantling the separation of the sensory body in space and the cultural inscriptions of that space. The map and the body are unified in a sensory-inscribed experience of the urban space.

The fact that *Biomapping* utilizes mobile technologies as its primary interface is significant in transforming the site of the map into a sensory-inscribed mode of implacement. The collaboration between the mobile device and GPS satellites positions the human body within space, yet it is the experience of that space coupled with a reading of the location that imparts meaning to the space. To elaborate, the act of walking through San Francisco offers one mode of sensory-inscribed engagement; to walk through the city with a mobile device provides further levels of implacement and signification. That is, while using a mobile device to trace my exact movements through a city and chart my emotional state, I experience my body in the city as being inscribed by the technologies that locate me. With these technologies, users are able to precisely know their location in space and time through GPS satellites. Simultaneously, users have to contend with the fact that they are being surveilled constantly, not only by the satellites but also by the people monitoring their emotional state through the GSR device and by passersby who inscribe the user's interactions with the mobile devices with certain significance (usually trying to "read" what you're doing and why you're there).

Another striking art project that works to redefine the uses of maps and representations of space is Paula Levine's *San Francisco<>Baghdad,* which is part of her series *Shadows from Another Place*. This project overlays a map of the city of Baghdad onto a map of San Francisco and, at each place where a bombing occurred in Baghdad, Levine maps corresponding points onto coordinates in San Francisco. Once these corresponding nodes have been created, Levine places a geocache container at each location. Her goal, one that resonates throughout her work as a whole, is to make the foreign something that is familiar. She writes, "Collapsing 'foreign' and 'domestic,' these maps bridge local and global, and allow walkers/viewers to experience spatial and narrative contiguity between separate and distant locations." This interplay between maps is drawn from the work in psychogeography by the Situationist International (SI), especially in the work of Guy Debord. Debord would encourage a wandering throughout the city (or, *dérive*), in which a wanderer would use a map from one city as the guide for another. The disjunction between the two would "contribute to clarifying certain wanderings that express not subordination to randomness but total *insubordination* to habitual influences." Debord continues: "A friend recently told me that he had just wandered through the Harz region of Germany while blindly following the directions of a map of London. This sort of game is obviously only a feeble beginning in comparison to the complete creation of architecture and urbanism that will someday be within the power of everyone." This reimagining of the relationship between wandering the city and the representation of the city space allowed for new embodied relationships to form between the wanderer and the urban landscape. As Mary Flanagan notes, "One of the significant intentions behind psychogeography, as Debord described it, was to be *mindful* of space in the method's open-ended, deliberately vague mission of encouraging people to explore their environment, usually the streets of the city." This mindfulness serves as a resistance for the inscriptions written into urban planning and design. Instead of following predetermined paths, which create predetermined relationships as prescribed bodies in space, the work of psychogeography seeks to find strategies to reimagine our relationship to urban space.

Levine's *San Francisco<>Baghdad* project, while offering a new mindfulness of the city, simultaneously subverts the militaristic foundations of GPS. By using a tool created by the United States military to critique the military, Levine's work allows participants to reimagine the uses of mobile and locative technologies and the ways we understand our representations of place. By mapping the city of Baghdad onto San Francisco using a mobile device, people engage the tension between embodied space and the tools used to signify place. Engaging this project also forces users to participate in an embodied way with the historical conflict between maps and empire. Here, subverting the map by using the very technologies designed by the power structures that typically draw the map, the grounded nature of the map as a static signifier comes into question. As Matthew Edney has argued in *Mapping an Empire*, "Imperialism and mapmaking intersect in the most basic manner. Both are fundamentally concerned with territory and knowledge." He continues by noting that the "maps came to define the empire itself, to give it territorial integrity and its basic existence. The empire exists because it can be mapped, the meaning of empire is inscribed into each map." In Levine's project, the map critiques the imperial agendas of the war in Iraq instead of reinforcing the power structures behind the map.

As seen in projects like *San Francisco<>Baghdad*, *Biomapping*, and *Amsterdam Realtime*, there are obvious correlations between representations of space and power structures. Maps are not simply representations of ontological reality; instead, they signify space in a very particular way that is designed to be read to fit with the current cultural hegemony. With mobile technologies, the ways that space is represented is a practice of lived space. The movement through space and the collaboration between material environment and representations of that environment inform an embodied meaning of space.

What these projects also demonstrate is that our experience of space is inherently tied to intersubjective modes of embodiment. Space is not only an individually lived experience but is always produced as a social experience. The sensory-inscribed body is developed out of a reciprocity that embodies the self as spatially related to others and also as inscribed as a particular body by others (as the self also inscribes the spaces and bodies around him or her). In fact, many of these spatial visualizations only find their true nexus when used by a community for a collective revisioning of lived space. Thus, there is a need for mobile mapping projects to move beyond the individual-centered design and begin to imagine the space of the mobile interface as a site for collaboration. Liqiu Meng, for instance, argues that "In mobile usage context, however, a geocentric map can hardly remain usable due to the following reasons: What a large target group needs is often much more than what is necessary for an individual user." To streamline the design and usability of a mobile map, it seems, it must be tailored for the individual. Again, such an approach prioritizes the mobile interface as designed for an individual and not as a community space. While this is understandable given the size and common usages of the mobile interface, such a statement overlooks the important ways that mobile devices and mobile maps can engage a community and become a space of dialog.

For example, when a massive earthquake hit the island country of Haiti in January of 2010, most emergency response organizations were unable to navigate through the destroyed landscape, since many of the roads in the area had not been adequately mapped by major mapping distributors like Google. The cartographers, using the crowdsourced mapping tool Open Street Map, responded to the need for emergency organizations to have maps that were not only accurate of the area (many roads, for example, were either not mapped, mapped incorrectly, or were no longer there) but could also be tailored to this situation. At that time, there were nearly 200,000 cartographers contributing to the Open Street Map project, many of whom worked directly with the Haiti earthquake crisis. The use of mobile phones for the mapping process after the earthquake allowed for rapid crowdsourcing of various information. For example, people would send Ushahidi, a volunteer organization that responds to global crises through digital technologies, a text message about emergencies and the status of roads. Ushahidi volunteers would then translate that information into visualizations on the Open Street Map of Haiti. One thing that is remarkable about this crowdsourced mapping project is how the stream of information involved people across vast geographical distances in a visualization of Haiti. The typical trajectory of one of the emergency SMS messages looked something like this: an SMS message is sent to Ushahidi's emergency number, 4636, that says, "I am with someone who was hit in the head. They pass out from time to time. Where can I find a neurologist? He's in Delmas 44, by the church Altagrace, which is across from the Texaco and the market Monsieur Henri." This message, however, was sent in Creole to the Ushahidi volunteers in Boston (none of whom spoke the language). Thus, Ushahidi mobilized many volunteers from the Haitian diaspora to translate the text message from Creole to English, to help categorize and rank the emergency, and to help locate the emergency on the map based on their knowledge of their homeland. The translated text would be sent back to Ushahidi, who would then send it on to the appropriate response groups such as the Red Cross or the Coast Guard.

As crowdsourced maps continue to emerge using mobile devices, it becomes evident that the mobile interface can become a collaborative space. Here, users can work together to create mobile representations that inform the lived space they traverse. In doing so, the digital space of the mobile device corresponds and permeates material space in meaningful ways. Likewise, as those identified as part of the Haitian diaspora, through interacting with these emergency maps, they are able to identify with a community that is geographically distant from them. They re-embody their former homeland, and by remembering the spatial relationships between landmarks, they can help create a visualization of the area that will help those on the ground in Haiti bring emergency relief to those in need. Here, we see that the phenomenologies of the imagination serve to embody our relationship to a place we consider home, no matter how distant, as well as link our body to the body of the community.

Producing Information Landscapes

Our representations of place using mobile media demonstrate the ways that mobile interfaces are transforming the information landscape around us. Our interactions with the landscape as an information interface is still in its infancy; however, some technologies are pointing the way to what future instantiations of mobile technologies could look like. Recently, I had my graduate seminar make a collaborative map showing all of the surveillance cameras on our campus at the University of Maryland. They formed four groups and split the campus into quadrants. Most of the students in the class had never created or altered a map before, so I hoped that the processes of cartography would provide them with a different embodied relationship with a space they perceive as commonplace. As the students began compiling their images with location data and camera type, I was (somewhat foolishly) shocked at the number of cameras on our campus. Pulling back to take in all of the pinpoints layered on top of the digital campus map offered a very different visualization of the space of our university. The assignment was designed to allow students to visualize the space they move through on a daily basis in a different way and thus transform their very sense of embodiment in that space. The production of this map by this group of students provided a clear example of the sensory-inscribed body: by inscribing the space as a space of inscription (through surveillance), their sensory perceptions collaborated with the various modes of inscription that are involved in the production of embodied space.

The students' responses were varying and fascinating. One student's reaction was similar to the many frustrations people feel about the age of participatory surveillance we are living in. She said, "Though we are mapping these cameras, they don't necessarily represent the current threats to privacy with so much data surveillance, personal information on Facebook, and everyone having a camera in their pocket on their cell phone. It worries me because I feel helpless trying to identify where the power structure is located these days." Another student noted how odd it felt to take a picture of another camera, especially how that act was "read." This moment for her was very much a sensory-inscribed moment of watching the self being watched and documenting that process. This sensory-inscribed experience was heightened when she and another student decided to go into the bank on campus and take pictures of all of the surveillance cameras inside. This led to another student coming to the realization about what the cameras were being used for in the first place:

> While the cameras are being placed under the guise of protecting people on campus, they aren't there to protect us. They are there to protect the University's assets and infrastructure. When we decided to see what the cameras were actually looking at, we noticed that they were focused on areas of the campus with a large number of computers or highly sensitive research equipment.

For the student, this realization transformed his conception of the campus as a surveilled space: it wasn't necessarily the disciplinary structure that Foucault described as a means to create citizen subjects, but instead becomes about protection of assets. The embodied relationship to this space emerges, therefore, as always in relationship to commodities. Bodies are not of worth in the lens of these cameras; instead, bodies can only be potential threats to the assets of the university.

These moments exemplify the transformations that can take place through interactions of sensory-inscribed bodies with mapping technologies. Whether it be discovering the purposes of surveillance cameras by mapping them, connecting a historical image and moment to our current experience of that location, or the community mapping of a city (such as the emotion maps of San Francisco or the crisis maps of Haiti), the ways we experience these spaces has everything to do with the representations we interact with of those spaces. Developing information landscapes—especially spaces we can collaborate in and contribute to—demonstrates that context is never grounded, but is instead lived, ongoing, and enacted. The role of these context-rich environments in transforming landscapes into information interfaces also demonstrates the role these visualizations play in our experience of community space as sensory-inscribed.

Part 2: Interviews

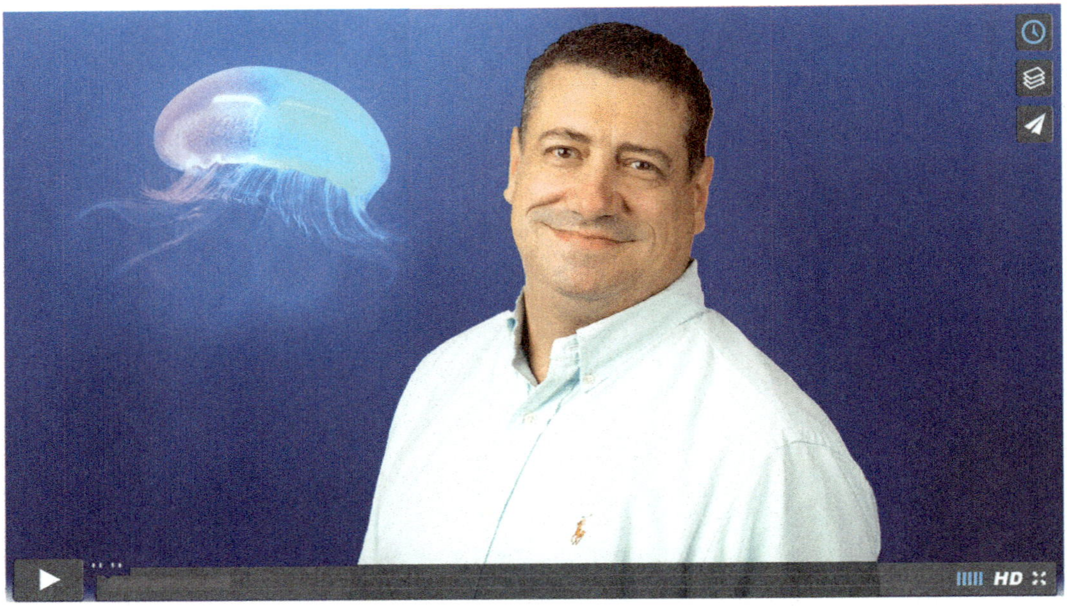

🔒 Sidney I. Dobrin on Augmented Reality

Sidney I. Dobrin is Chair of the Department of English at the University of Florida. He is the Director of the Trace Innovation Initiative, a research endeavor in UF's Department of English that supports interdisciplinary research at the intersections of ecology, posthumanism, writing studies, and media studies. He is the author and editor of many books and articles about these subjects.Dobrin image © 2016 by Sidney I. Dobrin and Jellyfish image by NG. Unsplash. Used by permission.

AURASMA
Scan this page to watch

Interview 1: Sidney I. Dobrin

Sean Morey: To start off with, can you tell us your background in academic textbook publishing?

Sid Dobrin: In 2003/2004, I published two readers with a small independent publisher, Mayfield Publishing. That experience taught me a lot about how to think about textbooks and the textbook industry. Soon after, I started experimenting with different ways to think about the function of textbooks, particularly in terms of media integration and the interfaces students use to access educational content.

In 2008, I co-authored a technical writing textbook for Pearson that was designed to really focus on the technological aspects of writing. During the course of writing that book and producing the second edition in 2010, I had the opportunity to spend a lot of time with different divisions within Pearson and to learn more about how that industry operates, how a publisher the size of Pearson was anticipating changes in technology, and how those changes would affect textbook design and sales. Sometime during the revision of the technical writing textbook, Pearson's English division (at the time technical writing books were handled by a different Pearson division) asked to meet with me.

During our initial meeting, one of the editors asked me to write a short document explaining what I saw as the possibilities for the next two generations of textbooks in terms of content trends, media applications, and technological applications. I found the assignment intriguing and delivered a document that offered my opinion not about the next three generations of textbooks, but about the next nine generations. This document was the first place I began to envision uses for AR technologies in the textbook industry.

Those early conversations with Pearson's English division led to the development of a first-year composition rhetoric that I wrote called *Writing Situations*. It was released in January, 2014, and though it does not have any AR technologies tied to it yet, it does integrate digital technologies beyond what other writing textbooks have to date. It is likely, too, that subsequent editions of the book will be strictly digital and will have AR assets.

In addition to *Writing Situations*, Pearson contracted me to write three writing handbooks, all of which integrate digital technologies in ways not yet seen with handbooks, including some conversations about AR applications.

I have also been talking with several people at Pearson about an approach to AR content delivery that I have been developing called "Smart Worlds," but admittedly, that conversation is in its infancy, despite early enthusiastic response from tech editors at Pearson.

SM: When did you become interested in AR from an academic or scholarly perspective?

SD: Probably on September 28, 1987. I know that seems uncannily exact, but that was the night that "Encounter at Farpoint," the first episode of *Star Trek: The Next Generation*, aired, that double episode that introduced us to the TNG crew and had that quick cameo by DeForest Kelley as the 137-year-old Admiral Leonard McCoy to give us contextual relationship to the original series. Yes, some might bristle at my use of Science Fiction to talk about AR, but SF provides very useful metaphors for talking about stuff we don't yet have ways to talk about. Besides, I'm an SF junkie—junkie, not scholar.

That first episode introduced the holodeck, a technology I've been fascinated by since. You see, the holodeck introduced a plausible simulated reality. It uses matter replication, tractor beams, transporter technologies, and force fields in conjunction with holographic projection to create simulated environments. In the world of film and TV, by the time the holodeck was introduced, we had seen three years earlier the "heads-up" display that the Terminator used to access information and evaluate response options. Even the movie poster had Schwarzenegger wearing sunglasses with digital text visible in the right lens, a kind of early Google Glass. The same year we got the holodeck, we also got that moment in *Running Man* when the TV tech guys digitally map the faces of Schwarzenegger and another character on to the images of two other actors. And four years before that we had Natalie Wood's last movie *Brainstorm* in which there was a system for recording people's experiences and playing them back in another person's brain, depositing the experience into the "listener" brain.

At the time, I didn't know that the holodeck wasn't necessarily a new idea, though. Back in the mid-1960s, Ivan Sutherland developed an idea he called the "ultimate display." What Sutherland was getting at was the ability to replicate physical reality to such a degree that whatever was presented inside the display would physically function in the same way the represented artifact functioned outside of the display. Sutherland imagined the possibility of the computer being able to display matter in the same way that matter functions in "reality." That is, Southerland imagined a virtual reality.

At the time the holodeck appeared, I was teaching programming, nothing fancy, just introduction to Basic. But I was also reading spatial theory. Coincidentally, I was also playing around with rotoscoping for the first time. I think the convergence of these various kinds of layering methods started me thinking about what we now call AR, though at the time, for me it was just a way of thinking about constructions and augmentations of visible and physical reality and Sutherland's VR ideas were only on my radar by way of rumors of VR gaming. The SF representations got me thinking a lot about the idea of masking and layering—interestingly, two primary metaphors now used in image work with softwares like Photoshop. I was intrigued by the idea of layering one representation atop another to either enhance the base layer or to create a completely different whole or even camouflage the base layer. I think this idea of layering has been an undergirding thought in most of what I've done throughout my career, perhaps most evident in *Postcomposition* when I address platforming and layering.

SM: Given the many textbooks you've written, how has AR progressed within the textbook industry from your first textbook to your latest? How does this change compare with the treatment of AR in academia more broadly?

SD: It hasn't. That is to say, from what I've seen, the textbook industry is not yet ready for AR delivery. I think this grows from a number of places. First, despite the textbook industry's claim to be more in-tune with mobile technologies and ubiquitous computing, a lot of this, it seems to me, is mere lip service. We have to remember that the textbook industry is primarily interested in sales, and textbooks are adopted not by students, but by faculty, a majority of whom are not welcoming of new technologies in their classrooms—particularly in fields like English where traditions of print and writing process dominate the zeitgeist. Likewise, and I speak from experience here, textbook publishers, because of their marriage to content ownership, often cite high cost of app development even when free development softwares are readily available. The AR softwares that you and I use are not considered viable by the industry because of concerns regarding intellectual property rights.

That said, I do see a lot of possibilities for using AR technologies within that industry. Of course, there are some real problems in saying so. AR offers a number of possibilities for rethinking the interface between student, information, and the world, but to tie those possibilities to an industry structured around the ownership of information and delivery mechanism inherently limits those possibilities in many ways. I do think, though, that as we explore aspects of AR that we're just now beginning to work through, like cognitive recognition softwares such as image recognition and facial recognition, these possibilities will both grow and will be unavoidable for educational fields like the textbook industry. These are certainly areas I plan to pursue further in my own research.

I think for now, the best we can hope for from the textbook industry in the immediate future might be some text-based augmentation technologies bound to traditional textbooks. For instance, on-page content might be augmented with apparatus and further content accessible through mobile devices that reveal layered content. Or, depending upon how copyright and permissions issues play out, we'll probably see more and more QR coding in textbooks. But beyond those kinds of evident augmentations, I'm not sure we'll see much in the next couple of textbook cycles.

As to academia, more generally, I think we'll see a more rapid integration of AR technologies than in the textbook industry simply because there are fewer limitations for experimentation. I'm thinking of faculty using AR in classes other than programming classes for a variety of purposes, including John Tinnell's class I observed in which he teaches AR as a form of writing.

SM: Do you plan to use AR in any current or future textbooks or academic works?

SD: Absolutely. As I mentioned earlier, I've already begun talking with some people at Pearson about an AR platform I've been working on and am designing specifically for rethinking and remaking traditional textbooks which function simply as content delivery mechanisms rather than as organic learning interfaces. Of course, if I want to fulfill this kind of thinking, I would need to embrace Andries van Dam's idea that the ideal interface is no interface.

And, I should say, too, that part of my interest in doing so grows specifically from what appears to me to be an overlooked niche in AR applications. James Kent, in his monstrous book *The Augmented Reality Handbook: Everything You Need to Know about Augmented Reality*, explains that as of 2011 AR applications are commonly used in twelve areas, one of which he identifies as "Entertainment and Education." I find it interesting that these are grouped together. He says that AR is used to create visual objects in museums and exhibitions, theme park attractions, games, and books. Interestingly, Kent seems to attach "books" here as an afterthought and as the thing that gets augmented. In March of 2011, Intel Capital, Partech, iSource, and Elaia partners invested $5.5 million in an AR company called Total Immersion to further its work in AR development for digital marketing, consumer products, events, retail, amusement parks, and museums. But none of this investment is geared toward education. Kent identifies ten potential applications that he sees as possible extensions of AR technologies; education is not listed as one of these. Kent and Total Immersion identify the growth AR development is seeing, but fail to identify the potential for the educational materials market. My feeling is that AR offers a lot of possibilities for education and that educators need to take up the opportunity—whether educators do so independently or through the textbook industry. The problem, of course, is that educators—particularly those of us in the humanities—have generally not been at the fore of software and technology development, waiting instead to debate the uses and values of technologies developed elsewhere. That is, we tend not to be makers or programmers. I think this is a constraint we necessarily must

> *"Educators in the humanities should be compelled to start making augmented reality tech specifically for what we do in the humanities. Of course, that's not to devalue the role of hacking in innovation, but hacking needs to be complemented with invention."*

exceed. Otherwise, we remain in the position of having to adapt our purposes and methodologies to tools designed for other uses. Such adaptation inherently situates the function of the tool as dominant over the purpose and method and, thereby, rewrites the purpose and methodology in the image of the tool. Educators in the humanities should be compelled to start making AR tech specifically for what we do in the humanities. Of course, that's not to devalue the role of hacking in innovation, but hacking needs to be complimented with invention, as well.

SM: How does incorporating AR into your books change the way you write them?

SD: First, when writing, I no longer think of textbooks as "books." Rather, the traditional book object is but one node of a more complex ecology of learning interfaces. In fact, in many ways, the traditional textbook becomes obsolete; unconnected, singular content delivery mechanisms offering limited and narrowly linear ways of thinking about and enacting education. Instead, I think of delivering not a closed system of content from book to reader, but delivering a full program of which the content is only one part. AR lets me rethink the content I write as being only one layer of the larger educational program I hope to deliver. Much of that program can be thought of as directional portals; that is, the platform serves primarily to direct students to near-endless possibilities of interaction between their objects of study, the program's content delivered as an augmented layer, the teacher's content as a layer, and then the network of layers that can be sourced through the Internet. Likewise, what AR provides is an opportunity to work with teachers and students through the AR platform to make each program customizable to the needs of the curriculum, the teacher's objectives, and the student's learning strategies. I suppose I'd say that with the AR frames I want to use, the emphasis is less on the content than it is on the ecology of the layers through which that content flows, expands, and reveals.

SM: What kind of content do you include, or do you see incorporated, into books that use AR? Do you think such content makes full use of AR's technology, or do you see room for innovation?

SD: Innovation is like Jell-O: there's always room for innovation. The moment anyone neglects innovation and accepts any technology, any methodology, any platform, or any content as sufficient, that is the moment that the rest of us should be alert to the neglect as a maneuver of hegemony. This is why hacking is central to innovation. Innovation is democratic; it refuses to let us rest on what we have achieved as the sole answer or possibility. Technology always strives to be nostalgia. Technology's value comes from its endeavor to become obsolete in the face of the next technology.

No content can ever make full use of any technology, AR or otherwise, including orality and print. This is why we have to stop thinking about the role of textbooks as content delivery, or, that is, we need to move away from the compulsion to continue to develop content delivery technologies in the shadow of textbooks. To do so is to shackle the very idea of content delivery—or perhaps more precisely, circulation—to an ideology of print. Part of this ideology is an imposition of limit, a naming of space and imposing boundaries. If we model circulation mechanisms—like what we might conveniently call AR textbooks—on the spatial ideology of print, we impose boundaries. For textbooks, this traditionally meant accounting for page limits, printing costs, distribution costs, permissions, copyright, and so on, even the space where the book could be accessed. Content in the textbook model is determined in part by the old joke about the *New York Time*'s motto "All the news that's fit to print" that it should really be "All the news that fits." Textbook thinking dictates content boundaries and linear movement through that content. If we think about content in a more ecological fashion, we can acknowledge that content is limitless and that we need to invent and innovate technologies that can provide departure points and transparent directions for navigating specific content pathways without restricting the user with "stay on the trail" directives. Of course, this kind of thinking runs counter to technology theorists like Neil Postman who argue that too much content, too much information, is detrimental to the very idea of humanism. In my view Postman and others who take up such positions are operating under their own will to nostalgia expressed in a doctrine of right and wrong and the belief that the loss of past values is inherently detrimental. I find such thinking fundamentally dangerous.

SM: Where do you think the demand for AR in academic textbooks, if any, is coming from? Publishers? Colleges and Universities? Students? Teachers?

SD: I think the word "demand" is a bit optimistic. From my perspective—and I can't speak to what happens with textbooks in the sciences, in engineering, or in many other disciplines—there is no demand. In fact, I'd say that AR is just now showing up on a few publishers' radars and many of them are hesitant to fully embrace the possibilities yet. I think we are still very early in the AR era and it's going to take some time before we see a larger commitment from the industry.

There are a couple of models that explain this kind of response to technological innovation. One that I find particularly useful as a way of thinking through these kinds of changes is the familiar linear model of innovation which comes out of actor-network theory and ideas about social influence on the evolution of technology. This model simply proposes that technology moves from invention to innovation to diffusion. For AR technologies when it comes to textbooks, I think we have to admit that we are still very early in an innovation phase. Of course, movement through the phases of the linear model can be generated by either technological push in which the technology reveals the possibilities and the innovators develop uses for the technology or by the market-pull in which the market demands technologies be developed for specific needs or desires. For textbooks, we are seeing a technology push, not a market pull. This may shift at some point, but the conditions for such a change to occur are fairly complex and include a cultural and generational shift in textbook adopters who are less bound by the specter of print.

SM: We often hear the criticism that new technologies are too quickly introduced into the classroom without much forethought on their effects or best practices for their use. Do you think this is the case with AR? In other words, what do you think are its pedagogical benefits to students? What can AR do better than traditional classroom technologies, or at least those that are well entrenched and accepted?

SD: This is an interesting question, but I want to twist it a bit because the question seems to over-simplify the variables. That is, the question seems to define and defend classrooms, the institutions that manage the spaces of those classrooms, and the very idea of what constitutes pedagogy. That is, it seems to want to validate AR in particular kinds of pedagogical situations by way of those institutions.

When it comes to technology, any technology, there will always be criticism. There *should* always be criticism. Without criticism innovation is stymied. When it comes to things like classroom pedagogy, the kinds of criticisms of newly-introduced technologies you seem to allude to generally emanate from skepticism—and that's a good thing—and nostalgia—and that's a bad thing in this case. We should all always be skeptical about technology, about pedagogy, and about technologies used in partnership with pedagogy. But, we should not cling to the memories of previous technologies as somehow better or better for us than the new technologies simply because we have a place for them in our hearts. This kind of criticism, the kind that says bringing new technologies to classrooms removes the things that were already good about classrooms, can only stifle innovation.

Now, your question about technologies being too quickly introduced implies a concept of use-value situated in a culture of convenience. That is, you seem to imply that there is already an idea of what is useful to students and a question as to whether AR technologies can offer some benefit to such ends. To be honest, I don't really care whether they do or not. I am less interested in technological development for pedagogical purposes when those purposes pre-establish what pedagogy might be. That is, as I twist your question, I'm more interested in how AR—or other tech—might change how we think about and enact pedagogies. Thus, when you ask what are AR's pedagogical benefits, I'd have to say that its greatest benefit is its potential to not be part of the pedagogies we rely on, but to aid in the emergence of new pedagogies.

SM: AR has the potential, like many social media applications, for user-generated content, or in this case, student-generated content. Does AR provide a means through which students can truly interact with a textbook, or do you see it as simply another piece of information to study and consume as if it were any other content?

SD: As I suggested earlier, I don't view AR as either simply a new content delivery mechanism or as simply a kind of content itself. Rather, I think of AR as a way of rethinking the interface between content networks and various nodes within those networks, including but not limited to students and teachers. Thus, I don't see AR technologies as providing a more dynamic interaction between student and textbook, but I see this as the opportunity to stop thinking of textbooks as spatially constrained content vessels. Instead, content is endless and, yes, crowdsourced, which, of course, opens the doors to the same pitfalls we witness in any crowdsourced content. But, when framed within a specific academic context, it is not just the crowdsourced content with which students engage, but learning the ethics of crowdsourcing and the rigor of content scrutiny.

I think Vernor Vinge's *Rainbows End* does an excellent job of articulating a vision of how AR technologies, mobile technologies, ubiquitous computing, and networked technologies might cohabitate with pedagogy. Whether in classrooms or at home or wherever, most people are perpetually wired into the network through wearable technology. Most interactions occur through contact lenses and content is downloaded at near instant speeds with just the twitch of an eye. Thus, no matter the context, individuals are able to search content in every situation, including crowdsourced and interactive content. Likewise, all content can be verified through streams of users all working with the same content. What's great about Vinge's depiction is that it's neither apocalyptic nor utopian; it is functional.

SM: When we think of AR and textbooks, we probably mostly think of print-based AR, augmenting the textbook itself with images, video, or 3D models. How could location-based AR help make textbooks a mobile textbook, and what do you think might be the education benefits of this?

SD: This to me is the key. We're seeing a few textbooks start to incorporate the kinds of text-based AR that you're talking about. Some are including QR codes on pages, but even that is relatively new and is also already problematic because of copyright concerns regarding hot links either via URL or QR. However, location-based and mobile AR is what I see as having the most potential. This is specifically what I am thinking about with the Smart Worlds platform I mentioned earlier.

Essentially, these kinds of mobile AR technologies dissolve the idea of the textbook and the idea of the classroom. For many disciplines in which field work or archive work is predominant, these kinds of AR interventions show a lot of promise for redevising how we teach and how students learn outside of the classroom. Certainly, there are some fields where the applicability is not immediately evident—writing instruction, for example—but I imagine those will develop as well.

SM: I take your point about considering pedagogy beyond the classroom, at least as we traditionally understand it, and we can think of a future ubiquitous classroom as ubiquitous computing continues to grow. Thinking about how AR can introduce new pedagogies in this new idea of a ubiquitous classroom, I was wondering if you could talk more broadly about what you see as the relationship between pedagogy and AR?

SD: In response to the question (or the suggested question) about the relationship between AR and pedagogy, I'd have to say that my worry in asking such questions is that pedagogy will be reduced in this thinking to asking how AR can be used to teach students in traditional classroom settings as just another tool to use in traditional situations. I see why that is a practical kind of question, but I'm more interested in how AR will affect larger pedagogical approaches to interaction with the world. That is, I want to think about the possibilities that emerge when AR users begin to naturalize AR into the daily condition of experience. I mentioned before the image Vinge articulates regarding the use of AR and pedagogy, and what fascinates me about that articulation is that while, yes, he imagines the use of AR in the classroom, he also sees AR as a way of navigating daily life. That kind of navigation, I'd argue, requires a different kind of daily pedagogy, a kind that reconsiders traditional pedagogical approaches like recognition, recall, organization, analysis, evaluation, application, and scaffolding not necessarily as processes or even as progressive, but, perhaps, as saturation, as the primary mediation of access to "reality." That's the kind of pedagogy I'm more interested in than simply classroom application. But, of course, our current situation also demands attention to that traditional understanding of pedagogy. I'm ok with that because I know that the introduction of AR into those familiar classroom situations will open doors for other possibilities, particularly as students play with AR and see the possibilities for their lives outside of the classroom.

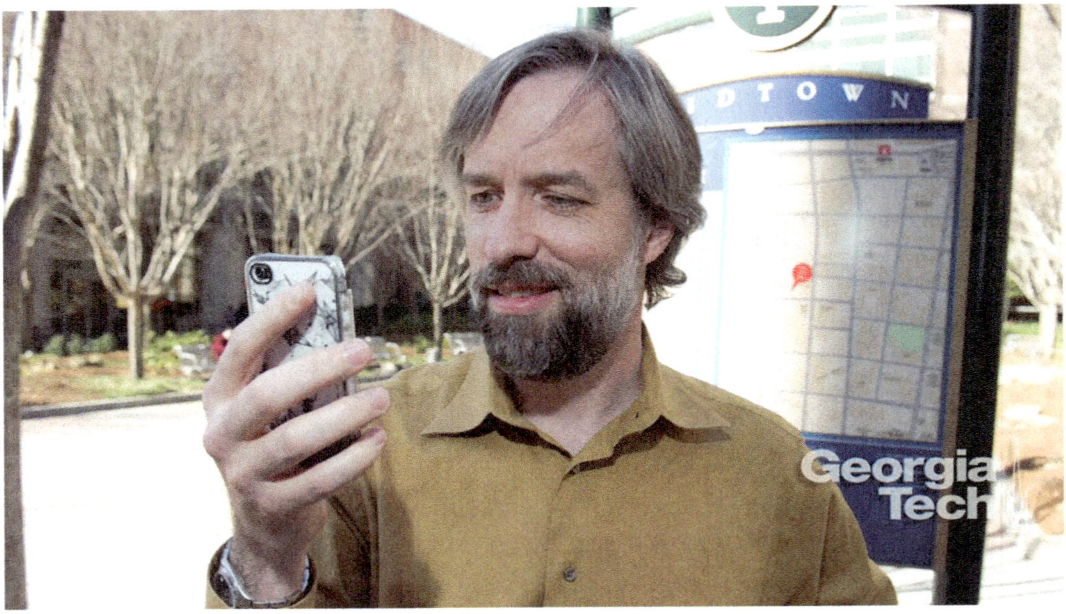

Blair MacIntyre is a Professor in the School of Interactive Computing in the College of Computing at the Georgia Institute of Technology. At Georgia Tech, he founded and directs the Augmented Environments Lab, which includes the Argon AR Web Project and the AR Game Studio. Along with Ian Bogost, he co-founded and co-directs the Georgia Tech Game Studio. His research focuses on the design and implementation of interactive mixed-reality and augmented-reality software, games and experiences, aimed at understanding the potential of AR as a new medium for games, entertainment, education, and work. He consults regularly with industry on topics related to AR, with companies big and small, in industries as diverse as chip manufacturing and video games. Photograph © 2011 by Georgia Tech. Used by permission.

AURASMA

Scan the image to watch

Interview 2: Blair MacIntyre

John Tinnell: In the early 1990s, you were among the first researchers in computer science to do work on augmented reality. What drew you to it so early?

Blair MacIntyre: My initial involvement with AR was mostly luck. When I arrived at Columbia University for graduate school, my advisor (Steven Feiner) had just started to work on AR. So I ended up being in the right place at the right time, and one of the first students working on AR in Steve's lab. VR was all the rage at the time. I look around now, and see the excitement with low cost devices like the Oculus Rift; everybody is talking about how VR is going to be the ultimate for games, but back then companies were making head mounted displays with trackers in them that you could hook up to a computer and use to play games. While the technology was a lot worse, people were pretty excited about VR back then, too. It didn't really interest me, however. For me, VR was all about cutting yourself off from the world. You could imagine that if VR reached the quality of the Star Trek holodeck, that it might be able to become a truly immersive experience—but VR was nowhere near that back then, and it is still a long way from that. A lot of the work that people were doing in VR with data gloves and other interaction devices didn't have an appeal for me, even though I was into 3D graphics and gaming. AR was much more about bringing stuff *out of the computer* and *into the world*. You can still create games and other 3D experiences, but with AR you could actually create immersive experiences without cutting people off from each another. So, AR held out the promise that, I can be sitting here looking at you and there can be graphics floating around us, is much more interesting and appealing to me than having us both putting on VR head-mounts and going into the holodeck together.

JT: Looking back almost 22 years later, has AR evolved in the way you expected it to? What have been some of the big surprises?

BM: Looking back, I don't think that any of us predicted smartphones. When I came to Georgia Tech 14 years ago, the AR community was fixated on head-mounts. The future was going to be one with see-through head mounts, where you would see graphics overlaid on the world around you. We knew the technology would get smaller, faster, and lighter; that was assumed. We all knew that batteries were going to be a perpetual problem, and they still are. But I don't think any of us, back then, predicted that smartphones would be the first major platform for AR. So now, instead of creating the head-worn ecosystems that we imagined when we built the Touring Machine (1997) and other outdoor AR experiences, we see something very similar delivered on a handheld platform.

JT: Do you think the progression toward the phone was just a matter of social convenience—using a device that people already carried around with them? Is that why it went that way?

BM: I started working on handheld AR in fall 2006, after a few other researchers had been exploring how to use them. But none of us felt that the phone was a great platform for AR. Even now, there are still people in the augmented reality research world that look down their noses at handhelds. You have to hold the phone up, it's not immersive, it's not hands-free, and so on. But we started to use the platform, and still do, because of exactly what you suggest; the idea that you could deliver *an* AR experience, even if it wasn't *the ideal* AR experience, to gadgets that people actually have and use. The fact that I have to take out my phone, fire it up, unlock it, go to an app, then finally look around—that still makes it impossible to do most of the things that you might want to do with AR. But still, the fact that you are carrying it around means that you can do *some* things.

JT: Let's talk more about what the rise of smartphones has meant for augmented reality, both in terms of academic research and popular culture. In a lot of recent publications, you write about the current state of AR with mobile apps in mind. How would you describe the relationship between the hardware marketed by the major tech companies, on the one hand, and, on the other hand, scholarship and computing prototypes developed in university research labs?

BM: There are still people using both platforms. There are more people in the research and commercial world doing computer vision and enabling technology research on the mobile phones right now than there used to be. It's exciting to see people trying to figure out how to solve these problems and figure out how to do things on these increasingly-powerful devices, which they couldn't have done even a short while ago.

There are probably two sides of the academic world. There are people who still insist that AR should be done on head-mounted displays, and work on head-mounted platforms. For example, Steve Feiner did some really good work a few years ago with Steve Henderson exploring how to create a jet engine repair system for the military, and they did a study of the effectiveness of AR along with it. I think most researchers in the academic world are focused on the mid- to distant future, and now that AR on phones is more mature, even my lab (the Augmented Environments Lab at Georgia Tech) is going to be doing a lot more work with head-mount displays in the near future, both by reviving a bunch of our old head mounts and by taking advantage of new devices like the Oculus Rift, by adapting them to support video-mixed AR. A lot of us began working with smartphones because when handhelds were a new platform, we thought they'd be useful, but nobody was doing much AR with them yet. There were some games, then Layar, Wikitude, and other AR browsers came along in the last few years. Now it's gotten to the point where, when you combine Qualcomm's Vuforia SDK with Unity3D, you have a full featured 3D game engine for AR, which opens the medium up to a huge variety of people. For me, as an academic, I have to be doing something that is a step ahead of industry or different; academic research should be pushing boundaries and not just competing with industry. A lot of the work that most of us have done over the last five or six years with handhelds is now possible for many people to do with Unity and Vuforia. So now many of the researchers like me are moving back to working with head mounts. I think it's partly because the head mounts are getting better and more accessible. Google Glass, as an example, doesn't support AR in the way that I think of AR. But it will open up the space for more people to explore what's possible with head mounts. I'm actually hoping that, once people start to see what is possible with Google Glass and what isn't possible with Google Glass, they will start to understand that there is a difference between a heads-up display

"Many researchers like me are moving back to working with head mounts . . . Google Glass, as an example, doesn't support augmented reality in the way that I think of AR. But it will open up the space for more people to explore what's possible with head mounts."

and being able to merge media with the world, especially for certain kinds of applications.

JT: And then focus might shift back to the newer head mounts being developed in university labs?

BM: It's interesting. Part of me is pessimistic that it's going to be really hard to go to the next step. When you look at what it would really take to build a head mount that could deliver an experience that would be stable, that people would wear, and that would look good—it's not clear to me how that's going to be possible. I actually don't see us going beyond Google Glass in the consumer space anytime soon. I actually like the design they did because they managed to do something that is self-contained and that will be able to deliver some set of experiences well. It's pretty much as good as it could be for something you can actually deliver right now.

JT: With the promise of wearable AR—in the far future perhaps—what is the value of projects being created for mobile AR today? (For example, some of the recent projects like *Voices of Oakland* that you've worked on at Georgia Tech.) Is it a matter of building up examples of what is possible, showing different use cases, or helping us imagine why we would want something like wearable AR?

BM: I think that phone-based AR (something like *Voices of Oakland* or a tour of Gettysburg) can provide a rich multimedia experience. I can have audio, video, and photographs on my phone. I can be walking around listening to the audio while taking in and appreciating my surroundings. Every now and again I can look at a video or look at pictures. Or I can hold up the phone and get an AR vignette. So for a focused tour experience where you are going to be stopping and engaging with a bit of AR content by looking through the phone for a minute and then moving on—I think that current hardware can be effective. You're not going to be able to deliver a fully immersed AR tour of Gettysburg because you can't walk around holding the phone up the whole time. But it's not clear to me that that's what you'd want anyway. When you are at a historic site, you'd really like to be looking at the place itself and talk to the people you're there with. So, things like historic tours and focused educational experiences will be able to deliver effective experiences on current mobile devices. Of course, there are still technical challenges such as tracking. How could I create 3D registered

AR experience in a cemetery, a historic battlefield, or in an old crumbled castle?

JT: Challenging in those cases because . . . you're dealing with surfaces that aren't flat and objects that aren't well defined?

BM: All of that. Computer vision based tracking is hard in natural environments. If you go somewhere like Oakland Cemetery, you have mausoleums and headstones that are generally fixed in place. They might fall over or get renovated or they might break, but that's a gradual change. Using something like Kinect Fusion, you can imagine putting a backpack on and just walking around the cemetery to build a huge real-time 3D model of the cemetery. Then you could imagine, every month or two, someone walks around again and updates as things break or shift. When depth sensors are integrated in phones, the updates could happen more regularly. So, I can imagine using a process like that for modeling and tracking. But even if you have a model like that, there are other issues such as lighting, changing seasons (do the trees have leaves or not?), debris on the ground, and people walking around. A real natural environment like that would just be *incredibly hard* to create a robust, reliable experience in. We're doing some Argon-based tour projects right now. One of the original motivations was that there are many applications, like tours of historic sites, for which building an app isn't feasible. Apps are expensive. Historic sites are usually non-profits and traditionally don't have a lot of money. And maintaining apps once they're developed is also expensive.

JT: They need a platform.

BM: Yes. And, ideally, it needs to be a platform that does not have the complexity and overhead associated with stand-alone apps. You can imagine Gettysburg or Oakland installing their own Wi-Fi network over the whole area. It's a little bit of overhead, but it's not that expensive—it's doable. Their Web servers already have all of their content on them. And so, delivering an experience using Web technologies is actually pretty feasible. It's certainly much more feasible than building a whole app, repurposing and bundling their content into the app, and having to deal with updates . . . a lot of that becomes untenable for non-profits. Consider how many people are using Layar's AR browser and similar apps right now. Layar is good for what it is; it is fine for putting virtual signage in the world. If you wanted to do a rich, dynamic multimedia project, something like the *Three Angry Men* project that we did or *AR Façade* (a room-sized game we built), or really any other complex system where you want to have complete control over the presentation and have it be a much richer multimedia experience, browsers like Layar and Wikitude aren't going to get you there. The thing that these browsers are really good at is discovery. But, beyond spatial discovery, authors also need to have complete control over everything—the presentation, the interaction, etc.—at least at the level the Web gives them. That's why we took the Web-based approach with Argon. We wanted to say, "You can build something, you can leave it on your website, you have complete control, you can update or tweak it as much as you want without having to go through much hassle, and people can just have one app where they can access it all." Cleary, in something like Argon, we need to have a method for spatial discovery. We could imagine building Layar channels that are just icons that link off and redirect into Argon. Better would be to build a geo-search kind of website, the equivalent of Google, for Argon.

JT: I'm in much the same position as those historical sites you mentioned. As a teacher who wants to do augmented reality projects in undergraduate multimedia courses, I can't expect my humanities students to build their own app. Having a robust and reliable platform that can support these projects is absolutely key. You've been mentioning Argon—the AR browser you've developed at the Augmented Environments Lab. Could you elaborate on how Argon is different from other AR browsers such as Wikitude and Layar?

BM: When we started the Argon project, we envisioned it as being like the other AR browsers, but being Web-centric rather than AR-centric. We referred to it as an AR Web browser back then. The idea was that you would start up in AR view but would have to explicitly go to a Web URL. Along the way, we created a modified version of KML called KARML that let you build Web-based AR experiences. You had a lot of the power of the native Web browser, supplemented with AR technology. Based on what we've learned from that initial version, we've moved away from the idea of an AR Web browser. Instead, we're focusing more on the key difference between something like Argon and AR browsers like Layar or Wikitude: the Web. We are taking an even more Web-centric approach now. We are still going to build and ship an app, Argon, which is best thought of as a Web browser like Dolphin, Mercury, or Chrome—except we are including an assortment of AR technology in it. The first version is built on top of Qualcomm's Vuforia, and will expose Vuforia up into JavaScript. But websites built with the Argon JavaScript libraries are created like normal websites, and Argon will be another Web browser on your phone. But when the webpage or Web app that you visit is written with our Argon JS library, it would notice that you are running on top of Argon and be able to access all of the AR functionality provided by the browser, just as websites can leverage plugins and other browser-specific functionality. The focus, then, is on exposing AR capabilities into the Web. The reason we are explicitly thinking of this separation between the JavaScript and the browser is that over time we want the JavaScript to run on as many browsers and platforms as possible, and support designers in adapting to the capabilities of those platforms. We've already got an initial version working on the desktop that sits on top of Google Street View instead of using live video and the phone's orientation and GPS sensors. The content can be written independently of the underlying technology when appropriate, so when you look around the Street View panoramic images, your AR content can be there and you can move around, just as if you were outside at that location.

JT: That seems like a great way to test an AR project, especially when you're working on something intended for a remote location you can't visit.

BM: Originally, we were thinking that this would be great for testing. But the other side of it is for delivery and re-use. One of the features we had in the first version of Argon was the support for geo-located panoramic images that we called "geospots." We started making a tour of campus using geospots. It's nice because you can build this geospot-based tour so that when you are standing at the geospot you have perfect tracking, because you've surveyed the point that the panorama was taken from. So when you look around, there's no error. With the new Web-centric approach, your content can be delivered regardless of whether someone is using something like Google Street View, Street Side View in Bing, or your panoramas. A historic site could build the entire tour, have it on their website, and people—not just those who physically come to the site—could get this entire experience and benefit from it.

JT: It seems like organizations would be more excited about creating really substantial AR projects if they can be on physical site *and* on the Web.

BM: We've talked to some historic sites and from an educational perspective they are very interested in this possibility. When you have a site that has a lot of classrooms full of kids coming, they are very interested in supporting pre- and post-experiences. Now you have a way to start creating teacher curricula or material for parents; they go and look at the website and get the kids educated or just excited to go visit. It can be the *same* content because it's in the *same* database on the *same* server app. When they go to the historic site, they can already have prepared a mobile curricula based on what they did on the Web. But now they can have AR bits aligned with where they actually are. To me, that is the key—the more we talk to people about real problems or real experiences, they rarely want to create something that is AR-centric—just like people don't talk about creating "3D" apps anymore. They might use 3D when it's the right thing to do. If you are doing an art project or something that is a self-contained experience, you can imagine it being AR-only. But imagine designing an AR maintenance app for a car engine, like the AR prototype we built in 1991 for printer maintenance. In a real system, the AR part only is going to be one mode of viewing, embedded inside a much larger app that will have all these other capabilities that you would use to support the repair task, such as looking things up or running diagnostics. Once you have the ability to have an AR mode, and then you combine that with the ability to have an AR mode that's on a desktop instead of on-site, then you can start supporting distributed collaboration. As soon as you just start thinking about adding AR to the Web and adding AR capabilities to different modes of presentation on the Web, all of the sudden you have a whole range of collaborative possibilities opening up to you, remotely or even just locally. It's really easy to do collaborative experiences on the Web; it's really easy to do persistent experiences on the Web. When you think about the difficultly you would have in creating stand-alone AR apps, especially in doing things like a persistent state or having two or three people collaborating or experiencing the same thing together or seeing different views on the same thing, it's horribly complicated to imagine doing that with the AR tools that we have right now. But when you compare it to the Web—if I wanted to have three people looking at the same document on the Web—it's kind of a no-brainer. Over time, I can easily imagine Argon, the browser, disappearing because there are a host of emerging Web standards that do a lot of what we're doing in Argon. There will be native code extensions at some point and the JavaScript compilers will get faster. There's Web RTC for doing video access. And there's WebGL for doing graphics, which we're using when we can. And so on. All of a sudden, at some point, you'll be able to run a Web app built with Argon on mobile Opera or mobile Firefox and get a mobile AR experience without having to install something new.

JT: That seems like it will be a much more feasible model of growth for AR—integrating AR into the Web rather than opposing it to the Web. Back to AR and education: the Web is impacting education at all levels in major ways (various e-leaning initiatives, massive online open courses, etc.). How do you think AR (as a dimension of the Web) stands to enhance learning and education? Does it offer another version of getting beyond the traditional classroom—one that makes learning more experiential and place-based?

BM: I think it depends on the educational experience you are doing. At Georgia Tech, there's a few courses that we are running on Coursera right now. When the first set of these courses were being planned, they wanted me to do an AR course. I would love to, but I didn't at the time because if you were actually going to teach a class on AR, you'd want people to be *doing* AR. The current Coursera/Udacity/MOOC setup isn't really amenable to that. The thing I would love to do with an augmented reality MOOC is build a website or a Web application, like people are currently using for some MOOCs, but enable people to create AR exercises wherever they happen to be. Imagine a situation where you are teaching about outdoor AR experience design. Tell people "go to a street corner near them and mark its location." Then go 200 feet up one street and 200 feet up the other street, and now they're led to create something on that street corner. So you can lead people through exercises where you send them off to "find things that match the template of an experience" and then they tailor it to their local culture and setting. Or imagine you have a unit where we're going to talk about the limitations of GPS. We can have them go outside and build small tests to study the effects. You can imagine creating more things like that, where you could literally have people create localized assignments all over the world and people could see each other's work if they happen to be near each other. Then there's another side to it. You could leverage AR to teach kids some basic Euclidian geometry—or anything that's spatial or has to do with measurement, or anything that maps well into the world. You could use AR to teach architecture, building management, construction, and all these outdoor topics. We actually built an AR version of Second Life years ago. We had an AR client that enabled you to map a part of second life into a physical space, and it let people from around the world come together in a live AR experience.

JT: You write about that in the collaborative essay with Jay Bolter in the book *Throughout: Art and Culture Emerging with Ubiquitous Computing*, right?

BM: Yes, there we were talking about digital performance and how we used this platform. The original motivation for that project was that I wanted to create a platform to allow people to create AR machinima. We figured, if we used an MMO, there could be a group of people sitting anywhere controlling the characters while the movie was being recorded live with the actors. It was a failure for that goal, actually, because in Second Life it's too hard to control avatars and objects precisely, but it was pretty cool in terms of what you could do with it in other ways. A lot of people were using Second Life as a platform for collaboration (or trying to). IBM had islands, and all these other companies had islands. There were a lot of education areas, and so on. It was like a massive platform that worked everywhere, that gave you 3D capabilities like spatialized sound. Any number of people could come together in these virtual spaces for free. You could have a "meeting" in these worlds. People had a sense that if the experience was more embodied, somehow, then remote collaboration might be better. At the same time, Sun Microsystems had created this system called Wonderland, which was also a collaborative 3D world but was not created in response to Second Life (it just happened to be created at around the same time). Unlike Second Life, Wonderland was actually designed for real work. You could use any of the OpenDoc file editors—their Java-based versions of Word and Excel—and actually have live documents on walls in an environment. They had much better controls over things like how people could hear each other in audio and how they could control awareness. It was easier to add media and so on. Sun open-sourced the project before they went out of business, so it's out there now; there's an Open Wonderland website you can go to download it and contribute to it. We experimented with creating a mixed reality experience to work with that platform. So, you and I are sitting here talking right now—imagine that we had a virtual world where people who aren't here could come and see us as avatars and we could see their avatars around us. Now, imagine further, we could have avatars sitting in the chairs beside us if we had head mounts on. They would see our avatars (or they may see video). We were mostly interested in experimenting with using the virtual world as the central structuring metaphor where all the content was to draw people together and facilitate collaborations where the remote participants didn't feel disenfranchised like they do with audio and video conferences. People who were in coffee shops or wherever could individually go there and they could have that sense of spatial collaboration and spontaneity. So, I go in there and I see your avatar. I can talk to you and ask you questions. (There has been research showing that the spatial nature and the social nature of these 3D environments does offer some benefit over a basic chat room.) Then, you could, at the same time, create physical team rooms that link into that space, so if there are groups together they get the benefits of co-located collaboration with the remote people being able to join in some ways. Going back to your previous question, I can imagine from a MOOCs perspective that's where the potential power could be. You could imagine a world like Second Life that could scale to 40,000 people and we could create this big, distributed world where all the people in Atlanta that are taking this MOOC could get together. You could then create these team rooms based on location. Or, you could do it not by geography but by teams people chose to form. When I log in, I could see the ten people in my group, and we can now collaborate together. If some of us are local, we could possibly meet up and be physically together. It was our original fantasy to create these mirror worlds. I think of it not as an augmented reality for MOOCs, but rather a kind of mixed reality, or mixture of AR and VR. That has a lot of interesting potential. The biggest problem with MOOCs right now is the dropout/failure rate. When you look at some of the numbers, they are having 40,000 to sign up, but then there is only a 1 or 2% completion rate. When you look at the demographics of those who complete MOOCs, it's clear that most MOOCs do not fulfill the original vision, which was making this content available to people who otherwise couldn't go to college. Most people doing MOOCs are people with college degrees who are doing them in the evening. Education is not just about content delivery; it requires a sense of community. I feel it's necessary for MOOCs to be broken down into smaller groups. I signed up for a MOOC on education that MIT is running right now and they break everyone down into groups, but even then it's all faceless; there's no sense that anyone cares if I'm there. I just can't help but feeling you need to have better support in terms of integrating it into your life, so that I can have casual conversations or if I pop in to see the content when I have time there might be some other people there. You could begin to create support systems to improve things.

JT: Could you describe the mission or goals of the Augmented Environments Lab at Georgia Tech, which you direct?

BM: Our lab is really interesting. We are trying to understand what makes for useful, usable experiences. It's focused on the experience of AR in the world. I decided to call it the "augmented *environments* lab" instead of an "augmented reality lab" because, when I started it, I was really interested in augmented reality as *one* aspect of this whole collection of off-the-desktop worlds. Back then, it was actually much simpler; there was AR and there was ubiquitous computing. I really liked the idea of mixing them. (I didn't want to just focus on AR, but, in the end, a lot of what we've done is AR.) The process that we've followed is to start with the tools. There is a long sequence of toolsets that we've built (such as DART, AR Second Life, and Argon) aimed at enabling people who aren't computer scientists to work with AR. We've tried especially hard to avoid caricatures of non-technologists (a lot of tools that you see are aimed at people who can't program). My experience of working with digital media designers and artists is that they are quite capable of doing a lot if the tools are well defined and robust. I'm always amazed at the kinds of things that people who aren't programmers can build in Flash and Director. They don't think of themselves as programmers, but they are programming because they are modifying scripts and behaviors. Our usual approach has been to find a toolset used by a group of people who are building non-AR experiences, and then try to add AR capabilities to that toolset. First, it was Director, then Second Life to a certain extent. And now it's the Web.

JT: Many Augmented Environments Lab projects feature collaboration with scholars in the arts, humanities, digital media studies, etc. How have these cross-disciplinary partnerships been important to your research and the Augmented Environments Lab at large?

BM: It's always been about collaboration. In some ways, collaboration has completely changed my life. It completely changed my research. Before I came to Georgia Tech, I had been collaborating, but only with technology people. When I first got to Georgia Tech, I had some ideas about traditional computer science work I was going to do. And the very first semester I was there, Jay Bolter gave a talk at the GVU Center's weekly Brown Bag on *Remediation*, the book of his that had just come out. As I was listening to the talk, I realized that even though he wasn't talking about AR, everything he said applies to AR. It's so easy to see how AR might evolve, if you just step back and ask what we know about other spatial media such as film or stage. Remediation introduced me to the notion that you build things in a new medium by, in effect, riffing on what the consumers of the media know. Like taking your understanding of what they know culturally, what they know about media, and leveraging that. I had no background in digital media, nor much in the humanities. I did a Math and CS degree at the University of Waterloo, which is very much a technology focused school, and then did a CS PhD, so I had no liberal arts background when I started at Georgia Tech. Fortunately, for me, Jay was the right person to collaborate with because he had both a technical and humanities background and was very interested in collaborating with technology folks. So, we just started teaching together; that next semester we co-taught a seminar. We've been collaborating ever since. I've also collaborated with Tony Tseng at the Savannah College of Art and Design's Atlanta Campus, where he does a lot of teaching in their Games program. If you look at all the projects I've done since I came to Georgia Tech, almost every one of them has been collaborative. To me, it's a very interesting comment on the university environment. Georgia Tech has always ensured that collaborative work counts toward the career of everyone involved (as opposed to a lot of universities, where collaborations count for nobody because it's not clear who does what). For me, in terms of the work I've done, collaboration is where all good ideas and good work comes from.

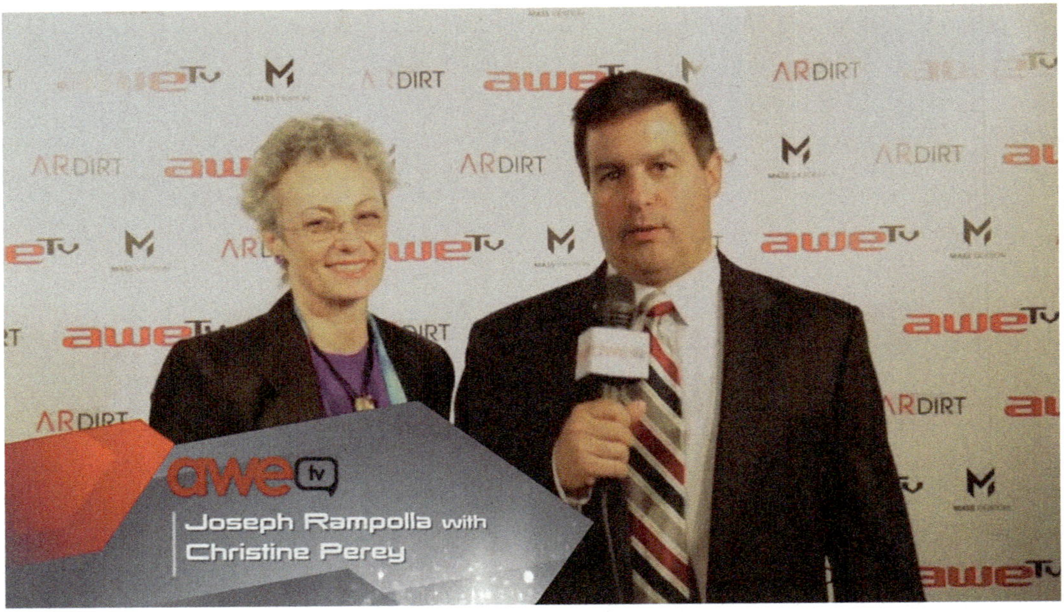

Christine Perey is an evangelist with over 20 years experience in new multimedia communications markets and technologies. Perey has authored over 100 feature articles on the topic of multimedia communications and is an invited speaker at industry events and serves on panels and committees dedicated to the advancement of rich media experiences in business and consumer markets. She founded and is the organizer of the Swiss Augmented Reality Meetup Group. She also founded Perey Research & Consulting and often collaborates with corporate research groups and universities to perform basic and applied research on Augmented and Mixed Reality technologies. Photograph of Christine Perey © 2014 by Augmented Reality.ORG.

AURASMA
Scan the image to watch

Interview 3: Christine Perey

John Tinnell: I imagine that many readers of this book may be a bit envious of your job—you travel around the world as a researcher and consultant, helping organizations leverage opportunities associated with emerging multimedia technologies such as mobile AR and smart objects.

Christine Perey: My lifestyle may appear (to some who are sitting comfortably reading this in an armchair or are unaccustomed to and don't have a high travel profession) attractive, but I can assure you that it's not as cushy as it seems! After they come to grips with the fact that a relentless travel schedule is exhausting and costly, people are more likely to scratch their heads and wonder why they should care at all. Is the question you are really asking "what it is she does . . . precisely?" I perform two roles: I do missionary work and am a consultant. As a consultant, I am usually in three modes of operation: project manager, detective and "scout," and producer. In the first, project management is heavily administrative and involves finding resources (technology, people, places, content, service providers) to make sure that the products (needed for "production") are what people need. Often there is poor alignment between what people, and companies representing groups of people, say they need, their timelines and budgets, and what they can use. The same goes for me. When I am looking for a new design to express an idea, I have grand concepts, but in the end, I can use very simple tools to communicate those ideas with others! In detective mode, I listen carefully. First, to the client, to read between the lines, to match up the goals of a company with their current position in the market and to narrow down from all possible paths (there are an infinite number) to those most likely to bring about the desired results. There's a lot of filtering and analysis in this process. Then, I put on my client's specially-tuned filter and listen. If necessary, I will search what I have gathered or can reach. For me, research is not a very organized process. It's low level, continuous. I'm searching through what I hear and see/read in reports, on the Web and during meetings, conferences, and tradeshows. I am always looking for patterns.

Information patterns build up, become figures, and move in flows. These representational blocks of the universe—and the "forces" acting on and between them—are then used in market landscapes and thought or business frameworks. Building, using, and adapting my frameworks to describe the future, including the professional networks that are tied to the various segments, I can produce different outputs. This is the last of my three modes: producer. I'm always pushing myself towards a product.

A deliverable can be an event, a meeting, a talk, for example. But most of the time the product is measured in terms of content. The reports or other outputs I'm producing have to become tools. They have to be put into action or I haven't achieved my goal. Most outputs have more than one component. There's always a component that depicts the present—the state of the art in mobile Augmented Reality with respect to other domains—and another that describes scenarios for the future. I can only fully come into my role as an advisor, as a strategic business development consultant, when I use the customized tools, or coach my clients on their direct use of the frameworks and models we produce. This brings me to what I call the "missionary" work. I am passionate about the future of AR. I do not ever question if AR is going to be ubiquitous. Every waking moment I'm focused on helping others change the way they think about both the digital and physical worlds, and to find ways to reduce barriers between the present and the future in which the two (digital data and the physical world) are so intimately connected that we often won't be able (and won't want) to distinguish them. There aren't enough hours in the day for me to think about the future when people will be able to discover, without searching, what they haven't yet asked, or anticipated that they would need or enjoy.

"Every waking moment I'm focused on helping others change the way they think about both the digital and physical worlds, and to find ways to reduce barriers between the present and the future in which the two (digital data and the physical world) are so intimately connected that we often won't be able (and won't want) to distinguish them."

JT: Could you give an overview of the objectives and interests that currently drive your work?

CP: In parallel with the client projects that are always fascinating and often open new areas of research for me, I'm an evangelist for emerging technology segments. Instead of serving or building a faith-based congregation, my goal is to develop new markets. I've been in this role for over 20 years, beginning with QuickTime and "multimedia." The markets in which I have worked barely exist or don't exist at all when my passion for them is born. There aren't sharp lines between these markets I've worked on since QuickTime in 1991-1993 and AR today. Everything builds upon the enablers that came before.

Right now, and since 2006, my focus is on making digital information accessible, useful, or entertaining for people in ways that involve the physical world. The physical world must be an integral part of the construction and delivery of an experience as the digital elements. The physical world is also three dimensional and changing, moving in real time. You know that this is Augmented Reality. I use the term *AR* to encompass all of Mixed and Augmented Reality. But I have to say that I am less interested in uses that are stationary, like the Dongfeng Nissan car launch event in spring 2013. It may seem like a subtle distinction, but I just can't get excited about experiences that have little or no resource constraints and are only designed for making a fleeting impression, a movie. The use of AR for a quick "wow" factor, even if it is to get a customer to turn a bottle of ketchup around or win points with a box of cereal, leave me cold.

So, let's get back to my objectives and the topics about which I hope to convey my passion. I can see that there isn't just one "AR market." In fact, AR should and will be adopted in all domains, horizontally, and in every facet of human life, even before we are born! The use of AR technology might, for example, help parents "see" a fetus in the womb for the first time. I'm working with many people around the world to lower barriers that stand in the way of having AR experiences be ubiquitous, in use daily in every facet of life. AR will use the resources at our fingertips and in the cloud (computational power, electricity, connectivity to other resources, digital data storage and transformation) to both discover our world and to interact with it in new and, I'm convinced, deeper ways.

AR could be as much of a game changer as the printing press was 600 years ago. Since we weren't around then, it's difficult for us to relate to how transformative that invention was to those who lived then and the hundreds of years that followed. But we can read about its impacts. Those who are not digital natives and reading this today might compare the way

AR will change daily life with the changes that came about in all aspects of life as a result of the Web. Back in the early days of the Web there was a lot of talk about convergence. I argue that the Web and our digital tools have brought about separation between information assets and the physical world. We used to rely largely on the physical world to provide information, but with the Web today, information moved away (became separated) from the physical world.

Information in digital format and the physical world are intersecting again. AR is the result of our powerful mobile devices (not just smartphones) tapping and leveraging ever increasing enabling technologies in the cloud. The best AR architectures rely at different levels on both; it is the result of decades of abstract information technologies converging once again with the physical world. There's another side of AR to consider. When tens of thousands of experience designers, individuals, and companies capturing and logging the world have had another five years of time to experiment with ubiquitous sensors and connectivity (with AR as one of the options for visualization), I predict digital data will no longer seem separate from the physical world.

JT: What aspects of AR do your clients tend to find most appealing?

CP: For the most part, my clients are building and providing enabling technologies. We work to improve enablers for both computer-vision based and geospatial AR. A lot of the work I do is "matching" between offerings of some businesses and the gaps of others. It feels like working on a jigsaw puzzle in which the pieces are constantly changing shapes! But the changes are usually following trends. The attraction and the primary reason people are expanding businesses [to provide AR experiences and tools for AR experience development and delivery] is that they want to make sure their companies are highly relevant to their current and future customers. I'm interested in a lot of commercial projects and study how AR will be embedded into urban information fabric.

Another area in which I'm developing my own vocabulary and learning from my clients is realism. Increasing realism of mobile AR experiences will bring them so close to reality that the user will be able to suspend their disbelief. We can't have and don't need realism everywhere. We ask ourselves when is realism most valuable and where can it be increased?

What are the components and qualities that contribute most to giving AR users realism?

JT: Why is the development of standards so crucial for the growth of AR? And what do you do to advance developments in this area?

CP: The reasons are really basic and apply to all domains where standards exist. It all has to do with where businesses can add their value to a market of customers. The more places and ways businesses can add incremental value, the greater the market grows. If the subsystems of a platform are well documented and, by definition, accessible universally on every user device in the same way, the innovation layer (where value creation begins) will be pushed above or below those interfaces. This simplifies (meaning it reduces cost) development, support, delivery, and everything else.

I compare the benefits of standards in AR to those on the Web, but since AR is not *only* relying on digital data formats (and the W3C defines data formats and interfaces for Web-based content), it is also instructive to think about industry-wide standards where they have advanced innovation. The two industries with which lay people are most familiar are in the construction industry or in automotive. As a result of there being a limited number of standard (widely adopted) options across an industry, businesses can innovate. There's a company that makes all the interiors of automobiles. They don't have to build a new factory or retool entirely when they begin manufacturing for BMW.

Innovation that leads to better or more numerous AR experiences, requiring a lower investment or cost in any way, will bring value to large numbers of individuals and companies. Where there can be value created, there are business models. Innovation can be in components, at many points in the hardware platform. Companies can innovate in physical size or interfaces and those will be options for a manufacturer as long as all the components use interfaces the MIPI Alliance publishes. Chip companies are already proposing hardware acceleration for specific algorithms and will differentiate themselves, most likely by reducing power consumption. Those innovations can be available to experience developers through the Khronos APIs for mobile software. Innovations will also be in experience delivery and in content. However, the end user will be able to change platform and still access the content in a totally different software environment, if the content is in a standard data format.

Open technology systems, such as those that use open source or internationally-ratified standards (e.g., Geographic Information Systems, content management systems, the Web, communication networks), dramatically increase opportunities for technology investors and entrepreneurs to profit from innovation in two ways:

1. The Total Addressable Market for a single product or service is larger because more end users will have the components necessary to access the innovation "out of the box" from more platforms. This boils down to there being more potential customers without more cost, and also increases the hardware and software options from which end users can choose.
2. The Total Available Market grows more quickly because the end users perceive and can actually access a larger ecosystem of products and content than a single provider could deliver. This gives end users deeper and wider content choices.

In his 2009 PhD dissertation entitled "Standards Battles for Complex Systems; Empirical Research on the Home Network," Geerten van de Kaa proved that when companies work together and develop standards, more companies benefit. His dissertation provides a framework that permits companies to predict the outcome of choices made in support of different proprietary and internationally-ratified standards. Van de Kaa offers a checklist for developing a company strategy for standards battles. Van de Kaa's research found that the diversity of the companies and institutions involved in and aware of a standard has a significant positive effect on the chances that the standard achieves dominance. This is intuitive but it also helps that this research supports the assumptions on which the AR Standards Community's work is based.

The AR Standards Community seeks to accelerate adoption of augmented reality through the development of open and interoperable data formats and interfaces for AR-ready content and experiences. Community members collaborate with a wide variety of Standards Development Organizations (SDO) and relevant industry groups that build or provide open interfaces and building blocks for AR experiences with a special emphasis on detecting complementary as well as overlapping work. The open community's resources, public mailing lists, and meeting archives are available on <http://www.arstandards.org>.

I run the portal and chair the regular face-to-face meetings that provide a neutral environment in which business and standards association leaders can learn about and coordinate activities. The portal and meetings directly increase the "community effect" that van de Kaa measured. Community members, including AR developers and stakeholders worldwide, can also provide inputs to SDOs and industries interested in open and interoperable AR.

JT: In many cases, AR is not a stand-alone medium; it is often incorporated in mobile apps as one among several other modes of displaying place-based information. When you work with organizations to develop their AR strategies, how do you propose to integrate the new possibilities that AR affords with already existing mobile and Web-based content?

CP: You hit the nail on the head: AR features will bring value to end users who can combine their digital content experience with the physical world, but this isn't always necessary or even valuable. If I want to research an abstract concept, I may not benefit in any way from having it in the physical world. And most valuable software only has visualization as one of the many features.

JT: Could you elaborate on a few of the concepts you draw upon when explaining what AR is and why it is significant, unique, or disruptive?

CP: When you search for something, anything, in a Web browser on a device that doesn't provide a well-defined position, results are returned in a list, probably in order of relevance. You can sort by other criteria (alphabetical, date, frequency of your friends that have looked at the results, etc.). If a user's search criteria include a geospatial element, both the query having a coordinate for the user's position and the results having a position, then a map view is most logical. There can and will be another "view": the camera view in which the results appear only when the device is oriented in the direction of the results (aka mobile AR).

As far as its potential to be disruptive, the keys are the manner in which AR builds upon a huge wealth of emerging and existing technology building blocks, and whether this new visualization and interaction paradigm is truly a step change. In some domains, for Fast Moving Consumer Goods, for example, it will bring value by dramatically lowering cost of design, testing, delivery, marketing, sales, and support of products or services. Another disruptive area will be in safety. By having an "intelligent" automobile, with AR in the windshield, the user will be able to see what the car is sensing without taking eyes off the road and physical world. While there remain many years of research before this is truly a safe solution, I have no doubt that the AR aspect is only one of many benefits of having a higher operating sensor platform (the car).

JT: At SXSW 2013, you described a class of applications for AR that would enable people to see how a particular place appeared at various historical periods. People could, for instance, simply swipe from one decade to another in order to see historical changes in the built environment, fashion, transportation, etc. Assuming use cases like these spread and improve, do you think AR carries with it a potential to enhance our historical awareness of places we might otherwise take for granted? If so, how might this new level of sensitivity to history inform content strategies in business, government, or education?

CP: Really great question! Our bodies can only exist in the present, in space, but our data can have a temporal dimension. Our minds can travel on the continuum of time, exploring the artifacts of the past and enriching our present state. Nearly everything that exists at this moment has a history. This is one of the core principles of *Spimes*. The original authority about and the person who coined the word Spime is Bruce Sterling. During his August 2004 address at SIGGRAPH, he introduced first *blojects*, objects that blog, and their evolutionary extension, Spimes. Rather than butcher Sterling's eloquent words, here's what he said, verbatim:

> In the future, an object's life begins on a graphics screen. It is born digital. Its design specs accompany it throughout its life. It is inseparable from that original digital blueprint, which rules the material world. This object is going to tell you—if you ask—everything that an expert would tell you about it. Because it *wants* you to become an expert. If you become an expert in wrangling that object, then, you will contribute to the advancement of the industry. The object will evolve faster, the industry will evolve faster . . . We can call [this object] a "Spime," which

> is a neologism for an imaginary object that is still speculative. A Spime also has a kind of person who makes it and uses it, and that kind of person is somebody called a "Wrangler." The most important thing to know about Spimes is that they are precisely located in space and time. They have histories. They are recorded, tracked, inventoried, and always associated with a story. Spimes have identities, they are protagonists of a documented process. They are searchable, like Google. You can think of Spimes as being auto-Googling objects.

As I've taken this concept of Spime Wrangling into my consulting practice, it suggests several outcomes. The first is that time, movement on the temporal axis, is an easy-to-measure metric for value. Going further back in time, or into a more precise time interval than the default setting (a date and time, for example), has more value than just going a short time interval. It's intuitive because historical artifacts, especially those that date pre-digital era, require a greater investment to bring into the digital domain. Further, they may have been stored longer. I've also expanded on Sterling's ideas with those of another great mind, Joe Pine III. Pine suggests in his book, *Infinite Possibilities,* that the temporal axis is as important as the spatial. I extended this idea to explore how trends, people, places, and things may also "go" into the future. Here it's not a linear relationship between the value and interval of time because the further out you go in the future, the higher the uncertainty.

JT: At present (April 2013), what factors seem to be limiting the widespread adoption of AR?

CP: The barriers to ubiquitous and pervasive AR can be put into four big groups. The first, and the one on which I have worked most over the past three years, is defined as getting all the technology components together and working smoothly. AR relies upon a large number of fundamental enabling hardware and software technologies. Then we have to add the content. If these three—hardware, software, and content—are out of balance, the stool will not stand. We are making rapid progress in the hardware and software domains, but content for AR is still very immature. There's an enormous amount left to do in the digital content domain to make it transparently accessible and useful to people using AR-assisted systems.

The second group of barriers involves user experience design: interfaces. Slow response time, poor tracking, or inaccurate positioning are all problems that technology will address almost without our focusing on them because the computational power of our devices increase with each generation. The user experience barriers I see are deeper than "where does the button go" or if the digital augmentation should be on the left or above an anchor in the physical world. Eyewear will address the problem of having to hold a smartphone up at eyelevel, but will also introduce a whole new set of very difficult new design problems, only a part of which have to do with registration and tracking.

Successful AR user interfaces will [go] along with or maybe will follow our developing a new and different vocabulary, and perhaps even some new social norms. These new interfaces could be more game changing than touch, and especially multi-touch, interfaces were for keyboards. Having multi-touch profoundly changed our relationships with keyboards in smartphones. Hands-free human interfaces with and without AR-assisted content will permit users to request access to and to manipulate small, very precise—you could call them "atomic"—units of information, some of them by manipulating the physical world.

The growth of AR has a number of business barriers. People ask if customers will pay significantly more for AR-assisted experiences than for what they need and can obtain without AR. That's an important question and there will be many studies on this because people pay for a lot of different units of value and we need to understand how this notion of value is evolving. In industrial uses, especially where there are complex systems, we can already demonstrate that the return on investment is fast, in some cases a few months. There will be new business models as businesses search for ways to quantify benefits and to reward those who provide the value to customers. But, I think many of our existing business models will be preserved and many educational and artistic AR experiences will be provided as public service. Across and threaded between these three groups of barriers, there are also very important legal, societal, and social barriers we need to address before AR will be widespread. I don't think these are in scope for this book, but they are enormously important to the long-term successful adoption of AR for consumers in public settings.

JT: Increasingly, graduate students who study new media are seeking research positions outside of universities. Could you offer them any advice about launching a career as a consultant? What are some of the challenges and the rewards of collaborating with a diverse array of researchers, publishers, businesses, and professional networks?

CP: There's a lot of uncertainty in the world so I don't want to make it sound as if consulting is the riskiest mode of working, but I will say that it's not a healthy choice for risk averse people. It requires taking risk and going down a lot of paths that are not sign-posted. Once you are engaged in a direction of research, whether alone, searching the Web, or with others, you have to judge for yourself, continually try to assess if the domain is sufficiently rich to lead to new business or new value to your existing clients.

I highly recommend that anyone considering consulting have a strong business and technology base. If you are an engineer, go to business school. If you are a business person, learn the science and engineering as well. Juggling is another good skill to have. I have at least four or five activities in related domains going at any time in order to leverage them against one another. Since I don't invoice clients on the basis of hours or days of work, but on the value I deliver, this makes it possible to mix some projects that have a lot of investment with others that are "low hanging fruit." I can't quantify these calculations but I know I am doing them intuitively every day. Another recommendation is to specialize in something about which you can stay passionate for a long time—years. You may need to move away from your areas of highest interest in order to work on projects for your clients, but be sure that you can quickly return to and catch up with your passions.

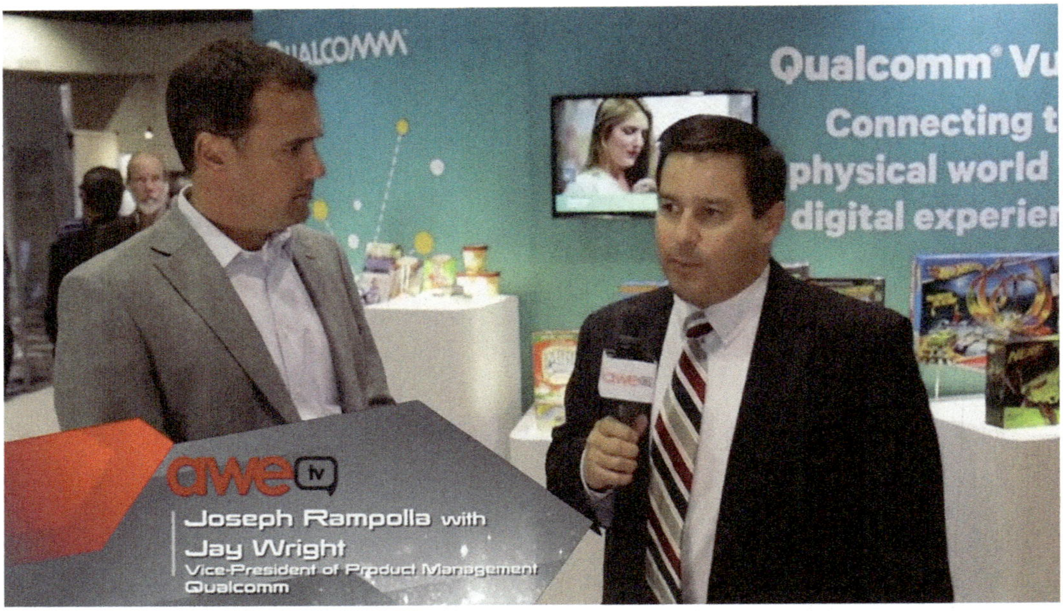

Jay Wright is president and general manager of Vuforia in the PTC Technology Platforms Group. In this role, Mr. Wright has global responsibility for driving the Vuforia business and maintaining Vuforia as the leading software platform for development of augmented reality applications. Previously, as Vice President of Business Development at Qualcomm, he managed the company's partnerships with innovators in industry and academia and led Qualcomm's efforts to enable augmented reality within the mobile ecosystem. An inventor and software engineer, Wright holds three patents—two of which encompass data synchronization between mobile devices and have been regarded as landmark patents in the field of wireless email. Photograph of Jay Wright © 2014 by Augmented Reality.ORG

AURASMA

Scan the image to watch

Interview 4: Jay Wright

John Tinnell: Qualcomm has positioned itself as an *enabler* of augmented reality. Could you describe what that enabler role entails, and how the mission of Vuforia (Qualcomm's AR software development engine) differs from or compliments AR browsers like Layar or Junaio?

Jay Wright: First, a brief, quick history of Qualcomm. We've been providing enablers for the mobile industry for 25 years. The biggest business we have and the biggest class of enablers happens to be chip sets that we provide for a large number of mobile devices—phones, tablets, and new classes of devices. Vuforia represents a different type of enabler. It's a software enabler for app developers and brands. The enabling piece that we are providing is a piece of software that we call the Vuforia Engine. And the Vuforia Engine is a component app developers put inside their applications; we describe it simply as giving apps the ability to see. The Vuforia Engine turns the camera, in essence, into an eye capable of recognizing certain objects in the camera's field of view. And then it's up to the app developer to determine what to do with the information that's been seen.

JT: So, you are more interested in supporting the development of individual apps rather than creating a general AR platform comparable to what Layar or Junaio are doing.

JW: That's absolutely right. We are behind-the-scenes. We are not building the applications ourselves. We're providing a component that app developers use inside their apps for the computer vision functionality.

JT: You manage Qualcomm's partnerships with innovators in industry and academia. How do you think about the relationship between software development and academic research?

> *"I think universities remain one of the best sources of innovation and new technology, period. There's only so much research and innovation that corporations can afford to do. We really rely on universities for a source of new technology, new ideas, and, of course, new employees."*

JW: University research is extremely important to us. We have made significant investments to be at the forefront of computer vision technology. And we've done that in conjunction with universities since the very beginning. One we've worked closely with was Georgia Tech, with Professor Blair MacIntyre. We've done quite a bit of work with him. We also formed an early relationship with Graz University of Technology in Austria. Austria has actually become quite a hotbed for computer vision. And actually, it was as a result of that university relationship and a company that had been spun out of that university that Qualcomm opened an office in Vienna. So we now have multiple university relationships around the world where we have various levels of funding and collaboration, and we do that in computer vision and, as a company, we do that in a lot of other areas as well. I think universities remain one of the best sources of innovation and new technology, period. There's only so much research and innovation that corporations can afford to do. We really rely on universities for a source of new technology, new ideas, and, of course, new employees.

JT: What major challenges in AR are developers trying to solve right now? Is it all about perfecting computer vision and image recognition?

JW: I'd put them in two different areas. I think one challenge is *robustness*. If you've played with some AR applications, you've probably experienced some of them being a bit finicky. It's really hard to deal with varying lighting conditions, when the device is moving, or when what you are looking at is moving—and that's something we spend a lot of time on. And then beyond robustness, we talk about making the device's camera more and more like your eye. Today, Vuforia has a pretty robust ability to recognize planar or flat images, as well as text and some simple 3D objects. But we want to be able to recognize every surface, every color, every object, every person. There's a lot of work to be done. So, we have multiple efforts around the world, R&D wise, on making computer vision algorithms that work with different types of objects and different types of environments.

JT: Beyond print-based surfaces, in other words?

JW: That's right. I think you'll see that, as the vision capabilities go beyond planar images, the types of experiences that will be possible are going to be increasingly interesting.

JT: That feeds into my next question: What is your sense of how the general public perceives AR technology right now? And, folding back into the previous question, what steps need to be taken for this medium to become really widespread?

JW: That's a great question. I think the people that had exposure to augmented reality functionality probably view it similar to scanning a barcode. They see it as a way they can use their phone to scan something and get more information. I think they understand the concept roughly in that sense, based on what we've seen from app developers (and now even some of these apps are getting large numbers of downloads). I think the application that really makes this break out—and I hate to say "killer app"—but the one that most people will probably use (and will look and feel like we think of as augmented reality) is for shopping—the ability to visualize products in my home, or wherever I may be, before I buy them.

JT: Like the Ikea app?

JW: Yes, like the Ikea app. And I think that goes even further; it goes beyond furniture. If you can imagine anytime you are shopping online—you are sitting at home with your tablet. Instead of putting something on your wish list that you want to go see in the store, you'll be able to visualize that right in front of you, look at the size, look at the color, look at the configuration. I would expect that you'd complete more transactions with that capability than you otherwise would have. I can tell you I personally would. I went through this personal struggle with a coffee maker. I wanted a coffee maker that would ground the beans, poured the milk, and the whole thing. And you start looking at these things online and the pictures are relatively different scales, and it's hard to get a sense of how big they are. So I think, "I'll have to wait until I go to the mall or the store so I can check this out." But if I have that kind of capability, I'm pretty sure I would have gotten much closer to the "buy" button.

JT: You've said elsewhere that AR supports *visual search*, and thus promises an alternative way of being online, perhaps analogous to the way Twitter's mode of "real-time search" differs from a basic Google search. How might AR—as a form of visual search—compare with the modes we're more familiar with?

JW: I'm not going to speak to who will deliver the functionality, but I can tell you we believe that pointing your device at something will become a pervasive means for interacting with it.

JT: Rather than typing keywords.

JW: That's right. So, if I want to find the app that works with whatever it is I'm looking at, or I want to buy whatever it is I'm looking at, or I want to interact with whatever it is I'm looking at, I will do that by pointing my device at it. And I believe that the recognition or the initiation of whatever transaction that I am going to have will be visual. In order to do that, you need a big database in the cloud that can hold lots of stuff. That's a capability that we offer with Vuforia, which allows developers now to build applications that can do visual search, if you will, against their own search space. And they can put over a million images in there and do these same kinds of experiences.

JT: So, it's almost like the environment and the physical assets in the world become the way of navigating digital content.

JW: That's one way of saying it. I think the other is this: objects will have digital content associated with them—whether that's apps or content I want to visualize on top of objects in our environment, be they books, consumer electronic devices, movie posters, etc. The way that you will access that digital information is by pointing your device at the object, and when your device is pointed at it, the camera will recognize it and allow you to see the information, or link to the associated experience.

JT: Speaking of AR and search, what kind of long-term impact do you anticipate from Google Glass and other AR eyewear currently being developed? Or is that transition too far off to plan for?

JW: I don't think it's too far off to plan for. There are many use cases we've seen with Vuforia that we can envision working in glasses or some sort of see-through display in the future. The generation of displays that really make things interesting, at least from a Vuforia and computer-vision perspective, are perhaps a generation (or several generations) beyond what we are seeing with Google Glass. While it's very interesting, and I think we are going to see some great applications, these are not experiences that are actually displaying graphics aligned with the underlying world that you're looking at. Primarily, I would describe them as *unregistered* experiences, to use the technical jargon. Glass is predominately a hands-free display for a voice interface and notification space UI. But once we go beyond that, and start looking at see-through displays that are actually capable of recognizing what's in the environment—allowing us to display graphics that are aligned with environments—then things get more interesting in the future. And we see Vuforia as an important part of that future technology stack.

JT: Absolutely, I'm excited for it.

JW: I can tell you there is a lot of work happening, and we've seen some *really* interesting things in the category of glasses.

JT: Setting aside future scenarios, one of the fascinating things about AR—as it exists today—is the capacity to turn any printed material into a networked hub for accessing digital content on-location and in the moment. As you already mentioned, many current examples are happening in retail and marketing. What aspects of AR do marketers tend to find most appealing with Vuforia or augmented reality in general?

JW: Let me tell you a little bit of what we've seen in print and then where I think this is going, maybe in a more interesting long term area. I think print overall has been declining in terms of published printed material. It's no secret that newspapers and magazines are down and some are ceasing to exist. So, I think publishers are excited about AR's potential to breathe some new light into the print experience. And we've seen quite a bit of Vuforia activity there. There's also been interesting activity with catalogue shopping because you can dramatically simplify the purchase process from catalogues and, perhaps more generically, you can turn any image or printed ad into a sort of digital storefront. One of the things that we're starting to see, with toys and then moving into consumer products, is not just using AR as a form of marketing, but actually seeing AR become a new digital layer that's part of the core product experience. Let me give you an example: the Magic Vision app that Johnson and Johnson did for Band Aid. This app is not about the Band Aid's advertising, it's not about the Band Aid's packaging, it's not about a Band Aid retail campaign. It's about *an AR experience* each and every time you use a Band Aid. You put the Band Aid on your child, presumably a child that's in some discomfort from being hurt. You pull out this Magic Vision app . . . pixie dust starts coming off the Band Aid and the little Muppet—this is working on the Muppet version of the Band Aids right now—jumps off the Band Aid onto your phone and starts singing a song to the child. And there's a neat photo shoot experience that's on there, too. This becomes something the child sees, gets entertained by, and is something that can happen every time a Band Aid is used. Also, for Band Aid, this is something that delivers on their core brand promise, which is about magic to make you feel better. So, there's the physical product that is making you feel better, and now there is the digital layer on top to reinforce that feeling. I think this is indicative of things to come. We are also seeing this in the toy industry where many toys now are including a digital layer, or an AR component, to make them relevant for a generation of kids that seem to find more interest in tablets and phones than in physical toys. That's an interesting thing—going beyond marketing to becoming a digital layer on top of physical products.

JT: In line with that, some media critics might worry that AR is solely about advertising, solely about consumer products. But the technology also enables similar innovations in the non-profit realm (museums, education, art, etc.). What are some promising areas for growth in those types of fields?

JW: I can tell you the one that is most exciting to me, and it uses a capability that we've just announced: text recognition, the ability to recognize words. And we showed this off with Sesame Workshop. Big Bird actually got on stage with Qualcomm's CEO Paul Jacobs. It was actually the original, same Big Bird since 1969—Caroll Spinney. He got up and showed "Big Bird's Words." Big Bird's Words is an app that helps young children learn how to read and build vocabulary. Sesame has done quite a bit of research with societal problems and educational issues with children. And they found there is a high correlation between maximum vocabulary size before kids start going to school and a very low income ceiling. So, they are trying to figure out how technology can be used to help [children] learn more words when they are younger. So with this "Big Bird's Words" app, they can go around the house and Big Bird would say, "Use my word-a-scope to go find the word 'cereal.'" So it challenged the child to go find the words in the house, and if they found a word that wasn't "cereal," the app would read it to them, tell them what it was, and give them some feedback. But the important thing about this is it allowed a child to have a reading experience that they could not have otherwise had without an adult there. To me, it is such a powerful learning tool. I was also really happy with it because we were able to show text recognition in a completely new app category—education for kids—as opposed to some of the other uses like menus or translations for business travelers. I think there is a lot of opportunity in education for instructional use, but the one that was most recently interesting to me was educating small kids and helping them read with the text recognition capability.

JT: Finally, because AR generally seeks to connect people with their immediate surroundings rather than a placeless Web, do you see AR and context-awareness as related research agendas? And, along those lines, is there a possibility for integrating Vuforia with Gimbal?

JW: I think they are very complimentary. At Qualcomm we talk about our sixth sense vision; we achieve the sixth sense by giving the device some of our own senses. So, the ability to see comes from the camera, the ability to hear can come from the microphone. There are also some specialized senses the device has. For example, humans don't have GPS. The way I think of Vuforia, in terms of context awareness, is that Vuforia is bringing the visual part of context. So, if you think about context taking our senses to the device, Vuforia is about transforming the camera into an eye. I think it's going to have a lot of traction because it's very visual and it has a wow effect.

JT: As opposed to just the simple push notification.

JW: Right. The grand vision for context is amazing and rich and promising, and I think a lot people really get excited about it. But it's very, very hard—today—to achieve some of the things we talk about beyond geofencing and other relatively straightforward uses of location. I think the challenge moving forward is really to learn how to fuse multiple data sources and application usage with data from the microphone and data from the camera, so that we can enable some of these further out things.

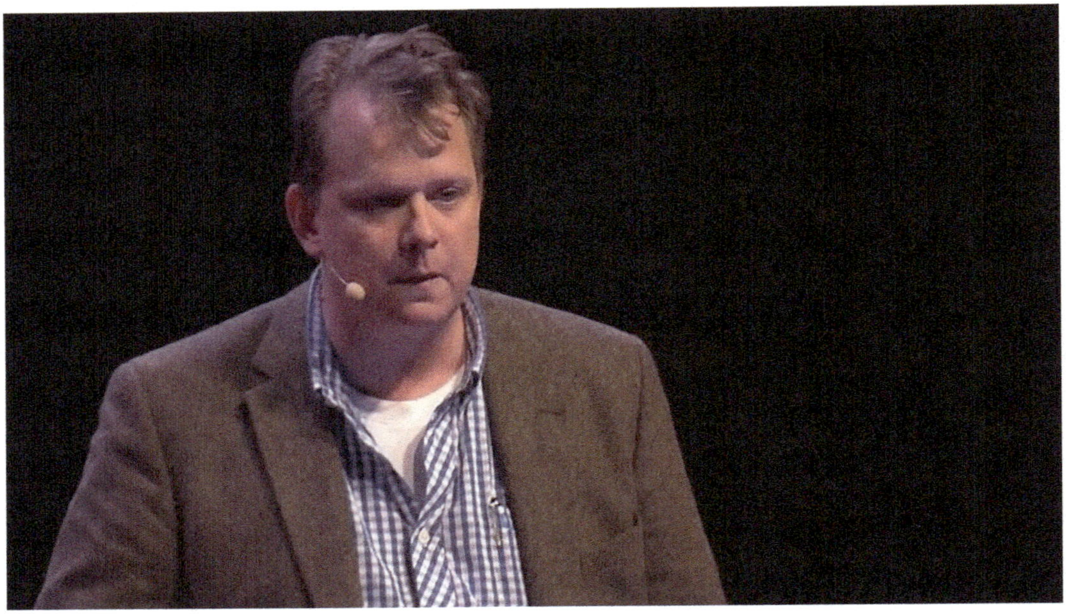

Maarten Lens-Fitzgerald co-founded the augmented reality platform Layar. Photograph of Maarten Lens-Fitzgerald. © 2012 by TED.

AURASMA
Scan the image to watch

Interview 5: Maarten Lens-Fitzgerald

John Tinnell: In the early 1990s, you helped companies create their first websites. This was at the dawn of Web browsers, and in 2009 your company (Layar) launched the world's first *AR* browser. How does your experience working with the Web in its early years inform or compare to your work at Layar today?

Maarten Lens-Fitzgerald: Yes, there are a lot of similarities involved with the emergence of a new medium and, to me, it's about knowing that it moves slow. Everybody thought so much was going to happen in the Web's early years—a lot of which didn't happen—and only now is the Web really coming of its first stage (there's bound to be a lot more). And the same goes, I think, for the medium of AR. So what really helps me here is to be knowledgeable of that, of the hype factor (which AR already has), but also with the fact of it being a new medium with lots of possibilities will attract lots of people with a lot of ideas which the medium is not right for yet. So with Layar specifically, also, what we are trying to do is make sure our foundation, our infrastructure, is good. My personal wish is that whatever AR will be in five years, that Layar will be like a DNS service of augmented reality (hopefully will be on the forefront, like on a Google level). It starts with good technology: making sure that it is well documented, and that it's not all proprietary, if we can help it, and really keeping it medium-focused and not just silo-focused, if you will.

JT: So in both cases, with the early days of the Web and AR today, do you find yourself facing challenges to convince people of the value of the new medium?

MLF: Just yesterday I had the Marketing VP of a very large magazine ask me to bring by some demo material. While he was trying it, one of the things he found interesting and was wondering about was how AR doesn't work when you move away the phone from the page. So that is, to me, *the* thing about AR. That moment was really interesting because it is so logical for him to ask that, so natural to wonder about that. I was thinking of how I could explain it well so he could relate to how logical it is for him to say that, but once he is using AR more regularly, he will not want it any other way. When I left I finally thought of how to explain it. When people just started creating websites, a lot of first timers did not like that, when they made a website, users could link away, that they could follow a link and *leave your website*. So, with that similarity in mind, it made me realize that, having been doing AR for so long, I really need to manage my expectations and manage my output with people who are just starting and really slowly have them do the basic steps to get into the medium.

JT: Yes, it's funny how when someone first encounters a new technology, the feature they end up being frustrated with sometimes becomes the feature that makes it what it is when it becomes popular.

MLF: Exactly.

JT: What initially drew you to AR?

MLF: A lot of things. I'm a science fiction reader. In the late 80s, I was reading Bruce Sterling and William Gibson. "Jacking in," "plugging in," and all that cyberspace terminology is what I grew up with. That's basically why I started on the Internet. For me, the Internet was a manifestation of that near-feature world that was actually not that alien or that far away. So, when me and my buddies (Raimo van der Klein and Claire Boonstra) went to start a company a while back, it was very logical to put AR on the list of stuff we wanted to do. What really made it possible was the introduction of the Android smartphone. I remember, the phone wasn't even live yet, but there was a demo online where you could, in street view, just move the phone, and it would move because it had a compass that could do that, which was also the earliest form of geo-based augmented reality. After seeing that, seeing the first apps come about with such AR utility, I started reading back into the all possibilities in sci-fi. I read Vernor Vinge's book *Rainbows End*, and I watched the anime *Dennou Coil*. Seeing all that, it was so clear to me that this is the future and it was going to happen now (this was toward the end of 2008). We were also thinking that App stores are going to be really tough to work with, because everyone is going to go there, and so we really saw that there has to also be a pre-install deal. And then there was the idea of combining AR with the old Web idea of having a browser with layers instead of pages. That was what really got Layar started.

JT: In 2009, you described the hype cycle for AR in terms of three levels: level 1 being *marker-based AR* (PC-webcam, mobile-QR codes, etc.); level 2 being *markerless AR* (the geo layers, some image recognition); and level 3, which perhaps hasn't happened yet, being *wearable AR* or what you called "augmented vision." From a technical standpoint, what needs to be done in order to make the leap from level 2 to level 3—from *markerless* to *wearable*?

MLF: First off, I was recently revisiting that article and I was like, "Wait just give me an extra week off to rethink everything and rephrase and write the next version of that." Right now, mobile augmented reality is pretty much done with the basic innovations. Meaning that visual augments are really good. It will get bigger, faster, and easier—but that's the only technical advancements you'll see there. The next innovation that will come is when you easily can recognize and augment 3D stuff. So, for example, augmenting faces and augmenting buildings (which people are starting to do already), but then to have it work both day and night and in a stable manner that is, I think, where the next step will be as far as augmenting is concerned. The phone will be the first device where everything will happen, but, of course, glasses are very interesting. And yet, what I am really learning now with Layar currently is that these innovations are logical things to look at from a lab or R&D point of view. But what's really key now is that people learn and know that it's good to pull out their phone and scan something—it's fun, it's useful. It's all about turning that gesture into a habit. Today, before many of us went to work or wherever, we checked our Facebook. That is something we learned—a new habit. And so the new habit of scanning, I think, right now is actually the key thing for augmented reality to really take off. That's, again, really where I am happy where Layar's position right now. All those other technologies will come later in a logical progression, as long as people know they can pull out their phones and see something.

"I used to embrace all the forward-looking stuff, from the TED talks to the singularity stuff and all that. While that's all great, I've learned that it's also about what you can do now. If you can move the world now just a quarter of an inch, that's amazing."

JT: So you think the near future of AR really has more to do with social factors rather than technological ones?

MLF: I don't know if it's social, but it's definitely human.

JT: Does this idea of AR's hype cycle play a role in Layar's recent decision to focus primarily on interactive print?

MLF: Definitely on a certain level. I think interactive print, to come back to what I said earlier, has such reach. Magazines, for instance, have such strong relationships with their readers, and AR fits so well into their value chain. I sometimes even say that, in the beginning of Layar, we were looking up and away almost to where it was going. We were also just talking about what the future of AR will be. Today, what we are doing basically is focusing down and looking at the world, seeing where AR fits *right now*. That's something I've learned as an entrepreneur. I used to embrace all the forward-looking stuff, from the TED talks to the singularity stuff and all that. While that's all great, I've learned that it's also about what you can do *now*. If you can move the world now just a quarter of an inch, that's amazing. And even if you can make a living out of it, and if you can make a billion or a million people pull out their phone—we have 29 million installs now—those kinds of things are very important, apart from R&D.

JT: Why is AR attractive to writers, editors, and publishers? What have they been saying about it?

MLF: They like it because they can share more. Any editor hates not being able to tell their whole story or show all their pictures. They also like that they can include videos and basically have more engagement with the reader. Another thing editors like is getting feedback and statistics from readers. So, just as you have the "like" button and "share" button on the Web, now this is possible in print. Not everyone does that yet, but it's so logical to have that little share/like bar you see on Web articles to appear on print articles. From a commercial standpoint, publishers really like AR because they can upsell ads.

JT: On that note, with AR, a lot of magazines are overlaying their pages with online shopping features. Some readers of this book might worry about that trend because the printed page has been such a vital site for the exchange of ideas. Some of these use cases, however, seem to direct readers more to the act of buying and consuming products—the printed page becomes a store front. Does that trouble you at all, or do you see that as just one of many ways of utilizing the technology?

MLF: I think for a reader to have a regular, good experience they need to trust their magazine brand. Magazines need to have a good level of balance between editorial, real information and commercially motivated information. We are doing several getting-started programs with magazine teams to find that balance in the augmented layer, which they have always done in their magazines. So, I'm not really worried. At Layar, we also have a sponsored program, which grants free use for students or educational endeavors. Also, artists and nonprofit organizations can use Layar for free. We really find that very important. Key insights have been given to us by artists who are using our platform, so that is such a key thing for AR and for Layar to keep doing. And we will keep doing that. On that note, one of the unique things that AR does is that it liberates space. So for the first time *anybody* can do stuff with any physical space. Artists, as well as university students, will be the first to explore this unique dimension. We welcome anyone trying to experiment and do new things with Layar because it's so important to the growth of the medium.

JT: Yeah, that's great. And I totally agree. Has an AR artwork in Layar ever inspired you to think differently about Layar or AR and its possibilities for creative expression?

MLF: Yes, artists gave us that key insight about the liberation of space by AR. Specifically, Sander Veenhof, with his invasion of MoMA in New York. We would not have gotten that insight if we had just played around with Layar ourselves. When we announced and published our app, we knew we had opened this little door to a humongous world that we had no idea how to populate on our own. So who better than artists, along with the rest of the world, to find out how it works? And that idea is still at the core of the company. We don't want to be a silo for this—it really is for everyone to explore and use.

JT: And that speaks to the importance of content, both in terms of interactive print and geo-layers. What are some of Layar's strategies for promoting interesting content?

MLF: We can do stuff in app, but we don't actively do that. The most important thing, and that is again one of the unique aspects of AR, is the *contextual call to action*. That is, if there is a geo-layer at the entrance of a building, something should be printed on the wall that invites people to pull out their phone to view a historical image of that place, for example. Or, in the case of magazine, there should be a call to action printed on the page that says something like, "Scan this to buy it." I think that is the key method to promote your AR content. It just doesn't make sense to have a promotion that prompts people to download a layer so they can scan a magazine *later,* or, *later*, when they're at a location, they can do this or that. The call to action needs to be made in context.

JT: What kind of impact do you expect from Google Glass and other AR eyewear currently being developed? Will geo-layers become more pervasive? What sort of long-term impact do you envision?

MLF: I have no clue. This morning I saw a good friend of mine from Holland, who is a photographer. She got accepted into the program to try Google Glass. I know her and can visit her regularly when I'm in Amsterdam and check it out. I've tried Google Glass on already, and I think I'm going to be disappointed. I wear the Jawbone UP, I have a Nike Fuel, and I'm now discovering, a little after a year, that those wearable technologies don't really impact as much as they did in the beginning. And, I'm afraid, specifically with Google Glass, which is so simple . . . It's not actually AR yet, so there I think there will be some disappointment. The last person who asked a question at the SXSW session on Google Glass said, "Yeah, that was a very underwhelming demo. When are you going to do the kick ass stuff?" I think here we have a good example of AR's overhype. This morning I saw a video of a group from London who have a quadcopter with a camera, and they steer it around and do great flyovers of places. In this video, they did a flyover of Amsterdam; they flew under the bridges and canals—it was amazing. That's a great application and such use cases are so logical. That's where goggles really work—when you need that remote, immersed, contextual view. But for us to wear glasses ourselves . . . we'll have to wait and see. I think there will be specific use cases that will work, but this year a billion people will get a new iPhone or a new phone. *That's a market*. The other one—glasses—is just an idea still.

JT: Many location-based apps, which are here for the mobile phone and are very popular, in the future might likely include some AR features, for example, I'm talking about apps like Foursquare or Highlight which display information posted in real-time by the people who surround you at that moment. If these practices become widespread, then it's bound to change the way people experience their own identities—that is to say, the ways we define ourselves to others and the ways others perceive us. Do you think people are eager to live like that (i.e., wearing their status updates like clothing)?

MLF: Yesterday, I was looking at a slidedeck about the liberation of space and it had an image of a line of people waiting for the bus, and the last one in the line is a big monster . . . because he felt like he should be a monster today. And everyone who sees him in AR, whether through the phone or the glasses, will see him like that. Specifically in New York, there are always people who will like to express themselves in various ways, be it a Mohawk or be it an augmented reality whatever. And even in the further future it's going to be really normal, and there might even be a format. Think of something like a lapel or the metals that sergeants wear. If you point your phone or glasses at that, you would be able to see whatever that person wants to share, visually, about themselves. Formats like that will definitely become possible and people will use them. But it's going to be a slow progression. It's going to be ten years for that really to settle in somewhere. (Already people are wondering about Google Glass and expressing concerns about it, which is logical.) But I think some people (myself included) will love to express themselves in a non-invasive way to only certain people. That's initially what I really liked about Twitter, for instance; that is how I met Raimo (one of the Layar co-founders). Early on, there was really a select group of people who knew about that channel. And that natural filter gave it something special and something similar will probably happen with some applications of AR.

JT: Have you observed any differences between how mobile AR is taking off in Europe vs. in the United States?

MLF: Yes, but they're just my personal observation, so there's no research here. That's where you need universities. What I see is that, in the US, people perceive that your phone, in general, is something to use when you call or when you check Facebook or do email, and to do other kinds of things they need something very . . . well gimmicky is maybe judgmental . . . but something like Four Square that has the check-in to make people do something new. In Holland and other places in Europe, I see people more readily trying new things with their phones than in the US.

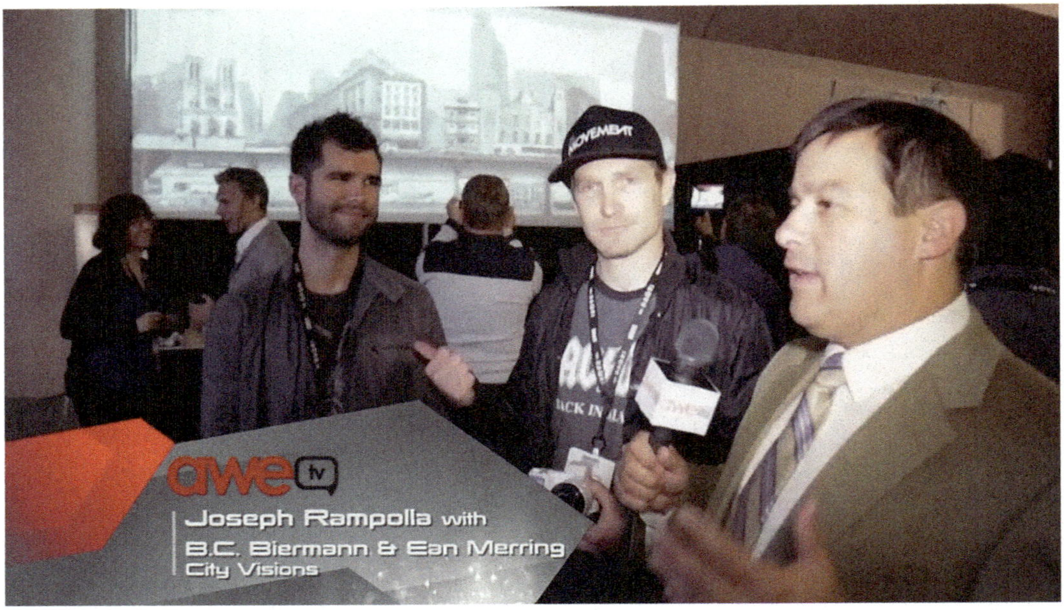

BC Biermann possesses an interdisciplinary background that comprises academia, technology, and the arts. With a PhD in Humanities (intermedia/cultural analysis) from the Universiteit van Amsterdam, BC ("Heavy") has worked as both a university professor and a tech developer in Anaheim, Prague, and Saint Louis. Since 2007, BC has internationally presented his academic work, which explores augmented reality, art, and semiotics in public space. As a kind of synthesis between scholarly inquiry and emerging media, BC founded The Heavy Projects to investigate how the fusion of creativity and technology can uncover new modes of relaying ideas. In collaboration with NYC's Public Ad Campaign (PAC), BC's "AR|AD Takeover" channel filtered outdoor advertising and replaced it with original street art (by Ron English, John Fekner, PosterBoy, Doctor D, and OX) and received attention in CNet, PC World, Popaganda, and Juxtapoz. "Re*Public," BC's current project with Jordan Seiler and Ean Mering, is a mobile device application that digitally resurfaces buildings in urban centers in order to turn architecture into locations for meaningful cultural exchange. Image of BC Biermann & Ean Merring. © 2014 by Augmented Reality.ORG.

Scan the image to watch

Interview 6: BC Biermann

John Tinnell: Every work of art, in whatever medium, might inspire discussions about that medium's aesthetic affordances or general characteristics. This is an especially vital dimension of artworks created *via* an emerging medium. As one of the artists pioneering AR work, do you approach your projects, at least in part, as a critical exploration of the medium?

BC Biermann: I don't know if I directly approach it in that way. I would say we do have an ideological interest that drives what we do. Our interest, ideologically, is in reappropriating public space for artists. We saw augmented reality as a way to do that—to basically break private property boundaries, to make incursions, and allow artists to participate in public space in ways they never could before. That's really what drives what we do artistically. Technically, AR is just the medium that currently allows us to do this. Along the way—as we're figuring out what AR can be as an art form—we explore the medium itself, but I don't think that is the driving factor.

JT: The movie *Minority Report* depicts a future in which AR has become a vehicle for pervasive advertising; digital ads address people by name and pitch them products related to where they are and what they're doing. One of your projects, *The AR/AD Takeover*, creates a very different relationship between AR and advertising.

BC: *The AR/AD Takeover* is a project I did with our partner Jordan Seiler, who heads up the PublicAdCampaign in NYC (and he's also a street artist). The PublicAdCampaign has done physical takeovers of ads in the past, and our project was the first digital version. Outdoor advertising, as we see it, is the last bastion of unfiltered commercial messaging that you can't turn off. So, we are seeing what we are doing as the first baby steps in undercutting the value or need for public, physical advertising. Personally, I'm not totally opposed to commercial advertising—I'm just opposed to it being in my face when I can't get rid of it. With AR, we now have a mechanism or system where artists, private individuals, companies, and commercial outlets can participate in this digital system of advertising where there is a filter. If I don't want to see any ads I don't have to. If I want to, I can see them digitally, and not everyone has to see the ads I'm looking at. That is the value, for us, for this type of technology in terms of how it might ultimately fit in with commercial advertising and art. I think the market will drive what people want to see, hopefully. We want to make some of the first splashes into this, artistically, just to show people that there can be other things you can see besides ads. We're aware that there will be a commercial side to this; people are already using AR for commercial purposes. That's going to happen, but right when technology gets going, it's important that people get exposed to alternative uses of it because that tends to be a long-term, driving factor in the way that they envision the technology. If all they see are commercial uses, then that's all it's going to be to most people. We want to show them that there are other things you can do with AR. You don't have to do what we're doing—we are sort of making it up as we go along—but we want to show people some of what is possible.

JT: Might we think of recent AR art as a kind of open laboratory that can inspire all kinds of work in design and development in all kinds of fields as the medium evolves?

"We don't want augmented reality to become just a commercial medium or just an artistic medium, but rather something people feel they can participate in. That's going to be a long-term driving factor or at least a sustainable criterion. People need to feel that they can add content and that we are not the only content creators."

BC: Maybe not all kinds of fields, but *the first use cases are the drivers*. If people see some of the first use cases as interactive art, that may have a lasting effect on how they intellectually understand the medium. When we demo our AR projects, some people get it immediately and some people still have no idea what they are looking at. They think it's some digital stuff on the screen that has no attachment to the world. There's still a steep learning curve as to what AR is, what you can do with it, what the value of it is, and what it is going to be moving forward—there is Google Glass, Microsoft has a patent, contact lenses will come out. We don't want this to become *just* a commercial medium or *just* an artistic medium, but rather something people feel they can participate in. That's going to be a long-term driving factor or at least a sustainable criterion. People need to feel that they can add content and that we are not the only content creators.

JT: Why are texts and images in public spaces such a critical site for artistic intervention?

BC: Because they're public. We've lost the sense of common spaces—it's an old concept. For instance, the idea that even with privately held structures, the outsides of them exist in common visual space. People own the buildings, but they don't own site lines. This is a big problem in Los Angeles, where there is so much illegal advertising. I did a lot of academic work on the difference between graffiti and commercial illegal billboards. The idea that we all have to look at it makes it common space—it's common visual space. We've lost the sense, especially in the US, of art in public spaces. I don't have to like every piece of public art—that's not what's important. What's important is the fact that people are participating and creating art as part of the public messaging that people see. Now, with AR, we are creating this digital landscape that has a physical attachment to spaces, which is very important because it maintains this notion of aura—that you have to go *there* to see. But, again, with AR not everybody has to see it. If people just want to see their physical world, they can do that. The content isn't permanent. I don't know if that's a good or bad thing, that the content can be changed or swapped out. It sits on a server somewhere and it doesn't have to be there for eternity, so maybe it loses a bit of its aura in that sense. On the other hand, people get sick of stuff, so the idea that content can be changed, and the fact that AR is dynamic is important to us (i.e., Re+Public).

JT: When you talk about creating first use cases, in order to inspire AR content creation in public spaces by the public at large, what kind of shift in mindset do you think it will take for people to really become content creators?

BC: We see the city as a canvas. There won't be separate ad spaces like billboards; I think there won't be a need for that. In terms of content creation, this is a problem. How do you filter out things? You don't want to look around your digital environment and see that it's just cluttered with crap. So how do you create a filter? And how do you create something that allows new info in, so that it doesn't become just an echo chamber of things you want to see? The closest analogy to that right now in the tech world is the genome project in music—like Pandora. I use Pandora because it adds new content that I wouldn't have thought of. It's still in line with what I'm already picking but it's adding new content, and I really like that. Essentially, we would need an image genome project. You could look around your physical landscape with the digital overlay, but maybe it's now adding in new content—it could be commercial content of products you wouldn't have thought of, it could be artistic content, etc. You could filter the images and have some measure of control, but at the same time, it's providing you with things you didn't directly have to add in yourself. I think that's very important—striking a balance between, on the one hand, an overload of unrelated content and images, and, on the other hand, having just this echo chamber of only things you've personally programmed. It's a tough balance to strike, but an important one.

JT: *The AR|AD Takeover* has a very scalable quality—it suggests a model for other people to "takeover" ads in other cities. Is that scalability something you aim for when you are developing a new project?

BC: That'd be great. We typically get sort of tunnel-visioned on what we are doing and putting it out there in the world. If others can replicate it, that's great, because, again, our interest with these types of projects is in re-imagining public space. We can only be in one place at a time, and there are only three of us. If it can be replicated in other cities, all the better. If we create something that seeds other virtual takeovers, that would be great for us.

JT: Because of the local/situated nature of AR, it seems especially important to document projects on the Web—not as a substitute for experiencing the work on location, but in order to provide people in other parts of the world with a model that they might extend or adapt. What is the challenge of documenting a live-experience-based form and how is that documentation important to the growth of AR in its early stages?

BC: It's super important. It's really the most important thing in terms of allowing others to see what this is and how is works. We try to be as authentic as possible in the documentation. We film it as it's working in the streets rather than creating an aftereffects version of it. We do real demos. (For example, when Google Glass first released their video it was a concept piece; it wasn't a real demo.) Sometimes we just record the tablet's screen, though that's not always the best way to go because the surfaces are very reflective and it's hard to see what's happening on the screen. What we did in Miami was just pull the video feed directly from the app and recorded that. The problem is that sometimes people forget or don't know what they are looking at because it's coming directly out of the app. So we try and create a narrative with each video. We show the murals on the building, the person with their tablet, and then we go inside the tablet—straight to the video feed. We try to create a story of what the project is and how it works. For us, the video documentation is critically important.

JT: What are some of things that frustrate you when working with current mobile AR apps?

BC: It's hard. Working with buildings is especially hard because of the environmental factors like lighting and the weather. It's not always consistent because of those factors. We're working with an object that exists in the real world, plus we overlay digital assets and animation and touch events. And we are designing for mobile, which makes it a little more difficult, as opposed to designing for desktop. With designing for mobile, you've got multiple platforms. Android and iOS are the two major ones, so you've got to sort of make two apps. Also, your digital assets have to be very, very optimized. Just having the camera open takes up power. Plus, the digital assets are always being tracked so the perspective remains correct. That takes up a lot of processing. And then the assets themselves, such as the animations, take up more processing. For mobile, you have to optimize super light assets so they work correctly. All those things make it difficult.

JT: What about if you are using a GPS system to tag the content in urban environments? Do you ever run into problems?

BC: We don't use GPS for those reasons. For what is it, it's pretty accurate (it's coming from space). But feature tracking is much more precise. It has its own sets of problems but, for us, the problems are less than the payoff in terms of having things stick. Once it registers the structure then it's really accurate. With GPS, the digital overlay floats a lot. It might come up 12 feet too far to the left one time and 30 feet too far to the right another time.

JT: What technical developments—either in hardware or software—do you think are critical to AR's growth as a medium for artistic expression and civic engagement?

BC: Right now the hardware is lagging behind the software. So I would say hardware—glasses that look good and that function. Right now, I think Google Glass is just going to be an informational service that pushes the information to the glasses. It doesn't do much for us. What I have in mind are glasses that are just like your smartphone, but are worn as head mounted displays. People aren't going to want to hold up their tablets and do what we do. We are just doing it because we are anticipating this next generation of hardware to come. And it is coming. We're just hoping it gets here and it works—people start using it and so forth. Ultimately, I love the digital world, but I also love the physical world. I want AR to be a nice mixture of the two. I don't want the digital content to overwhelm people's physical experience. We see it as an *addition to,* not a *replacement of*. But no one knows the trajectory of this thing.

JT: In terms of aesthetics, why is creating work in AR different from making a painting to be displayed in a gallery or animation for the Web in a desktop environment?

BC: Because it's virtual but it still has a locality. For us, that's why we like it. When we design, we're trying to make it appropriate for the space. You have this digital overlay and it should have some connection to the space itself. We try to choose buildings that have some meaning, are culturally or historically significant, or a place where something significant is happening. That gives us a starting point from which to build out the digital content. Without that, the spatial relationship becomes meaningless. If the building doesn't matter and you just slap something on top of it digitally, then why use that building? We want the digital connection to have a tie-in to the physical location. That's why AR, for us, is powerful.

JT: Media critics sometimes refer to Situationist practices when commenting on locative media art. Are there any artistic movements that particularly inform your AR work?

BC: Not consciously. But aesthetically, I am a Minimalist. My partners have their own aesthetic. When we work together, there is a creative tension. We come up with what we think is appropriate for the space. We don't ever sit down with an aesthetic or artistic style in mind. When we augment existing murals, like we did in Miami, we try and use the existing style as the starting point and stay true to it. When you look a mural and then look at the digital overlay we've created, the overlay should be an extension of that mural. We aren't trying to juxtapose what we do with the existing mural; we are trying to add to it, with 3D and interactive elements. We did one mural in Miami where we basically took the elements and pulled everything apart. In AR, it looks like you can see behind the content that was on the mural—like you can see the levels that possibly would have been there. So, we are creating new artistic content in 3D that is an extension of what you see in 2D. But we don't really set out with any specific style in mind.

JT: You often collaborate with organizations and groups beyond academia. Do you find that AR—because it can occur in public spaces—facilitates collaboration between university professors and community organizations?

BC: It does. There are several projects I'm working on in St. Louis that are pulling in multiple organizations. There is still a learning curve. You have to teach people what AR is and what the value of it can be. You are taking totally 2D static art and you can make it totally interactive and you can give it a life of its own. I think AR can really facilitate collaboration between artists and cities. That's really what I'm trying to push. Cities should understand that: (1) public art is a good thing, and (2) now there can be another added layer of digital content.

JT: I think a lot of the work you guys are doing certainly makes the value of AR projects more apparent and will make it easier for people to follow in your footsteps.

BC: I hope so. Hopefully we can pave that road and make it easier for other people. It's been difficult in a lot of ways. It's been exciting because it's so new, but that's also the hard part. It's so new that people don't know what the hell they are looking at.

JT: Could you describe a project you're working on now or one that you've recently completed?

BC: The one we did here [in Austin, TX, at South by Southwest 2013] was for IEEE and Open Stand. We augmented the Driskill Hotel. We did everything remotely, which made it difficult. We worked with some very abstract concepts and we had to tie them all together. That was new for us because usually we create all the content without much direction. In this case, we took this project on because we believe in what Open Stand is doing. There was certain content that we had to try to include and that made it trickier. This project was sort of a one-time thing. Usually we are doing multiple spaces, either murals or buildings. And sometimes the discussion comes up about "Is it derivative or is it new art?" I lean toward the idea that all art is derivative of some kind. Whether it's a building or an ad or a piece of art—that's the source that we use as a trigger. The digital overlay that's revealed off of it has to be derivative because it's spatial. We are making a connection to what you see in the real world. What we create off of it is something that's new. The original mural can't move; we can make it move. We can create a 3D world that the mural might live in, which extends out from it. For us, the interactivity, the motion, the animation, the 3D qualities are all ways we can bring 2D stuff to life. That's what interests us.

Part 3: Artwork

BC Biermann

Augmented Architecture [NYC + LA, 2012]

As part of the Re+Public collaboration between The Heavy Projects and Jordan Seiler's PublicAdCampaign, Heavy digitally resurfaced, or "skinned" physical buildings in urban centers by overlaying 3D content onto the physical environment. Creatively harnessing augmented reality (AR) technology, Heavy turned architecture into locations for meaningful cultural exchange and, in doing so, provides the user with a new way of seeing public space as a more open and democratic media environment.

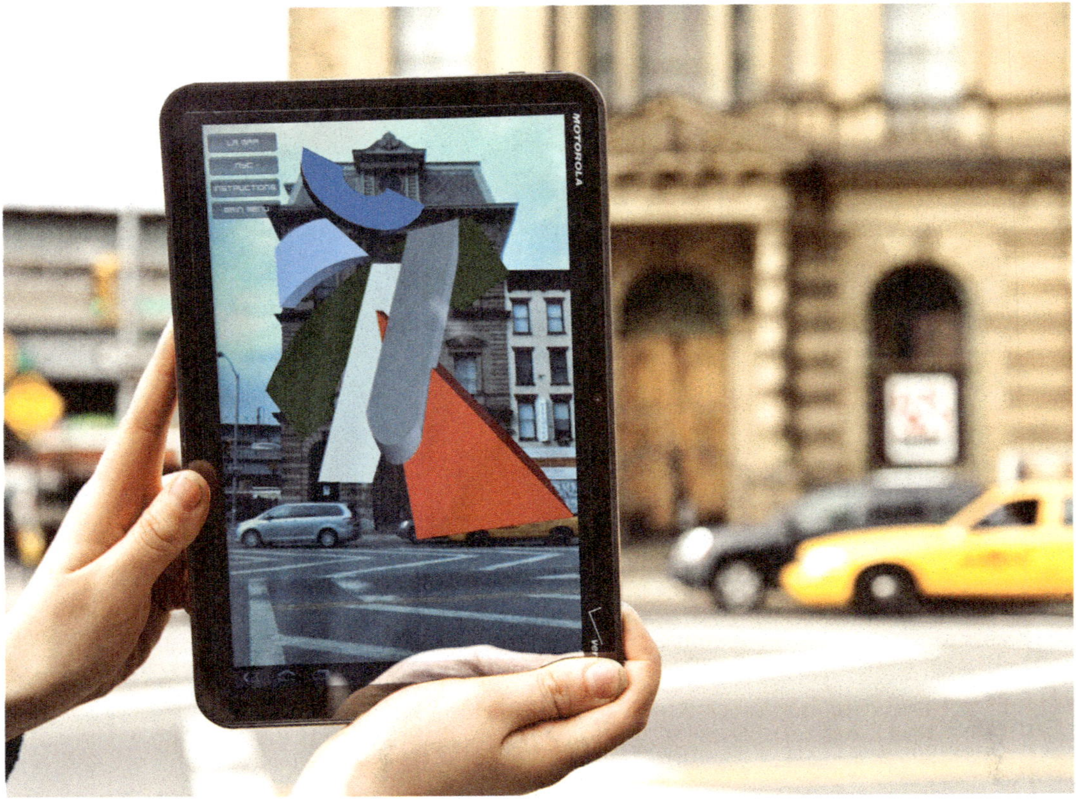

Augmented Architecture, by BC Biermann, Williamsburg Art and Design Building, Brooklyn, New York, 2012. © 2012 by BC Biermann.

Scan the image to view

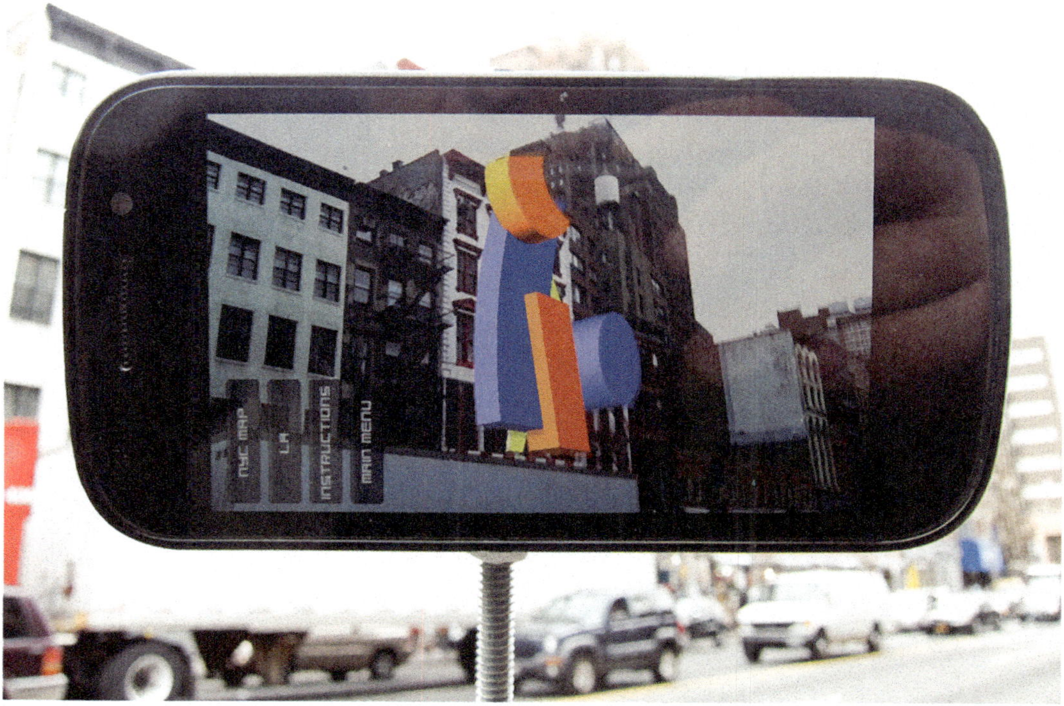

Augmented Architecture, by BC Biermann, Pearl Paint Building, Manhattan, New York, 2012. © 2012 by BC Biermann.

BC Biermann

Bowery Wall [NYC, 2012]

In 1982, Keith Haring painted the first mural on the Houston & Bowery Street wall in New York City. Since the original Haring piece, the wall was bombed by ads and tags. However, in 2008, the wall was restored through the hard work of the wall's owner Tony Goldman and curator Jeffrey Deitch. The Goldman projects have collaborated with such artists as Os Gemeos, Shepard Fairey, Barry McGee, Sace, Kenny Scharf, JR, Faile, and Retna. In June 2012, as part of the Re+Public collaboration between The Heavy Projects and Jordan Seiler's PublicAdCampaign, Heavy used augmented reality to create a virtual history of the famous mural site. Users are able to take a virtual tour of the wall and view each piece as it originally appeared. Our project is dedicated to Tony Goldman (1943-2012).

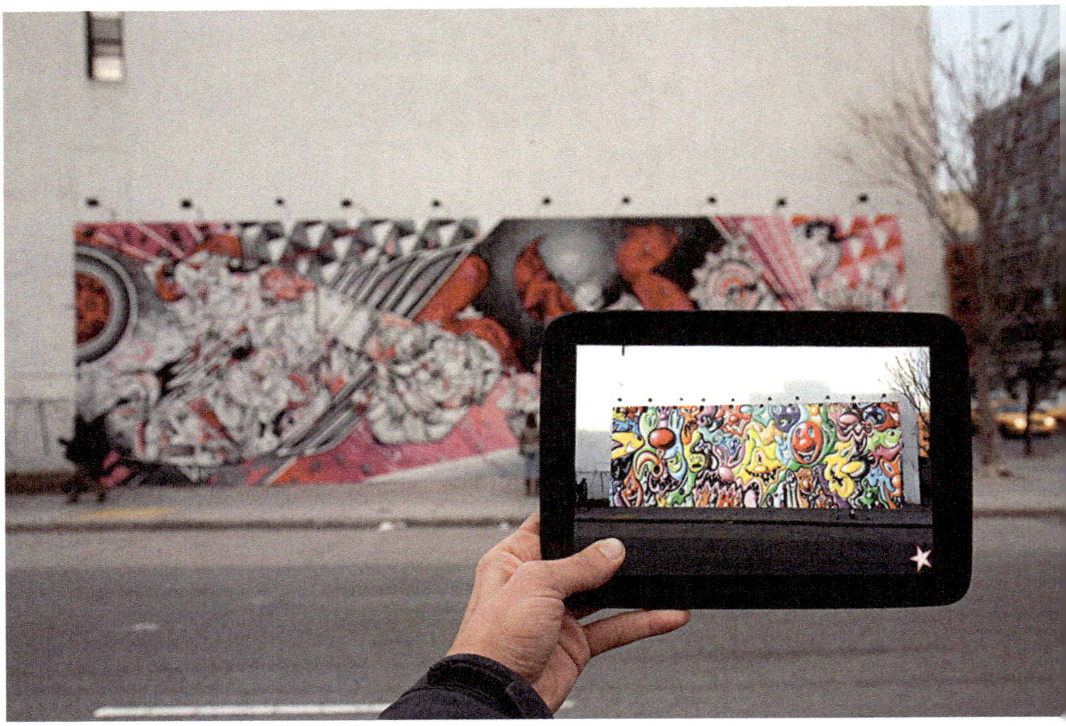

Bowery Wall, by BC Biermann, New York, 2012. © 2012 by BC Biermann.

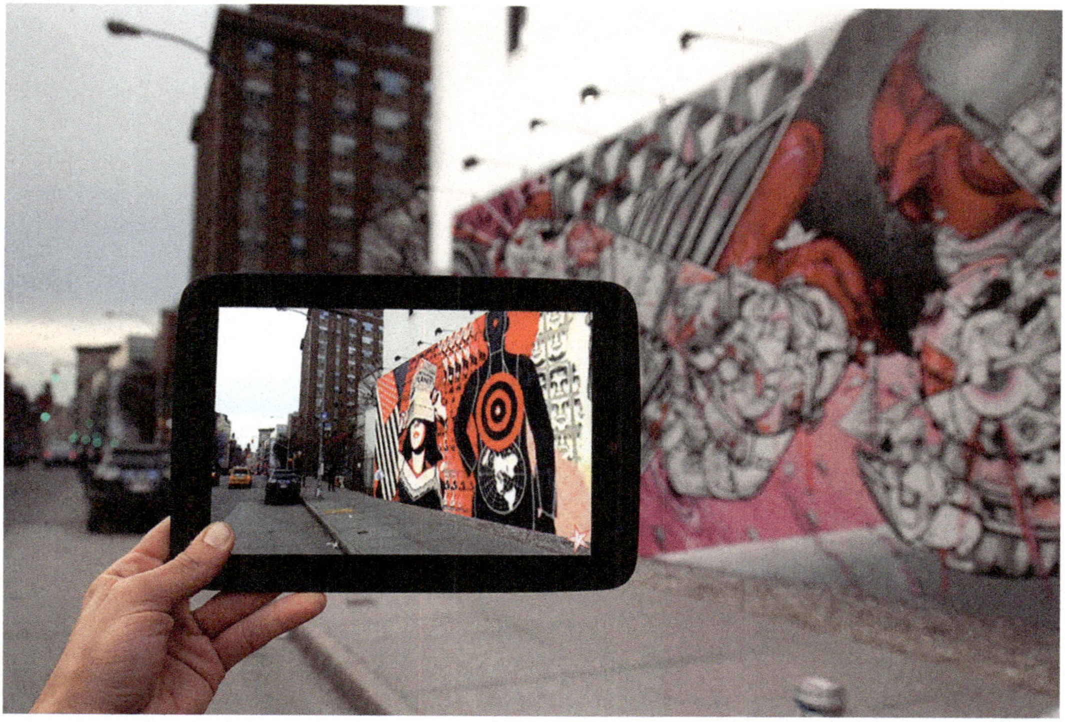

Bowery Wall, by BC Biermann, New York, 2012. © 2012 by BC Biermann.

BC Biermann

Wynwood Walls @ Art Basel [Miami, 2012]

As part of the Re+Public collaboration between The Heavy Projects and Jordan Seiler's PublicAdCampaign, during the Art Basel event, Heavy digitally augmented and animated five murals (How & Nosm, Aiko, Retna, Ryan McGinness, and Momo). Additionally, we resurrected the Shepard Fairey mural that he recently painted over. This project was in collaboration with Goldman Properties.

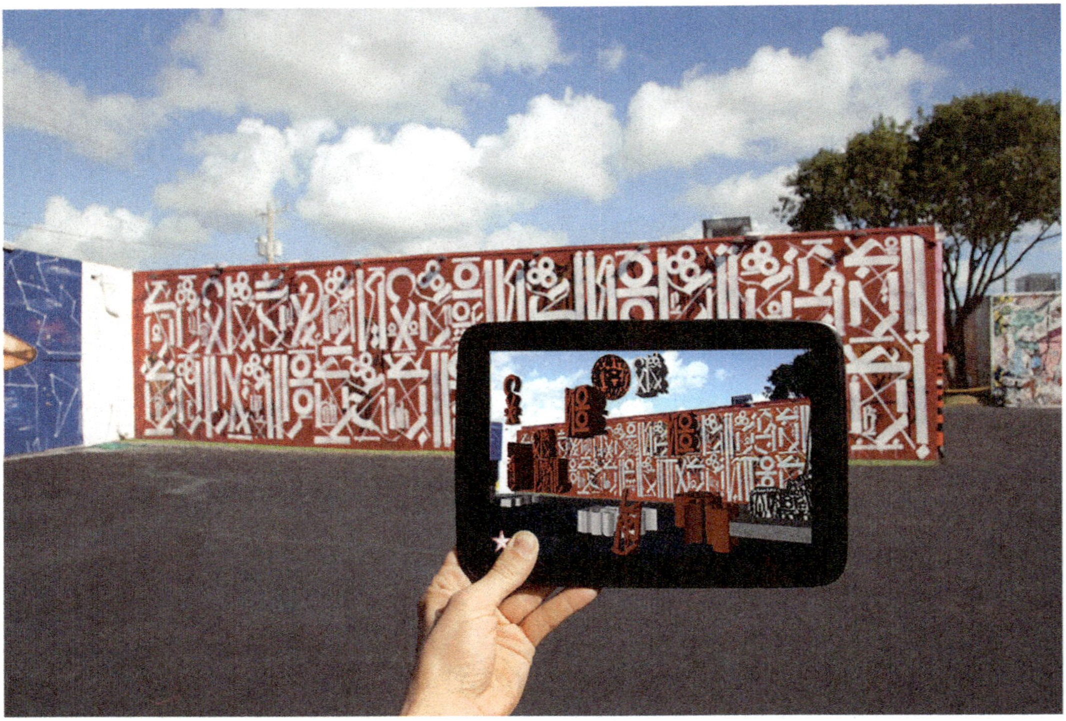

Wynwood Walls at Art Basel, by BC Biermann, Miami, Forida, 2012. © 2012 by BC Biermann.

Scan the image
to view

Tamiko Thiel

Shades of Absence [Venice, Istanbul, Brooklyn, Los Angeles, 2011]

In these pavilions of absence, images of contemporary artists whose public artworks have been censored are reduced to gold silhouettes and placed in the midst of terms of transgression. Each erased silhouette stands for countless unknown or lesser known artists who face censorship or persecution with no public support.

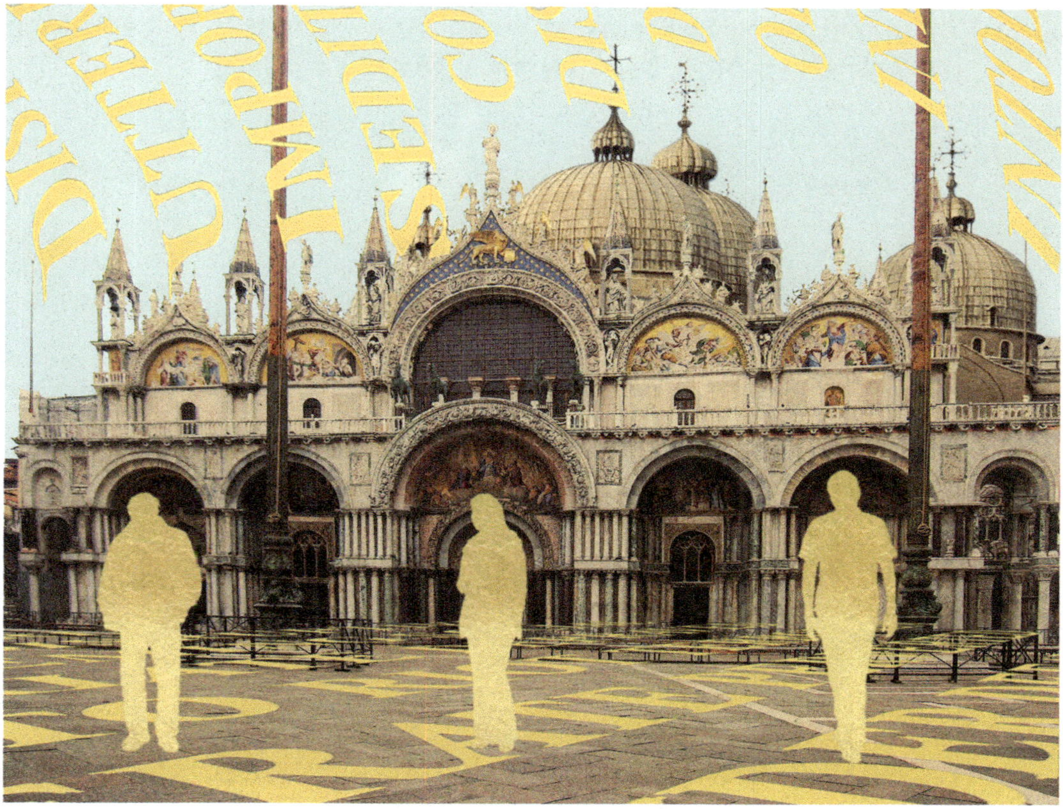

Shades of Absence: Public Voids, by Tamiko Thiel, Augmented Reality, Venice, Italy, 2011. In Piazza San Marco for the 2011 Venice Biennale intervention.

Scan the image to watch

Tamiko Thiel

Clouding Green [Singapore, 2012-2013]

The world's computing power is moving into the Cloud—but where does the Cloud get its energy? The artwork *Clouding Green* floats a massive augmented reality cloud—in colors ranging from sooty carbon black to brilliant renewable green—over eight major Silicon Valley cloud computing providers cited in the Greenpeace report "How Clean is Your Cloud?"

The augmented image in the book shows the 15.3% Clean Energy Index cloud over Apple Headquarters in Silicon Valley.

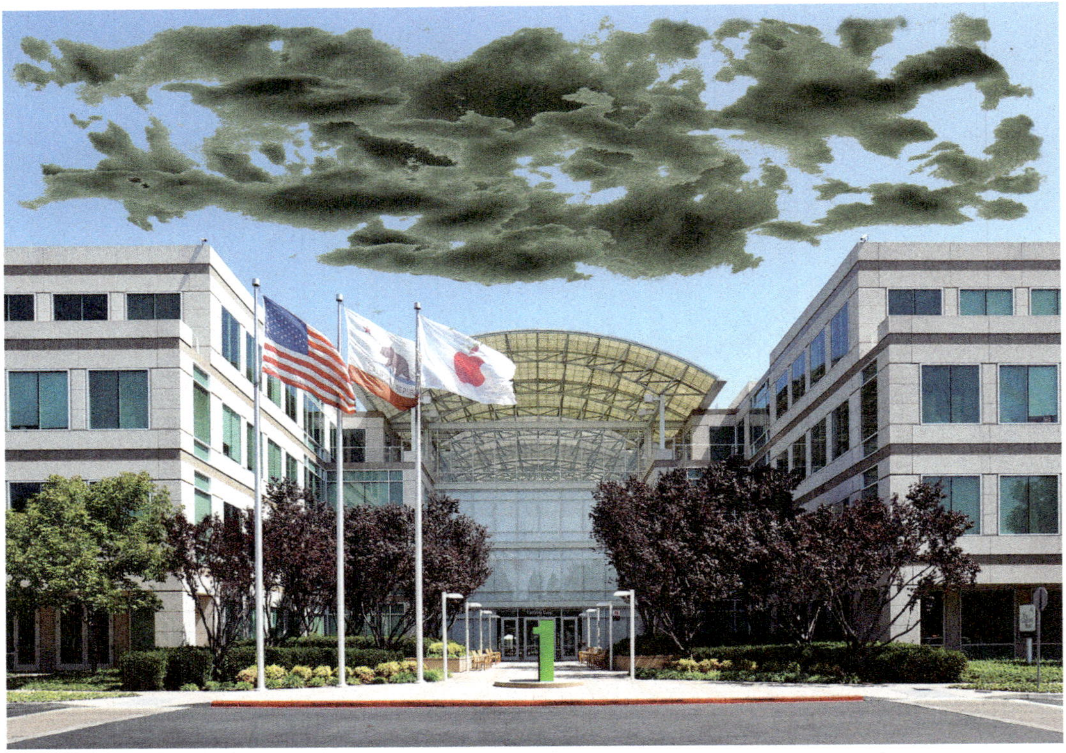

Clouding Green, by Tamiko Thiel, Augmented Reality, 2012. Seen with 15.3% Clean Energy Index at Apple HQ. Photo by Joe Ravi, license CC-BY-SA 3.0. © 2012 by Tamiko Thiel.

Tamiko Thiel

Reign of Gold [NYC, Berlin, Los Angeles, Sydney, Tampa, 2012]

Reign of Gold is an AR art project in conjunction with the Occupy Wall Street movement and can be viewed anywhere in the world set against your favorite object of protest. Touch the augmented image in the display of your mobile device to get a geolocative AR layer that surrounds you with a rain of $50 US gold eagle coins.

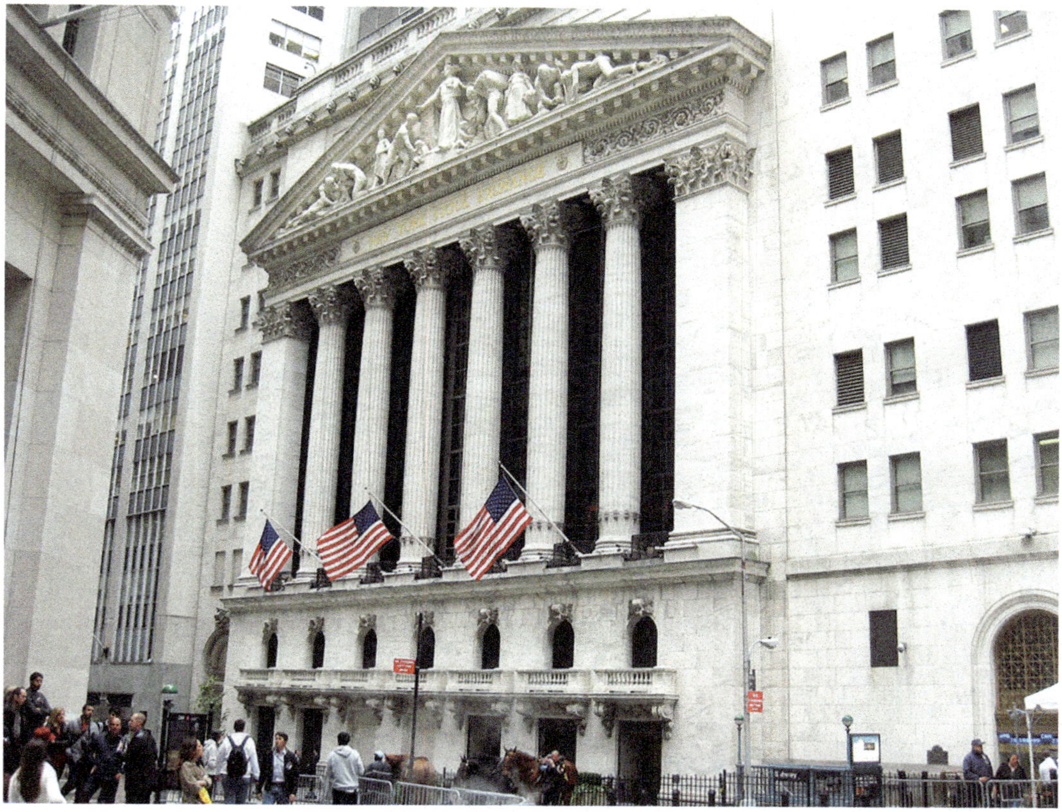

Reign of Gold, by Tamiko Thiel, Augmented Reality, NYC, 2011. Seen at the New York Stock Exchange on Wall Street as part of AR Occupy Wall Street. © 2012 by Tamiko Thiel.

Scan the image to view

Tamiko Thiel

Jasmine Rain (Birdcage) [Cairo, Tunis, Beijing, Boston, NYC, 2011]

A sweet rain of jasmine flowers promises freedom and celebrates the Jasmine Revolutions of the Arab Spring. Touch the augmented image and you will find yourself enclosed in a golden cage until the revolution fulfills its promise.

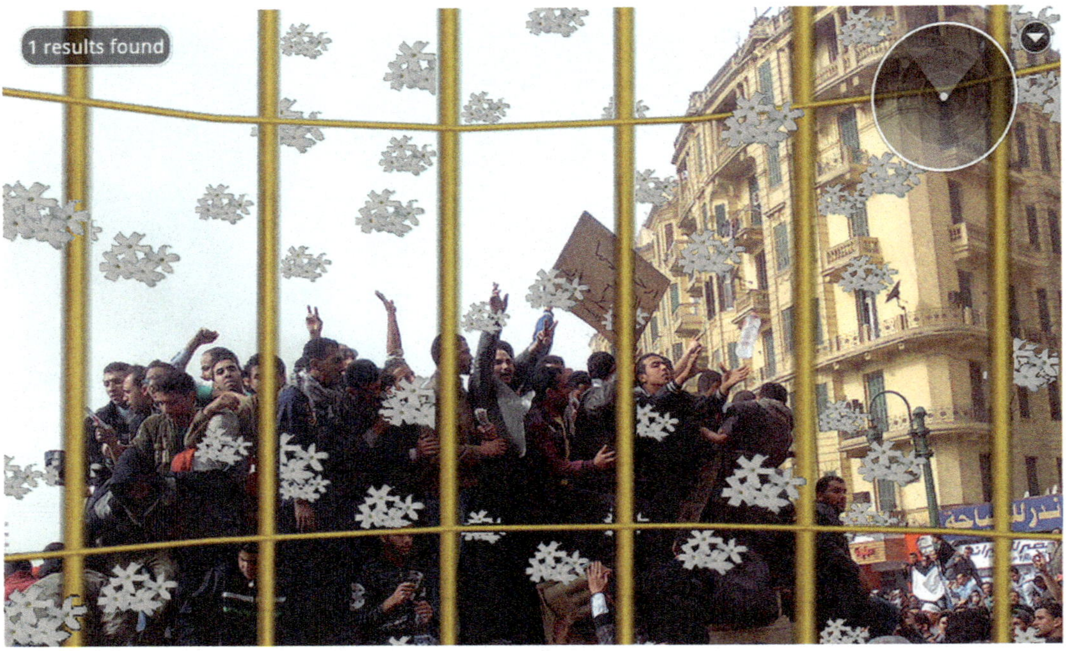

Jasmine Rain (Birdcage), by Tamiko Thiel, Augmented Reality, Cairo, Egypt, 2011. Seen at Tahrir Square, Cairo, Egypt. Photo by Ramy Raoof, 2011. © 2011 by Tamiko Thiel.

Scan the image to watch

Tamiko Thiel

Carnation Rain [Lisbon, 2011]

Carnation Rain commemorates the "Carnation Revolution" with an animated rain of virtual carnations geolocated in Largo do Carmo (Carmo Square), Lisbon. On April 25th, 1974, the "Carnation Revolution" broke out in Largo do Carmo as a leftist military coup toppled the Salazarist dictatorship that had ruled Portugal for around 50 years, ushering in changes that brought democracy to Portugal. Carnations, stuck in the barrels of the guns to show their peaceful intent, became the symbol for this first bloodless revolution in twentieth century Europe.

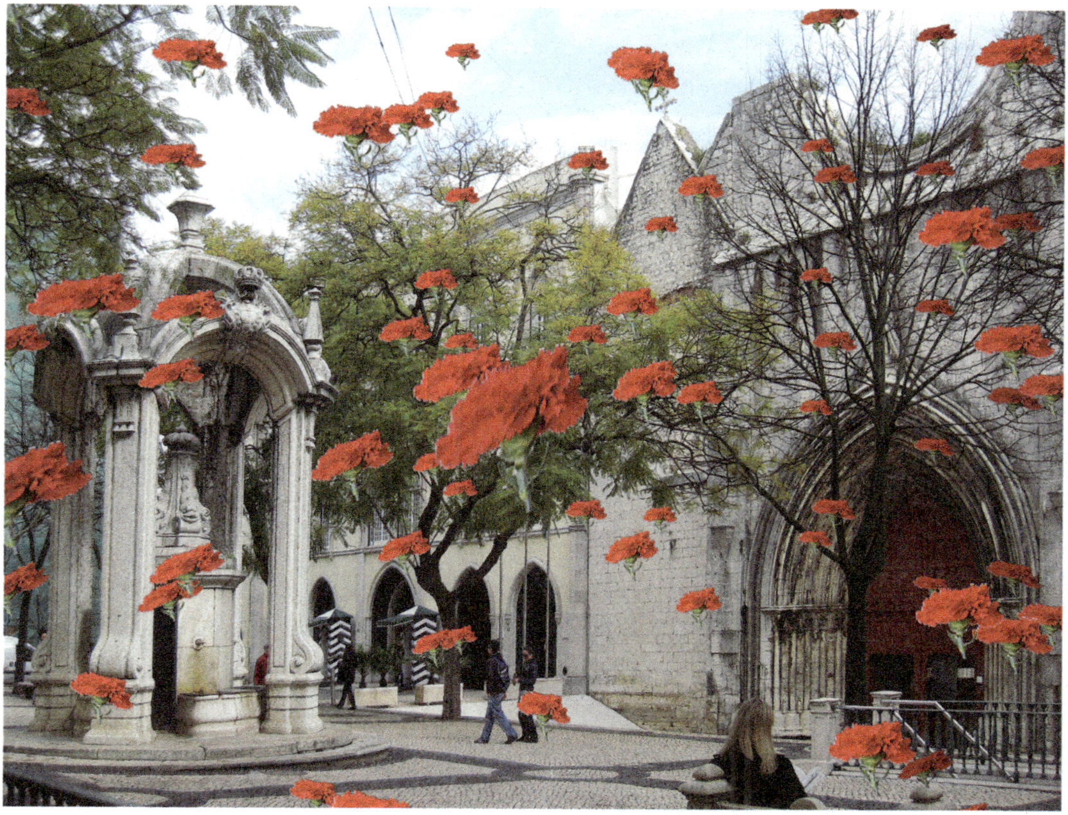

Carnation Rain, by Tamiko Thiel, Augmented Reality, Largo do Carmo, Lisbon, Portugal, 2011. © 2011 by Tamiko Thiel.

Scan the image to watch

Conor McGarrigle

NAMAland [Dublin, 2010-2012]

NAMAland is a mobile AR artwork, built on the Layar platform, which uses Open Data and augmented reality to visualize and critique aspects of the Irish financial collapse through an overlayering of the city of Dublin with a database driven data layer identifying properties under the control of NAMA (The National Assets Management Agency).

NAMA is an Irish Government Agency established in December 2009 to acquire bad property loans from Irish banks with the aim of removing them from the banks' balance sheets as a bailout mechanism. The controversial agency acquired properties worth €40 billion but failed in its stated aim of bailing out the banks, culminating in Ireland entering an IMF/EU bailout program in November 2010 due to the imminent collapse of the banking system. Despite its central role in the financial collapse, NAMA was very secretive in its workings. Legally exempted from Freedom of Information requirements, the agency was intent on shielding its property portfolio, and the individuals and corporations involved, from public scrutiny under the guise of "commercial sensitivity." *NAMAland* set out to make this information available to the public in an easily accessible format. The project was built on an unofficial database of NAMA properties which I refined, augmented, and geotagged, creating the first and, to date, only mapping of NAMA properties.

NAMAland sought to visualize this one aspect of the Irish financial collapse by overlaying an augmented layer of NAMA property data over the physical space of Dublin. This served to make concrete what has become an abstract account of financial transactions by associating it with real buildings and lands which can be interrogated in real space on any smartphone.

NAMAland succeeded in capturing the popular imagination in Ireland. It received extensive coverage in the mainstream media on TV, radio, and print culminating in an interview and report on the Nine O'Clock News on RTE (the Irish national broadcaster). The title "*NAMAland*" has even entered common usage as a descriptor for the post IMF bailout situation. The project also included a series of very successful guided walks, facilitated through the app, which addressed NAMA and the issues at the heart of the financial collapse, opening the project to a wider constituency who may not necessarily have access to the requisite technology to view the work.

Central to the project's success was its ability to function as a conduit which reconnected NAMA with the space of the city, a connection which had been deliberately severed, to preserve the idea of the agency as a by-product of obscure international financial dealings. What *NAMAland* contributed was an opening up of previously unavailable data and a re-connecting of this data with the fabric of the city itself. This served to add specificity in place of generalization, fueling debate through the provision of an infrastructure on which specific spatial critiques could be structured, supplying a point of entry hitherto unavailable.

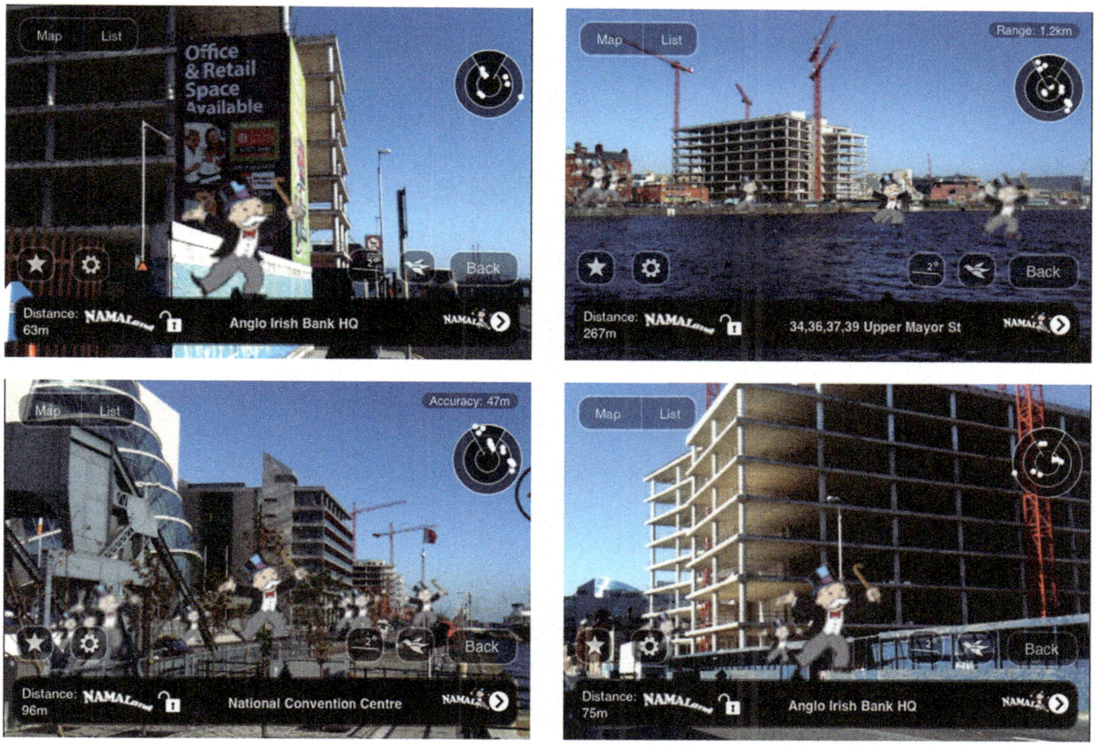

NAMAland, by Conor McGarrigle, Dublin, 2010-2012. ©2012 by Conor McGarrigle.

Scan the image to watch

Conor McGarrigle

Walking Stories [Dundrum, 2011]

Walking Stories is an augmented reality soundwalk through Dundrum village guided by a location-aware smartphone app, a printed map with downloadable audio files and situated QR codes.

Dundrum is a village in South County Dublin; it is home to Dundrum Town Centre, the largest shopping centre in Ireland, which has transformed the locality into a busy shopping destination. The project was commissioned for the Unfolding Narratives exhibition which explored the impact of such unprecedented development on a community's vision of itself through considering both the visible and the hidden narratives of Dundrum as a place.

Starting at the historic Carnegie Library, the soundwalk unfolded in Dundrum village leading participants on a narrative trail which recounts the personal stories that connect people to specific locations. *Walking Stories* revealed a virtual world of memories, associations, and connections that underpin a community. *Walking Stories* asked what is it that connects us to the spaces we live and work in and invited us to share in the personal memories that create a place.

The project was available as an augmented reality mobile app working on the Layar platform, as a series of situated QR codes that played the story for each location when scanned, and as a printed map and website that allowed users to download story MP3 files to personal audio players to be used in conjunction with the map.

Walking Stories was curated by Annette Moloney and Maeve Mulrennan and commissioned by Dun Laoghaire Rathdown County Council.

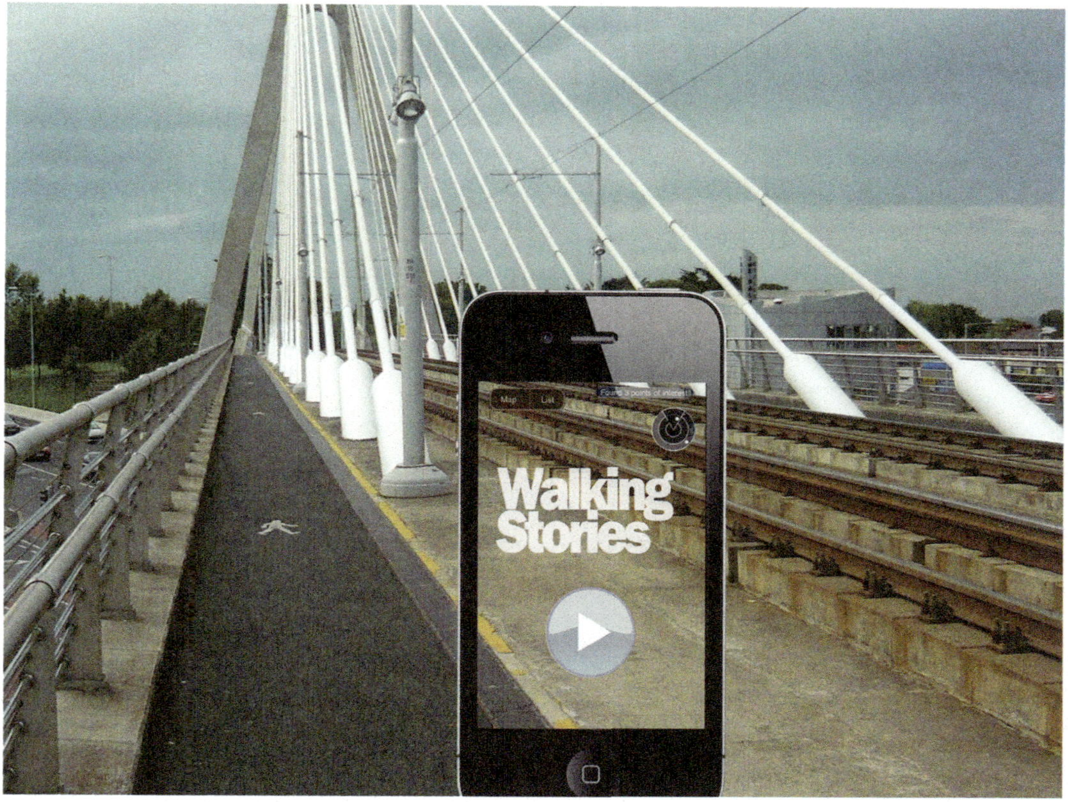

Walking Stories, by Conor McGarrigle, Dundrum, Ireland, 2011. © 2011 by Conor McGarrigle.

Conor McGarrigle

Vineland [2013]

Vineland is a data driven AR artwork which overlays a number of cities (mainly in the US) with their geo-tagged Vine videos (Vines are video tweets, six-second long status updates which are posted directly to Twitter), with each video viewable in the location in which it was posted.

The project is created through scraping large amounts of Vine data from Twitter and filtering out Vines which have been precisely geo-tagged and can be located in real space. The work overlays these ephemeral six-second videos over real space to create a data-generated portrait of the city as told through its vines.

Vineland raises concerns about the permanency of data in the era of PRISM when nothing is forgotten. While Vines are an ephemeral form, once created they persist in the network, despite the expectation that as fleeting gestures they are soon forgotten. Vine is in many ways the bleeding edge of the Internet, a technically sophisticated tool which is easy to use and seamlessly integrated within a social media infrastructure, used to produce these ephemeral moments.

Through data scraping techniques, *Vineland* appropriates Vine's geo-tagged content, thus mirroring the logic of enterprises driven by user generated content, to produce a work generated by algorithmic processes from which emerges a locative portrait of social media and the richness of the social activity of so many individuals, in effect a snapshot of everyday life with all its humor, banality, and brilliance.

Vineland is live in the cities of Atlanta, Berlin, Boston, Chicago, Denver, Dublin, London, Los Angeles, Mountain View, New York City, Paris, Portland, San Francisco, and Seattle.

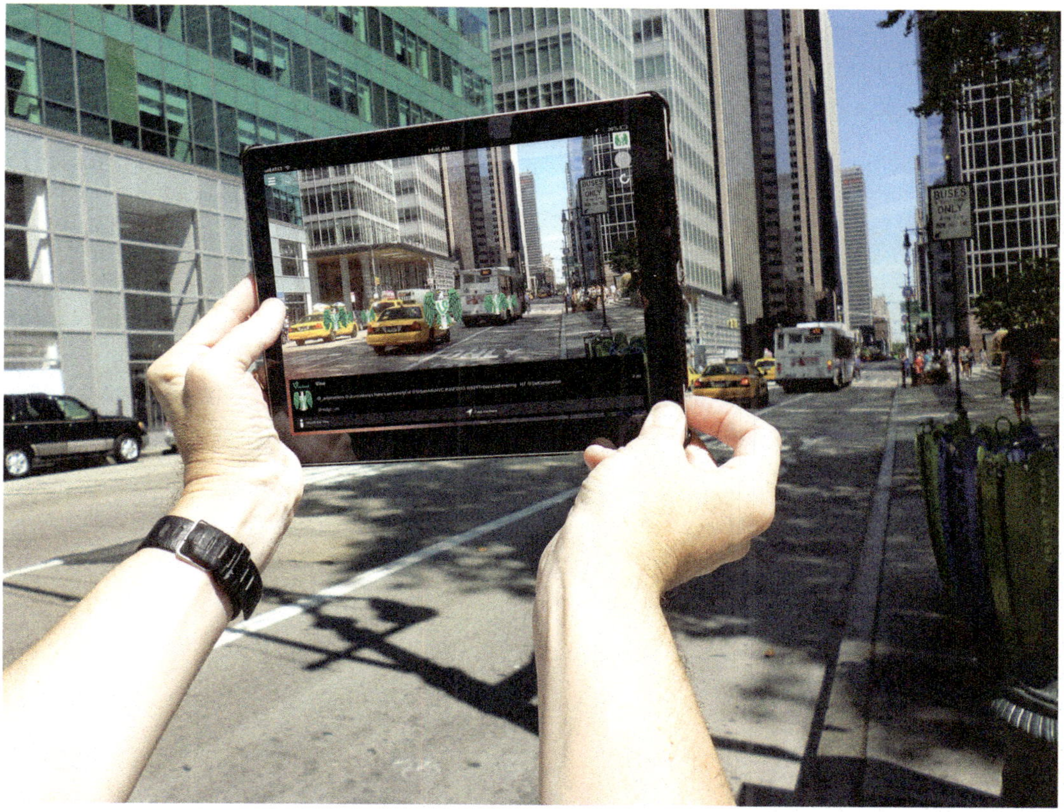

Vineland, by Conor McGarrigle, NYC, 2013. © 2013 by Conor McGarrigle.

Conor McGarrigle

Where's Franco? [VENICE, 2011]

Where's Franco? is an augmented reality pervasive game that placed actor and artist James Franco at various locations throughout Venice for the duration of the Biennale of Art 2011. The project responded to the hype surrounding Franco's much anticipated on-again-off-again debut at the Biennale, with a whimsical project that allowed users to take a photograph of themselves with the actor in various locations throughout Venice.

The project is perhaps best described by the original project text:

> James Franco, actor, artist, academic, a modern day renaissance man who can rock a tash better them [*sic*] most. We know Franco is in Venice for the Biennale, but where?
>
> Where's Franco is an augmented reality pervasive game which has placed Franco at various locations throughout Venice for the duration of the Biennale of Art. Use it to explore Venice while finding Franco and seeing him in his native habitat, the centre of the international art world!
>
> Just in case the invite for that Franco party gets lost in the post don't go home without that all important photo of you hanging out with the man during the Biennale.

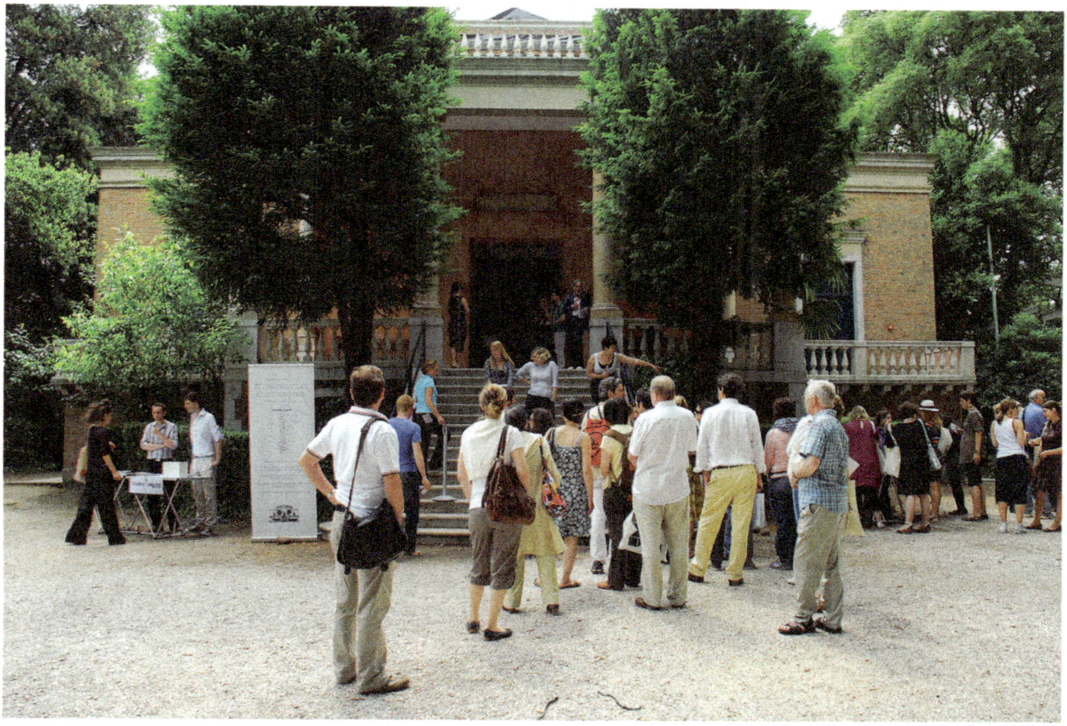

Where's Franco? by Conor McGarrigle, Venice Biennale, 2011. © 2011 by Conor McGarrigle

Scan the image
to view

John Craig Freeman

Orators, Rostrums, and Propaganda Stands [2012-2013]

Orators, Rostrums, and Propaganda Stands is based of the work of Gustav Gustavovich Klucis, including his designs for screen-radio orators, rostrums, and propaganda stands from 1922. Klucis was a pioneering member of the Russian Constructivist avant-garde in the early twentieth century. As Russian politics degenerated under the Stalin dictatorship in the 1920s and 30s, Klucis came under increasing pressure to devote his artwork to state propaganda. Despite his loyal service to the Communist Party, Klucis was arrested in Moscow on January 17, 1938. His whereabouts remained a mystery until 1989, when it was discovered that he had been executed by Stalin just after his arrest. Each of the four virtual objects display a black and white animation from a contemporary mass uprising: Tank Man near Tiananmen Square in Beijing in 1989, the assassination of Neda Agha-Soltan, who was gunned down in the streets of Tehran during the 2009 Iranian election protests, scenes from Tahrir Square in Cairo during the 2011 Arab Spring, and the 2011 Occupy Wall Street uprising. Each of these images are juxtaposed, in montage, with frames from the Odessa Steps scene of Sergei Eisenstein's historic Battleship Potemkin film. When touched, the virtual objects play sound from the uprising. The stands call up both the resurgence and nostalgia of current worldwide political idealism as they reimagine the public square, now augmented with the worldwide digital network.

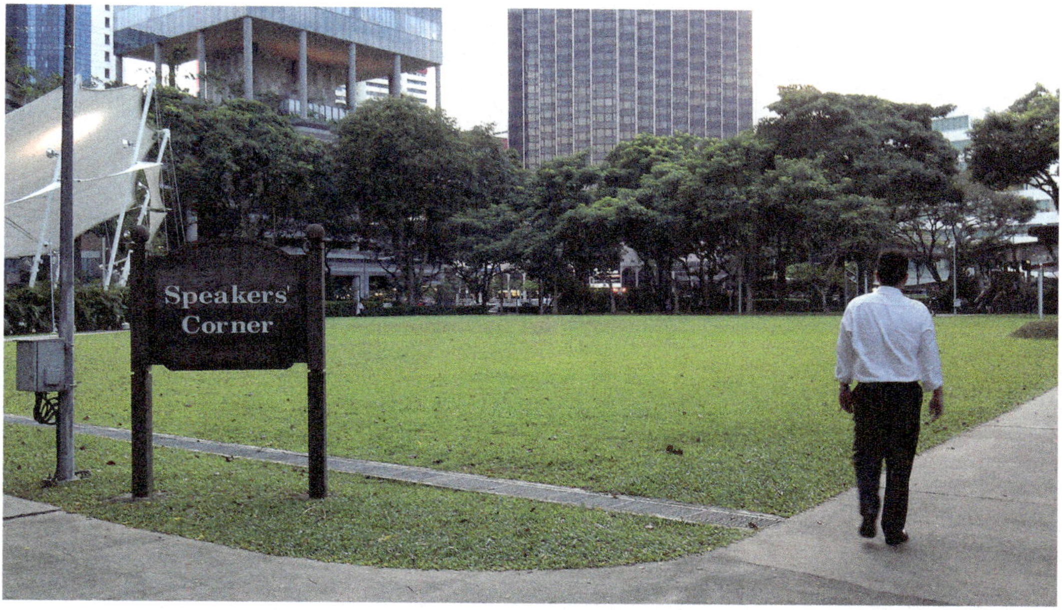

Orators, Rostrums, and Propaganda Stands, by John Craig Freeman, 2012-2013. Commissioned by the Los Angeles County Museum of Art. © 2013 by John Craig Freeman.

Scan the image to view

John Craig Freeman

Flotsam & Jetsam [Singapore, Massachusetts, 2013]

Flotsam is floating wreckage of a ship or its cargo. Jetsam is part of a ship, its equipment, or its cargo that is purposefully cast overboard or jettisoned to lighten the load in time of distress and that sinks or is washed ashore by the Coriolis Effect: planetary vorticity along with horizontal and vertical friction. Marking the contour of the expected sea level fifty years from now, *Flotsam & Jetsam* is a clarion call for the denizens of the world to take seriously the science of climate change and other abuses to the global environment by envisioning the debris left by storm surge and other manifestations of the incoming tide.

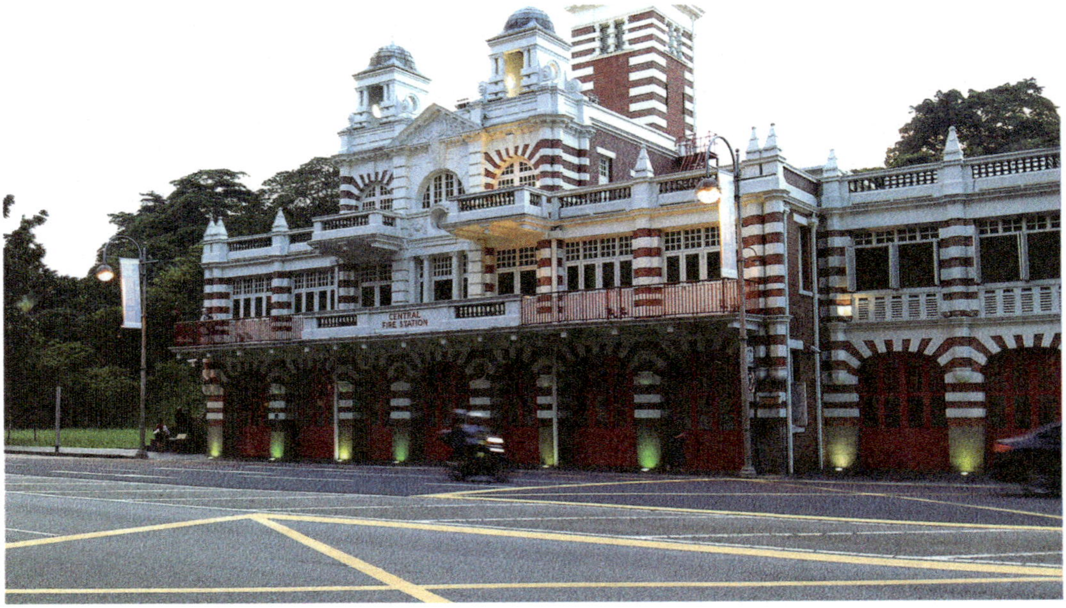

Flotsam & Jetsam, by John Craig Freeman, Digital Arts Week, Singapore, 2013. © 2013 by John Craig Freeman. Placement: Below previous paragraph.]

Scan the image
to view

John Craig Freeman

EEG AR: Things We Have Lost [Liverpool, 2013]

EEG AR: Things We Have Lost allows participants to conjure up virtual objects by simply imagining them into existence using brainwave sensor technology. As part of the research, development, and community engagement of this project, in 2012 we selected people at random in the streets of Liverpool and simply asked, "What have you lost?"

The location was recorded, a virtual lost object was created based on the response, and the objects were then placed back in the exact GPS coordinates using augmented reality technology, creating a citywide network of lost things. Though this process, a database of lost things was generated, including pensions, empires, dodo birds, etc. During the experimental phase of the project, test subjects were outfitted with EEG-reading brainwave sensors and ask to think deeply about what he or she has lost. Once our software detects a measurable and consistent pattern, it issues a database call to instantiate a virtual lost object at random from the database. The virtual object then appears in front of the participant, viewable on any iPhone or Android device.

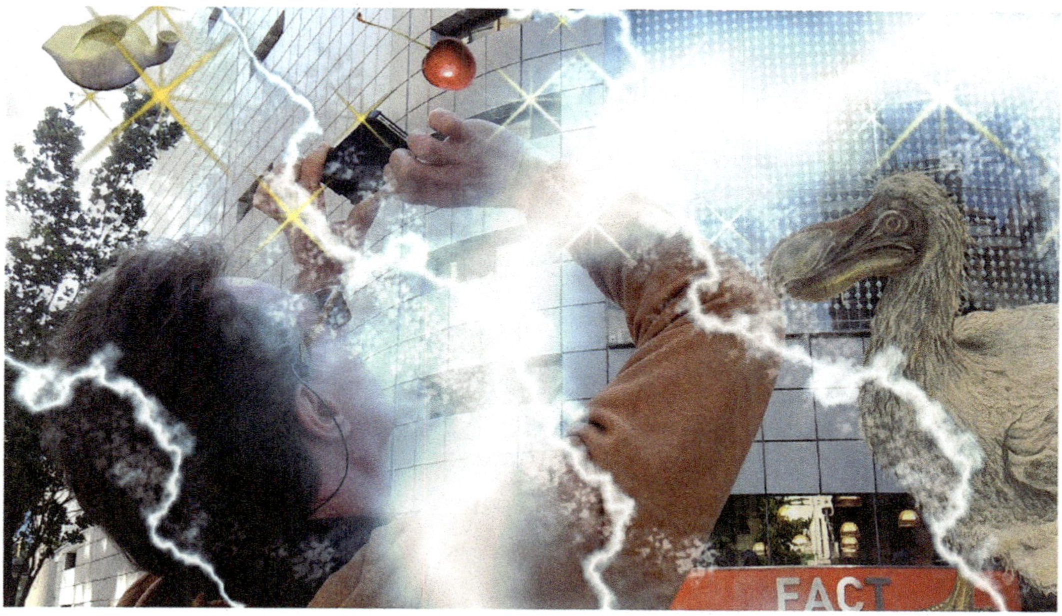

EEG AR: Things We Have Lost, by John Craig Freeman, Liverpool, England, 2013. © 2013 by John Craig Freeman.

Scan the image to view

John Craig Freeman

Border Memorial: Frontera De Los Muertos [Arizona, 2012]

Border Memorial: Frontera de Los Muertos is an augmented reality public art project and memorial, dedicated to the thousands of migrant workers who have died along the US/Mexico border in recent years trying to cross the desert southwest in search of work and a better life.

This project allows people to visualize the scope of the loss of life by marking each location where human remains have been recovered.

Based on a traditional form of woodcarving from Oaxaca, the virtual object consists of life-sized, three dimensional geometric models of a skeleton effigy or *calaca*. Calacas are used in commemoration of lost loved ones during the Mexican Día de los Muertos, or Day of the Dead festivals. According to indigenous belief, despite the tragedy, death should always be celebrated. In the tradition of Día de los Muertos, the Border Memorial project is designed to honor, celebrate, and remember those who have died and to vault this issue into public consciousness and American political debate. The project is intended to provide a kind of lasting conceptual presence in an otherwise ephemeral physical environment and cultural discourse.

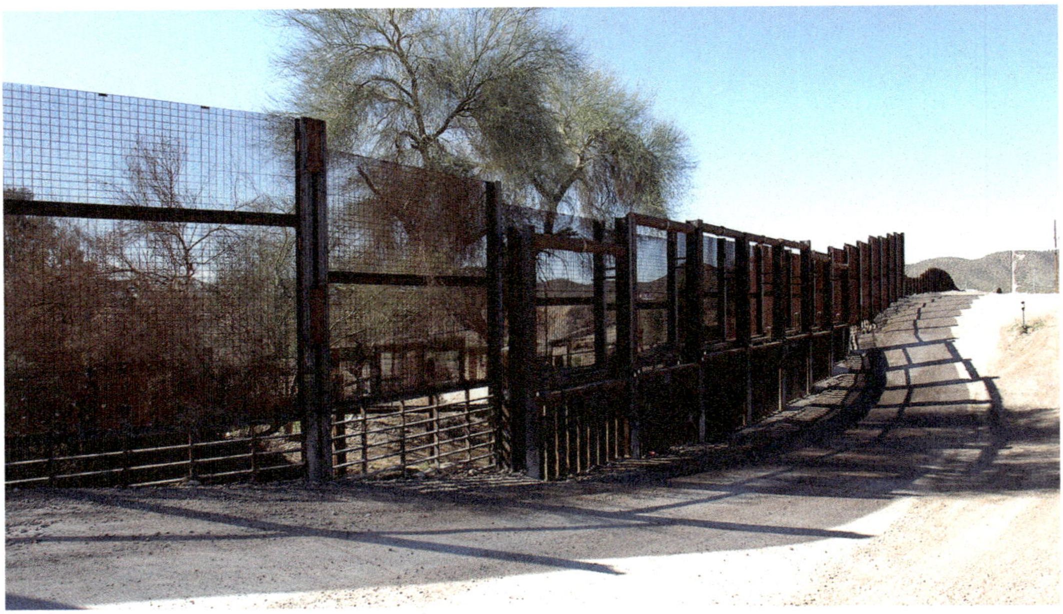

Border Memorial: Frontera de Los Muertos, by John Craig Freeman, Southern Arizona, 2012. © 2012 by John Craig Freeman.

Scan the image to view

John Craig Freeman

Water wARs [Venice Biennial and Brooklyn, 2011]

Water wARs anticipates the flood of environmental refugees into the developed world caused by environmental degradation, global warming, and the privatization of the world's drinking water supply by multinational corporations like Bechtel.

The project consists of a sprawling virtual shanty pavilion for undocumented artists/squatters and water war refugees.

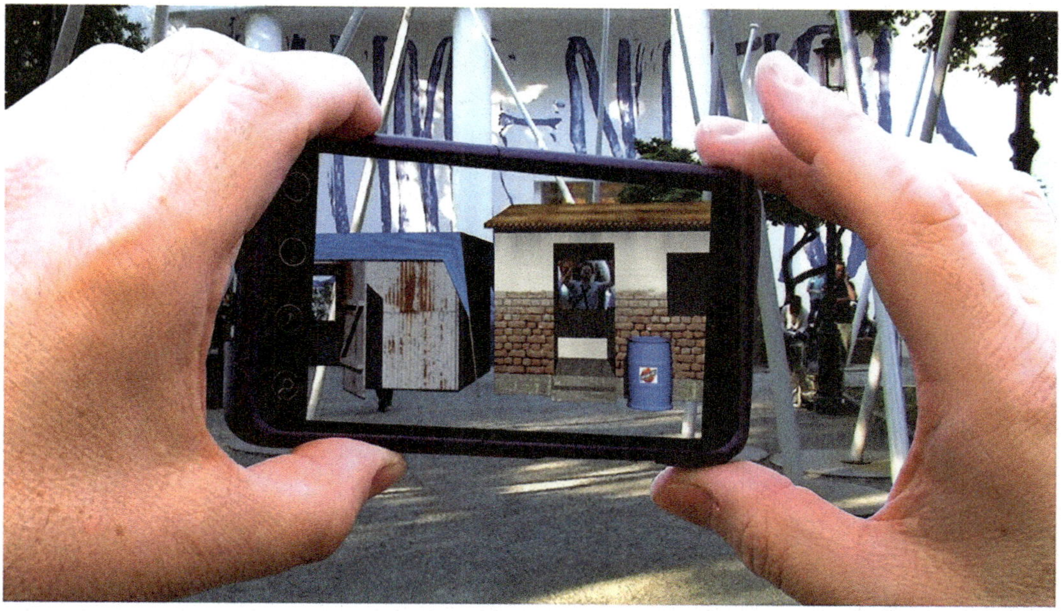

Water wARs, by John Craig Freeman, Venice Biennale, 2011. © 2011 by John Craig Freeman.

Scan the image to view

John Craig Freeman

Tiananmen SquARed (Attributed to) 4 Gentlemen [Beijing, 2010]

Tiananmen SquARed is a two part augmented reality public art project and memorial, dedicated to human rights and democracy worldwide. The project includes virtual replicas of the Goddess of Democracy and Tank Man from the 1989 student uprising in Tiananmen Square. Both augmentations have been placed in Beijing at the precise GPS coordinates where the original incidents took place. The Goddess of Democracy was a thirty-three foot tall statue, constructed in only four days out of foam and papier-mâché over a metal armature. Students from an art institute created the statue, placing it to face toward a huge picture of the late Communist Party chairman Mao Zedong. Tanks later flattened the statue when China's military crushed the protest. Tank Man was an anonymous man who stood in front of a column of Chinese Type 59 tanks the morning after the Chinese military forcibly removed protestors from in and around Beijing's Tiananmen Square on June 5, 1989. The man achieved widespread international recognition due to the videotape and photographs taken of the incident.

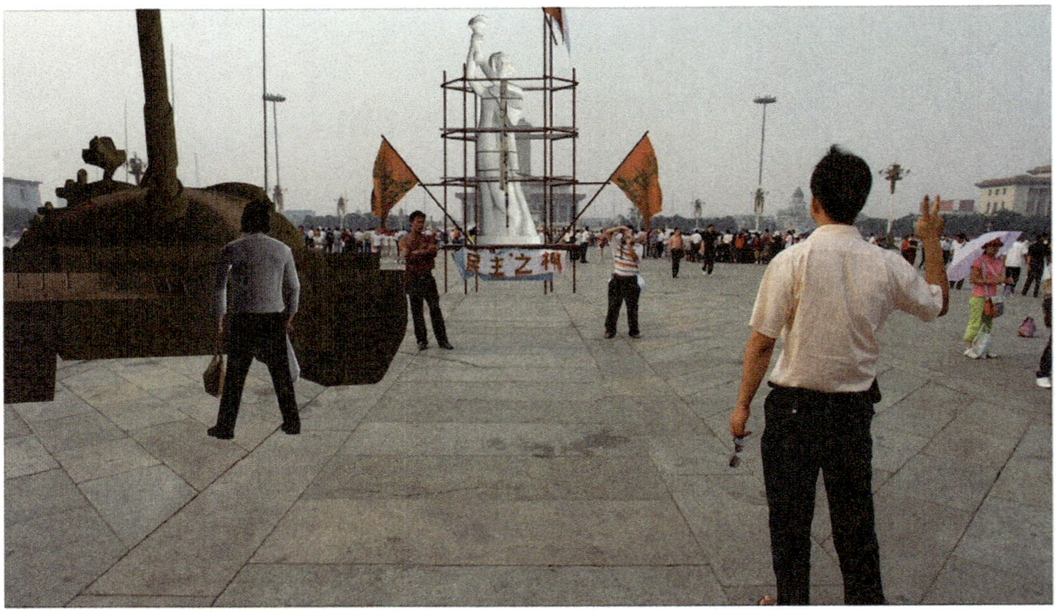

Tiananmen SquARed (Attributed to) 4 Gentlemen, by John Craig Freeman, Beijing, 2010. © 2010 by John Craig Freeman.

John Craig Freeman

Peace Doors [Belfast, 2010]

With nine locations along the Peace Line in West Belfast, *Peace Doors* addresses the ongoing conflict between the Catholic and Protestant communities there. The Peace Line is constructed of walls, fences, industrial complexes, and even a shopping mall, designed to separate the Protestant Shankill neighborhood to the north from the Catholic Falls Road neighborhood to the south. The first Peace Line barriers were built in 1969, following the outbreak of the 1969 Northern Ireland riots and "The Troubles." They were built as temporary structures because they were indeed meant to be temporary, lasting only six months, but due to their effective nature they have become more permanent, wider, and longer across the city.

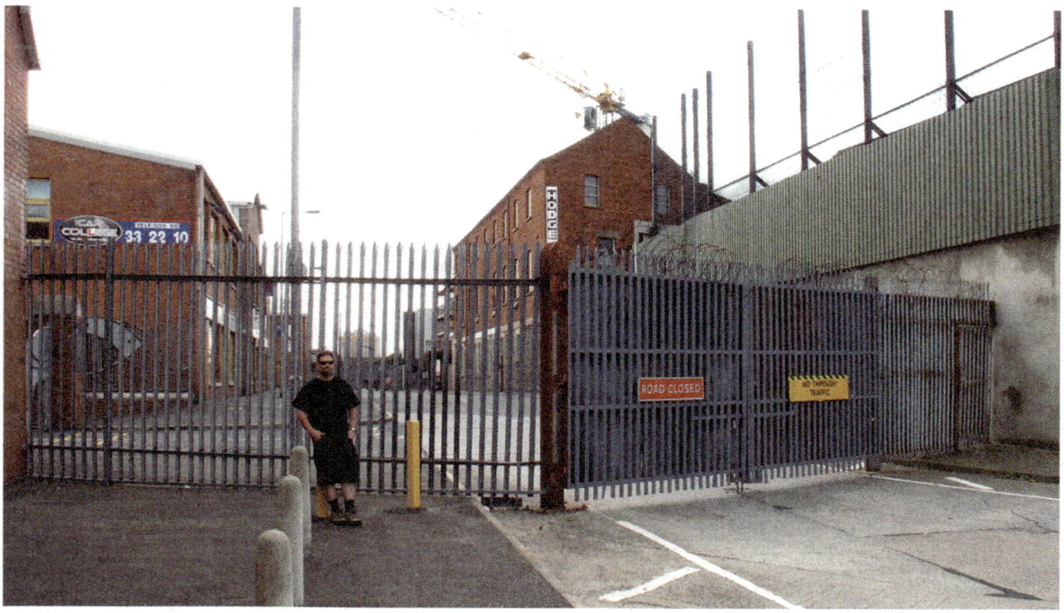

Peace Doors, by John Craig Freeman, Belfast, 2010. © 2010 by John Craig Freeman.

Scan the image to view

Bryan Leister

Goldman Sachs (Giant Blood Sucking Vampire Squid) [Denver, 2012]

This project was a site-specific augmented reality installation for Redline Denver's Material Engagements exhibition curated by Harmony Hammond. Visitors to the gallery are invited to download the application from the Apple App store or Google Play to their mobile device. Pointing their device at the charcoal drawing on the wall reveals a hidden world where hundreds of invisible people work to suck the life out of everything that we know.

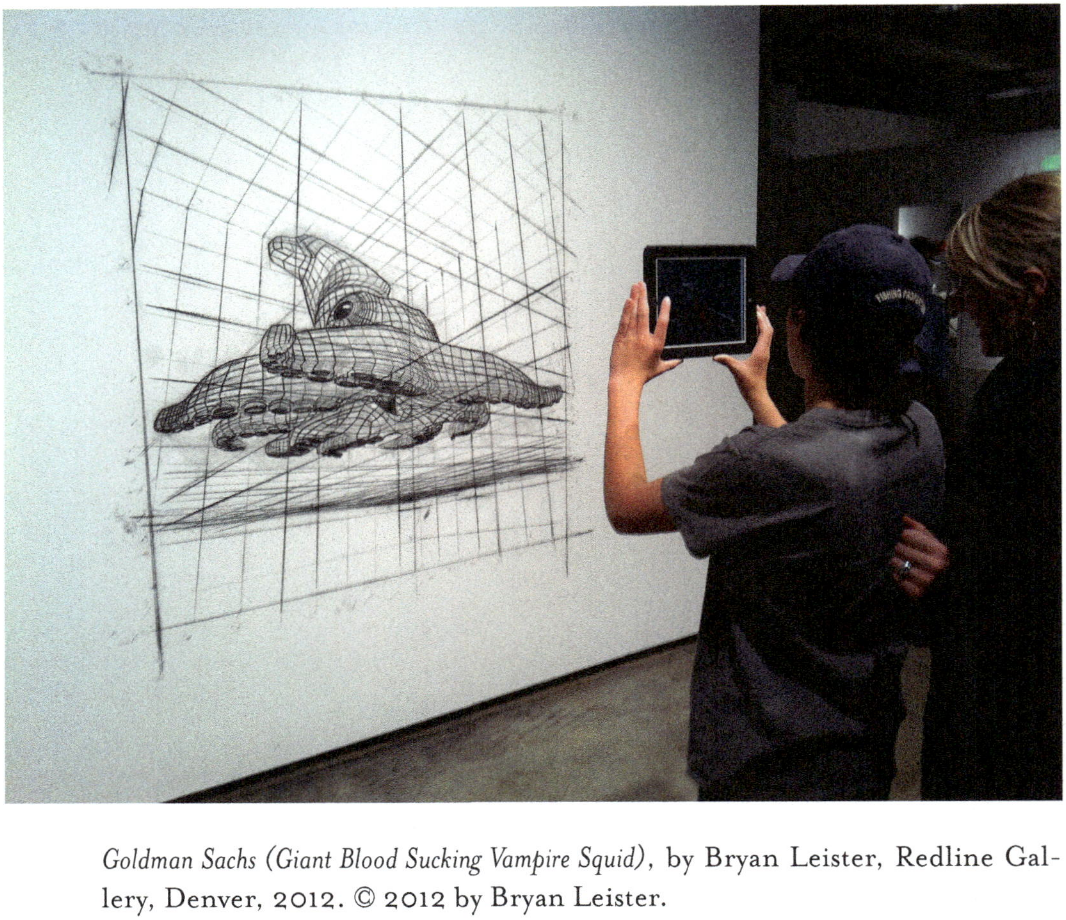

Goldman Sachs (Giant Blood Sucking Vampire Squid), by Bryan Leister, Redline Gallery, Denver, 2012. © 2012 by Bryan Leister.

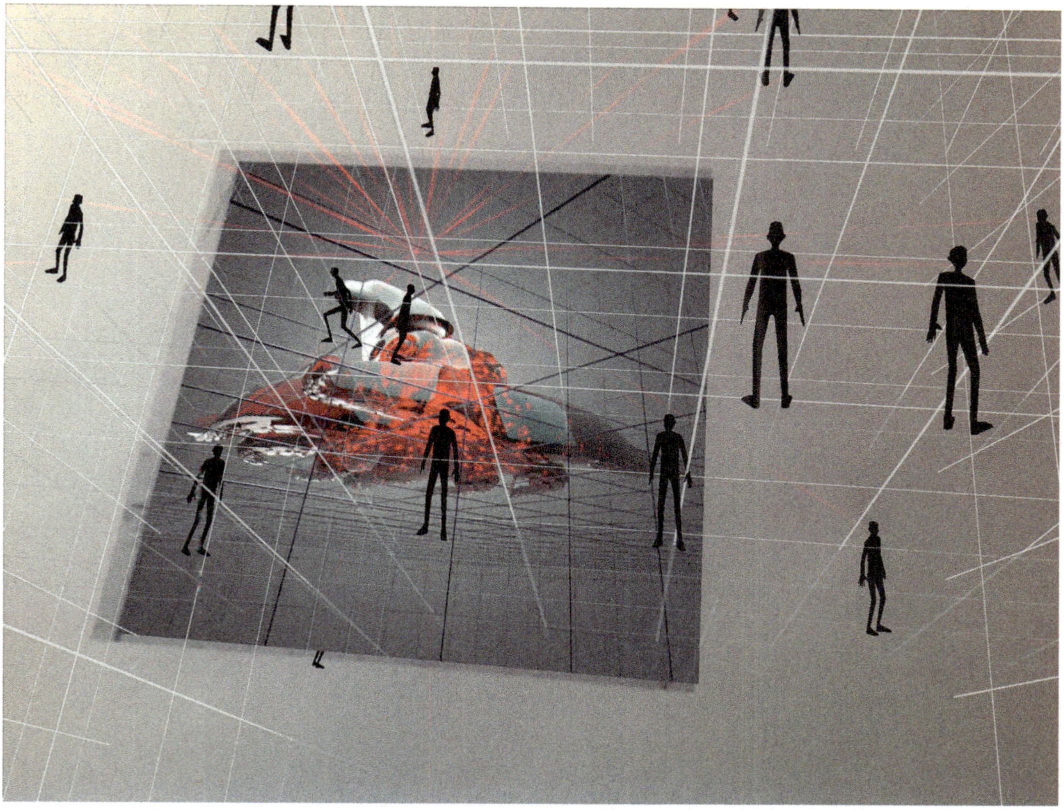

Screenshot from *Goldman Sachs (Giant Blood Sucking Vampire Squid)*, by Bryan Leister, Redline Gallery, Denver, 2012.

Bryan Leister

Mood Analyticator [Denver, 2012]

This augmented reality application was created for the 2012 Blacktop Festival held in Denver. Attendees were able to download the mobile application and point their device at t-shirts printed with original heart drawing artwork by Clemente Guzman. The application would then display that person's live, beating heart and it was able to determine, after a time, if the person was good or bad. Once the application has been downloaded to your mobile device, point the camera of the device at Clemente Guzman's heart drawing on my website.

Programming: Bryan Leister
Heart drawing: Clemente Guzman
Anatomical heart animation: Travis Vermilye
Additional animations: Bryan Leister, Ethan Zink, and Jacob Imlay

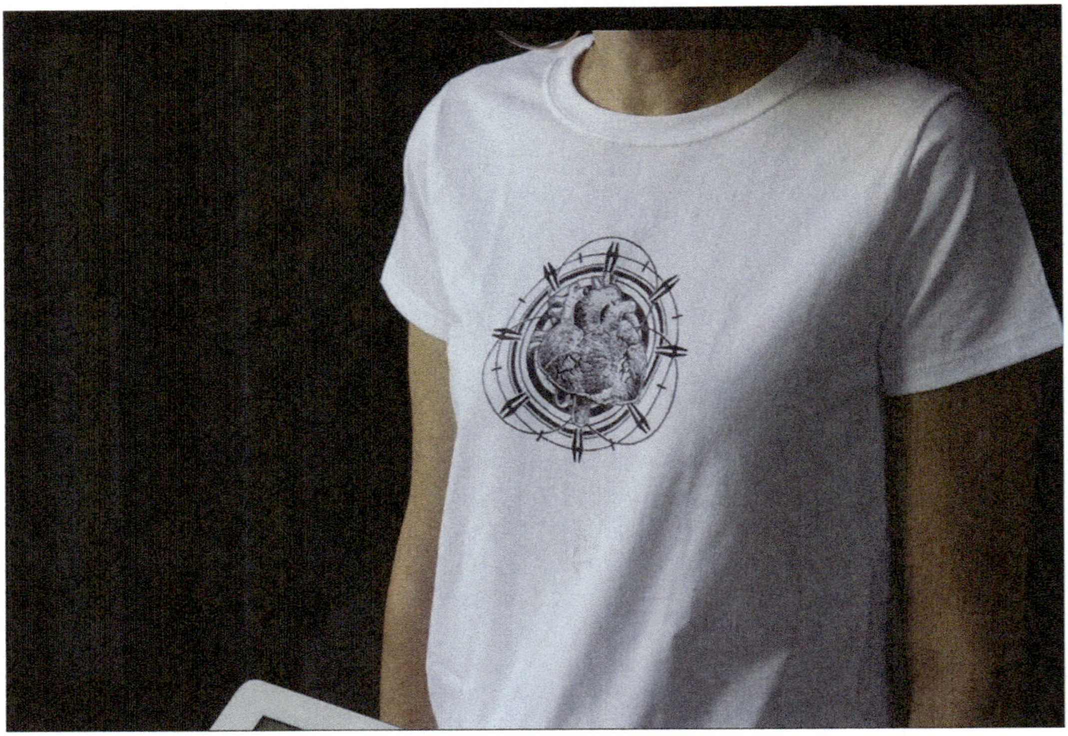

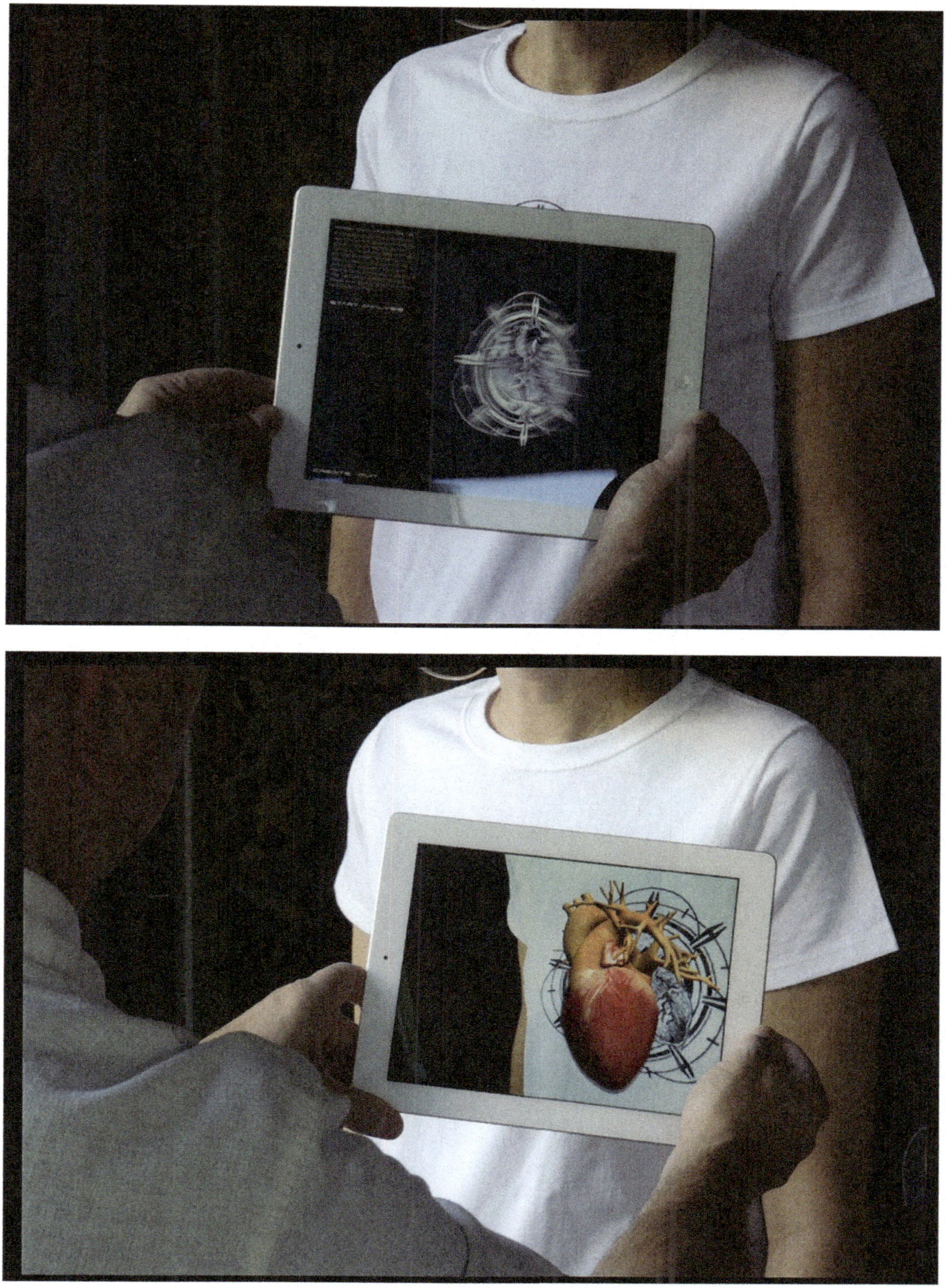

Mood Analyticator, by Bryan Leister, Denver, 20W2.

Mark Skwarek

#arOCCUPYWALLSTREET [NYC, 2011]

Protesters were not allowed to protest at Wall Street, forcing them blocks from the New York Stock Exchange [NYSE] to the Zuccotti Park. Wall Street was barricaded off. Only part of the sidewalk is accessible to the public and there is a constant police presence around both the protesters and the NYSE at all times. *#arOCCUPYWALLSTREET* takes the protest to the heart of the financial district, placing them directly in front of the NYSE. Augments now blanket the entire financial district. Augmented reality gives protesters a global voice.

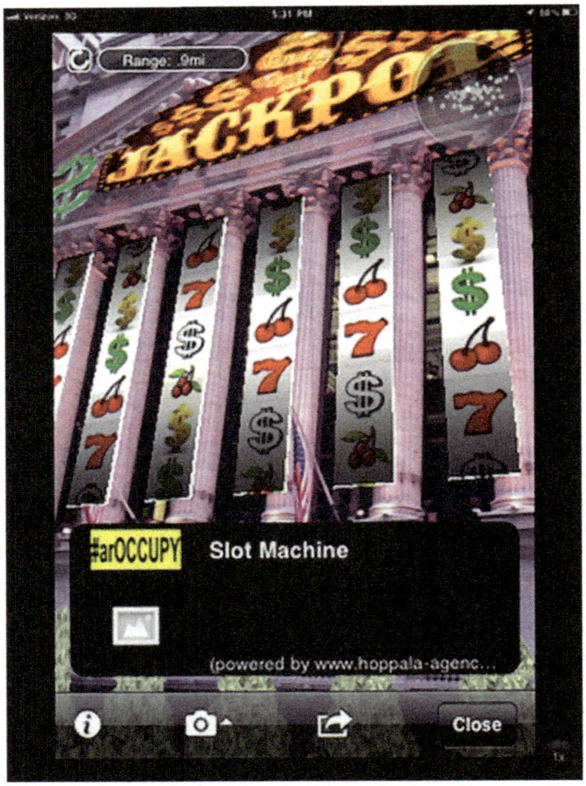

Screenshot from *#arOCCUPYWALLSTREET*, by Mark Skwarek, NYC, 2011. © 2011 by Mark Skwarek.

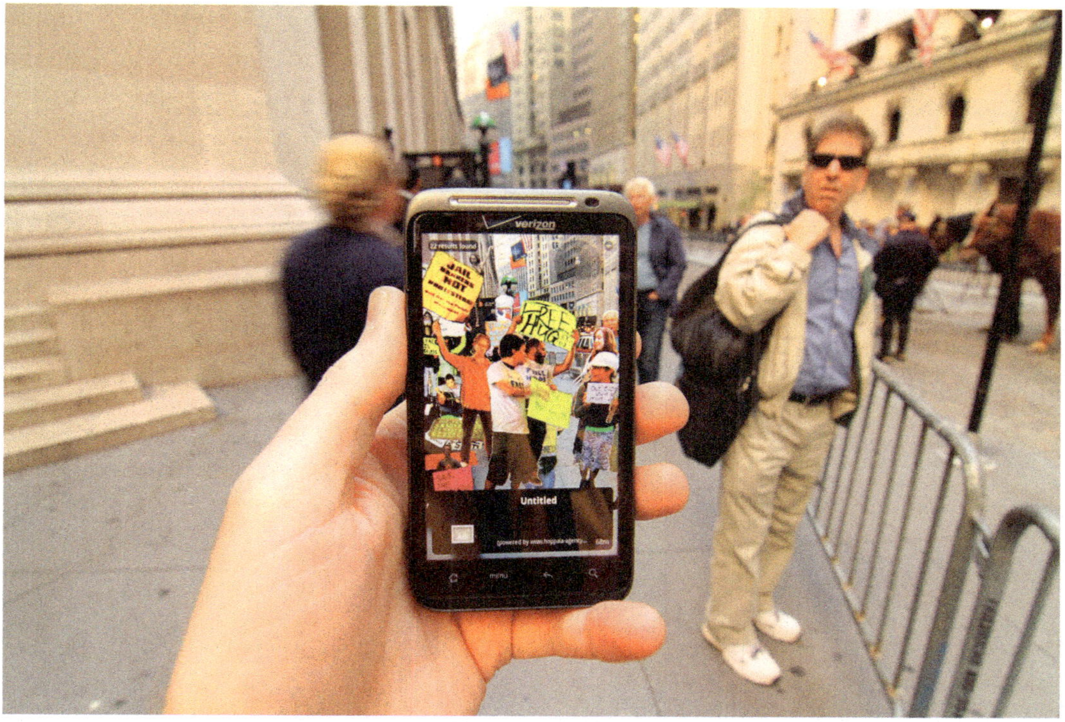

#*arOCCUPYWALLSTREET*, by Mark Skwarek, NYC, 2011. © 2011 by Mark Skwarek.

Scan the image
to view

Mark Skwarek

The Bottomless Pit [Zero1 Biennial, 2012]

A hole was made through the earth connecting San Jose, CA USA to Mexico, to China, to Tunisia, to Japan, and to Brooklyn, NY. Viewers can experience the work with augmented reality seen on smartphones and tablets. People who participate can throw objects of their choosing into the hole and choose where they fall to. The objects were chosen by the people at each hole location and were things that were positive about that location's culture. A main goal of the project is to connect people in distant lands with augmented reality and to strengthen the global community.

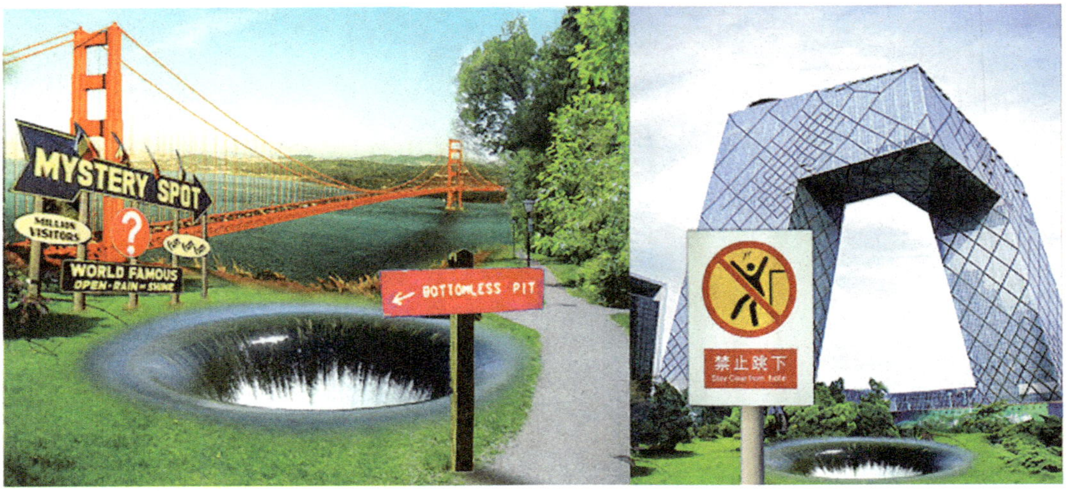

The Bottomless Pit, by Mark Skwarek, ZERO1 Biennial, San Jose, CA, 2012. © 2012 by Mark Skwarek.

Scan the image to view

Mark Skwarek

erasAR [USA, 2010]

The *erasAR* project is an augmented reality artwork that will erase different objects from the face of the earth [but not limited to the earth]. The project will erase a number of things including physical objects such as the Virginia coal mountains. The erasAR project will also erase ideas like people's dreams. erasAR pioneered diminished reality on mobile devices in 2010. The public is invited to submit objects they wish to be deleted from their daily existence to be included to the project. The project is ongoing in multiple locations.

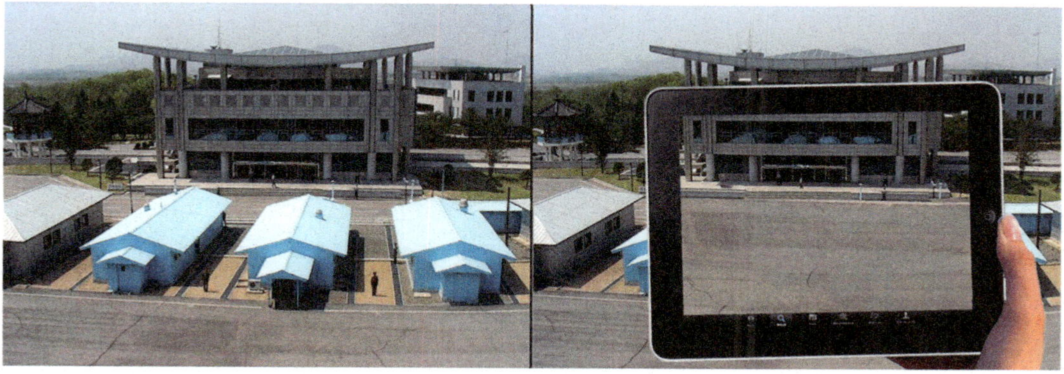

erasAR, by Mark Skwarek, Panmunjom on North/South Korean border, 2010.

Scan the image
to view

Notes

1 Introduction: A Medium in the Making

3 ***The final scene of* Vanilla Sky**: *Vanilla Sky*, directed by Cameron Crowe (2001; Hollywood, CA: Paramount Home Entertainment, 2002), DVD.

6 ***Jurgenson (2012) ultimately argues that social networks***: Nathan Jurgenson, "When Atoms Meet Bits: Social Media, the Mobile Web and Augmented Revolution," *Future Internet* 4, no. 1 (2012): 83-91.

6 ***With his colleague John Seely Brown, Weiser proclaimed***: Mark Weiser and John Seely Brown, "The Coming Age of Calm Technology," *Beyond Calculation*, eds. Peter J. Denning and Robert M. Metcalfe (New York: Copernicus, 1997), 7.

8 ***Noting critical differences between locative AR apps and standard Web browsers, Madrigal concludes***: Alexis Madrigal, "The World is Not Enough: Google and the Future of Augmented Reality," *The Atlantic*, October 25, 2012, accessed 18 Nov. 2012, http://www.theatlantic.com/technology/archive/2012/10/the-world-is-not-enough-google-and-the-future-of-augmented-reality/264059/.

12 ***In this work—which makes too many important points to be adequately summarized in this brief review—Manovich seeks***: Lev Manovich, "The Poetics of Augmented Space," *Visual Communication* 5, no. 2 (2006): 219.

12 ***Another important aspect that Manovich offers***: Ibid., 223.

13 ***Manovich feels that unlike previous forms***: Ibid., 232.

13 ***Thus, ultimately Manovich argues***: Ibid., 237.

14 ***Whereas Manovich deals mainly with multimedia installations***: Adriana de Souza e Silva, "From Cyber to Hybrid: Mobile Technologies as Interfaces of Hybrid Spaces," *Space and Culture* 9, no. 3 (2006): 265.

14 ***From Foursquare to Tapln, emerging mobile apps have reimagined the architecture of digital networks***. Ibid., 266.

14 ***Creating AR or MR compositions, for Anders, is a matter of integrating***: Peter Anders, "Cybrid Principals: Guidelines for Merging Physical and Cyber Spaces," *International Journal of Architectural Computing* 3, no. 3 (2005): 22-4.

15 ***He believes a "tighter coupling of material and cyber spaces" increases***: Ibid., 26.

15 ***Highlighting the "written, coded quality of ubicomp," they align QR codes and AR apps***: Christian Ulrik Andersen and Søren Pold, "The Scripted Spaces of Urban Ubiquitous Computing: The Experience, Poetics, and Politics of Public Scripted Space," *Fibreculture Journal* 19 (2011): 110.

15 ***Invented in 1914, the first electric traffic lights were wired***: "First Electric Traffic Signal," *History.com*, This Day in History, accessed 1 Nov. 2012, http://www.history.com/this-day-in-history/first-electric-traffic-signal-installed.

15 ***Major cities began to computerize their traffic lights***: "Toronto Traffic FAQ," *Toronto.ca*, Transportation, accessed 1 Nov. 2012.

16 ***Despite ubicomp's capacity to support scripted spaces***: Christian Ulrik Andersen and Søren Pold, "The Scripted Spaces of Urban Ubiquitous Computing: The Experience, Poetics, and Politics of Public Scripted Space," *Fibreculture Journal* 19 (2011): 121.

16 ***That is, engaging with mobile devices qua PCs, people move***: Ibid.

16 ***Rather than linking primarily to information pertaining to various remote contexts***: Ibid.

16 ***While people often read and add to the blogosphere***: Ibid.

17 ***To do so requires us to invent***: Ibid.

17 ***That artists are pioneering much of the early innovative work with AR browsers should come as no surprise***: Marshall McLuhan, "The Playboy Interview: Marshall McLuhan," *Mcluhanmedia.com/*, 1969, accessed 15 Oct. 2012.

17 ***As a curator, she envisions a new breed of exhibits***: Simona Lodi, "Spatial Art: An Eruption of the Digital into the Physical," *Leonardo Electronic Almanac* 19, no. 2 (2013). 20.

17 ***Aesthetic experience and social critique accrue on-location***: Ibid., 26.

17 ***Collectively, in addition to their value as individual artworks, they model***: Ibid., 26.

18 ***While cultural critics writing about emerging technologies commonly employ historical practices***: Jay David Bolter, Maria Engberg, and Blair MacIntyre, "Media Studies, Mobile Augmented Reality, and Interaction Design," *Interactions* 20, no. 1 (2013): 37.

18 ***In addition to posing analogies and contrasts***: Ibid., 37.

18 ***After charting the emergence of panoramic paintings***: Ibid., 41.

Chapter 2: Designing, Arranging, and Assessing Augmented Places through Mobile Media Alignment

28 ***How such space is represented and visualized has everything to do with how that space is embodied***: Jason Farman, *Mobile Interface Theory: Embodied Space and Locative Media* (New York: Routledge, 2012), 35.

28 ***Space today exists in a constant state of interplay***: Ibid., 36.

28 ***This perceptual shift—from human conceptualizations of embodiment***: Elizabeth A. Grosz, *Architecture from the Outside: Essays on Virtual and Real Space* (Cambridge, MA: The MIT Press, 2001), 76.

29 ***With mobile technologies, the user is able to move***: Eric Gordon and Adriana de Souza e Silva, *Net Locality: Why Location Matters in a Networked World* (West Sussex, United Kingdom: Wiley-Blackwell, 2011), 3.

30 ***This chapter will build primarily from the definitions proposed by Tuan***: Yi-Fu Tuan, *Space and Place: The Perspective of Experience* (Minneapolis, MN: University of Minnesota Press, 1977), 6.

30 ***Space, from this perspective, therefore can be likened to movement***: Ibid., p. 6-7.

31 ***Even that expansive umbrella label can be debatable***: Adriana de Souza e Silva, "From Cyber to Hybrid Mobile Technologies as Interfaces of Hybrid Spaces," *Space and Culture* 9, no. 3 (2006): 264.

31 ***In this chapter, the base understanding of the concept comes from Milgram***: Paul Milgram and Herman Colquhoun, "A Taxonomy of Real and Virtual World Display Integration," in *Mixed Reality: Merging Real and Virtual Worlds*, ed. Yuichi Ohta and Hideyuki Tamura (Berlin: Springer-Verlag, 1999), 2.

31 ***Within hybrid reality are hybrid spaces***: Adriana de Souza e Silva, "From Cyber to Hybrid Mobile Technologies as Interfaces of Hybrid Spaces," *Space and Culture* 9, no. 3 (2006): 265-266.

31 ***This is a situation in which a real-world context***: Eric Klopfer and Kurt Squire, "Environmental Detectives—the Development of an Augmented Reality Platform for Environmental Simulations," *Educational Technology Research and Development* 56, no. 2 (2008): 205.

31 ***This is not a situation in which virtual experiences are enhanced***: David Drascic and Paul Milgram, "Perceptual Issues in Augmented Reality," *Electronic Imaging: Science & Technology* (International Society for Optics and Photonics, 1996), 123.

31 ***Within these hybrid spaces are the hybrid places***: Mark Bilandzic and Marcus Foth, "A Review of Locative Media, Mobile and Embodied Spatial Interaction," *International Journal of Human-Computer Studies* 70, no. 1 (2012): 68.

31 ***While a place might be static long enough for examination***: Allan Pred, "Place as Historically Contingent Process: Structuration and the Time Geography of Becoming Places," *Annals of the Association of American Geographers* 74, no. 2 (1984): 279.

31 ***Place, therefore, needs to be understood as an embodied relationship***: Tim Cresswell, *Place* (Malden, MA: Blackwell Publishing, 2004), 37.

32 ***Instead, pockets of different contexts exist***: N. Katherine Hayles in Adriana de Souza e Silva, "From Cyber to Hybrid Mobile Technologies as Interfaces of Hybrid Spaces," *Space and Culture* 9, no. 3 (2006): 269.

32 ***Augmented reality, as a concept, not a specific technology***: Thomas Olsson *et al.*, "User Evaluation of Mobile Augmented Reality Scenarios," *Journal of Ambient Intelligence and Smart Environments* 4, no. 1 (2012): 29.

32 ***It can be considered one of the core forms***: Mark Weiser, "The Computer for the 21st Century," *Scientific American* 265, no. 3 (1991): 94-104.

33 ***The major augmented reality systems***: Augmented reality, as a concept, not a specific technology: Thomas Olsson *et al.*, "User Evaluation of Mobile Augmented Reality Scenarios," *Journal of Ambient Intelligence and Smart Environments* 4, no. 1 (2012): 29-30.

33 ***Those generally can be categorized as implementation errors***: Paul Milgram and David Drascic, "Perceptual Effects in Aligning Virtual and Real Objects in Augmented Reality Displays," *Proceedings of the Human Factors and Ergonomics Society Annual Meeting*, (SAGE Publications, 1997): 3; Ernst Kruijff, JE Swan, and Steven Feiner, "Perceptual Issues in Augmented Reality Revisited," *Mixed and Augmented Reality (ISMAR), 2010 9th IEEE International Symposium on*, (IEEE, 2010): 3.

33 ***In turn, user acceptance of augmented reality is equivalently low***: Thomas Olsson *et al.*, "User Evaluation of Mobile Augmented Reality Scenarios," *Journal of Ambient Intelligence and Smart Environments* 4, no. 1 (2012): 29-30.

34 ***Audiences, though, still are not accepting***: Ibid., 32.

34 ***The environment offers cues***: Ernst Kruijff, JE Swan, and Steven Feiner, "Perceptual Issues in Augmented Reality Revisited," *Mixed and Augmented Reality (ISMAR), 2010 9th IEEE International Symposium on*, (IEEE, 2010): 3.

34 ***From a user experience perspective***: Thomas Olsson *et al.*, "User Evaluation of Mobile Augmented Reality Scenarios," *Journal of Ambient Intelligence and Smart Environments* 4, no. 1 (2012): 30.

35 ***In a generic classroom context, Shaffer and Resnick***: David Williamson Shaffer and Mitchel Resnick, "'Thick' Authenticity: New Media and Authentic Learning," *Journal of Interactive Learning Research* 10, no. 2 (1999): 197.

35 ***It happens whenever a person breaks from routine***: Mike Sharples, Dan Corlett, and Oliver Westmancott, "The Design and Implementation of a Mobile Learning Resource," *Personal and Ubiquitous Computing* 6, no. 3 (2002): 220.

35 ***That description illustrates the natural alliance***: Ibid.

35 ***The presence of a hidden reality***: Michael Polyani, *The Tacit Dimension* (NY: Doubleday, 1966), 24.

36 ***Even beyond the realm of explicitly documented and expressed knowledge***: Ibid., 4.

36 ***When flowing through space***: Michael Polanyi, *Personal Knowledge: Towards a Post-Critical Philosophy* (NY: Routledge, 1962), 316.

36 ***Humans have been inscribing and ascribing***: Fred Lukermann, "The Concept of Location in Classical Geography," *Annals of the Association of American Geographers* 51, no. 2 (1961): 196-197.

37 ***That legislation meant that wireless carriers***: Eric Gordon and Adriana de Souza e Silva, *Net Locality: Why Location Matters in a Networked World* (West Sussex, United Kingdom: Wiley-Blackwell, 2011), 41.

37 ***So while a map, and other media technologies***: Ibid., 12.

42 ***Related activities can be physical***: Thomas Olsson *et al.*, "User Evaluation of Mobile Augmented Reality Scenarios," *Journal of Ambient Intelligence and Smart Environments* 4, no. 1 (2012): 30.

42 ***With mobile media, as with archaeology, context is essential***: Anne Galloway and Matt Ward, "Locative Media as Socialising and Spatialising Practices: Learning from Archaeology," *Leonardo Electronic Almanac—Locative Media Special* 14, no. 3 (2006): 1.

43 ***Mobile media alignment might be a way to positively affect***: David Williamson Shaffer and Mitchel Resnick, "'Thick' Authenticity: New Media and Authentic Learning," *Journal of Interactive Learning Research* 10, no. 2 (1999): 195.

Chapter 3: Potential Panels: Toward a Theory of Augmented Comics

49 ***In* Augmented Reality: An Emerging Technologies Guide to AR, *Gregory Kipper and Joseph Rampolla offer***: Gregory Kipper and Joseph Rampolla, *Augmented Reality: An Emerging Technologies Guide to AR* (Waltham, MA: Syngress, 2013), 3.

49 ***I have explored this conversation more fully elsewhere***: see my forthcoming article in *Digital Humanities Quarterly*.

49 ***Will Eisner, a major figure in comics theory***: Will Eisner, *Comics and Sequential Art: Principles and Practices from the Legendary Cartoonist* (NY: W.W. Norton, 2008), 39.

50 ***Harvey finished his 1994* The Art of The Funnies**: Robert C. Harvey, *Art of the Funnies: An Aesthetic History* (Oxford, MS: University Press of Mississippi, 1994), 9.

57 ***In a recent conversation with Marvel Comics writer Jonathan Hickman***: Jonathan Hickman, e-mail message to author, July 28, 2013.

60 ***David Carrier has argued that even a single panel***: David Carrier, *The Aesthetics of Comics* (University Park, PA: Pennsylvania State University Press, 2000), 11-25.

Chapter 4: "Sergey Brin is Batman": Google Glass & the Rhetoric of Adoption in Popular Networked Culture

66 ***Brin is also mythologized***: Matt Lynley, "Googlers Are Passing Around A Crazy Rumor About Sergey Brin Working On Architecture," *Business Insider*, October 25, 2011, accessed August 7, 2013, http://www.businessinsider.com/googlers-are-passing-around-a-crazy-rumor-about-sergey-brin-working-on-architecture-2011-10.

66 ***Glass has also graced the face***: Michael Gorman, "Google Glass Shows How Diane von Furstenberg is Living, What It's Like at New York Fashion Week," *Engadget*, September 14, 2012, accessed August 7, 2013, http://www.engadget.com/2012/09/14/google-glass-diane-von-furstenberg-new-york-fashion-week-video.

66 ***Having been viewed more than 20 million times***: Google, "Project Glass: One Day...," *YouTube*, April 4, 2012, accessed August 7, 2013, https://www.youtube.com/watch?v=9c6W4CCU9M4.

67 ***In one blog post, Google states***: Sergey Brin, "Personal Blog," *Google.com*, April 4, 2012, accessed July 31, 2013, https://plus.google.com/+GoogleGlass/posts/aKymsANgWBD.

68 ***Provocative headlines emerged***: Chloe Albanesius, "Google 'Project Glass' Replaces the Smartphone with Glasses," *PC Magazine*, April 4, 2012, accessed August 7, 2013, http://www.pcmag.com/article2/0,2817,2402613,00.asp; Martin LaMonica, "Google X Labs: First Project Glass, Next Space Elevators?," *CNET.com*, April 24, 2012, accessed August 7, 2013, http://www.cnet.com/news/google-x-labs-first-project-glass-next-space-elevators.

69 ***Glenn Stillar writes that "Rhetoric deals***: Glenn Stillar, *Analyzing Everyday Texts: Discourse, Rhetoric and Social Perspectives* (California: Sage, 1998), 62.

69 ***Here we offer a basic reading of the One Day video***: Kenneth Burke, "Poem" (Definition of Humanity), in *The Legacy of Kenneth Burke*, ed. Herbert W. Simons and Trevor Melia (Madison: University of Wisconsin Press, 1989), 263.

70 ***Finally, Pedersen and Simcoe argue***: Isabel Pedersen and Luke Simcoe, "The Iron Man Phenomenon, Participatory Culture, & Future Augmented Reality Technologies," in *CHI 2012 Extended Abstracts on Human Factors in Computing Systems* (NY: Association of Computing Machinery, 2012), 291-300.

71 ***In this vein, Katherine Hayles writes***: N. Katherine Hayles, *How We Think: Digital Media and Contemporary Technogenesis* (Chicago: University of Chicago Press, 2012), 123.

72 ***Basing his "definition of human" partly on the Aristotelian notion of entelechy***: Kenneth Burke, *On Symbols and Society* (Chicago: University of Chicago Press, 1989), 71; Kenneth Burke, *A Grammar of Motives* (Berkeley: University of California Press, 1945), 261.

72 ***He ironically labels us "Rotten with Perfection"***: Kenneth Burke, "Poem" (Definition of Humanity), in *The Legacy of Kenneth Burke*, ed. Herbert W. Simons and Trevor Melia (Madison: University of Wisconsin Press, 1989), 263.

72 ***Humans attach this sense of entelechy***: Glenn Stillar, *Analyzing Everyday Texts: Discourse, Rhetoric and Social Perspectives* (California: Sage, 1998), 87.

72 ***Also influenced by Burke, Michael Hyde***: Michael Hyde, *Perfection: Coming to Terms with Being Human* (Waco, TX: Baylor University Press, 2010), 4.

73 ***A "media event" has been defined***: Daniel Dayan and Elihu Katz, *Media Events: The Live Broadcasting of History* (Boston: Harvard University Press, 1994), 212.

73 ***Manuel Castells conceptualizes the network society***: Manuel Castells, "The Network Society: From Knowledge to Policy," in *The Network Society: From Knowledge to Policy*,

ed. Manuel Castells and Gustavo Cardoso (Washington, DC: Johns Hopkins Center for Transatlantic Relations, 2006), 3.

74 ***The first chapter of Everett M. Rogers's work***: Everett M. Rogers, *Diffusion of Innovations*, 5th ed. (NY: Free Press, 2003), 1.

75 ***On October 25, 2011,* Business Insider *published***: Matt Lynley, "Googlers Are Passing Around A Crazy Rumor About Sergey Brin Working On Architecture," *Business Insider*, October 25, 2011, accessed August 7, 2013, http://www.businessinsider.com/googlers-are-passing-around-a-crazy-rumor-about-sergey-brin-working-on-architecture-2011-10.

76 ***In a sense, the meme functions***: Kenneth Burke, *A Grammar of Motives* (Berkeley: University of California Press, 1945), 26-29.

76 ***By naming the substance, the whatness***: Kenneth Burke, *A Grammar of Motives* (Berkeley: University of California Press, 1945), 23.

76 ***Rupert Till explains the definition***: Rupert Till, *PopCult: Religion and Popular Music* (London: Continuum, 2010), 47.

77 ***According to Aristotle***: Aristotle, *Rhetoric*, trans. Rhys Roberts (Mineola, NY: Dover Publications, 2004), 1.2.p. 7.

77 ***Ethos is a highly contested term***: Craig Smith, "Ethos Dwells Persuasively: A Hermeneutic Reading of Aristotle on Credibility," in *The Ethos of Rhetoric*, ed. Michael Hyde (Columbia, SC: University of South Carolina Press, 2004).

77 ***However, Craig Smith emphasizes how Aristotle***: Ibid., 2.

80 ***While applicable research has been conducted***: Jonas Hedman and Gregory Gimpel, "The Adoption of Hyped Technologies: A Qualitative Study," *Information Technology and Management* 11, no. 4, (2010): 161-175.

Chapter 5: Life through the Screen: Location-Based Information and the Personalization of Space

84 ***Throughout the day, I also perform many Google searches***: Alexander Halavais, *Search Engine Society* (Cambridge, MA: Polity, 2009); Siva Vaidhyanathan, *The Googlization of Everything: (And Why We Should Worry)* (Berkeley, CA: University of California Press, 2011).

84 ***It may seem like a minor point***: Josephy Turow, *The Daily You: How the New Advertising Industry Is Defining Your Identity and Your Worth* (NY: Yale University Press, 2012).

84 ***This concern has been called the "filter bubble"***: Eli Pariser, *The Filter Bubble: What the Internet Is Hiding from You* (NY: Penguin Books, 2011); Siva Vaidhyanathan, *The Googlization of Everything: (And Why We Should Worry)* (Berkeley, CA: University of California Press, 2011).

84 ***However, what is relatively new***: Jordan Frith, "Splintered Space: The Smartphone as the Screen to the City," *Mobilities* 7, no. 1 (2012): 131–149; Adriana de Souza

e Silva and Jordan Frith, *Mobile Interfaces in Public Spaces: Locational Privacy, Control and Urban Sociability* (NY: Routledge, 2012).

84 ***As researchers have noted, digital information***: Jason Farman, *Mobile Interface Theory* (NY: Routledge, 2012); Eric Gordon and Adriana de Souza e Silva, *Network Locality: How Digital Networks Create a Culture of Location* (Boston, MA: Blackwell Publishers, 2011).

84 ***We use smartphones to manipulate the digital data***: Adriana de Souza e Silva and Jordan Frith, *Mobile Interfaces in Public Spaces: Locational Privacy, Control and Urban Sociability* (NY: Routledge, 2012).

86 ***One of the most influential conceptualizations of the public***: Jeff Weintraub, "The Theory and Politics of the Public/private Distinction," in *Public and Private in Thought and Practice: Perspectives on a Grand Dichotomy*, ed. Jeff Weintraub and Krishan Kumar (NY: University of Chicago Press, 1997), 23.

86 ***As Sennett writes, urban public spaces***: Richard Sennett, *The Fall of Public Man* (NY: Knopf, 1977), 48.

86 ***Jane Jacobs, in her seminal book***: Jane Jacobs, *The Death of Life of Great American Cities* (NY: Random House, 1961), 30.

87 ***The difference we confront while in the public spaces***: Richard Sennett, "The Civitas of Seeing," *Places* 5, no. 4 (1989): 82–84.

87 ***Homophily can be best understood***: Miller McPherson, Lynn Smith-Lovin, and James M. Cook, "Birds of a Feather: Homophily in Social Networks," *Annual Review of Sociology* 27 (2001): 415–444.

87 ***For example, boyd details***: danah boyd, "White Flight in Networked Publics? How Race and Class Shaped American Teen Engagement with MySpace and Facebook," in *Race After the Internet*, ed. Lisa Nakamura, Peter Chow-White, and Alondra Nelson (NY: Routledge, 2011).

87 ***Rather than engaging with differing opinions***: Alexander Halavais, *Search Engine Society* (Cambridge, MA: Polity, 2009).

87 ***Sites like Facebook provide a new form of public space***: danah boyd, "Why Youth <3 Social Network Sites: The Role of Networked Publics in Teenage Social Life," in *Youth, Identity, and Digital Media*, ed. David Buckingham (Cambridge, MA: The MIT Press, 2008) 119–142.

88 ***My argument in this chapter***: Daniel M. Sutko and Adriana de Souza e Silva, "Location-aware Mobile Media and Urban Sociability," *New Media & Society* 13, no. 5 (2011): 807–823.

88 ***These forms of informational filtering and sorting***: Adriana de Souza e Silva and Jordan Frith, *Mobile Interfaces in Public Spaces: Locational Privacy, Control and Urban Sociability* (NY: Routledge, 2012).

88 ***Gordon refers specifically to urban spaces***: Jordan Frith, "Splintered Space: The Smartphone as the Screen to the City," *Mobilities* 7, no. 1 (2012): 131–149.

89 ***As smartphones become increasingly popular***: Adriana de Souza e Silva and Jordan Frith, "Re-narrating the City Through the Presentation of Location," in *Digital Storytelling with Mobile Media: Locative Technologies and Narrative Practices*, ed. Jason Farman (NY: Routledge, 2013).

89 ***Differential mobility refers to groups' unequal access***: Kevin Hannam, Mimi Sheller, and John Urry, "Mobilities, Immobilities and Moorings," *Mobilities* 1, no. 1 (2006): 1–22.; Doreen Massey, *Place, Space, and Gender* (Minneapolis, MN: University of Minnesota Press, 1994).

90 ***Their check-ins are shared***: Jordan Frith, "Turning Life into a Game: Foursquare, Gamification, and Personal Mobility," *Mobile Media and Communication* 1, no. 2 (2013): 248–262.

90 ***Dodgeball did not use GPS to locate people***: Lee Humphreys, "Mobile Social Networks and Urban Public Space," *New Media & Society* 12 (2010): 763–778; Lee Humphreys, "Mobile Social Networks and Social Practice: A Case Study of Dodgeball," *Journal of Computer-Mediated Communication* 13 (2007).

91 ***Unlike ideal public spaces in which people may encounter otherness***: Alice Crawford, "Taking Social Software to the Streets: Mobile Cocooning and the (an) Erotic City," *Journal of Urban Technology* 15, no. 3 (2007): 89.

92 ***Humphreys found that Dodgeball contributes***: Lee Humphreys, "Mobile Social Networks and Social Practice: A Case Study of Dodgeball," *Journal of Computer-Mediated Communication* 13 (2007); Lee Humphreys, "Mobile Social Networks and Urban Public Space," *New Media & Society* 12 (2010): 776.

92 ***As Farman writes, these types of mobile applications***: Jason Farman, *Mobile Interface Theory* (NY: Routledge, 2012), 73.

93 ***This is important because, as the Foursquare engineers explained***: Justin Moore, "Building a Recommendation Engine, Foursquare Style," *Foursquare Engineering Blog*, March 22, 2011, accessed January 12, 2015, http://engineering.foursquare.com/2011/03/22/building-a-recommendation-engine-foursquare-style.

94 ***However, the results returned on these searches***: Daniel M. Sutko and Adriana de Souza e Silva, "Location-aware Mobile Media and Urban Sociability," *New Media & Society* 13, no. 5 (2011): 818.

96 ***My argument is not that this will be inherently bad***: Adriana de Souza e Silva and Jordan Frith, *Mobile Interfaces in Public Spaces: Locational Privacy, Control and Urban Sociability* (NY: Routledge, 2012).

Chapter 6: "Augpunk": Imagining Alternative Futures for Augmented Reality through Science Fiction

99 ***William Gibson coined the term "cyberspace,"***: William Gibson, *Neuromancer* (NY: Ace Books, 1984), 69.

100 ***In 2007, characters in Gibson's novel* Spook Country**: William Gibson, *Spook Country* (NY: G.P. Putnam's Sons, 2007), 22.

101 ***According to Istvan Csicsery-Ronay***: Istvan Csicsery-Ronay, *The Seven Beauties of Science Fiction* (Middletown, CT: Wesleyan University Press, 2008), 3.

101 ***A recent Internet meme shows***: See "Star Trek: Predicting the Future Since 1966," *Weknowmemes*, July 13 2013, accessed August 28 2013, http://weknowmemes.com/2013/07/star-trek-predicting-the-future-since-1966.

101 ***For many scholars of science fiction, these properties allow***: Istvan Csicsery-Ronay, *The Seven Beauties of Science Fiction* (Middletown, CT: Wesleyan University Press, 2008), 74.

101 ***By contrast, sf is "a zone of playful game-rules***: Ibid.

101 ***The recent short film "Sight,"***: Eran May-raz and Daniel Lazo, "Sight," Youtube video, 7.53, posted by "The CGBros," August 1, 2012, https://www.youtube.com/watch?v=lK_cdkpazjI.

102 ***Suvin draws on Berthold Brecht's definition of* estrangement**: Darko Suvin, "On the Poetics of the Science Fiction Genre," *College English* 34, no. 3 (1972): 374.

102 ***While myth and fantasy also estrange their audiences***: Ibid., 375; For an extended analysis of Suvin's theory of cognitive estrangement, see Carl H. Freedman, *Critical Theory and Science Fiction* (Hanover, NH: Wesleyan University Press, 2000).

103 ***In 2009, AR blogger and sf author Thomas K. Carpenter***: See Thomas K. Carpenter, "The AR Reading List," *Thomaskcarpenter.com*, September 21, 2009, accessed August 30, 2013, http://thomaskcarpenter.com/2009/09/21/ar-reading-list.

103 ***In addition, augpunk may also catalyze new ideas***: Mark Pesce makes this argument in "Magic Mirror: The Novel as a Software Development Platform," MIT Communications Forum, accessed August 28, 2013, http://web.mit.edu/comm-forum/papers/pesce.html.

104 ***For cyberpunk ringleader and longtime AR booster Bruce Sterling***: Bruce Sterling, *Mirrorshades: The Cyberpunk Anthology* (NY: Arbor House, 1986), 345.

104 ***Sterling writes, "Cyberpunk comes from***: Ibid., 346.

104 ***Similarly, augpunks no longer desire***: William Gibson, "Google's Earth," *New York Times*, August 31, 2010, accessed August 28, 2013, http://www.nytimes.com/2010/09/01/opinion/01gibson.html?_r=0.

104 ***Artist Anthony Antonellis captures this***: Kyle VanHemert, "Watch: This Guy Has a Digital Tattoo Viewable Only by Cellphone," *Wired*, August 23, 2013, accessed August 28, 2013, http://www.wired.com/2013/08/watch-theres-digital-art-embedded-in-this-guys-hand-thanks-to-an-rfid-implant.

104 ***Cyberpunk 1.0's influence on both sf and popular culture***: See James P. Kelly and John Kessel, *Rewired: The Post-Cyberpunk Anthology* (San Francisco, CA: Tachyon Publica-

tions, 2007); Also, Graham J. Murphy and Sherryl Vint, *Beyond Cyberpunk: New Critical PERSPECTIVES* (NY: Routledge, 2010).

104 ***Cyberpunk draws on punk music's DIY***: William Gibson, *Burning Chrome* (NY: Arbor House, 1986), xx.

105 ***Banksy's admirers note***: Paul Gough, *Banksy: The Bristol Legacy* (Bristol: Redcliffe, 2012), 9.

105 ***For the augpunks depicted in "Paintwork,"***: Ibid.

105 ***To those who would label his graffiti***: Ibid., 9-10.

105 ***Maughan pays direct homage to Banksy***: Tim Maughan, *Paintwork* (Bristol, England: Tim Maughan, 2011), 20.

106 ***In order to retain his anonymity***: Ibid., 5.

106 ***This surveillance software is programmed***: Ibid., 5-7.

106 ***"Between disgruntled pensioners posting***: Ibid., 7.

106 ***In a database culture in which movement***: N. Katherine Hayles, *How We Became Posthuman: Virtual Bodies in Cybernetics, Literature, and Informatics* (Chicago: University of Chicago Press, 1999).

107 ***While graffiti artists have always***: Tim Maughan, *Paintwork* (Bristol, England: Tim Maughan, 2011), 6.

107 ***3Cube's first piece***: Ibid., 9.

107 ***Through this widening breach***: Ibid.

107 ***3Cube's effort is part of a trilogy***: Ibid., 34.

108 ***For 3Cube, the aesthetic experience***: Ibid., 10.

108 ***Accordingly, he prefers***: Ibid., 11.

108 ***Each burn is a direct, tonally-inverted response***: Ibid., 27.

108 ***They variously depict Bristol's Barton Hill skyline***: Ibid., 36.

108 ***The writer "Artefackt," for example***: Ibid., 25.

108 ***Likewise, Tera tells 3Cube***: Ibid., 33.

108 ***3Cube eventually comes to recognize***: Ibid., 37.

108 ***Artefackt and Tera seek to restore***: Walter Benjamin, "The Work of Art in the Age of Mechanical Reproduction," *Marxists.org*, 1936, accessed August 31, 2013, https://www.marxists.org/reference/subject/philosophy/works/ge/benjamin.htm.

109 ***3Cube is left alone***: Tim Maughan, *Paintwork* (Bristol, England: Tim Maughan, 2011), 38.

109 ***Perhaps even the story's hardline 2D artists***: See Sweza, "Graffyard," Sweza.com, April 27, 2010, accessed August 28, 2013, http://sweza.com/graffyard.

109 ***In a June 2013 interview, Maughan***: Philip Bates, "Interview with Tim Maughan, Bristol Science Fiction Champion," *Guide2Bristol*, July 10, 2013, accessed August 28, 2013, http://www.guide2bristol.com/news/3018/Interview-with-Tim-Maughan-Bristol-Science-Fiction-champion---part-one.

110 ***For Frederic Jameson, this element of cyberpunk***: Fredric Jameson, *Postmodernism, Or, the Cultural Logic of Late Capitalism* (Durham, NC: Duke University Press, 1991), 38.

110 ***Even for those players not in the gold farming business***: Nick Yee, "The Labor of Fun: How Video Games Blur the Boundaries of Work and Play," *Games and Culture* 1, no. 1 (2006): 70.

111 ***In the more robust definition of the locative media interface developed by Jason Farman***: Jason Farman, *Mobile Interface Theory: Embodied Space and Locative Media* (NY: Routledge, 2012), 77.

111 ***Marcus whets the international gaming community's appetite***: Tim Maughan, *Paintwork* (Bristol, England: Tim Maughan, 2011), 77.

111 ***Once Marcus leaks***: Ibid., 78.

111 ***The gamer Paul's mech***: Ibid., 72.

112 ***Paul is under pressure from the Cuban government***: Ibid., 81.

113 ***By insisting on the creative autonomy of the AR gamer***: Jason Farman, *Mobile Interface Theory: Embodied Space and Locative Media* (NY: Routledge, 2012), 92.

113 ***"Havana Augmented" and other augpunk stories provide***: Ibid., 90.

113 ***Cyberpunks augment themselves not to pursue a commercial image of beauty***: William Gibson, *Neuromancer* (NY: Ace Books, 1984), 59.

114 ***More interesting for our purposes***: *Oxford English Dictionary Online*, s.v. "augur."

114 ***The augpunk's interventions are "a practical contribution***: qtd. in Jan R. Holmevik, *Inter/vention: Free Play in the Age of Electracy* (Cambridge, MA: MIT Press, 2012), 28.

114 ***Kurzweil's visions of "spiritual machines"***: See Ray Kurzweil, *The Age of Spiritual Machines: When Computers Exceed Human Intelligence* (NY: Viking, 1999); Also, Ray Kurzweil, *The Singularity Is Near: When Humans Transcend Biology* (NY: Viking, 2005).

115 ***In addition, these visions allow us***: John Tinnell, "All the World's a Link: The Global Theater of Mobile World Browsers," *Enculturation*, December 14, 2011, accessed September 1, 2013, http://www.enculturation.net/all-the-worlds-a-link.

115 ***Further, sf is a powerful vehicle for exploring***: Ibid.

115 ***Interestingly, cyberpunk author Bruce Sterling***: Tish Shute, Ori Inbar, and Bruce Sterling, "Augmented Reality—Transitioning Out of the Old-fashioned 'Legacy Internet': Interview with Bruce Sterling" *UgoTrade*, May 6 2011, accessed September 1, 2013, http://www.ugotrade.com/2011/05/06/augmented-reality-transitioning-out-of-the-old-fashioned-legacy-internet-interview-with-bruce-sterling.

116 ***Sterling would do well to remember Donna Haraway's dictum***: Donna J. Haraway, *Simians, Cyborgs, and Women: The Reinvention of Nature* (NY: Routledge, 1991), 149.

Chapter 7: Gathering Memories with Augmented Reality

120 ***In this vision, ubiquitous computing***: Adam Greenfield, *Everyware: The Dawning Age of Ubiquitous Computing* (Berkeley, CA: New Riders Press, 2006), 1.

120 ***As such, ubiquitous computing and augmented reality***: Evan Barba, Blair MacIntyre, and Elizabeth D. Mynatt, "Here We Are! Where Are We? Locating Mixed Reality in the Age of the Smartphone," *Proceedings of the IEEE* 100, no. 4 (2012): 929.

120 ***For example, the rhetorical art of memory***: Frances A. Yates, *The Art of Memory* (Chicago, IL: University of Chicago Press, 1966).

120 ***Uricchio, for instance, argues***: William Uricchio, "Imag(in)ing the City: Simonides to the Sims," in *Cities in Transition: The Moving Image and the Modern Metropolis*, ed. Andrew Webber (London: Wallflower Press, 2008), 110.

121 ***Pedersen addresses the concept of augmented memory***: Isabel Pedersen, *Ready to Wear: A Rhetoric of Wearable Computers and Reality-Shifting Media* (Anderson, SC: Parlor Press, 2013), 28.

121 ***In doing so, I do not attempt to contradict Pedersen's insights***: Ibid., 121.

122 ***By superimposing digital objects onto the real world***: Jason Farman, *Mobile Interface Theory: Embodied Space and Locative Media* (NY: Routledge, 2013).

122 ***In commenting on the influence of world browsers, Tinnell writes***: John Tinnell, "All the World's a Link: The Global Theater of Mobile World Browsers," *Enculturation*, December 14 2011, accessed September 1, 2013, http://www.enculturation.net/all-the-worlds-a-link.

122 ***Indeed, Olick stipulates that the media of memory***: Jeffrey K. Olick, *The Politics of Regret: On Collective Memory and Historical Responsibility* (NY: Routledge, 2007), 98.

123 ***The materiality of media actively shapes memory***: Ibid., 104.

123 ***Nevertheless, recent scholarship has begun to argue***: Joanne Garde-Hansen, Andrew Hoskins, and Anna Reading, *Save as . . . Digital Memories* (NY: Palgrave Macmillan, 2009), 1.

123 ***Given the "amorphous" qualities of memory***: Jacques Le Goff, *History and Memory*, trans. Elizabeth Claman and Steven Rendal (NY: Columbia University Press, 1992), 51.

123 ***Here, I turn to metaphors used to describe***: Isabel Pedersen, *Ready to Wear: A Rhetoric of Wearable Computers and Reality-Shifting Media* (Anderson, SC: Parlor Press, 2013), 119.

123 ***For instance, Garde-Hansen, Hoskins, and Reading argue***: Joanne Garde-Hansen, Andrew Hoskins, and Anna Reading, *Save as . . . Digital Memories* (NY: Palgrave Macmillan, 2009), 3.

123 ***They thus advocate "a concept of digital memory***: Ibid., 7.

124 ***The concept of digital network memory emphasizes***: Andrew Hoskins, "Digital Network Memory," in *Mediation, Remediation, and the Dynamics of Cultural Memory*, ed. Astrid Erll and Ann Rigney (Berlin: de Gruyter, 2009), 92.

124 ***Hoskins argues that digital network memory***: Ibid., 94.

124 ***In so doing, digital network memory temporally***: Ibid., 95.

124 ***Digital network memory works within a culture of connectivity***: Jose Van Dijck, *The Culture of Connectivity: A Critical History of Social Media* (Oxford: Oxford University Press, 2013), 12.

126 ***Farman writes, "By utilizing technologies***: Jason Farman, *Mobile Interface Theory: Embodied Space and Locative Media* (NY: Routledge, 2013), 44.

126 ***HistoryPin juxtaposes experience and memory***: Helen Liggett, *Urban Encounters* (Minneapolis, MN: University of Minnesota Press, 2003), 109.

126 ***Or as Solnit comments***: Rebecca Solnit, *Infinite City: A San Francisco Atlas* (Berkeley, CA: University of California Press, 2010), 5.

126 ***Farman refers to this mode of embodiment***: Jason Farman, *Mobile Interface Theory: Embodied Space and Locative Media* (NY: Routledge, 2013), 13.

126 ***Importantly, the sensory-inscribed body***: Ibid., 14.

126 ***Digital network memory regards the moment***: Andrew Hoskins, "7/7 and Connective Memory: Interactional Trajectories of Remembering in Post-scarcity Culture," *Memory Studies* 4, no. 3 (2011): 272.

126 ***According to Hoskins, remembering becomes***: Ibid.

126 ***Digital network memory and interactional trajectories demonstrate***: Andrew Hoskins, "Anachronisms of Media, Anachronisms of Memory: From Collective Memory to a New Memory Ecology," in *On Media Memory: Collective Memory in a New Media Age*, ed. Motti Neiger, Oren Meyers, and Eyal Zandberg (NY: Palgrave Macmillan, 2011), 283.

128 ***Rickert thus advances the concept of ambience***: Thomas Rickert, "In the House of Doing: Rhetoric and the Kairos of Ambience," *Journal of Advanced Composition* 24, no. 4 (2004): 903.

128 ***Following the metaphor of ambience***: Ibid.

128 ***Here, ambience implies an enmeshing of memory***: Ibid., 904.

128 ***An ambient rhetoric highlights***: Ibid., 906.

128 ***As such, ambience signals***: Thomas Rickert, *Ambient Rhetoric: The Attunements of Rhetorical Being* (Pittsburgh, PA: U of Pittsburgh Press, 2013), xi.

129 ***As Rickert suggests, "If the network metaphor***: Thomas Rickert, "In the House of Doing: Rhetoric and the Kairos of Ambience," *Journal of Advanced Composition* 24, no. 4 (2004): 904.

129 ***A digital ambient memory better acknowledges***: Andrew Hoskins, "Digital Network Memory," in *Mediation, Remediation, and the Dynamics of Cultural Memory*, ed. Astrid Erll and Ann Rigney (Berlin: de Gruyter, 2009), 96.

129 ***Rickert employs the concept of dwelling***: Thomas Rickert, *Ambient Rhetoric: The Attunements of Rhetorical Being* (Pittsburgh, PA: U of Pittsburgh Press, 2013), xiii.

129 ***Similarly, when HistoryPin compels me***: Gilles Deleuze, *The Fold: Leibniz and the Baroque*, trans. Tom Conley (Minneapolis, MN: University of Minnesota Press, 1993), 19.

130 ***Medial will to power is not a networked intention***: Matthew Fuller, *Media Ecologies: Materialist Energies in Art and Technoculture* (Cambridge, MA: The MIT Press, 2007), 56.

130 ***Medial will to power is the force***: Ibid., 63.

130 ***And moving things across thresholds invents***: Ibid.

130 ***In his explication of ambient rhetoric, Rickert posits***: Thomas Rickert, "In the House of Doing: Rhetoric and the Kairos of Ambience," *Journal of Advanced Composition* 24, no. 4 (2004): 911.

130 ***Here, the present refers to***: Nathan Stormer, "Recursivity: A Working Paper on Rhetoric and Mnesis," *Quarterly Journal of Speech* 99, no. 1 (2013): 28.

133 ***Chun suggests that the enduring ephemeral marks***: Wendy Chun, *Programmed Visions* (Cambridge, MA: MIT Press, 2012), 170.

133 ***Ernst writes, "There is no ending online***: Wolfgang Ernst, "Dis/continuities: Does the Archive Become Metaphorical in Multi-media Space?," in *New Media, Old Media: A History and Theory Reader*, ed. Wendy Hui Kyong Chun & Thomas Keenan (NY: Routledge, 2006), 110.

133 ***Hoskins suggests that this unending digital archive***: Andrew Hoskins, "Media, Memory, Metaphor: Remembering and the Connective Turn," *Parallax* 17, no. 4 (2011); Andrew Hoskins, "7/7 and Connective Memory: Interactional Trajectories of Remembering in Post-scarcity Culture," *Memory Studies* 4, no. 3 (2011).

133 ***Andrejevic refers to this as the "digital enclosure,"***: Mark Andrejevic, *iSpy: Surveillance and Power in the Interactive Era* (Lawrence, KS: University Press of Kansas, 2009), 2.

133 ***Lacey suggests that the digital enclosure***: Kimberly Lacey, "Making Memory: Techne, Technology, and the Refashioning of Contemporary Memory" (PhD diss., Wayne State University, 2011), 164, http://digitalcommons.wayne.edu/oa_dissertations/246.

133 ***Whereas the metaphor of the network implies links and linking***: Thomas Rickert, "In the House of Doing: Rhetoric and the Kairos of Ambience," *Journal of Advanced Composition* 24, no. 4 (2004): 915.

134 ***The street photographer Garry Winogrand once said***: Helen Liggett, *Urban Encounters* (Minneapolis, MN: University of Minnesota Press, 2003), 120.

134 ***Bogost interprets this to mean***: Ian Bogost, "Seeing Things-OOOIII," Vimeo video, 6:46, posted by "Ian Bogost," September 15, 2011, http://vimeo.com/29092112.

134 ***Bogost argues that wonder***: Ian Bogost, *Alien Phenomenology, or What It's Like to Be a Thing* (Minneapolis, MN: University of Minnesota, 2012), 122.

Chapter 8: The Dream Deferred: Augmented Reality as Rhetorical Realism

138 ***Swift describes their first experiment***: Jonathan Swift, *Gulliver's Travels into Several Nations of the World. With a Memoir of the Author* (Cambridge: Oxford UP, 2006), 214.

138 ***Rather than work within the structures of existing discourse***: Ibid.

138 ***Since words are only names for things***: Ibid., 215.

138 ***While this new method makes longer discourses***: Ibid.

139 ***"The room where company meet who practise this art***: Ibid.

139 ***Bishop's answering machine has a stock of marbles***: Paul Dourish, *Where the Action Is: The Foundations of Embodied Interaction* (Cambridge, MA: MIT Press, 2001), 40-41; see also Andy Clark, *Natural-Born Cyborgs: Minds, Technologies, and the Future of Human Intelligence* (NY: Oxford University Press, 2003), 48-50.

139 ***As Paul Dourish notes, the goal behind augmented reality***: Paul Dourish, *Where the Action Is: The Foundations of Embodied Interaction* (Cambridge, MA: MIT Press, 2001), 41.

140 ***Though realism has become some something of a devil term***: James Hikins argues that realism "weaves a persistent thread" through the history of rhetoric and that rhetorical practice is ("esoteric" theory not withstanding) realist through and through. Because rhetoric always emerges out of lived experience, any theory of rhetoric must, Hikins insists, "adequately account for what we know about the natural world in which we all reside" (24). Hikins also acknowledges the many forms realism has taken in the rhetorical and philosophical traditions. Though not categorized as such, virtually all of the realist traditions Hikins identifies are epistemological in nature. As I argue in this chapter, this effectively leaves ontological realism off the rhetorician's table. More recent work by Rickert, for example, who also offers a cogent critique of Hikins (see 193-199), aims to break the hold epistemology has had on rhetoric for much of last century and in so doing open rhetoric up to ontological questions and discussions.

141 ***That is, we should also use the occasion***: Martin Heidegger, "The Way to Language," in *Basic Writings*, ed. David Farrell Krell, trans. David Farrell Krell (NY: HarperCollins, 1993), 398.

141 ***Unlike the rhetorics of disembodiment***: Isabel Pedersen, "Dehumanization, Rhetoric, and the Design of Wearable Augmented Reality Interfaces," in *Small Tech: The Culture of Digital Tools*, ed. Byron Hawk, David Rieder, and Ollie Oviedo (Minneapolis, MN: University of Minnesota Press, 2008), 166.

141 ***Apps such as Tagwhat, Acrossair, Layar, and Wikitude World Browser***: Sarvesh Chandra, "Top 20 Augmented Reality Apps for Android and iPhone/iPad Users," *DeepKnowHow*, April 4, 2013, accessed August 15, 2013, http://bit.ly/2eisR2M.

142 ***As Paul Dourish explains, in augmented reality***: Paul Dourish, *Where the Action Is: The Foundations of Embodied Interaction* (Cambridge, MA: MIT Press, 2001), 38.

142 ***Put somewhat differently, the key innovation***: Andy Clark, *Natural-Born Cyborgs: Minds, Technologies, and the Future of Human Intelligence* (NY: Oxford University Press, 2003), 53.

142 ***As Jay Bolter and Richard Grusin have argued***: Jay David Bolter and Richard Grusin, *Remediation: Understanding New Media* (Cambridge, MA: MIT Press, 2000), 24.

143 ***Such a realism assumes***: Lee Braver, *A Thing of This World: A History of Continental Anti-Realism* (Evanston, IL: Northwestern University Press, 2007), 15-19; Braver includes two additional theses in his definition of realism: bivalence and the passive knower. Though both of these have resonance with rhetoric, particularly with Wilkins's attempts to definitively categorize concepts into a universal language, for the sake of length I have chosen to focus on just the first three of his realist theses.

143 ***Though Ramus leaves a small role for rhetoric to play***: Walter Ong, *Ramus, Method, and the Decay of Dialogue* (Chicago, IL: University of Chicago Press, 2004), 291.

144 ***Words, he says, "plainly force and overrule***: Francis Bacon, *The New Organon. The Works of Francis Bacon*," ed. James Spedding, Robert Ellis, and Douglas Heath (NY: Garrett, 1968), 1 43.

144 ***As does the art of rhetoric***: John Locke, *An Essay Concerning Human Understanding* (Philadelphia, PA: Kay and Troutman, 1849), 328.

144 ***Rhetoric, he laments, is that "powerful instrument***: Ibid.

144 ***These explicit contributions to rhetorical theory not withstanding***: John Wilkins, *An Essay Toward a Real Character and a Philosophical Language, 1668* (Menston, UK: Scolar, 1968), 13.

145 ***According to Arika Okrent***: Arika Okrent, *In the Land of Invented Languages* (NY: Spiegel and Grau, 2010), 26.

145 ***There, you would find the symbol for dog***: Ibid., 51-52.

145 ***As Stanley Fish suggests in a discussion of Wilkins***: Stanley Fish, *Doing What Comes Naturally: Change, Rhetoric, and the Practice of Theory in Literary and Legal Studies* (Durham, NC: Duke University Press, 1989), 477.

146 ***When augmented reality specialists and researchers in distributed cognition argue***: Andy Clark, *Natural-Born Cyborgs: Minds, Technologies, and the Future of Human Intelligence* (NY: Oxford University Press, 2003).

146 ***Richard Rorty offers a succinct and representative example***: Richard Rorty, *Contingency, Irony, and Solidarity* (Cambridge, UK: Cambridge University Press, 1989), 5; Rorty's equivocation on the issue of mind-independent reality is a common move for anti-realists. Indeed, Rorty's ability to separate issues of knowledge from metaphysical notions of reality follows numerous Kantian thinkers who have adapted Kant's transcendental philosophy, which acknowledges the existence of things-in-themselves (noumenon) while at the same time arguing that

such things are fundamentally unknowable and therefore not relevant to phenomenal inquiry. As Braver notes, however, these equivocations make it difficult for anti-realists to avoid all tenets of realism. As Rorty demonstrates, realist ideas are almost always lurking in the background, even in the staunchest anti-realist arguments.

147 ***Whereas epistemological realism argues***: Levi R. Bryant, *The Democracy of Objects* (Ann Arbor, MI: Open Humanities Press, 2011), 18.

147 ***According to Levi Bryant, ontological realism***: Ibid., 18-19.

148 ***Here is how the developers of Tagwhat***: "Tagwhat Frequently Asked Questions," *Tagwhat*, 2013, accessed August 15, 2013, http://www.tagwhat.com/faq.php.

149 ***In* Ambient Rhetoric*, Thomas Rickert draws attention***: Thomas Rickert, *Ambient Rhetoric: The Attunements of Rhetorical Being* (Pittsburgh, PA: University of Pittsburgh Press, 2013), 159.

150 ***In* Being and Time*, for example, Heidegger characterizes***: Martin Heidegger, *Being and Time*, trans. John Macquarrie and Edward Robinson (NY: Harper and Row, 1962), 204; Quoted in Thomas Rickert, *Ambient Rhetoric: The Attunements of Rhetorical Being* (Pittsburgh, PA: University of Pittsburgh Press, 2013), 171.

150 ***As Rickert suggests, passages such as this indicate***: Thomas Rickert, *Ambient Rhetoric: The Attunements of Rhetorical Being* (Pittsburgh, PA: University of Pittsburgh Press, 2013), 171.

150 ***Language is our means of engaging world***: Ibid., 163.

151 ***Heidegger's best known, but least understood, statement on language***: Martin Heidegger, "Letter on Humanism," in *Basic Writings*, ed. David Farrell Krell, trans. Frank A. Capuzzi (NY: HarperCollins, 1993), 217.

151 ***Paraphrasing Heidegger, Rickert argues against such interpretations***: Thomas Rickert, *Ambient Rhetoric: The Attunements of Rhetorical Being* (Pittsburgh, PA: University of Pittsburgh Press, 2013), 102.

151 ***He continues***: Martin Heidegger, "The Way to Language," in *Basic Writings*, ed. David Farrell Krell, trans. David Farrell Krell (NY: HarperCollins, 1993), 411.

151 ***Out of unspokeness or the unsaid***: Ibid., 411; Ibid., 413.

151 ***This is* language**: Ibid., 419.

152 ***Though he resists the tradition of realism***: In *Being and Time*, Heidegger admonishes realism for insisting that only one kind of Being is real. For the realist, what is present-at-hand acquires the meaning of "Reality," leaving all other aspects of Being on the outside looking in (see 244-256). Again, following Heidegger's lead, Rickert also raises doubts about the usefulness of realism for an ontological rhetoric, suggesting that an ontological approach to rhetoric must reach beyond explanations about language's connection to world (197). While Rickert's critique of realism makes sense given many of its traditional forms, his argu-

ment is actually much more in tune with more recent discussions of ontological realism such as Bryant's.

152 ***Thus when the Tagwhat user responds***: Martin Heidegger, "The Way to Language," in *Basic Writings*, ed. David Farrell Krell, trans. David Farrell Krell (NY: HarperCollins, 1993), 411.

Chapter 9: SAZoo-AR, *Ethea*, and Computer Vision

156 ***Even the simple act of using a computer keyboard***: Paul Dourish, *Where the Action Is: The Foundations of Embodied Interaction* (Cambridge, MA: MIT Press, 2001), 110.

156 ***The world's most popular developer of AR***: "Features," *Layar*, 2013, accessed April 15, 2013, http://www.layar.com.

156 ***An early news release on Geomedia's blog***: Jeremy Kenisky, "Augmented Reality Zoo Exhibits and Zoo-AR," *Geomedia*, August 13, 2012, accessed August 15, 2013, http://bit.ly/2fvRXbr; emphasis in original.

157 ***The video features Marybeth Green (PhD)***: Ibid., 1:03.

158 ***Donald Hawkins, a PhD candidate from Education Service Center***: Ibid., 1:20.

158 ***Given the successful implementation of all of these factors***: "Our Company," "About," Geomedia, accessed August 15, 2013, http://bit.ly/2eAupQY.

158 ***It is true that many textbooks and popular novels tend to minimize***: James M. Lang, "The Benefits of Making It Harder to Learn," *The Chronicle of Higher Education*, June 3, 2012, accessed August 20, 2012, http://bit.ly/2fPCXt5.

158 ***Along different lines, Gardner's "multiple intelligences" theory***: See Lynn Waterhouse, "Multiple Intelligences, the Mozart Effect, and Emotional Intelligence: A Critical Review," *Educational Psychologist* 41, no. 4 (2006): 207-225.

159 ***Echoing Donna Haraway, Bruno Latour suggests***: Bruno Latour, *The Pasteurization of France*, trans. Alan Sheridan and John Law (Cambridge, MA: Harvard University Press, 1988), 193.

161 ***In AR's blending of the physical and digital means of perception***: Lev Manovich, "The Poetics of Augmented Space," *New Media and Society* 5, no. 2 (2006): 219-200.

162 ***Consequently, Zoo-AR offers statements such as***: "AR Education" "*Zoo-AR*," Geomedia, 2013, accessed August 15, 2013, http://zoo-ar.com/education.html.

162 ***One local newspaper report***: Rene A. Guzman, "Zoo Animals Just a Touch Away," *San Antonio Express-News*, May 24, 2013, accessed August 15, 2013, http://bit.ly/2fztJQn.

162 ***Such ontological assumptions produce***: "AR Education" "*Zoo-AR*," Geomedia, 2013, accessed August 15, 2013, http://bit.ly/2fkguzT.

163 ***Anne Friedberg writes***: Anne Friedberg, *The Virtual Window: From Alberti to Microsoft* (Cambridge, MA: MIT Press, 2006), 232.

163 ***In* Existential Technics*, Ihde declares***: Quoted in Donna Haraway, "Crittercam: Compounding Eyes in NatureCulture," in *PostPhenomenology: A Critical Companion to Ihde*, ed. Evan Selinger (Albany, NY: SUNY Press, 2006), 175.

164 ***In the context of mobile media studies, Richardson illustrates infolding***: Ingrid Richardson, "Faces, Interfaces, Screens: Relational Ontologies of Framing, Attention and Distraction," *Transformations* 18 (2010): http://www.transformationsjournal.org/journal/issue_18/article_05.shtml.

164 ***Richardson instead articulates a space of co-production***: Ibid.; see Bruno Latour, *We Have Never Been Modern* (Cambridge, MA: Harvard University Press, 1993).

164 ***Koreans value* nunchi**: Stella Ting-Toomey and Atsuko Kurogi qtd. in Jaz Hee-jeong Choi, "Approaching the Mobile Culture of East Asia," *M/C Journal* 10, no. 1 (2007): http://journal.media-culture.org.au/0703/01-choi.php.

165 ***The unique way that SAZoo-AR infolds us***: Ingrid Richardson, "Faces, Interfaces, Screens: Relational Ontologies of Framing, Attention and Distraction," *Transformations* 18 (2010): http://www.transformationsjournal.org/journal/issue_18/article_05.shtml.

165 ***To take an analogy, it may alternately deviate***: Ibid.

165 ***They likely enacted what Erving Goffman has called***: Erving Goffman, *Interaction Ritual: Essays on Face-to-Face Behavior* (NY: Pantheon Books, 1967), 31-32.

166 ***The screen creates a specific sense of involvement***: Lucas D. Introna and Fernando M. Ilharco, "The Ontological Screening of Contemporary Life: A Phenomenological Analysis of Screens," *European Journal of Information Systems* 13 (2004): 225.

166 ***Postphenomenology "calls for a certain kind of inattention***: Eugénie Shinkle qtd. in Ingrid Richardson, "Faces, Interfaces, Screens: Relational Ontologies of Framing, Attention and Distraction," *Transformations* 18 (2010): http://www.transformationsjournal.org/journal/issue_18/article_05.shtml.

167 ***These observations are in keeping with Harper and Richardson's***: Ingrid Richardson and Carly Harper, "Corporeal Virtuality: The Impossibility of a Disembodied Ontology," *Body Space and Technology* 2, no. 2 (2002); Ingrid Richardson, "Telebodies & Televisions: Corporeality and Agency in Technoculture," (PhD diss., University of Western Sydney, 2003).

167 ***Not in the context of AR apps***: Ingrid Richardson, "Faces, Interfaces, Screens: Relational Ontologies of Framing, Attention and Distraction," *Transformations* 18 (2010): http://www.transformationsjournal.org/journal/issue_18/article_05.shtml.

167 ***An analogy can be found in Haraway's discussion***: Donna Haraway, "Crittercam: Compounding Eyes in NatureCulture," in *PostPhenomenology: A Critical Companion to Ihde*, ed. Evan Selinger (Albany, NY: SUNY Press, 2006), 180.

168 ***However, Haraway suggests that these perspectives are misleading***: Ibid., 186.

168 ***Attaching a camera to an animal makes us part of the animal***: Ibid.

168 ***Haraway writes, "[T]he infolding of others***: Ibid., 176.

169 ***Mark B. Hansen argues that any digital image is processual***: Mark B. N. Hansen, *New Philosophy for New Media* (Cambridge, MA: MIT Press, 2004), 11.

169 ***"Computer vision is about enabling***: Frank Gillett qtd. in Christina Bonnington, "What's a 'Computer Vision Specialist' and Why Does Apply Need One?," *Wired Gadget Lab*, April 18, 2012, accessed August 15, 2013, http://www.wired.com/2012/04/apple-3d-specialist.

169 ***By contrast, CMOS devices possess transistors***: Karim Nice, Tracy V. Wilson, and Gerald Gurevich, "How Digital Cameras Work," *How Stuff Works*, 2013, accessed August 15, 2013, http://bit.ly/2eIYalK.

170 ***iPhones employ a color filter array***: "iPhone 5—Technical Specifications," *Apple*, October 24, 2013, accessed April 15, 2013, http://apple.co/2fPxJxi.

170 ***Bogost writes, "Because the Bayer sensor's method***: Ian Bogost, *Alien Phenomenology, Or What It's Like to Be a Thing* (Minneapolis, MN: University of Minnesota Press, 2012), 72.

171 ***Bogost offers a parallel to a bat's vision***: Ibid.

171 ***Bogost concludes, "Irrespective of the underlying electro-optical mechanisms***: Ibid.

172 ***The first goal of most computer vision***: See Tony Lindeberg, "Scale-space," *Encyclopedia of Computer Science and Engineering Vol. 4*, ed. Benjamin Wah (NY: John Wiley and Sons, 2009), 2495–2504; David G. Lowe, "Distinctive Image Features from Scale-Invariant Keypoints," *International Journal of Computer Vision* 60, no. 2 (2004): 91-110.

172 ***For example, Layar's official blogger Adrienne Goetz***: Adrienne Goetz, "Introducing: LayarVision, and a $55,000 Creation Challenge," *Layar Blog*, August 2, 2011, accessed August 15, 2013, http://bit.ly/2eiz0vT.

172 ***Analogous to the guesswork of the Bayer filter***: David G. Lowe, "Distinctive Image Features from Scale-Invariant Keypoints," *International Journal of Computer Vision* 60, no. 2 (2004): 91.

172 ***However, unlike human eyes, computer vision***: Ibid., 191.

173 ***OpenCV regulates the update speed***: "OpenCV Tutorials," *OpenCV*, 2013, accessed August 15, 2013, http://docs.opencv.org/doc/tutorials/tutorials.html.

173 ***If a corner detector can easily pick out straight lines***: Ibid.

174 ***Code is "hypocritical," Wendy Chun writes***: Wendy Chun, *Programmed Visions* (Cambridge, MA: MIT Press, 2012), 24.

174 ***Drawing on Heidegger, Charles E. Scott offers***: Charles E. Scott, *The Question of Ethics: Nietzsche, Foucault, Heidegger* (Bloomington, IN: Indiana University Press, 1990), 143-145.

175 ***In the context of education***: Ibid., 144.

Chapter 10: When Geolocation Meets Visualization

178 ***When Geolocation Meets Visualization***: This chapter is excerpted from Chapter 2 of Jason Farman, *Mobile Interface Theory: Embodied Space and Locative Media* (NY: Routledge Press, 2012). Reproduced with permission.

179 ***For Elizabeth Grosz, this dissolve takes place***: Elizabeth Grosz, *Architecture from the Outside: Essays on Virtual and Real Space* (Cambridge, MA: MIT Press, 2001), 76.

179 ***By interrogating whether or not the "computer screen***: Ibid., 88, 79.

180 ***Here, we must complicate***: Ibid., 86.

180 ***The term virtual is drawn***: *Oxford English Dictionary Online*, s.v. "Virtual, adj. (and n.)."

180 ***They write, "Because the Internet was mostly accessed***: Adriana de Souza e Silva and Daniel Sutko, "Theorizing Locative Technologies Through Philosophies of the Virtual," *Communication Theory* 21 (2011): 25.

181 ***De Souza e Silva and Sutko note***: Ibid., 26.

181 ***As Umberto Eco has argued***: Umberto Eco, cited in Adriana de Souza e Silva and Daniel Sutko, "Theorizing Locative Technologies Through Philosophies of the Virtual," *Communication Theory* 21 (2011): 29.

181 ***As John Rajchman writes, citing Proust***: John Rajchman, "The Virtual House," *Constructions* (Cambridge, MA: MIT Press, 1998), 116.

181 ***Rajchman continues: "The actual is then what manifests***: Ibid.

181 ***Virtuality is experienced as a multiplicity***: Ibid.

182 ***This experience of virtuality***: Gilles Deleuze, *Difference and Repetition* (NY: Columbia University Press, 1994).

183 ***These forms of visualization, according to artist Tom Corby***: Tom Corby, "Landscapes of Feeling, Arenas of Action: Information Visualization as Art Practice," *Leonardo* 41, no. 5 (2008): 462.

185 ***This loss of place is "tantamount***: Edward Casey, *Getting Back into Place: Toward a Renewed Understanding of the Place-World* (Bloomington: Indiana University Press, 2009), 36–37.

187 ***As Derrida has argued***: Jacques Derrida, "Signature Event Context," in *Margins of Philosophy*, trans. Alan Bass (Chicago, IL: University of Chicago Press, 1982), 310.

187 ***By utilizing technologies that draw on a person's location***: Though I am distinguishing here between digital and material spaces, this is more of a gesture toward the relationship between digital information and hardscapes. The digital must be understood as material, since the infrastructure that makes it possible and the interfaces that allow us to interact with data are always material.

188 ***This extends Lev Manovich's distinction***: Lev Manovich, *The Language of New Media* (Cambridge, MA: MIT Press, 2001), 25.

189 ***As Paul Jahshan notes***: Paul Jahshan, *Cybermapping and the Writing of Myth* (NY: Peter Lang, 2007), 53.

190 ***As Jean Baudrillard noted***: Jean Baudrillard, *Simulacra and Simulation*, trans. S.F. Glaser (Ann Arbor, MI: The University of Michigan Press, 1994), 1.

190 ***As Raymond B. Craib argues***: Raymond B. Craib, "Cartography and Power in the Conquest and Creation of New Spain," *Latin American Research Review* 35, no. 1 (2000): 8.

191 ***He specifically draws on examples like Esther Polak's* Amsterdam Realtime**: Drew Hemment, "Locative Arts," *Leonardo* 39, no. 4 (2006): 349–350.

191 ***In his article on the uses of information visualization***: Tom Corby, "Landscapes of Feeling, Arenas of Action: Information Visualization as Art Practice," *Leonardo* 41, no. 5 (2008): 465.

192 ***As Chris Perkins writes about the project***: Chris Perkins, "Community Mapping," *The Cartographic Journal* 44, no. 2 (2007): 128.

192 ***Corby develops the consequences of user-generated mapping***: Tom Corby, "Landscapes of Feeling, Arenas of Action: Information Visualization as Art Practice," *Leonardo* 41, no. 5 (2008): 465.

192 ***As I have argued elsewhere***: Jason Farman, "Mapping the Digital Empire: Google Earth and the Process of Postmodern Cartography," *New Media and Society* 12, no. 6 (2010).

194 ***She writes, "Collapsing 'foreign' and 'domestic,' these maps bridge***: Paula Levine, "Shadows from Another Place," *Proceedings of the Media in Transition 4 Conference*, http://web.mit.edu/comm-forum/mit4/papers/levine.pdf.

194 ***The disjunction between the two***: Guy-Ernest Debord, "Introduction to a Critique of Urban Geography," *The Situationist International Text Library*, http://bit.ly/2eiCE8P.

194 ***Debord continues***: Ibid.

194 ***As Mary Flanagan notes***: Mary Flanagan, *Critical Play: Radical Game Design* (Cambridge, MA: MIT Press, 2009), 195.

195 ***He continues by noting that the "maps***: Matthew Edney, *Mapping an Empire: The Geographical Construction of British India, 1765–1843* (Chicago, IL: University of Chicago Press, 1990), 2.

195 ***Liqiu Meng, for instance, argues***: Liqiu Meng, "Egocentric Design of Map-Based Mobile Services," *The Cartographic Journal* 42, no. 1 (2005): 7.

196 ***At that time, there were nearly 200,000 cartographers***: Christian Heipke, "Crowdsourcing Geospatial Data," *ISPRS Journal of Photogrammetry and Remote Sensing* 65 (2010): 550–557.

196 ***The typical trajectory of one of the emergency SMS messages***: This SMS message was sent to Ushahidi on January 23, 2010 and is chronicled, along with the English translation and the pinpoint on the Open Street Map, at: http://haiti.ushahidi.com/reports/view/1772.

Tamiko Thiel

272 ***The artwork Clouding Green floats***: "How Clean is Your Cloud?," *Greenpeace*, Greenpeace.org, April 2012, http://bit.ly/2fd7NtM.

Bibliography

3Satva. *Retinex*. Volume 1. Los Angeles, CA: Michael Satva Hanfling, 2010.

Albanesius, Chloe. "Google 'Project Glass' Replaces the Smartphone with Glasses." *PC Magazine*, April 4, 2012. http://www.pcmag.com/article2/0,2817,2402613,00.asp.

Anders, Peter. "Cybrid Principals: Guidelines for Merging Physical and Cyber Spaces." *International Journal of Architectural Computing* 3, no. 3 (2005): 391-406.

Anderson, Matthew Tobin. *Feed*. Cambridge, MA: Candlewick Press, 2002.

Andrejevic, Mark. *iSpy: Surveillance and Power in the Interactive Era*. Lawrence, KS: University of Kansas. 2009.

"AR Education." *Zoo-AR*. Geomedia. 2013. http://zoo-ar.com/education.html.

Aristotle. *Rhetoric*. Translated by Rhys Roberts. Mineola, NY: Dover Publications, 2004.

Azuma, Ronald T. "A Survey of Augmented Reality." *Presence: Teleoperators and Virtual Environments* 6, no. 4 (1997): 355-85.

Bacon, Francis. *The New Organon. The Works of Francis Bacon*. Edited by James Spedding, Robert Ellis, and Douglas Heath. New York: Garrett, 1968.

Barba, Evan, Blair MacIntyre, and Elizabeth D. Mynatt. "Here We Are! Where Are We? Locating Mixed Reality in the Age of the Smartphone." *Proceedings of the IEEE* 100, no. 4 (2012): 929–36.

Bates, Philip. "Interview with Tim Maughan, Bristol Science Fiction Champion." *Guide2Bristol*. http://bit.ly/2eiBRom.

Baudrillard, Jean. *Simulacra and Simulation*. Translated by S.F. Glaser. Ann Arbor, MI: The University of Michigan Press, 1994.

Bayus, Barry L., Sanjay Jain, and Ambar G. Rao. "Truth or Consequences: An Analysis of Vaporware and New Product Announcements." *Journal of Marketing Research* 38, no. 1 (2001): 3-13.

Beaty, Bart. *Comics Versus Art*. Toronto: University of Toronto Press, 2012.

Benjamin, Walter. "The Work of Art in the Age of Mechanical Reproduction." *Marxists.org*. http://bit.ly/2fPHfRh.

Bilandzic, Mark, and Marcus Foth. "A Review of Locative Media, Mobile and Embodied Spatial Interaction." *International Journal of Human-Computer Studies* 70, no. 1 (2012): 66-71.

Bogost, Ian. *Alien Phenomenology, or What It's Like to Be a Thing*. Minneapolis, MN: University of Minnesota, 2012.

———. *Persuasive Games: The Expressive Power of Videogames*. Cambridge, MA: MIT Press, 2010.

———. "Seeing Things-OOOIII." Vimeo video, 6:46. Posted September 15, 2011. http://bit.ly/2fvZPK3.

Bolter, Jay David and Richard Grusin. *Remediation: Understanding New Media*. Cambridge, MA: MIT Press, 2000.

Bolter, Jay David, Maria Engberg, and Blair MacIntyre. "Media Studies, Mobile Augmented Reality, and Interaction Design." *Interactions* 20, no. 1 (2013): 36-45.

Bonnington, Christina. "What's a 'Computer Vision Specialist' and Why Does Apply Need One?" *Wired Gadget Lab*, April 18, 2012. http://www.wired.com/2012/04/apple-3d-specialist.

boyd, danah. "White Flight in Networked Publics? How Race and Class Shaped American Teen Engagement with MySpace and Facebook." In *Race After the Internet*, edited by Lisa Nakamura, Peter Chow-White, and Alondra Nelson, 203-222. New York: Routledge, 2011.

———. "Why Youth <3 Social Network Sites: The Role of Networked Publics in Teenage Social Life." In *Youth, Identity, and Digital Media*, edited by David Buckingham, 119-142. Cambridge, MA: MIT Press, 2008.

Braver, Lee. *A Thing of This World: A History of Continental Anti-Realism*. Evanston, IL: Northwestern University Press, 2007.

Brin, David. *Earth*. New York: Bantam Books, 1990.

Brin, Sergey. "Personal Blog." Google.com, April 4, 2012. https://plus.google.com/ +GoogleGlass/posts/aKymsANgWBD.

Bryant, Levi R. *The Democracy of Objects*. Ann Arbor, MI: Open Humanities Press, 2011.

Burke, Kenneth. *A Grammar of Motives*. Berkeley, CA: University of California Press, 1945.

———. *On Symbols and Society*. Chicago, IL: University of Chicago Press, 1989.

———. "Poem." In *The Legacy of Kenneth Burke*, edited by Herbert W. Simons and Trevor Melia, 263-266. Madison, WI: University of Wisconsin Press, 1989.

Callahan, Timothy. "When Worlds Collide: Marvel's Augmented Reality." *Comic Book Resources*, April 2, 2012. http://www.comicbookresources.com/?page=article&id=37936.

Carpenter, Thomas K. "The AR Reading List." *Thomas K. Carpenter*. 2009. Web. 30 Aug 2013.

Carrier, David. *The Aesthetics of Comics*. University Park, PA: Pennsylvania State University Press, 2000.

Casey, Edward. *Getting Back into Place: Toward a Renewed Understanding of the Place-World*. Bloomington, IN: Indiana University Press, 2009.

Castells, Manuel. "The Network Society: From Knowledge to Policy." In *The Network Society: From Knowledge to Policy*, edited by Manuel Castells and Gustavo Cardoso, 3-22. Washington, DC: Johns Hopkins Center for Transatlantic Relations, 2005.

Chandra, Sarvesh. 'Top 20 Augmented Reality Apps for Android and iPhone/iPad Users." *DeepKnowHow*, April 4, 2013. http://deepknowhow.com/2013/04/04/top-20-augmented-reality-apps-for-android-and-iphoneipad-users.

Choi, Jaz Hee-jeong. "Approaching the Mobile Culture of East Asia." *M/C Journal* 10, no. 1 (2007).

Christian Ulrik Andersen, and Søren Pold. "The Scripted Spaces of Urban Ubiquitous Computing: The Experience, Poetics, and Politics of Public Scripted Space." *Fibreculture Journal* 19 (2011): 110-25.

Chun, Wendy. *Programmed Visions*. Cambridge, MA: MIT University Press, 2012.

Cicero, Marcus Tullius. *On the Ideal Orator*. Translated by James M. May and Jacob Wisse. New York: Oxford University Press, 2001.

Clark, Andy. *Natural-Born Cyborgs: Minds, Technologies, and the Future of Human Intelligence*. New York: Oxford UP, 2003.

Corby, Tom. "Landscapes of Feeling, Arenas of Action: Information Visualization as Art Practice." *Leonardo* 41, no. 5 (2008): 462.

Craib, Raymond B. "Cartography and Power in the Conquest and Creation of New Spain." *Latin American Research Review* 35, no. 1 (2000): 8.

Crawford, Alice. "Taking Social Software to the Streets: Mobile Cocooning and the (an) Erotic City." *Journal of Urban Technology* 15, no. 3 (2007): 89.

Cresswell, Tim. *Place*. Malden, MA: Blackwell Publishing, 2004.

Csicsery-Ronay, Istvan. *The Seven Beauties of Science Fiction*. Middletown, CT: Wesleyan University Press, 2008.

Cusumano, Michael. "Technology Strategy and Management: The Evolution of Platform Thinking." *Communications of the Association for Computing Machinery* 53, no. 1 (2010): 32-34.

Dayan, Daniel and Elihu Katz. *Media Events: The Live Broadcasting of History*. Boston, MA: Harvard University Press. 1994.

de Certeau, Michel. *The Practice of Everyday Life*. Berkeley, CA: University of California Press, 1984.

de Souza e Silva, Adriana. "From Cyber to Hybrid Mobile Technologies as Interfaces of Hybrid Spaces." *Space and Culture* 9, no. 3 (2006): 261-78.

de Souza e Silva, Adriana, and Jordan Frith. *Mobile Interfaces in Public Spaces: Locational Privacy, Control and Urban Sociability*. New York: Routledge, 2012.

——. "Re-narrating the City through the Presentation of Location." In *Digital Storytelling with Mobile Media: Locative Technologies and Narrative Practices*, edited by Jason Farman. New York: Routledge, 2013.

de Souza e Silva, Adriana and Daniel Sutko. "Theorizing Locative Technologies through Philosophies of the Virtual," *Communication Theory* 21 (2011): 25.

Dead Space. Video Game. Developer Visceral Games. Publisher Electronic Arts. 2008-2013.

Debord, Guy-Ernest. "Introduction to a Critique of Urban Geography." *The Situationist International Text Library*. http://library.nothingness.org/articles/SI/en/display/2.

Derrida, Jacques. "Signature Event Context." In *Margins of Philosophy*, translated by Alan Bass. Chicago, IL: University of Chicago Press, 1982.

Deleuze, Gilles. *Difference and Repetition*. New York: Columbia University Press, 1994.

——. *The Fold: Leibniz and the Baroque*. Translated by Tom Conley. Minneapolis, MN: University of Minnesota Press, 1993.

Dickinson, Greg, Carole Blair, and Brian Ott. *Places of Public Memory: The Rhetoric of Museums and Memorials*. Tuscaloosa, AL: University of Alabama Press, 2010.

Dourish, Paul. *Where the Action Is: The Foundations of Embodied Interaction*. Cambridge, MA: MIT Press, 2001.

Draaisma, Douwe. *Metaphors of Memory: A History of Ideas about the Mind*. Cambridge, UK: Cambridge University Press, 2000.

Drascic, David and Paul Milgram. "Perceptual Issues in Augmented Reality." *Proceedings of the International Society for Optics and Photonics* 2653, Stereoscopic Displays and Virtual Reality Systems III, 123 (1996): doi:10.1117/12.237425

Edney, Matthew. *Mapping an Empire: The Geographical Construction of British India, 1765–1843*. Chicago, IL: University of Chicago Press, 1990.

Eisner, Will. *Comics and Sequential Art: Principles and Practices from the Legendary Cartoonist*. New York: W.W. Norton, 2008.

Encheva, Lyuba and Isabel Pedersen. "'One Day . . .': Google's Project Glass, Integrated Reality, and Futuristic Visions in Predictive Advertising." *The 37th Annual Meeting of the Semiotic Society of America*, Toronto, November 1-4, 2012.

Ernst, Wolfgang. "Dis/continuities: Does the Archive Become Metaphorical in Multi-media Space?" In *New Media, Old Media: A History and Theory Reader*, edited by Wendy Hui Kyong Chun and Thomas Keenan, 105-124. New York: Routledge, 2006.

Etherington, Darrell. "Apple Patent a Reminder That It's Working on Google Glass-Style Wearable Tech, Too." *Mobile Phone Advisor*, December 7, 2012. http://mobilephoneadvise.com/apple-patent-areminder-that-its-working-on-google-glass-stylewearable-tech-too.

Farman, Jason. "Mapping the Digital Empire: Google Earth and the Process of Postmodern Cartography." *New Media and Society* 12, no. 6 (2010): 869–888.

——. *Mobile Interface Theory: Embodied Space and Locative Media*. New York: Routledge, 2012.

Iron Man. DVD. Directed by Jon Favreau. Hollywood, CA: Paramount, 2008.

"Features." *Layar*, 2013. http://www.layar.com.

"First Electric Traffic Signal." *History.com*. This Day in History. http://www.history.com/this-day-in-history/first-electric-traffic-signal-installed.

Fish, Stanley. *Doing What Comes Naturally: Change, Rhetoric, and the Practice of Theory in Literary and Legal Studies*. Durham, NC: Duke University Press, 1989.

Flanagan, Mary. *Critical Play: Radical Game Design*. Cambridge, MA: MIT Press, 2009.

Freedman, Carl H. *Critical Theory and Science Fiction*. Hanover, NH: Wesleyan University Press, 2000.

Friedberg, Anne. *The Virtual Window: From Alberti to Microsoft*. Cambridge, MA: MIT Press, 2006.

Frith, Jordan. "Splintered Space: The Smartphone as the Screen to the City." *Mobilities* 7, no. 1 (2012): 131–149.

——. "Turning Life into a Game: Foursquare, Gamification, and Personal Mobility." *Mobile Media and Communication* 1, no. 2 (2013): 248–262.

Fuller, Matthew and Sónia Matos. "Feral Computing: From Ubiquitous Calculation to Wild Interactions." *The Fibreculture Journal* 19 (2011).

Fuller, Matthew. *Media Ecologies: Materialist Energies in Art and Technoculture*. Cambridge, MA: MIT Press, 2007.

Galloway, Anne and Matt Ward. "Locative Media as Socialising and Spatialising Practices: Learning from Archaeology." *Leonardo Electronic Almanac—Locative Media Special* 14, no. 3 (2006).

Garde-Hansen, Joanne, Andrew Hoskins, and Anna Reading. *Save as . . . Digital Memories*. New York: Palgrave Macmillan, 2009.

Gibson, William. *All Tomorrow's Parties*. New York: G.P. Putnam's Sons, 1999.

——. *Burning Chrome*. New York: Arbor House, 1986.

——. "Google's Earth." *New York Times,* August 31, 2010. http://www.nytimes.com/2010/09/ 01/opinion/01gibson.html?_r=0.

——. *Neuromancer*. New York: Ace Books, 1984.

——. *Spook Country*. New York: G.P. Putnam's Sons, 2007.

——. *Virtual Light*. New York: Bantam Books, 1993.

Baldwin, Robert. "Sergey Brin Finally Lets Someone Else Wear Google Glass." *Wired,* May 29, 2012. http://www.wired.com/2012/05/sergey-brin-finally-lets-someone-else-wear-google-glass/.

Goetz, Adriene. "Introducing: LayarVision, and a $55,000 Creation Challenge." *Layar Blog,* August 2, 2011: https://www.layar.com/news/blog/2011/08/02/introducing-layar-vision-and-a-55000-creation-challenge.

Goffman, Erving. *Interaction Ritual: Essays on Face-to-Face Behavior*. New York: Pantheon Books, 1967.

Google. "Google Explorer Program." *Google*. February 2013.

———. “Project Glass: Live Demo at Google I/O.” YouTube video, 11:26. Posted June 27, 2012. https://www.youtube.com/watch?v=D7TB8b2t3QE.

———. “Project Glass: One Day...,” YouTube video, 2:30. Posted April 4, 2012. https://www.youtube.com/watch?v=9c6W4CCU9M4.

———. “Project Glass: Trampoline Video.” *Google Plus* video, 0:15. Posted May 23, 2012. https://plus.google.com/u/0/s/project%20glass%3A%20trampoline.

Gordon, Eric. *The Urban Spectator: American Concept Cities from Kodak to Google*. Lebanon, NH: Dartmouth College, 2010.

Gordon, Eric and Adriana de Souza e Silva. *Net Locality: Why Location Matters in a Networked World*. West Sussex, UK: Wiley-Blackwell, 2011.

———. *Network Locality: How Digital Networks Create a Culture of Location*. Boston, MA: Blackwell Publishers, 2011.

Gorman, Michael. “Google Glass Shows How Diane von Furstenberg is Living, What It’s Like at New York Fashion Week.” *Engadget*, September 14, 2012. http://www.engadget.com/2012/09/14/google-glass-diane-von-furstenberg-new-york-fashion-week-video.

Gough, Paul. *Banksy: The Bristol Legacy*. Bristol: Redcliffe, 2012.

Greenberg, Saul and Bill Buxton. “Usability Evaluation Considered Harmful (Some of the Time).” In *Proceedings of the SIGCHI Conference on Human Factors in Computing Systems 2008*, 111-120. New York: Association of Computing Machinery, 2008.

Greenfield, Adam. *Everyware: The Dawning Age of Ubiquitous Computing*. Berkeley, CA: New Riders Press, 2006.

Grosz, Elizabeth A. *Architecture from the Outside: Essays on Virtual and Real Space*. Cambridge, MA: MIT Press, 2001.

Groten, Dirk and Ronald Van Der Lingen. “Layar on Google Glass: It’s Not Augmented Reality.” *Layar*, June 25, 2013. https://www.layar.com/news/blog/2013/06/25/layar-on-google-glass.

Guzman, Rene A. “Zoo Animals Just a Touch Away.” *San Antonio Express-News*, May 24, 2013. http://www.mysanantonio.com/life/article/Zoo-animals-just-a-touch-away-4547455.php.

Halavais, Alexander. *Search Engine Society*. Cambridge, MA: Polity, 2009..

Halo (Series). Video Game. Developer Bungie Studios, 343 Industries. Publisher Microsoft Studios. 2001-2013.

Hannam, Kevin, Mimi Sheller, and John Urry. “Mobilities, Immobilities and Moorings.” *Mobilities* 1.1 (2006): 1–22.

Hansen, Mark B. N. *New Philosophy for New Media*. Cambridge, MA: MIT Press, 2004.

Haraway, Donna J. “Crittercam: Compounding Eyes in NatureCulture.” In *PostPhenomenology: A Critical Companion to Ihde*, edited by Evan Selinger, 175-188. Albany, NY: SUNY Press, 2006.

———. *Simians, Cyborgs, and Women: The Reinvention of Nature*. New York: Routledge, 1991.

Harvey, Robert C. *Art of the Funnies: An Aesthetic History*. University Press of Mississippi, 1994.

Hayles, N. Katherine. *How We Became Posthuman: Virtual Bodies in Cybernetics, Literature, and Informatics*. Chicago: University of Chicago Press, 1999.

———. *How We Think: Digital Media and Contemporary Technogenesis*. Chicago: University of Chicago Press. 2012.

Hedman, Jonas, and Gregory Gimpel. "The adoption of hyped technologies: A qualitative study." *Information Technology and Management*, 11, no. 4 (2010): 161-175.

Heidegger, Martin. *Being and Time*. Translated by John Macquarrie and Edward Robinson. New York: Harper and Row, 1962.

———. "Letter on Humanism." In *Basic Writings*, edited by David Farrell Krell, translated by Frank A. Capuzzi, 217-65. New York: HarperCollins, 1993.

———. "The Way to Language." In *Basic Writings*, edited by David Farrell Krell, translated by Frank A. Capuzzi, 387-426. New York: HarperCollins, 1993.

Heipke, Christian. "Crowdsourcing Geospatial Data," *ISPRS Journal of Photogrammetry and Remote Sensing* 65 (2010): 550–557.

Hemment, Drew. "Locative Arts." *Leonardo* 39, no. 4 (2006): 349–350.

Hernandez, Damon. "Retinex: Augmented Reality Comic Book." *Metaverse One*, July 12, 2010. http://damonhernandez.blogspot.com/2010/07/retinex-augmented-reality-comic-book.html.

Hikins, James W. "Realism and Its Implications for Rhetorical Theory." In *Rhetoric and Philosophy*, edited by Richard A. Cherwitz, 21-77. New York: Routledge, 1990.

Holmevik, Jan R. *Inter/vention: Free Play in the Age of Electracy*. Cambridge, MA: MIT Press, 2012.

Horrigan, John B. and Ellen Satterwhite. "Adoption Paths: The Social Forces that Shape the Uptake of Technology." *Telecommunications Policy Research Conference*, 2010. http://ssrn.com/abstract=1989632.

Hoskins, Andrew. "7/7 and Connective Memory: Interactional Trajectories of Remembering in Post-scarcity Culture." *Memory Studies* 4, no. 3 (2011): 269–280.

———. "Anachronisms of Media, Anachronisms of Memory: From Collective Memory to a New Memory Ecology." In *On Media Memory: Collective Memory in a New Media Age*, edited by Motti Neiger, Oren Meyers, and Eyal Zandberg, 278-288. New York: Palgrave Macmillan, 2011.

———. "Digital Network Memory." In *Mediation, Remediation, and the Dynamics of Cultural Memory*, edited by Astrid Erll and Ann Rigney, 91-106. Berlin: de Gruyter, 2009.

———. "Media, Memory, Metaphor: Remembering and the Connective Turn." *Parallax* 17, no. 4 (2011): 19–31.

"How Clean is Your Cloud?" *Greenpeace*, April 2012. http://www.greenpeace.org/international/ Global/international/publications/climate/2012/iCoal/How-CleanisYourCloud.pdf.

Humphreys, Lee. "Mobile Social Networks and Social Practice: A Case Study of Dodgeball." *Journal of Computer-Mediated Communication* 13 (2007).

——. "Mobile Social Networks and Urban Public Space." *New Media & Society* 12 (2010): 763–778.

Hyde, Michael. *Perfection: Coming to Terms with Being Human*. Waco, TX: Baylor University Press. 2010.

Ihde, Don. *Technics and Praxis: A Philosophy of Technology*. New York, NY: Springer, 1978.

——. *Technology and Lifeworld: From Garden to Earth*. Bloomington, IN: Indiana University Press, 1990.

Introna, Lucas D., and Fernando M. Ilharco. "The Ontological Screening of Contemporary Life: A Phenomenological Analysis of Screens." *European Journal of Information Systems* 13 (2004): 221-234.

Jacobs, Jane. *The Death of Life of Great American Cities*. New York: Random House, 1961.

Jahshan, Paul. *Cybermapping and the Writing of Myth*. New York: Peter Lang, 2007.

Jameson, Fredric. *Postmodernism, Or, the Cultural Logic of Late Capitalism*. Durham: Duke University Press, 1991.

Johnson, Larry, Rachel Smith, Holly Willis, Alana Levine, and Keene Haywood. *The 2011 Horizon Report*. Austin, TX: The New Media Consortium, 2011.

Johnson, Steven. *Where Good Ideas Come From: The Natural History of Innovation*. New York: Riverhead, 2010.

Jurgenson, Nathan. "When Atoms Meet Bits: Social Media, the Mobile Web and Augmented Revolution." *Future Internet* 4, no. 1 (2012): 83-91.

Karapanos, Evangelos, John Zimmerman, Jodi Forlizzi, and Jean-Bernard Martens. "User Experience Over Time: An Initial Framework." *Proceedings of the SIGCHI Conference on Human Factors in Computing Systems*. New York: Association of Computing Machinery, 2009. 729-38.

Kelly, James P. and John Kessel. *Rewired: The Post-Cyberpunk Anthology*. San Francisco, California: Tachyon Publications, 2007.

Kenisky, Jeremy. "Augmented Reality Zoo Exhibits and Zoo-AR." *Geomedia*, August 13, 2012. http://geomedia.com/2012/08/13/augmented-reality-zoo-exhibits-and-zoo-ar.

Kipper, Gregory and Joseph Rampolla. *Augmented Reality: An Emerging Technologies Guide to AR*. Waltham, MA: Syngress, 2013.

Klopfer, Eric, and Kurt Squire. "Environmental Detectives—the Development of an Augmented Reality Platform for Environmental Simulations." *Educational Technology Research and Development* 56, no. 2 (2008): 203-28.

Kruijff, Ernst, J. Edward Swan, and Steven Feiner. "Perceptual Issues in Augmented Reality Revisited." *Mixed and Augmented Reality (ISMAR), 2010 9th IEEE International Symposium*, Seoul, Korea, October 13-16, 2010.

Kujala, Sari, Virpi Roto, Kaisa Väänänen-Vainio-Mattila, and Arto Sinnelä. "Identifying Hedonic Factors in Long-term User Experience." In *Proceedings of the 2011 Conference on Designing Pleasurable Products and Interfaces*, Article 17. New York: Association for Computing Machinery, 2011.

Lacey, Kimberly. "Making Memory: Techne, Technology, and the Refashioning of Contemporary Memory." PhD diss., Wayne State University, 2011. http://digitalcommons.wayne.edu/oa_dissertations/246.

LaMonica, Martin. "Google X Labs: First Project Glass, next space elevators?" *CNET.com*, April 24, 2012. http://www.cnet.com/news/google-x-labs-first-project-glass-next-space-elevators.

Lang, James M. "The Benefits of Making It Harder to Learn." *The Chronicle of Higher Education*, June 3, 2012. http://chronicle.com/article/The-Benefits-of-Making-It/132056.

Lanier, Jaron. *You Are Not A Gadget: A Manifesto*. New York: Vintage, 2011.

Latour, Bruno. *The Pasteurization of France*. Translated by Alan Sheridan and John Law. Cambridge, MA: Harvard University Press, 1988.

Le Goff, Jacques. *History and Memory*. Edited by Elizabeth Claman. New York: Columbia University Press, 1992.

Levine, Paula. "Shadows from Another Place," In *Proceedings of the Media in Transition 4 Conference*, Cambridge, MA, May 6-8, 2005. http://web.mit.edu/comm-forum/mit4/papers/levine.pdf.

Liggett, Helen. *Urban Encounters*. Minneapolis, MN: University of Minnesota Press, 2003.

Lindeberg, Tony. "Scale-space." *Encyclopedia of Computer Science and Engineering Vol. 4*. Edited by Benjamin Wah, 2495-2504. New York: John Wiley and Sons, 2009.

Locke, John. *An Essay Concerning Human Understanding*. Philadelphia, PA: Kay and Troutman, 1849.

Lodi, Simona. "Spatial Art: An Eruption of the Digital into the Physical." *Leonardo Electronic Almanac* 19, no. 2 (2013).

Lowe, David G. "Distinctive Image Features from Scale-Invariant Keypoints." *International Journal of Computer Vision* 60, no. 2 (2004): 91-110.

Lukermann, Fred. "The Concept of Location in Classical Geography." *Annals of the Association of American Geographers* 51, no. 2 (1961): 194-210.

Lynley, Matt. "Googlers Are Passing Around A Crazy Rumor About Sergey Brin Working On Architecture." *Business Insider*, October 25, 2011. http://www.businessinsider.com/googlers-are-passing-around-a-crazy-rumor-about-sergey-brin-working-on-architecture-2011-10.

Madrigal, Alexis. "The World is Not Enough: Google and the Future of Augmented Reality." *The Atlantic*, October 25, 2012. http://www.theatlantic.com/technology/archive/2012/10/the-world-is-not-enough-google-and-the-future-of-augmented-reality/264059.

Manovich, Lev. *The Language of New Media*. Cambridge, MA: MIT Press, 2001.

——. "The Poetics of Augmented Space." *Visual Communication* 5, no. 2 (2006): 219-240.

Marvel's The Avengers. DVD. Directed by Joss Whedon. Burbank, CA: Buena Vista Home Entertainment, 2012.

Massey, Doreen. *Place, Space, and Gender*. Minneapolis, MN: University of Minnesota Press, 1994.

Maughan, Tim. *Paintwork*. Bristol, England: Tim Maughan, 2011.

May-raz, Eran and Daniel Lazo. "Sight." Youtube video, 7.53. Posted by "The CG-Bros," August 1, 2012. https://www.youtube.com/watch?v=lK_cdkpazjI.

McCloud, Scott. *Understanding Comics: The Invisible Art*. New York: Harper Perennial, 1994.

McLuhan, Marshall. "The Playboy Interview: Marshall McLuhan." *Mcluhanmedia.com*, 1969. http://www.mcluhanmedia.com/m_mcl_inter_pb_01.html.

——. *Understanding Media: The Extensions of Man*. Edited by Terrence Gordon. Corte Madera, CA: Ginko Press, 2003.

McPherson, Miller, Lynn Smith-Lovin, and James M. Cook. "Birds of a Feather: Homophily in Social Networks." *Annual Review of Sociology* 27 (2001): 415–44.

Meng, Liqiu. "Egocentric Design of Map-Based Mobile Services," *The Cartographic Journal* 42, no. 1 (2005).

Meskin, Aaron. "Defining Comics?" *The Journal of Aesthetics and Art Criticism* 65, no. 4 (2007): 369-79.

Milgram, Paul, and Herman Colquhoun. "A Taxonomy of Real and Virtual World Display Integration." In *Mixed Reality: Merging Real and Virtual Worlds*, edited by Yuichi Ohta and Hideyuki Tamura, 5-30. Berlin: Springer-Verlag, 1999.

Milgram, Paul, and David Drascic. "Perceptual Effects in Aligning Virtual and Real Objects in Augmented Reality Displays." In *Proceedings of the Human Factors and Ergonomics Society Annual Meeting*, 1239-1243. SAGE Publications, 1997.

Milgram, Paul, and Fumio Kishino. "A Taxonomy of Mixed Reality Visual Displays." *IEICE Transactions on Information Systems* E77-D, no. 12 (1994).

Moore, Justin. "Building a Recommendation Engine, Foursquare Style." *Foursquare Engineering Blog*, March 22, 2011. http://engineering.foursquare.com/2011/03/22/building-a-recommendation-engine-foursquare-style.

Murphy, Graham J. and Sherryl Vint. *Beyond Cyberpunk: New Critical Perspectives*. New York, New York: Routledge, 2010.

Negroponte, Nicholas. *Being Digital*. New York: Vintage Books, 1995.

Nice, Karim, Tracy V. Wilson, and Gerald Gurevich. "How Digital Cameras Work." *How Stuff Works*, 2013. http://electronics.howstuffworks.com/cameras-photography/digital/digital-camera.htm.

Okrent, Arika. *In the Land of Invented Languages*. New York: Spiegel and Grau, 2010.

Olick, Jeffrey K. *The Politics of Regret: On Collective Memory and Historical Responsibility*. New York: Routledge, 2007.

Olsson, Thomas, Tuula Kärkkäinen, Else Lagerstam, and Leena Ventä-Olkkonen. "User Evaluation of Mobile Augmented Reality Scenarios." *Journal of Ambient Intelligence and Smart Environments* 4, no. 1 (2012): 29-47.

Ong, Walter. *Ramus, Method, and the Decay of Dialogue*. Chicago: University of Chicago Press, 2004.

"OpenCV Tutorials." *OpenCV*, 2013. http://docs.opencv.org/doc/tutorials/tutorials.html.

"Our Company." *Geomedia*. http://geomedia.com/welcome-to-geomedia.

Pariser, Eli. *The Filter Bubble: What the Internet Is Hiding from You*. New York: Penguin Books, 2011.

Pedersen, Isabel. "Dehumanization, Rhetoric, and the Design of Wearable Augmented Reality Interfaces." In *Small Tech: The Culture of Digital Tools*, edited by Byron Hawk, David Rieder, and Ollie Oviedo, 166-178. Minneapolis, MN: University of Minnesota Press, 2008.

———. *Ready to Wear: A Rhetoric of Wearable Computers and Reality-Shifting Media*. Anderson, SC: Parlor Press, 2013.

Pedersen, Isabel and Luke Simcoe. "The Iron Man Phenomenon, Participatory Culture, & Future Augmented Reality Technologies." *CHI 2012 Extended Abstracts on Human Factors in Computing Systems*. New York: Association of Computing Machinery, 2012: 291-300.

Perkins, Chris. "Community Mapping," *The Cartographic Journal* 44, no. 2 (2007): 127-137.

Pesce, Mark. "Magic Mirror: The Novel as a Software Development Platform." *MIT Communications Forum*. http://web.mit.edu/comm-forum/papers/pesce.html.

Polanyi, Michael. *Personal Knowledge: Towards a Post-Critical Philosophy*. New York, NY: Routledge, 1962. Print.

Polyani, Michael. *The Tacit Dimension*. New York: Doubleday, 1966.

Pred, Allan. "Place as Historically Contingent Process: Structuration and the Time Geography of Becoming Places." *Annals of the Association of American Geographers* 74, no. 2 (1984): 279-97.

Predator. DVD. Directed by John McTiernan, Beverly Hills, California: Twentieth Century Home Entertainment, 2010.

Quintilian. *Institutes of Oratory*. Edited by Lee Honeycutt. Translated by John Selby Watson. http://rhetoric.eserver.org/quintilian.

Rajchman, John. *Constructions*. Cambridge, MA: MIT Press, 1998.

Rhetorica Ad Herennium. Translated by Harry Caplan. Cambridge, MA: Harvard University Press, 1954.

Richardson, Ingrid. "Faces, Interfaces, Screens: Relational Ontologies of Framing, Attention and Distraction." *Transformations* 18 (2010). http://www.transformationsjournal.org/ journal/issue_18/article_05.shtml.

———. "Telebodies & Televisions: Corporeality and Agency in Technoculture." PhD diss., University of Western Sydney, 2003.

Richardson, Ingrid and Carly Harper. "Corporeal Virtuality: The Impossibility of a Disembodied Ontology." *Body Space and Technology* 2, no. 2 (2002).

Rickert, Thomas. *Ambient Rhetoric: The Attunements of Rhetorical Being*. Pittsburgh, PA: University of Pittsburgh Press, 2013.

———. "In the House of Doing: Rhetoric and the Kairos of Ambience." *Journal of Advanced Composition* 24, no. 4 (2004): 901–927.

Rogers, Everett M. *Diffusion of Innovations*, 5th ed. New York: Free Press, 2003.

Rorty, Richard. *Contingency, Irony, and Solidarity*. Cambridge, UK: Cambridge University Press, 1989.

Schuiten, François. *La Douce*. Tournai, Belgium: Casterman, 2012.

Scott, Charles E. *The Question of Ethics: Nietzsche, Foucault, Heidegger*. Bloomington, IN: Indiana University Press, 1990.

Blade Runner. DVD. Directed by Ridley Scott. Burbank, California: Warner Home Video, 1999.

Sennett, Richard. "The Civitas of Seeing." *Places* 5, no. 4 (1989): 82–84.

———. *The Fall of Public Man*. New York: Knopf, 1977.

Shaffer, David Williamson and Mitchel Resnick. "'Thick' Authenticity: New Media and Authentic Learning." *Journal of Interactive Learning Research* 10, no. 2 (1999): 195-215.

Sharples, Mike, Dan Corlett, and Oliver Westmancott. "The Design and Implementation of a Mobile Learning Resource." *Personal and Ubiquitous Computing* 6, no. 3 (2002): 220-234.

Shute, Tish, Ori Inbar, and Bruce Sterling. "Augmented Reality—Transitioning out of the old-fashioned 'Legacy Internet': Interview with Bruce Sterling." *UgoTrade*, 6 May 2011. http://www.ugotrade.com/2011/05/06/augmented-reality-transitioning-out-of-the-old-fashioned-legacy-internet-interview-with-bruce-sterling.

Singer, Laura. "Eye/Mind/Screen: Toward a Phenomenology of Cinematic Scopophilia." *Quarterly Review of Film and Video* 12, no. 3 (1990): 51-67.

Skyfall. DVD. Directed bu Sam Mendes. Beverly Hills, CA: MGM Pictures, 2012.

Smith, Craig. "Ethos Dwells Persuasively: A Hermeneutic Reading of Aristotle on Credibility." In *The Ethos of Rhetoric*, edited by Michael Hyde, 1-19. Columbia, SC: University of South Carolina Press, 2004.

Solnit, Rebecca. *Infinite City: A San Francisco Atlas*. Berkeley, CA: University of California Press, 2010.

"Star Trek: Predicting the Future Since 1966." *Weknowmemes*, July 13,2013. http://weknowmemes.com/2013/07/star-trek-predicting-the-future-since-1966.

Sterling, Bruce. *Mirrorshades: The Cyberpunk Anthology*. New York: Arbor House, 1986.

Stillar, Glenn. *Analyzing Everyday Texts: Discourse, Rhetoric and Social Perspectives*. Thousand Oak, CA: Sage. 1998.

Stormer, Nathan. "Recursivity: A Working Paper on Rhetoric and Mnesis." *Quarterly Journal of Speech* 99, no. 1 (2013): 27–50.

Sutko, Daniel M. and Adriana de Souza e Silva. "Location-aware Mobile Media and Urban Sociability." *New Media & Society* 13, no. 5 (2011): 807–823.

Suvin, Darko. *Metamorphoses of Science Fiction*. New Haven, CT: Yale University Press, 1979.

——. "On the Poetics of the Science Fiction Genre." *College English* 34, no. 3 (1972): 372-382.

Sweza. "Graffyard." *Sweza*, April 27, 2010.

Swift, Jonathan. *Gulliver's Travels into Several Nations of the World. With a Memoir of the Author*. Cambridge, UK: Oxford University Press, 2006.

"Tagwhat Frequently Asked Questions." *Tagwhat*, 2013. http://www.tagwhat.com/faq.php.

The Dark Knight. DVD. Directed by Christopher Nolan. Burbank, CA: Legendary Pictures, 2008.

The Terminator. DVD. Directed by James Cameron. Los Angeles, CA: Orion Pictures, 1984.

Till, Rupert. *PopCult: Religion and Popular Music*. London: Continuum, 2010.

Ting-Toomey, Stella and Atsuko Kurogi. "Facework Competence in Intercultural Conflict: An Updated Face-Negotiation Theory." *International Journal of Intercultural Relations* 22, no. 2 (1998): 187-225.

Tinnell, John. "All the World's a Link: The Global Theater of Mobile World Browsers." *Enculturation*, December 14, 2011. http://www.enculturation.net/all-the-worlds-a-link.

Top Gun. DVD. Directed by Tony Scott. Hollywood, CA: Paramount Pictures, 1986.

"Toronto Traffic FAQ." *Toronto.ca*, 2015. http://www1.toronto.ca/wps/portal/contentonly?vgnextoid=80c7a84c9f6e1410VgnVCM10000071d60f89RCRD.

Total Immersion AR. "Star Wars Comics Featuring Augmented Reality Experience with Luke Skywalker and Darth Vader." YouTube video, 1:10. Posted April 9, 2010. http://www.youtube.com/watch?feature=player_embedded&v=RPEmBadE-bY.

Tuan, Yi-Fu. *Space and Place: The Perspective of Experience*. Minneapolis, MN: University of Minnesota Press, 1977.

Turow, Joseph. *The Daily You: How the New Advertising Industry Is Defining Your Identity and Your Worth*. New York: Yale University Press, 2012.

Uricchio, William. "Imag(in)ing the City: Simonides to the Sims." In *Cities in Transition: The Moving Image and the Modern Metropolis*, edited by Andrew Webber, 102-112. London: Wallflower Press, 2008.

Vaidhyanathan, Siva. *The Googlization of Everything: (And Why We Should Worry)*. Berkeley, CA: University of California Press, 2011.

Van Dijck, Jose. *The Culture of Connectivity: A Critical History of Social Media*. Oxford: Oxford University Press, 2013.

VanHemert, Kyle. "Watch: This Guy Has a Digital Tattoo Viewable Only by Cellphone." *Wired*, August 23, 2013: http://www.wired.com/2013/08/watch-theres-digital-art-embedded-in-this-guys-hand-thanks-to-an-rfid-implant.

Vinge, Vernor. *Rainbows End*. New York: Tor, 2006.

Virilio, Paul. *The Information Bomb*. Translated by Chris Turner. New York: Verso, 2000.

Waterhouse, Lynn. "Multiple Intelligences, the Mozart Effect, and Emotional Intelligence: A Critical Review." *Educational Psychologist* 41, no. 4 (Fall 2006): 207-225.

Weintraub, Jeff. "The Theory and Politics of the Public/Private Distinction." In *Public and Private in Thought and Practice: Perspectives on a Grand Dichotomy*, edited by Jeff Weintraub & Krishan Kumar, 1-42. New York: University of Chicago Press, 1997.

Weiser, Mark and John Seely Brown. "The Coming Age of Calm Technology." In *Beyond Calculation*, edited by Peter J. Denning and Robert M. Metcalfe, 75-85. New York: Copernicus, 1997.

Weiser, Mark. "The Computer for the 21st Century." *Scientific American* 265, no. 3 (1991): 94-104.

"What Is Zoo-AR? Teaser." *Zoo-AR*. Geomedia, 2013. http://geomedia.com/2012/08/13/ augmented-reality-zoo-exhibits-and-zoo-ar/.

Whyte, William. *The Social Life of Small Urban Spaces*. Washington, DC: Conservation Foundation, 1980.

Wilkins, John. *An Essay Toward a Real Character and a Philosophical Language, 1668*. Menston, UK: Scolar, 1968.

Yates, Frances A. *The Art of Memory*. Chicago, IL: University of Chicago Press, 1966.

Yee, Nick. "The Labor of Fun: How Video Games Blur the Boundaries of Work and Play." *Games and Culture*. 1, no. 1 (January 2006): 68-71.

Zelizer, Barbie. "Reading the Past Against the Grain: The Shape of Memory Studies." *Critical Studies in Mass Communication* 12 (1995): 214–239.

Contributors

Scot Barnett is Assistant Professor of English at Indiana University. His research interests include histories and theories of rhetoric, phenomenology and speculative realism, and digital arts and rhetorics. His most recent work focuses on new media aesthetics and performativity (in particular the intersections of dance and technology) and their implications for rhetorical understandings of action and embodiment. His work has appeared in the journals *Kairos*, *Enculturation*, and *Itineration*, as well as in several edited book collections. He is the co-editor of *Rhetoric, Through Everyday Things* (University of Alabama Press, 2016) and the author of *Rhetorical Realism: Rhetoric, Ethics, and the Ontology of Things* (Routledge, 2017).

BC [heavy] Biermann is an educational technologist, academic, and digital artist. With a PhD in Humanities (Intermedia Analysis) from the Universiteit van Amsterdam, he derives his alias from his love for philosophical discussion. With an interdisciplinary background that comprises technology, philosophy, and the arts, he has worked as both a university professor and a tech developer. In 2005, BC founded The Heavy Projects as a means to technologically explore his internationally presented academic research, which investigates the intersection of emerging technologies and semiotics.

Jason Farman is Associate Professor in the Department of American Studies at the University of Maryland, College Park. He is also the Director of the Design Cultures & Creativity Program and a faculty member with the Human-Computer Interaction Lab. He is author of the book *Mobile Interface Theory: Embodied Space and Locative Media* (Routledge, 2012 — winner of the 2012 Book of the Year Award from the Association of Internet Researchers). He is the editor of the books *The Mobile Story: Narrative Practices with Locative Technologies* (Routledge, 2014) and *Foundations of Mobile Media Studies: Essential Texts on the Formation of a Field* (Routledge, 2016). He has published scholarly articles on such topics as mobile technologies, the history of technology, digital maps and cultural geography, locative and site-specific art, videogames, digital storytelling, performance art, social media, and surveillance. Farman has been a contributing author for *The Atlantic*, *Atlas Obscura*, and *The Chronicle of Higher Education*. He has been interviewed on NPR's *Marketplace* and has been a frequent media expert on how technology is transforming culture for ABC News, the Associated Press, the Christian Science Monitor, the Baltimore Sun, and the Denver Post, among others. He received his PhD from UCLA's School of Theater, Film, and Television.

John Craig Freeman is a public artist with over twenty years of experience using emergent technologies to produce large-scale public work at sites where the forces of globalization are impacting the lives of individuals in local communities. His work seeks to expand the notion of public by exploring how digital networked technology is transforming our sense of place. He has produced work and exhibited around the world including in Venice, Istanbul, Xi'an, Belfast, Los Angeles, Beijing, Zurich, New York City, Taipei, São Paulo, Warsaw, Kaliningrad, Miami, Bilbao, Havana, Atlanta, Calgary, Buffalo, Boston, Mexico City, London and San Francisco. In 1992, he was awarded an Individual Artist Fellowship from the National Endowment for the Arts. His work has been reviewed in *The New York Times, El Pais, Liberation, Wired News, Artforum, Ten-8, Z Magazine, Afterimage, Photo Metro, New Art Examiner, Time, Harper's,* and *Der Spiegel*. His writing has been published *in Rhizomes, Leonardo, the Journal of Visual Culture,* and *Exposure*. He is an Associate Professor of New Media at Emerson College.

Jordan Frith is Assistant Professor at the University of North Texas. His research focuses on location-aware mobile media, particularly location-based social networks. He is particularly interested in the intersections of online social networking and mobile communication. He has published two books (*Smartphones as Locative Media* and *Mobile Interfaces in Public Spaces*) and has published in journals in Sociology, Composition, Geography, Communication, and Technical Communication.

Jason Helms is Assistant Professor of English at Texas Christian University where he teaches courses on the history of rhetoric, multimedia authoring, visual rhetoric, gaming, comics, rhetoric and philosophy, and writing. His research focuses on the interplay of rhetoric and technology, especially in comics and visual rhetorics. His work has appeared in *Digital Humanities Quarterly*, *Itineration*, *Kairos*, and *Philosophy & Rhetoric*. His digital monograph *Rhizcomics: Rhetoric, Technology, and New Media Composition* will be published by the University of Michigan Press and Sweetland Digital Rhetoric Collaborative in January of 2017.

Steve Holmes is Assistant Professor of Rhetoric and Composition at George Mason University. His scholarship connects issues in rhetorical history and theory; mobile media studies; videogames and virtual worlds; material rhetorics, and cultural studies. He has several publications in these areas, including a recent book chapter on rhetorical 'allegorithms' in Markus Persson's *Minecraft* and an article in *The Fibreculture Journal* on the political philosophy of Jacques Rancière and griefing.

Jason Kalin is Assistant Professor in the Department of Writing, Rhetoric, & Discourse and the program in New Media Studies at DePaul University. His research interests include rhetorical theory, visual rhetorics, digital rhetorics, memory studies, and new media studies.

Bryan Leister works across a broad range of media reflecting his education in design and his career as an illustrator and artist. His work has been commissioned for the covers of many national and international magazines, including Time, BusinessWeek, Forbes, Der Spiegel and the Atlantic Monthly. He has won over 100 awards from competitions such as Communication Arts, the Art Directors Club of Washington DC, the Illustrators Club of Washington DC, AIGA, Graphis, PRINT and a gold and silver medal from the Society of Illustrators in NYC. His installations and animations have been shown at the Urban Institute for Contemporary Arts, Grand Rapids, MI, The Denver Museum of Nature and Science, The Corcoran Gallery of Art, Provisions Gallery, Warehouse Gallery, The Pyramid Atlantic, The Woolly Mammoth Theater and the Arlington Arts Center. He is Assistant Professor of Visual Arts at the University of Colorado Denver, where he teaches Digital Design and Transmedia.

Conor McGarrigle is a new media artist and researcher working at the intersection of digital networks and real space. He is Lecturer in Fine Art in the Dublin School of Creative Arts at the Dublin Institute of Technology. His work is concerned with the integration of digital technologies into the everyday and the spatial implications of location aware mobile devices. Recent work takes the form of urban interventions mediated through digital technologies and projects have involved, mapping, walks, iPhone apps, augmented reality, guerilla video projection and net art. He has exhibited widely internationally including: the Lebanese Pavilion at the 2011 Venice Biennale, SITE Santa

Fe, SIGGRAPH, Fundacio La Caixa, Barcelona; Fundacio Miro, Mallorca; FILE, St Etienne Biennale of Design, The Seoul Net Festival, D/Art Sydney, The Werkleitz Biennale, The Science Gallery, Dublin; EV+A, Limerick; Arthouse Multimedia Centre for the Arts, Dublin and as part of the 'Game On/ Renewing Media Art' and 'Unrealised Projects' touring exhibitions.

Sean Morey is Assistant Professor of English at the University of Tennessee, Knoxville where he teaches writing and digital media. His research focuses on developing theories of electracy, the intersection between digital media, rhetoric, composition, and the environment, as well as the role of visual rhetoric in constructions of nature and environment. He is the author of *Rhetorical Delivery and Digital Technologies: Networks, Affect, Electracy* (Routledge, 2016), *The New Media Writer* (Fountainhead Press, 2014), *The Digital Writer* (Fountainhead Press, 2017), and has co-edited the collection *Ecosee: Image, Rhetoric, Nature* (SUNY Press, 2009).

Brett Oppegaard, PhD, Assistant Professor at the University of Hawaii, studies augmented reality, ubiquitous computing, and mobile media. He was the individual recipient of the regional and national 2012 George and Helen Hartzog Award for his research into mobile app development and media delivery systems within the National Park Service as well as the national 2013 John Wesley Powell Prize winner for outstanding achievement in the field of historical displays. He was chosen for a National Endowment for the Arts fellowship as a journalist and also has earned National Endowment for the Humanities' grants as a scholar for his innovative mobile media research projects. Those projects include collaborations with America's first national park, Yellowstone, and the National Park Service's Harpers Ferry Center, the Interpretive Design Center of the federal agency. He now works in the School of Communications, within the College of Social Sciences at University of Hawaii's flagship Manoa campus.

Isabel Pedersen, PhD, is Canada Research Chair in Digital Life, Media, and Culture at the University of Ontario Institute of Technology. Currently, she holds a Social Sciences and Humanities Research Council (SSHRC) standard grant for her research into reality-shifting media. She has a PhD in Language and Literature from the University of Waterloo, an MA in Language and Professional Writing from the University of Waterloo, and a BA in English from

Trinity College, University of Toronto. She recently published her first book *Ready to Wear: A Rhetoric of Wearable Computer and Reality-Shifitng Media* (Parlor Press). She has been fascinated with computers, wearable technology, and popular culture since she spent her youth playing video games in the arcades on Yonge Street in downtown Toronto.

Mark Skwarek is an artist working to bridge the gap between virtual and physical world with augmented reality. His art explores the translation our everyday digital experience into the physical world using mobile augmented reality. He organized the augmented reality artist group manifest.AR, the arOCCUPYWALLSTREET movement, and co-organized We AR in MoMA. Skwarek earned his MFA. from Rhode Island School of Design's Digital Media Department. He is full time faculty at New York University Polytech, where he teaches 3D Graphics and the Augmented Reality Grad Class. His artwork has been written about by the *New York Times, Art in America, Boing Boing, WIRED,* the *Boston Globe, The Huffington Post,* NPR, BBC, *Leonardo,* and *Creative Capital*. Skwarek has exhibited in various venues, including: the Institute of Contemporary Art, Boston; ISEA; Dumbo Arts Festival, UCLA Digital Grad Gallery; the CyberArts Festival; the Sunshine International Art Museum, Beijing; and the Krannert Art Museum at the University of Illinois. Upcoming shows include FACT in Liverpool England, Siggraph 2013, The 2013 Augmented World Expo, and The Corocran Gallery of Art.

Tamiko Thiel is a visual artist exploring the interplay of place, space, the body and cultural identity. She expresses herself in a variety of media including digital prints, videos, interactive 3d virtual worlds and augmented reality. In 2007 she was awarded a major grant from the Hauptstadtkulturfonds (Berlin Capital City Cultural Funds) to create an interactive 3D installation on the Berlin Wall, *Virtuelle Mauer/ReConstructing the Wall*. This artwork won the IBM Innovation Award for Artistic Creation in Art and Technology at the 2009 Boston Cyberarts Festival. A founding member of the cyberartist group Manifest.AR, she participated in the pathbreaking augmented reality exhibit "We AR in MoMA," an uninvited guerilla takeover of MoMA New York. Videos of Thiel's "Art Critic Face Matrix" were featured in articles in the *New York Times* and on *WNYC* (National Public Radio). In 2011 she led the Manifest.AR Venice Biennial AR Intervention, placing her work series "Shades of Absence," on censorship in the visual arts, in the Venice Giardini and in the German National Pavilion (which won the Golden Lion Award for best national pavilion).

John Tinnell is Assistant Professor of English at the University of Colorado Denver. His forthcoming book, *Actionable Media* (Oxford UP, 2017), theorizes a new wave of digital communication emerging in the wake of ubiquitous computing. His research examines technocultural practices that integrate with the built environment to affect urban life; he emphasizes the opportunities and challenges these modes of media production raise for rhetoricians, communication scholars, and public intellectuals across the humanities. He has incorporated augmented reality composition into his undergraduate courses and published articles on new media in *Computers and Composition*, *Enculturation*, *Convergence*, *Computational Culture*, and *Reflections*.

Douglas Trueman has a BA in English from the University of Calgary, an MA in Creative Writing from City University in London and a Master's Degree in Professional Communication from the University of Ryerson. He is a veteran video games reviewer writing for such magazines as *Electronic Gaming Monthly*, the *Official Xbox Magazine* and the *Official PlayStation Magazine* as well as *Nintendo Power*. He also authored strategy guides for Prima Publishing, BradyGames and Ziff-Davis Publishing. His goal is to see games gain wide stream cultural acceptance as works of art.

Joseph P. Weakland is an independent scholar and works as Editorial Associate at the Center for Environmental and Sustainability Education at Florida Gulf Coast University. His research draws on science fictional thought processes in order to explore the rhetorical possibilities opened up by emerging technologies. He is interested in modes of anticipatory engagement with education, meaning making, and rhetorical exchange in a socio-ecological world transformed by accelerating technological change. He has presented on emergent technologies and science fiction at the Modern Language Association annual convention and the Conference on College Composition and Communication. Presently, he works in Atlanta as a communications specialist for a software company that develops logistical solutions for public transportation systems.

Index

3

3Cube, 105–108, 114, 311n
3D, 10–11, 19, 49, 105, 108, 157–159, 162, 212, 215, 217–219, 222, 224, 242, 251, 263–264, 266
3D animation, 10, 19

A

actionable content, 148
aesthetics, 9, 12, 15–16, 18, 21, 49, 51, 108, 114, 120, 122, 130, 134, 148, 257, 262, 311n
Alonso, Alex, 56
Althusser, Louis, 170
Ambient Research Room and Wearable Eye Display Lab, 139
Anders, Peter, 14, 301n
Andersen, Christian Ulrik, 15–16, 301n, 302n
Anderson, M.T., 100–101, 313; *Feed*, 100, 101
Andrejevic, Mark, 71, 133, 315n
Antonellis, Anthony, 104, 310n
Apple Computers, 10, 114, 272, 292, 321N
AR: marker-based, 251; markerless, 251; wearable, 9, 218, 251
AR Façade (project), 220
AR Standards Community, 234
Argon (project), 214, 220, 221, 223, 226
Aristotle, 72, 306n
Ark of the Covenant (book), 48
Art Basel event, 270
Artefackt, 108, 311N
Atlantic, 8, 301n
augmented architecture, 266–267
Augmented Environments Lab (Georgia Tech), 18, 214, 217, 220, 226–227
augmented reality, medical uses of, 11
Augmented Reality Handbook, 207
augmented space, 12, 13, 14, 21, 29, 31–33, 35–39, 42–43, 114
Augmented World Expo, 115
Aurasma (AR app), 7, 55
Avengers vs. X-men (comic), 55–56, 60
Azuma, Ronald T., 9, 11, 12

B

Balnnibarbi, 138, 139
Banksy, 105, 311
Barnett, Scot, 22, 137
Barthes, Roland, 155, 167, 172; *Camera Lucida*, 172
Barton Hill Estate, 107
Batcave, 66, 75, 79
Batcave (as metaphor), 66, 75, 79
Batman, 20, 65–66, 70, 75, 77–79, 305n
Baudrillard, Jean, 70, 190, 323n
Bayeux Tapestry, 51–52
Beatty, Bart, 52
Benjamin, Walter, 108, 311n, 321N
Biermann, B. C., 256–257, 266–270
Big Bird, 246
Biomapping project (Nold), 191–193, 195
biotechnology, 4
Bishop, Durrell, 139, 144, 316n
Blade Runner (film), 101

Blair, Carole, 17, 122, 214–215, 242, 302n, 313n
blogosphere, 16, 302n
Bluetooth, 165
Bogost, Ian, 134, 159, 170, 214, 316n, 321n
Bolter, Jay David, 17–18, 142, 224, 227, 302n, 317n
Bond, James, 78–79
Boonstra, Claire, 250
Bowery Wall, 268–269
Brainstorm (film), 204
Brecht, Berthold, 102, 310n
Brewster Apartments, 125
bricoleur, 113
Brin, Sergey, 20, 65–66, 68, 70–72, 7578, 100, 101, 305–307n
broadband, 11
Brown, John Seely, 6, 120, 301
Bryant, Levi, 147, 318–319n
Buckingham Palace, 183, 187–188
Burke, Kenneth, 69, 72, 76, 173, 306–307n
Business Insider (magazine), 75, 305n, 307

C

Calvino, Italo, 58
Carpenter, Thomas K., 103, 113, 310n
Carrier, David, 60, 305n
Casey, Edward, 184, 322n
Castells, Manuel, 73, 307n
Chrome (web browser), 221
Chronicle of Higher Education, 158
Cicero, 120, 144; *De Oratore*, 120
Claremont, Chris, 47
Coca-Cola, 106, 107
cognitive estrangement, 102, 310n
Comics and Sequential Art (Eisner), 305n
Comics vs. Art (book), 52
Coming Age of Calm Technology (Mark Weiser), 301n
contextual alignment, 39, 42
Corby, Tom, 183, 191, 322–323n
Coursera (software), 223
Craib, Raymond B., 190, 192, 323
Cranmer, Thomas, 185
Crawford, 91, 94, 309n
CritterCam (*National Geographic*), 167
Cruise, Tom, 74
cyberspace, 6, 7, 21, 37, 99, 100, 103–104, 106, 111, 179, 189, 250, 310n

D

Dam, Andries van, 207
Dark Knight (movie), 80
Darth Vader, 53–54
Dasein, 150–151, 184
Dassault Systèmes, 52
Dead Space (game), 74
Death and Life of Great American Cities (Jacobs), 86
Debord, Guy, 13, 194, 323n
deconstruction, 4
Deitch, Jeffrey, 268
Derrida, Jacques, 4
Designing, Arranging, and Assessing Augmented Places Through Mobile Media Alignment (Oppegaard), 19, 27, 302n
Detective Comics, 307n
Dickinson, Greg, 122
Diffusion of Innovations (book), 74, 307
digital culture, 3, 9, 186
digital life, 65, 72
digital, the, 7, 28, 31, 35, 42, 84, 87–88, 90, 107, 129, 130, 133, 169–170, 180, 189–190, 192, 197,

230–231, 237–238, 246, 260–263, 308n, 315n
Director (software), 114, 226
discourse, 9, 19, 20, 30, 43, 69–70, 76, 78–80, 113, 115, 138, 150, 156, 159, 169, 175, 288, 316n
DJ-DEO-dominatrix-mafiosa Daunt, 54
Dobrin, Sidney I., 202–203
Doctor D, 256
Dodgeball (service), 90–92, 309
Dolphin (web browser), 221
Dourish, Paul, 139, 142, 156, 316–317n, 319n
Dream Deferred: Augmented Reality as Rhetorical Realism (Barnett), 22, 137, 316n
Driskill Hotel (Austin), 263
Droid (cellphone), 101
drones (unmanned aerial vehicles), 106

E

Eco, Umberto, 181, 322n
e-commerce, 8
Edney, Matthew, 195, 323n
Egyptian Revival, 125
Eisner, Will, 49, 50, 305n
Electronic Arts, 74
embodied spatial interaction, 31
Emerging Technologies Guide to AR (book), 49, 305n
Engberg, Maria, 17, 302n
English, Ron, 164, 196, 202–203, 205, 256, 310n, 312n, 322n, 324n
entelechy, 72, 306n
epistemology, 22, 140, 143–144, 146–149, 152, 316n, 318n
Esquire, 8
Essay Concerning Human Understanding (Locke), 137, 317n
ethos, 20, 68, 77–78, 174
Extent of Presence, 10
Eyeborg (book), 75

F

Facebook, 84–85, 87, 90, 132, 149, 198, 251, 255, 308n
Fade (rasta graffiti artist), 54
Fairey, Shepard, 268, 270
Fall of Public Man (book), 86, 308n
familial substance, 76
Family Circus (comic), 50
Farman, Jason, 23, 92, 111, 113, 126, 177, 302n, 308–309n, 312–314n, 322n, 323n
Far Side (comic), 50
FCC (Federal Communications Commission), 37
Feiner, Steve, 215, 217, 304n
Fekner, John, 256
fiber optic cables, 11
Field Trip (app), 8
Field Trip (Google app), 8
film, 3–5, 72, 74, 78, 101–103, 110, 169, 170, 204, 227, 260, 284, 310n
Filter, Bayer, 307
Finger, Bill, 78
Fish, Stanley, 145–146, 165, 167–168, 317
Flash (software), 226
Foursquare, 14, 21, 86, 89–90, 92–95, 254, 301n, 309n; Explore, 90, 92–96; Latitude, 90; Loopt, 90
Fox, Lucius, 79
Freeman, John Craig, 17, 284–291
Freeman, Morgan, 17
Friedberg, Anne, 163, 320n
Frith, Jordan, 20, 83, 308n, 309n
Fürstenberg, Diane von, 66

G

Gall-Pteres Projection Map, 189
gamification, 22, 157, 159
Gardner, Howard, 158, 162–163, 319n
Gartner's Hype Cycle for Emerging Technologies, 18
Gates, Bill, 77–78
Gathering Memories with Augmented Reality (Kalin), 21
Gemeos, Os, 268
Geomedia, 22, 156–164, 166–167, 171, 174, 319n, 320n
GeoPedia (app), 185
geo-publishing, 8
Georgia Tech Game Studio, 214
geospots, 221
geotagged, 7, 85, 124, 141, 186, 276
geotagging, 7, 85, 116, 124, 141, 186, 276
gestural prefigurement, 165
Gettysburg, 36, 218–219
Gibson, William, 99, 100, 103–104, 250, 310–312; *All Tomorrow's Parties*, 106; *Neuromancer*, 99, 104, 109, 114, 310n, 312n; *Spook Country*, 100, 103, 310; *Virtual Light*, 100
Gillet, Frank, 169, 321n
Gimbal, 247
Gizmodo, 65
Glass (Google), 8, 11, 20, 61, 65, 67–68, 70, 72, 74–77, 80, 95–96, 101, 104–106, 122, 130, 132–133, 142, 204, 217–218, 244, 254–255, 258, 260, 262, 305n
Glass as Jeeves (character), 72
Global Positioning System (GPS), 5, 10, 13–14, 37, 90, 95, 126, 148, 187–188, 190–191, 193–194, 221, 223, 247, 261, 287, 290, 309n
Goetz, Adrienne, 172, 321n
Goffman, Erving, 165, 320n
Goldman, Tony, 268, 270, 292–293
Google, 8, 11, 20, 61, 65–80, 84, 89, 95–96, 101, 104–107, 114, 122, 125, 130, 132–133, 141, 189, 191, 196, 204, 217–218, 220–221, 237, 243–244, 249, 254–255, 258, 260, 262, 292, 301n, 305n, 306n, 307n, 310n, 323n
Google Explorer Program, 67
Google Glass, 8, 11, 20, 61, 65–67, 68, 70, 72, 74–77, 80, 95–96, 101, 104–106, 122, 130, 132–133, 142, 204, 217–218, 244, 254–255, 258, 260, 262, 305n
Google X, 67–68, 75, 79, 306n
Google X-Labs: First Project Glass, 306n
Grand Academy of Lagado, 138
Granov, Adi, 55
Graz University of Technology in Austria, 242
Green, Marybeth, 157, 272, 319n, 324n
Grosz, Elizabeth A., 179, 302n, 322n
Groten, Dick, 11
Grusin, Richard, 142, 317n
Guild, Sakura, 110, 112, 114
Gutenberg's printing press, 156

H

Halo (game), 74
Hansen, Mark B., 169, 321n
Haraway, Donna, 116, 159, 161, 163, 167–168, 313n, 319n, 320n, 321n
Haring, Keith, 268
Harvard University, 158, 306n, 319n, 320n
Harvey, Robert, 50–51, 305n

Havana Augmented (Maughan), 21, 109–111, 113–114, 312n
Hawkins, Donald, 158, 319n
Hayles, Katherine, 71, 182, 303n, 306n, 311n
Head-Mounted display, 67
head-mounted displays, 7, 11, 217
Heavy Projects, 256, 266, 268, 270
Heidegger, Martin, 22, 128, 138, 140–141, 149–152, 156, 158, 160, 163, 174, 184, 316n, 31n8, 319n, 322n; *Being and Time*, 150, 318n
Helms, Jason, 19, 47
Hemment, Drew, 190, 323n
Henderson, Steve, 217
Hergé (Georges Remi), 57
heterogeneity, 87, 91, 97
Hickman, Jonathan, 57, 305n
Hi-Definition Television (HDTV), 10
Highlight (app), 254
HistoryPin (app), 21, 125–127, 129, 133, 314n, 315n
Holmes, Steve, 23, 155
homophily, 87–88, 92–93, 96
Horizon Report, 8
Horizon Report (2011), 8
How We Think: Digital Media and Contemporary Technogenesis (Hayles), 306n
Human-Computer Interaction, 68
hybrid reality, 31, 30n3
Hyde, Michael, 72, 306n, 307n
hyperimmersion, 162

I

IBM, 224
Idols of the Market-Place, 143
Ihde, Don, 160, 163, 166, 320n, 321n; *Existential Technics*, 163, 320n; *Technology and Lifeworld*, 163
Ikea (app), 243
Information Bomb (book), 71
Innis, Harold, 164
Instagram (app), 122, 124, 129–130, 133
Intel, 114, 207
interfaces, 6, 14, 17, 23, 28–29, 35, 43, 89, 92, 94, 124, 126–127, 181, 182, 186–188, 197, 199, 203, 207–208, 233–234, 238, 323n
Internet, 6, 67, 73, 83–84, 101, 133, 180, 182, 208, 250, 280, 301n, 307n, 308n, 310n, 312n, 322n
iPhone, 10, 67, 161, 169, 183, 188, 254, 287, 317n, 321n
Iron Man (Marvel character), 48, 55, 60–62, 70, 78–79, 306n
iSource, 207
iSpy (book), 71, 315nn

J

Jacobs, Jane, 86–87, 308n
Jacobs, Paul, 246
Jahshan, Paul, 189, 323
javascript, 221, 223
Jawbone UP, 254
Jobs, Steve, 77–78
Johnson, Steven, 155–156, 245
Junaio (AR app), 7, 33, 120, 122, 241

K

Kaa, Geerten van de, 234–235
Kalin, Joseph, 21, 119
Kane, Bob, 78
Kelley, DeForest, 204
Kenisky, Jeremy, 157, 319n
Kent, James, 207
Kinect Fusion, 219
Kipper, Gregory, 49, 305n

Kishino, Fumio, 9–12
Krazy Kat (comic), 62
Kurzweil, Ray, 114, 312n

L

La Douce (Francois Schuiten), 19, 52, 58, 62
Lacey, Kimberly, 133, 315n
Land Warrior (system), 75
Lanham, Richard, 144
Lanier, Janon, 71
Latour, Bruno, 71, 159, 164, 169, 174, 319n, 320n; *Pasteurization*, 319n
Lawnmower Man (film), 142
Layar (AR app), 7, 11, 21, 33, 86, 89, 95, 120, 122, 124–127, 133, 141, 156, 172, 183, 217, 219–220, 241, 248–253, 255, 276, 278, 317n, 319n, 321n
Lee, Jim, 47, 309n, 317n
Lens-Fitzgerald, Maarten, 248–249
Les Cités Obscures (comic), 57–58
Levinas, Emmanuel, 160
Levine, Paul, 193–195, 323n
Life through the Screen: Location-Based Information and the Personalization of Space (Frith), 20, 83
ligne claire, 57
Lincoln Park, 125
Lingen, Ron van der, 11
Lingis, Alphonso, 160
Locke, John, 137–138, 144, 146, 317n
Lodi, Simona, 17, 302n
London Royal Society, 139, 144
London Street Museum, 10

M

MacIntyre, Blair, 17, 214–215, 242, 302n, 313n
Madrigal, Alexis, 8, 301n
Magic Vision (app), 245
Magneto, 48, 55, 60–61
Mann, Steve, 75
Manovich, Lev, 12–14, 88, 133, 161, 166, 188, 301n, 319n, 323n
Marble Answering Machine, 139
Marvel Comics, 48, 52, 55, 57, 78, 305n
materiality, 28, 122, 179, 181–182, 185, 313n
Matrix, The (1999), 9
Maughan, Tim, 21, 104–106, 109, 113–115, 311n, 312n
McCloud, Scott, 50, 51
McGarrigle, Conor, 276–283
McGee, Barry, 268
McLuhan, Marshall, 17, 51, 164, 302n
Mechwarrior (game), 110
media theory, 5
meme, 75, 101, 307n, 310n
Meng, Liqiu, 195, 323n
Mercator, Gerardus, 189
Mercury (web browser), 221
Mering, Ean, 256
Meskin, Aaron, 51–52
Microsoft, 114, 258, 320n
Milgram, Paul, 9–12, 31, 303n, 304n
minimalist, 50
Minority Report (film), 257
Mirrorshades (anthology), 104, 310n
MIT Media Lab, 139
mixed reality (MR), 10–11, 14, 28, 29, 31, 225, 301n
Mixed Reality Visual Displays, A Taxonomy of (Milgrim and Kishino), 9
MMORPG (Massively Multiplayer Online Role-Playing Game), 110
mnemotechnics, 129

mobile devices, 14, 16, 28, 35, 37, 42, 85, 94, 101, 156, 166, 170, 178, 183, 186, 190–191, 193, 196, 206, 218, 240, 241, 299, 302n
Mobile Interfaces in Public Spaces: Locational Privacy, Control and Urban Sociability, 308n, 309n
mobile media alignment, 29, 35, 37, 44
mobile Web, 6–7
Mœbius (Jean Girard), 57
MoMA (Museum of Modern Art) Invasion (art intervention), 17
MOOCs (Massive Open Online Courses), 223, 225
Morey, Sean, 3, 119, 203
Motorola (cellphone company), 101
Myspace, 87

N

Naja, Robert Del, 105
nano-gloss, 106
Nathan Jurgenson, 5–6, 301n
Negroponte, Nicholas, 84
neologisms, 103, 106, 113, 237
New York City, 96, 268, 280
New York Times, 83
Nike Fuel Band, 254
Nolan, Christopher, 79
Nold, Christian, 191–193
nomos, 163
Norman, Donald, 142

O

Obama, Barack, 73
Oculus Rift, 215, 217
Olick, Jeffrey, 122, 313n
Ong, Walter, 143, 317n
Open Stand, 263
Open Street Map, 196, 324n
OpenCV (Open Source Computer Vision Library), 172–173, 321n
Oppegaard, Brett, 19, 27
Orkent, Arika, 145, 317n
ossification, 116
Ott, Brian, 122

P

Paintwork (Maughan), 21, 104–105, 106, 108–111, 114, 311n, 312n
Pandora, 5, 260
Pandora (website), 5, 260
Pankhurst, Emmeline, 183, 187–188
Paparazzi (Maughan), 21, 109
PARC, 139
Parker, Peter (Spider-Man), 78
Partech, 207
Pearl Paint Building, 267
Pedersen, Isabel, 20, 65, 70, 121, 141, 306n, 313n, 316n; *Ready to Wear: A Rhetoric of Wearable Computers and Reality-Shifting Media*, 70, 141, 313n
Peeters, Benoit, 57–58
Perey, Christine, 228–229
Perfection: Coming to Terms with Being Human (Hyde), 72, 306n
Perkins, Chris, 191, 323n
phenomenology, 160, 170
Phillyhistory.org, 86
physis, 163
Playboy, 8, 302
Pleasantville (film), 72
Polak, Esther, 190, 323n; *Amsterdam Realtime*, 190, 195, 323n
Pold, Soren, 15–16, 301n, 302n
popular culture, 4
postcomposition, 202, 205
PosterBouy, 256

Postman, Neil, 209
Potential Panels: Toward a Theory of Augmented Comics (Helms), 19, 47, 305n
Predator (film), 100
propaganda, 284
Public Ad Campaign, 256

Q

Quick Response, 15, 49, 57, 105–109, 186, 206, 212, 278, 301n
Quintilian, 120
Quintilian: *Institutes of Oratory*, 120

R

Rajchman, John, 181, 322n
Ramism, 143
Rampolla, Joseph, 49, 305n
Ready to Wear: A Rhetoric of Wearable Computers and Reality-Shifting Media (Pedersen), 70, 141, 313n
Reddit, 84
Reductionism, 29
Reebie Storage Warehouse, 125
Remediation (Bolter and Grusin), 227, 314n, 315n, 317n
Remembrance Agent (book), 75
Renaissance and Enlightenment, 143–144
Reproduction Fidelity, 10
Resnick, Mitchel, 35, 304n, 305n
Retinex, 52, 54, 55, 57, 60
rhetoric, 8–10, 16, 18–22, 29, 39, 54, 68, 70–71, 74, 76–77, 80, 108, 120–123, 128, 130, 132, 134, 140, 142–144, 146–150, 152, 162–163, 173, 203, 313n, 314n, 315n, 316n, 317n, 319n
Rhetorica ad Herennium, 120
rhetoricity, 140–142, 149, 152–153
Richardson, Ingrid, 160, 164, 167, 320n
Rickert, Thomas, 22, 128–130, 149–151, 314n, 315n, 316n, 318n, 319n; *Ambient Rhetoric*, 149, 314n, 315n, 318n
robotics, 11, 103
Rogers, Buck, 307n
Rogers, Everett M., 74, 307n
Rolling Irion (game), 111–112
Rorty, Richard, 146–147, 151, 317n
Running Man (film), 204

S

Salvation Army, 184
San Antonio Zoo, 22, 156, 166–167, 169, 174
Saussure, Ferdinand de, 145
Scharf, Kenny, 268
Schuiten, Francois, 52, 57–58
SCNB type 12 (book), 58
Scott, Charles E., 50, 174, 322n
Second Life (virtual reality software), 5, 141, 224, 226
Seiler, Jordan, 256–257, 266, 268, 270
sequential art, 50–52, 60
Sesame Street, 246
Shaffer, David Williamson, 35, 304n, 305n
Sienkiewicz, Bill, 62
SIGGRAPH (Special Interest Group on GRAPHics and Interactive Techniques), 236
Silva, de Souza e, 14, 31, 88–89, 92, 96, 180, 301n, 303n, 305n, 308n, 309n, 322n
Singer, Laura, 165
Skwarek, Mark, 296–299

Skywalker, Luke, 53
Slate.com, 84
smart objects, 229
Smartphone with Glasses, 306n
smartphones, 6–8, 10, 13, 37, 49, 55, 62, 84, 89, 94, 215–217, 232, 238, 298, 308n, 309n
Smith, Craig, 77, 307n
social media, 6, 65, 67, 69, 71, 211, 280
social networks, 6, 14–15, 31, 43, 80, 91, 124, 152, 301n
software, 4–7, 10, 91–92, 106, 129, 133, 148, 161, 164, 167, 171, 173, 180, 207, 214, 233–235, 237, 240–241, 262, 287, 311n
spatiotemporal, 7
Spence, Rob, 75
Spiderman, 58
spiders (Web), 13
Spinney, Carroll, 246
Splintered Space: The Smartphone as the Screen to the City, 308n, 309n
Star Trek, 72, 101, 204, 215, 310n
Star Wars (movie and comic), 52–55
Stark, Tony (Iron Man), 78–79, 100
Starner, Thad, 75
Stations of the Cross in Israel, 36
Stava, Michael Tres, 52, 54, 60
Sterling, Bruce, 104, 115–116, 236–237, 250, 310n, 312n, 313n
Stillar, Glenn, 69, 306n
Stray Toasters (book), 62
Street Iron (game), 110–112
Subreddits, 84
Sutherland, Ivan, 205
Suvin, Darko, 102, 310n
Sweza, 109, 311n
Swift, Jonathan, 138–140, 145, 316n
Swiss Augmented Reality Meetup Group, 228
SxSW Festival, 90, 236, 254

T

Tagwhat (app), 22, 141, 148–149, 152–153, 317–319n
Tangible Media Center, 139
Tapln (app), 14, 301n
techne, 120, 163
Technics and Praxis, 163
technosoma, 165
technosomatic involvement, 164–165
Theurer-Wrigley House, 125
Thiel, Tamiko, 271–275, 324n
Three Angry Men (project), 220
Till, Rupert, 76, 307n
Tinnell, John, 3, 115, 119, 122, 206, 215, 229, 241, 249, 257, 312n, 313n
Tintin (comic), 57
Top Gun (film), 74
Total Immersion, 52–55, 207
Touring Machine (1997; AR experience), 216
transductive relationships, 7
Tron (film), 142
Trueman, Douglas, 20, 65
Tseng, Tony, 227
Tuan, Yi-Fu, 30, 303n
Turing Machine, 161
Turkle, Sherry, 7

U

ubicomp, 15, 16, 301n, 302
ubiquitous computing, 28, 30, 32, 35, 39, 80, 100, 103, 115, 119, 120–121, 139–140, 142, 205, 212–213, 226, 230–232, 237, 313n

Udacity (software), 223
Uncanny (book), 47
Understanding Comics (McLoud), 50
Unity 3D, 217
UrbanSpoon (app), 95
utopian, 20, 72, 84, 97, 103, 104, 105, 158, 212

V

van der Klein, Raimo, 250
Vanilla Sky (film), 3, 4, 5, 7, 9, 301n
Vinge, Vernor, 100, 212–213, 250; *Rainbows End*, 100, 212, 250
Virilio, Paul, 71
virtual agoras, 16
virtual environment, 9–11, 31
virtual reality, 5–6, 9, 10–11, 110, 141, 205, 215, 225
virtual worlds, 4–5, 74, 225, 278
Visual Memory Prosthetic (book), 75
visual search, 243–244
Voices of Oakland (project), 218
Vufoiria SDK, 217, 221, 241–242, 244–245, 247
Vuforia Engine (app), 241
Vuzix, 75

W

Walkman (Sony), 96
WALL-E (film), 102
Wayne, Bruce (Batman), 78–79
Weakland, Joseph P., 21, 99
wearable computers, 9, 20, 66, 68, 70, 75, 78, 80, 121, 141, 212, 218, 251, 254
Weintraub, Jeff, 86, 308n
Weiser, Mark, 6, 32, 120, 137, 139, 142, 301n, 304n
When Geolocation Meets Visualization (Farman), 23, 177, 322n
Whyte, William, 86
Wikipedia, 84, 89, 122, 124–125, 141, 147–148, 185
WikipediaWorld, 125, 130
Wikitude World Browser, 141, 317n
Wilkins, Bishop John, 139, 144–146, 153, 317n
Williamsburg Art and Design Building, 266
Wind of Blades (game), 110, 112
Window on the World (displays), 11
Winogrand, Garry, 134, 315n
Witte Museum, 159
Wonderland (system), 224
Wood, Natalie, 204
World of Warcraft (game), 5, 110
Wright, Jay, 240, 241
Wrigley Jr., William, 125
Wrigley, Philip K., 125
Wynwood Walls, 270

X

X-Men (film), 60

Y

Yelp (app), 86, 89, 95, 122
You Are Not a Gadget (book), 71
YouTube, 53, 66, 69, 111, 306n

Z

zeitgeist, 206
Zelizer, Barbie, 122

CPSIA information can be obtained
at www.ICGtesting.com
Printed in the USA
BVOW05s1705010817
490644BV00008B/80/P

9 781602 355569